T0325004

Serverless Computing Concepts, Technology, and Architecture

Rajanikanth Aluvalu
Chaitanya Bharathi Institute of Technology, India

Uma Maheswari V.
Chaitanya Bharathi Institute of Technology, India

A volume in the Advances in Systems Analysis,
Software Engineering, and High Performance
Computing (ASASEHPC) Book Series

Published in the United States of America by
   IGI Global
   Engineering Science Reference (an imprint of IGI Global)
   701 E. Chocolate Avenue
   Hershey PA, USA 17033
   Tel: 717-533-8845
   Fax: 717-533-8661
   E-mail: cust@igi-global.com
   Web site: http://www.igi-global.com

                    Library of Congress Cataloging-in-Publication Data

CIP Pending
ISBN: 979-8-3693-1682-5
EISBN: 979-8-3693-1683-2

This book is published in the IGI Global book series Advances in Systems Analysis, Software Engineering, and High Performance Computing (ASASEHPC) (ISSN: 2327-3453; eISSN: 2327-3461)

British Cataloguing in Publication Data
A Cataloguing in Publication record for this book is available from the British Library.

For electronic access to this publication, please contact: eresources@igi-global.com.

Advances in Systems Analysis, Software Engineering, and High Performance Computing (ASASEHPC) Book Series

Vijayan Sugumaran
Oakland University, USA

ISSN:2327-3453
EISSN:2327-3461

MISSION

The theory and practice of computing applications and distributed systems has emerged as one of the key areas of research driving innovations in business, engineering, and science. The fields of software engineering, systems analysis, and high performance computing offer a wide range of applications and solutions in solving computational problems for any modern organization.

The **Advances in Systems Analysis, Software Engineering, and High Performance Computing (ASASEHPC) Book Series** brings together research in the areas of distributed computing, systems and software engineering, high performance computing, and service science. This collection of publications is useful for academics, researchers, and practitioners seeking the latest practices and knowledge in this field.

COVERAGE

- Metadata and Semantic Web
- Engineering Environments
- Computer System Analysis
- Human-Computer Interaction
- Parallel Architectures
- Computer Networking
- Enterprise Information Systems
- Storage Systems
- Computer Graphics
- Virtual Data Systems

IGI Global is currently accepting manuscripts for publication within this series. To submit a proposal for a volume in this series, please contact our Acquisition Editors at Acquisitions@igi-global.com or visit: http://www.igi-global.com/publish/.

Titles in this Series

For a list of additional titles in this series, please visit:
www.igi-global.com/book-series/advances-systems-analysis-software-engineering/73689

Advanced Applications in Osmotic Computing
G. Revathy (SASTRA University, ndia)
Engineering Science Reference • © 2024 • 370pp • H/C (ISBN: 9798369316948) • US $300.00

Omnichannel Approach to Co-Creating Customer Experiences Through Metaverse Platforms
Babita Singla (Chitkara Business School, Chitkara University, Punjab, India) Kumar Shalender (Chitkara Business School, Chitkara University, India) and Nripendra Singh (Pennsylvania Western University USA)
Engineering Science Reference • © 2024 • 223pp • H/C (ISBN: 9798369318669) • US $270.00

Uncertain Spatiotemporal Data Management for the Semantic Web
Luyi Bai (Northeastern University, China) and Lin Zhu (Northeastern University, China)
Engineering Science Reference • © 2024 • 518pp • H/C (ISBN: 9781668491089) • US $325.00

Bio-Inspired Optimization Techniques in Blockchain Systems
U. Vignesh (Vellore Institute of Technology, Chennai, India) Manikandan M. (Manipal Institute of Technology, India) and Ruchi Doshi (Universidad Azteca, Mexico)
Engineering Science Reference • © 2024 • 288pp • H/C (ISBN: 9798369311318) • US $300.00

Enhancing Performance, Efficiency, and Security Through Complex Systems Control
Idriss Chana (ESTM, Moulay Ismail University of Meknès, Morocco) Aziz Bouazi (ESTM, Moulay Ismail University of Meknès, Morocco) and Hussain Ben-azza (ENSAM, Moulay Ismail University of Meknes, Morocco)
Engineering Science Reference • © 2024 • 371pp • H/C (ISBN: 9798369304976) • US $300.00

Frameworks for Blockchain Standards, Tools, Testbeds, and Platforms
Yanamandra Ramakrishna (School of Business, Skyline University College, Sharjah, UAE) and Priyameet Kaur Keer (Department of Management Studies, New Horizon College of Engineering, India)
Engineering Science Reference • © 2024 • 244pp • H/C (ISBN: 9798369304051) • US $285.00

Machine Learning Algorithms Using Scikit and TensorFlow Environments
Puvvadi Baby Maruthi (Dayananda Sagar University, India) Smrity Prasad (Dayananda Sagar University, India) and Amit Kumar Tyagi (National Institute of Fashion Technology, New Delhi, India)
Engineering Science Reference • © 2024 • 453pp • H/C (ISBN: 9781668485316) • US $270.00

701 East Chocolate Avenue, Hershey, PA 17033, USA
Tel: 717-533-8845 x100 • Fax: 717-533-8661
E-Mail: cust@igi-global.com • www.igi-global.com

Table of Contents

Detailed Table of Contents

Chapter 1
    Radhika Kavuri, Chaitanya Bharathi Institute of Technology, India
    Satya kiranmai Tadepalli, Chaitanya Bharathi Institute of Technology, India

The chapter provides a comprehensive exploration of the dynamic and efficient realm of serverless computing. Beginning with a historical context, the chapter delves into the serverless fundamentals, limitations of traditional computing and the emergence of serverless solutions. The core components of serverless computing, including computer services, storage services, and event triggers, are explained. The chapter navigates through serverless architecture, drawing comparisons with microservices and monolithic structures, and highlights the role of serverless frameworks in facilitating development. Major serverless platforms, including Amazon web services, Microsoft Azure, and Google Cloud Platform, are explored in detail. The chapter addresses considerations such as cold starts, vendor lock-in, security concerns, and monitoring/debugging challenges. Real-world case studies provide practical insights into successful serverless implementations. In conclusion, the chapter discusses the future trajectory of serverless computing.

Chapter 2
    Ramu Kuchipudi, Chaitanya Bharathi Institute of Technology, India
    Ramesh Babu Palamakula, Chaitanya Bharathi Institute of Technology, India
    T. Satyanarayana Murthy, Chaitanya Bharathi Institute of Technology, India

This book chapter introduces readers to the dynamic and transformative world of serverless computing. With the focus on agility, scalability, and cost-effectiveness for developing and deploying applications, serverless computing has become a game-changer. The chapter's introduction to serverless computing provides a clear understanding of its fundamental principles and concepts, setting it apart from conventional computing models. Specifically, it explores the fundamental aspects of serverless architectures, emphasizing critical components such as functions as a service (FaaS), event driven programming, and the involvement of cloud providers in this setting. The chapter discusses the potential of serverless systems to optimize resource usage, speed up development, and adapt to changing user preferences while minimizing operational expenses. The chapter highlights practical use cases and success stories that demonstrate how serverless has been successfully implemented in various industries and domains.

Chapter 3

Nidhi Niraj Worah, Thakur College of Engineering and Technology, India
Megharani Patil, Thakur College of Engineering and Technology, India

This chapter serves as a comprehensive initiation into serverless computing, a revolutionary paradigm in cloud computing. It begins by elucidating the foundational concepts, breaking down its architecture that simplifies development through modular functions triggered by specific events. The narrative unfolds, highlighting the myriad benefits, such as enhanced efficiency, seamless scalability, and liberating developers from intricate server management. A comparative analysis with traditional cloud computing underscores serverless computing's unique attributes. However, the chapter maintains balance by addressing challenges like cold start latency, execution duration limits, and potential vendor lock-in. The exploration concludes by showcasing real-world applications in domains like real-time data processing, backend APIs, batch processing, image and video processing, and chatbots. Offering a nuanced understanding of serverless computing, this chapter stands as an invaluable resource for readers exploring its advantages, challenges, and diverse applications.

Chapter 4

Vishal Goar, Engineering College Bikaner, Bikaner, India
Nagendra Singh Yadav, Engineering College Bikaner, Bikaner, India

As the landscape of computing continues to evolve, serverless computing emerges as a paradigm shift, offering a transformative approach to application development and deployment. Serverless computing has revolutionized the way businesses build & deploy applications. With its promise of seamless scalability, reduced operational overhead, and cost optimization, serverless systems have become a dominant paradigm in cloud computing. A focal point of this exploration is the examination of the myriad benefits that serverless computing brings to the table. This chapter focuses on the Introduction to Serverless computing, core concepts of serverless computing, Advantages of serverless computing, Challenges in Serverless Computing, Use Cases and Industry Adoption, Best Practices for Serverless Development, and Future Trends in Serverless Computing.

Chapter 5

S. Boopathi, Muthayammal Engineering College, India

This chapter provides a comprehensive overview of the evolving landscape of serverless computing, focusing on the technologies and tools that shape its ecosystem. Starting with an introduction to serverless architecture, the chapter delves into the benefits and challenges of adopting serverless computing. It explores key technologies such as function-as-a-service (FaaS), backend-as-a-service (BaaS), and event-driven architecture, highlighting their roles in enabling scalable and cost-effective solutions. Additionally, the chapter discusses popular tools and platforms used for developing, deploying, and managing serverless applications. Through this exploration, readers gain insights into the latest trends, best practices, and considerations for leveraging serverless computing effectively in modern IT environments.

Chapter 6

    Sai Samin Varma Pusapati, Chaitanya Bharathi Institute of Technology, India

This chapter delves into the synergy between containerization and serverless computing, pivotal for advancing cloud-native application deployment. It outlines the architectural foundations and benefits of each paradigm, emphasizing their combined impact on scalability, efficiency, and agility. The discussion progresses to technical integrations, focusing on container orchestration and serverless platforms, enhancing management and deployment. Addressing challenges like security and operational complexity, it highlights strategies for navigating these issues. Real-world examples illustrate the practical application across sectors, showcasing the integration's capacity to meet diverse computational needs. This convergence is posited as a significant driver for future cloud-native innovations, offering a glimpse into evolving trends and the potential reshaping of software development landscapes. The exploration underscores the critical role of this amalgamation in optimizing resource utilization and simplifying cloud infrastructure complexities.

Chapter 7

    Swapna Mudrakola, Matrusri Engineering College, India
    Krishna Keerthi Chennam, Vasavi College of Engineering, India
    Shitharth Selvarajan, Leeds University, India

Applications are developed and deployed on the specific stack of software, as virtualization creates an environment to run the designed stack of software. Virtualization requires the installation of the entire software to run the application. The environment setup time will take more than, the execution time. Memory and CPU time are not effectively utilized. The containers are replacing the drawback of installing the unnecessary services of the software, not requiring running applications. The container consists of only the required services software loaded in the container. Container security is also an important aspect of utilizing applications with portability features. Different tools are designed for different aspects of security issues.

Chapter 8

    Sai Prashanth Mallellu, Vardhaman College of Engineering, Hyderabad, India
    Maheswari V., Chaitanya Bharati Institute of Technology, Hyderabad, India
    Rajanikanth Aluvalu, Chaitanya Bharati Institute of Technology, Hyderabad, India
    M. V. V. Prasad Kantipudi, Symbiosis Institute of Technology, Symbiosis International
       University, India

Function as a service (FaaS) is a central component of serverless computing, reshaping the landscape of application development in the cloud. FaaS allows developers to create stateless functions responding to specific events, triggering execution without the need for direct infrastructure management. This architecture abstracts developers from underlying complexities, emphasizing code-centric development. The pay-per-use model, automatic scaling, and event-driven execution contribute to an efficient, cost-effective, and responsive application development process. This abstract presents an overview of the core principles of FaaS, emphasizing its transformative role in modern cloud computing. Function as a Service (FaaS) is an essential element of serverless computing, reshaping the landscape of cloud-based application development. FaaS empowers developers to craft concise, stateless functions tailored for specific tasks triggered by diverse events. By abstracting infrastructure management, developers can concentrate solely on coding.

Function as a service (FaaS) is a service of cloud computing that allows cloud customers to develop applications and establish functionalities. FaaS is commonly employed for deploying microservices and is popularly referred to as serverless computing. Here, the authors investigate the world of function as a service (FaaS) within cloud computing. They explore FaaS's evolution from its inception to its role in serverless computing, covering key concepts like serverless architecture, event-driven programming, and statelessness. The exploration involves gaining knowledge in establishing FaaS environments using AWS Lambda, IBM Bluemix OpenWhisk, Azure functions, Auth0 Webtask, and Google Cloud functions as the authors delve into design principles and best practices. Emphasis is placed on the advantages of adopting event-driven, serverless methodologies and optimization techniques involved in FaaS. For an experienced developer or novice, this chapter helps to understand function as a service, making it valuable to learn the insights of serverless computing.

Users who may be geographically distant from organizations must be provided with up-to-date info. Replication is one approach to make such data accessible. The process of duplicating and maintaining database items across many databases is known as distributed database replication. Distributed databases safeguard application availability while providing quick local access to shared data. Distributed databases are often divided up into pieces or replica divisions. In distributed databases, fragmentation is advantageous for utilization, effectiveness, parallelism, and security. Locality of reference is strong if data items are found in the location where they are utilized the most. Users may still query or edit the remaining pieces even if one is unavailable. It's critical to manage fragmented data replication availability even in the event of a failure. Failure scenarios include a server that responds improperly or returns an inaccurate value. Enabling fault tolerance and data management systems like SAS, Oracle, and NetApp is the only way to fix these errors. This study reviews the research on data replication and fragmentation techniques used in cloud environments. It is easy to implement, takes into consideration cloud databases, considers both fragmentation and replication strategies, and is focused on enhancing database performance. All the necessary information to implement the approach is included in the chapter.

Chapter 11

Unraveling the Complex Challenges and Innovative Solutions in Microservice Architecture:
Exploring Deep Microservice Architecture Hurdles 177

    Kaushikkumar Patel, TransUnion LLC, USA

This chapter delves into the challenges of microservice architecture within serverless computing, outlining strategic remedies. It underscores operational hurdles like sophisticated orchestration and service interactions, along with security concerns due to the system's decentralized fabric. The discourse extends to performance bottlenecks, focusing on resource management in serverless frameworks. Proposed solutions include advanced system monitoring, state-of-the-art security safeguards, and innovative optimization strategies. The chapter concludes with prospective research directions, emphasizing advanced service meshes and security enhancements, offering practitioners a pragmatic blueprint for microservice implementation in serverless infrastructures. This analysis is crucial for professionals navigating the intricacies of microservice deployment.

Chapter 12

NodeJS and Postman for Serverless Computing 195

    Rajesh Kannan Kannan, Chaitanya Bharathi Institute of Technology (Autonomous), India
    Meena Abarna K. T., Annamalai University, India
    S. Vairachilai, VIT Bhopal University, India
    R. Vijayalakshmi, Mahatma Gandhi Institute of Technology (Autonomous), India

Node.js is a robust, open-source cross platform server-side JavaScript runtime environment. Node.js, which Ryan Dahl created in 2009, is incredibly popular because it makes it easier to create network applications that are both scalable and high-performing. Its event-driven architecture, which permits asynchronous I/O operations and makes it ideal for managing concurrent connections and delivering quick, real-time applications, is one of its main advantages. With Node.js, coders can leverage JavaScript for both the client and server- side scripting, promoting code reuse and resulting in a smoother development process.

Chapter 13

Serverless Computing: A Security Viewpoint 205

    Padmavathi Vurubindi, Chaitanya Bharathi Institute of Technology, Hyderabad, India
    Sujatha Canavoy Narahari, Sreenidhi Institute of Science and Technology, India

Recently, serverless computing has become a newfound computing platform for the cloud-based deployment of applications and it took over all other contemporary computing platforms. It has two significant advantages over its contemporary computing platforms. First off, it enables software developers to delegate to cloud service providers all infrastructure maintenance and operational chores, allowing them to concentrate solely on the business logic of their applications. The second is that it has a strict pay-per-use business model, where customers are only charged for the resources, they utilize. Despite its advantages, researchers have been deeply examining the actual security guarantees offered by the current defences employed to safeguard container-based infrastructures over the past few years. This led to the discovery of significant flaws in the security controls employed for network security and process isolation. In this chapter, the authors highlight the security attacks/issues with the investigated serverless architecture platforms and suggest potential countermeasures.

Applications that are serverless can be distributed (many services are connected for smooth operation), elastic (resources can be scaled up and down without limit), stateless (interactions and data aren't stored), event-driven (resources are allocated only when triggered by an event), and hostless (apps aren't hosted on a server). Serverless computing is becoming more and more popular as cloud adoption rises. In many respects, serverless computing unleashes the entire potential of cloud computing. we pay only for the resources consumed, and resources are allocated, increased, or decreased dynamically based on user requirements in real-time. It makes sure that when there are no user requests and the application is effectively dormant, resources are immediately scaled to zero. More scalability and significant cost reductions are the outcomes of this. According to research by Global industry Insights, the serverless industry is expected to reach $30 billion in market value by the end of the forecast period, growing at an above-average rate of 25% between 2021 and 2027.

Serverless applications require a good development environment and the right tools. This chapter guides serverless computing application developers through installing and utilising essential components and technologies. VSCode is a robust code editor and debugger. Easy installation provides developers with a diverse code editing and debugging platform. AWSToolkit for VS Code simplifies serverless application development, testing, and release on Amazon web services (AWS). Fast setup with step-by-step instruction makes AWS serverless development easy for developers. Node.js is needed for serverless apps. Developers require Node.js for local and cloud serverless operations. This chapter briefly describes installation. Postman is essential for serverless API testing. Postman installation and use for serverless API testing and troubleshooting are covered in this chapter. Developers seeking efficiency will benefit. These concepts let developers build a strong development environment, integrate AWS resources, and leverage SDKs to build serverless apps.

This chapter explores serverless computing, a transformative paradigm that revolutionizes application development, deployment, and management. It provides an overview of the core principles and advantages driving its adoption in contemporary technological ecosystems, including function as a service (FaaS) offering, orchestration tools, and serverless frameworks. These technologies enable developers to focus on code execution, abstracting infrastructure management complexities, and serve as a guide for elucidating the efficacy and scalability of serverless architectures. This narrative delves into the evolution of serverless technologies, from early frameworks to sophisticated tools, emphasizing their significance in scalability, operational efficiency, and resource optimization, providing a guide for technologists, developers, and researchers.

Preface

In the ever-evolving landscape of computing, the paradigm shift towards Serverless Computing stands as a transformative technology, surpassing traditional cloud computing models with its unparalleled advantages, including reduced costs, lower latency, and the elimination of server-side management overhead. As the adoption of containerization and microservices architectures becomes prevalent, the significance of serverless computing continues to grow exponentially. Serverless computing isn't just a buzzword; it's a revolution.

This edited reference book, titled "Serverless Computing Concepts, Technology and Architecture," authored by Rajanikanth Aluvalu and Uma Maheswari V from Chaitanya Bharathi Institute of Technology, India, fills a critical void in the academic and research landscape by providing a comprehensive exploration of serverless computing. The authors delve into fundamental concepts, characteristics, challenges, applications, and futuristic approaches of serverless computing, offering a valuable resource for both novice learners and seasoned professionals.

Key Features:

- Fundamentals of Serverless Computing Concepts: The book begins by introducing readers to the foundational principles of serverless computing, providing a solid understanding of its core concepts.
- Exploration of Containerization and its Benefits: Containerization is explored in detail, highlighting its significance, benefits, and a comparison with virtualization.
- Discussion on Microservice Architecture: The authors delve into microservices, covering its architecture, characteristics, benefits, implementation challenges, and a comparative analysis with monolithic architecture.
- Introduction to Technologies and Tools: The book introduces various technologies and tools crucial for the implementation of serverless computing, including Visual Studio Code, Node.js, Postman, and SDKs.
- Case Studies of Serverless Computing Implementation: Real-world case studies are presented to provide practical insights into the successful implementation of serverless computing.

This book is designed to cater to the needs of doctoral and post-doctoral research scholars, as well as undergraduate and postgraduate students pursuing Computer Science, Information Technology, Electronics & Communication Engineering, and related disciplines. Furthermore, IT professionals, computer science researchers, scholars, and government agencies will find this book to be a comprehensive reference point for understanding and implementing serverless computing.

We are excited about introducing this book in various conferences, workshops, and faculty development programs in India and abroad. The intent is to make this resource readily available to universities and institutes' libraries, ensuring its accessibility to a broad audience.

As editors, we sincerely hope that this book serves as a valuable guide, fostering a deeper understanding of serverless computing and encouraging further research and innovation in this dynamic field.

Chapter 1: Introduction to Serverless Computing

This chapter, authored by Radhika Kavuri and Satya kiranmai Tadepalli from Chaitanya Bharathi Institute of Technology, India, offers a comprehensive exploration of serverless computing. Starting with a historical context, it delves into the fundamentals, limitations of traditional computing, and the emergence of serverless solutions. Core components, including compute services, storage services, and event triggers, are explained. The chapter navigates through serverless architecture, drawing comparisons with microservices and monolithic structures. Major serverless platforms like AWS, Azure, and Google Cloud are explored, along with considerations such as cold starts, vendor lock-in, security, and monitoring challenges. Real-world case studies provide practical insights, and the chapter concludes by discussing the future trajectory of serverless computing.

Chapter 2: Resource Allocation in Serverless Computing

Authored by Ramu Kuchipudi, Ramesh Babu Palamakula, and T Satyanarayana Murthy from Chaitanya Bharathi Institute of Technology, India, this chapter introduces readers to the dynamic and transformative world of serverless computing. Focusing on agility, scalability, and cost-effectiveness, it explores fundamental aspects of serverless architectures, including functions as a service (FaaS), event-driven programming, and cloud provider involvement. The chapter highlights how serverless systems optimize resource usage, speed up development, and adapt to changing user preferences. Practical use cases and success stories demonstrate successful serverless implementations across industries and domains.

Chapter 3: Serverless Computing - Unveiling the Future of Cloud Technology

Authored by Nidhi Worah and Megharani Patil from Thakur College Of Engineering and Technology, India, this chapter provides a comprehensive initiation into serverless computing. It elucidates foundational concepts, breaking down serverless architecture and its benefits such as enhanced efficiency, seamless scalability, and liberation from intricate server management. A comparative analysis with traditional cloud computing is presented, addressing challenges like cold start latency, execution duration limits, and potential vendor lock-in. Real-world applications in various domains, including real-time data processing, backend APIs, batch processing, and chatbots, are showcased, making this chapter an invaluable resource for readers exploring serverless computing.

Chapter 4: Exploring the World of Serverless Computing - Concepts, Benefits, and Challenges

Authored by Vishal Goar and Nagendra Singh Yadav from Engineering College Bikaner, India, this chapter focuses on the introduction to serverless computing, core concepts, advantages, challenges, use cases, industry adoption, best practices, and future trends. It explores how serverless computing promises seamless scalability, reduced operational overhead, and cost optimization, making it a dominant paradigm in cloud computing. The chapter provides a comprehensive overview of the benefits that serverless computing brings to the table, shaping the landscape of application development and deployment.

Chapter 5: Unraveling the Fabric of Serverless Computing: Technologies, Trends, and Integration Strategies

Authored by Subhi B from BIT Autonomous, India, this chapter provides a comprehensive overview of the evolving landscape of serverless computing. It focuses on the technologies and tools shaping the serverless ecosystem, exploring key technologies like Function-as-a-Service (FaaS), Backend-as-a-Service (BaaS), and event-driven architecture. The chapter discusses popular tools and platforms for developing, deploying, and managing serverless applications. Readers gain insights into the latest trends, best practices, and considerations for leveraging serverless computing effectively in modern IT environments.

Chapter 6: Containerization in the Context of Serverless Computing

Authored by Sai Samin Varma Pusapati from Chaitanya Bharathi Institute of Technology, India, this chapter delves into the synergy between containerization and serverless computing. It outlines the architectural foundations and benefits of each paradigm, emphasizing their combined impact on scalability, efficiency, and agility. The discussion progresses to technical integrations, focusing on container orchestration and serverless platforms, addressing challenges like security and operational complexity. Real-world examples illustrate the practical application of this convergence, positioning it as a significant driver for future cloud-native innovations.

Chapter 7: Containerization, Containers as a Service, and Container Security

Authored by Swapna Mudrakola, Krishna Keerthi Chennam, and Shitharth Selvarajan from various institutions in India, this chapter explores the drawbacks of virtualization in application deployment and introduces containers as a solution. It discusses Containerization, Containers as a Service, and Container Security, emphasizing the importance of efficient resource utilization and security in modern computing environments. Different tools designed for various aspects of security issues are introduced.

Chapter 8: Function as a Service (FaaS) for Fast, Efficient, Scalable Systems

Authored by Sai Prashanth Mallellu, Uma Maheswari V, Rajanikanth Aluvalu, and MVV Prasad Kantipudi from various institutions in India, this chapter provides an overview of Function as a Service (FaaS), a central component of serverless computing. It emphasizes FaaS's transformative role in modern cloud computing, allowing developers to create stateless functions triggered by specific events without direct infrastructure management. The pay-per-use model, automatic scaling, and event-driven execution contribute to an efficient, cost-effective, and responsive application development process.

Chapter 9: Scalable and Microservice-Oriented Approach using FaaS

Authored by Swathi Sowmya Bavirthi, Bala Krishna Peesala, Santhosh V, and Swathi K from Chaitanya Bharathi Institute of Technology (Autonomous), India, this chapter explores the world of Function as a Service (FaaS) within cloud computing. It covers FaaS's evolution, serverless architecture, event-driven programming, and statelessness. The exploration involves establishing FaaS environments using AWS Lambda, IBM Bluemix OpenWhisk, Azure Functions, Auth0 Webtask, and Google Cloud Functions. The chapter emphasizes the advantages of adopting event-driven, serverless methodologies and optimization techniques involved in FaaS.

Chapter 10: Review of Grid-Cloud Distributed Environments - Fusion Fault Tolerance Replication Model and Fragmentation

Authored by Dharmesh Dhabliya, Ananta Ojha, Amandeep Gill, Asha Uchil, Anishkumar Dhablia, Jambi Ratna Raja Kumar, Ankur Gupta, and Sabyasachi Pramanik from various institutions in India, this chapter reviews Grid-Cloud Distributed Environments. It discusses the importance of data replication in providing up-to-date information to geographically distant users. The chapter covers distributed database replication, fragmentation, and the need for fault tolerance in fragmented data replication.

Chapter 11: Unraveling the Complex Challenges and Innovative Solutions in Microservice Architecture

Authored by Kaushikkumar Patel from TransUnion LLC, United States, this chapter delves into the challenges of microservice architecture within serverless computing. It outlines strategic remedies for operational hurdles, security concerns, performance bottlenecks, and resource management in serverless frameworks. Proposed solutions include advanced system monitoring, state-of-the-art security safeguards, and innovative optimization strategies. The chapter concludes with prospective research directions, offering a pragmatic blueprint for microservice implementation in serverless infrastructures.

Chapter 12: NodeJS and Postman for Serverless Computing

Authored by Rajesh Kannan Kannan, Meena Abarna K T, Vairachilai S, and Vijayalakshmi R from various institutions in India, this chapter focuses on Node.js and Postman for serverless computing. It provides insights into the robust, open-source, cross-platform server-side JavaScript runtime environment, Node.js. The chapter highlights Node.js's advantages, including its event-driven architecture, and how it facilitates code reuse for both client and server-side scripting. Postman, essential for serverless API testing, is also covered, providing developers with valuable tools for testing and troubleshooting serverless APIs.

Chapter 13: Serverless Computing - A Security Viewpoint

Authored by Padmavathi Vurubindi and Sujatha Canavoy Narahari from various institutions in India, this chapter examines serverless computing from a security viewpoint. It explores the advantages and challenges of serverless computing platforms and suggests potential countermeasures for addressing security attacks and issues. The chapter highlights the shift in infrastructure maintenance and operational chores to cloud service providers, focusing on security guarantees and flaws in current defense mechanisms.

Chapter 14: Applications of Serverless Computing - Systematic Overview

Authored by Kathirvel A from Karunya Institute of Technology and Sciences (Missing Country), this chapter provides a systematic overview of applications in serverless computing. It explores the characteristics of serverless applications, including distribution, elasticity, statelessness, event-driven nature, and hostlessness. The chapter emphasizes the growing popularity of serverless computing, predicting a market value of $30 billion by 2027, driven by scalability, cost reductions, and cloud adoption.

Chapter 15: Development Environment, Tools, and SDKs for Serverless Computing

Authored by Ashwin Raiyani, Sheetal Pandya, and Sampath Boopathi from various institutions in India, this chapter guides serverless computing application developers through the installation and utilization of essential components and technologies. It covers the use of VSCode as a robust code editor, the AWS Toolkit for VS Code for simplified serverless application development, and the importance of Node.js for local and cloud serverless operations. The chapter also introduces Postman for serverless API testing, providing developers with insights into building a strong development environment and leveraging SDKs for building serverless applications.

Chapter 16: A Study on Landscape of Serverless Computing: Technologies and Tools for Seamless Implementation

Authored by T. Kalaiselvi, G. Saravanan, T. Haritha, A.V. Santhosh Babu, M Sakthivel, and Sampath Boopathi from various institutions in India, this chapter explores the landscape of serverless computing. It provides an overview of the core principles and advantages driving the adoption of serverless computing, including Function as a Service (FaaS) offerings, orchestration tools, and serverless frameworks. The narrative delves into the evolution of serverless technologies, from early frameworks to sophisticated tools, emphasizing their significance in scalability, operational efficiency, and resource optimization. The chapter serves as a guide for technologists, developers, and researchers interested in understanding and implementing serverless computing.

The edited reference book, "Serverless Computing Concepts, Technology and Architecture," authored by Rajanikanth Aluvalu and Uma Maheswari V from Chaitanya Bharathi Institute of Technology, India, addresses a critical gap in academic and research literature. The comprehensive exploration of fundamental concepts, characteristics, challenges, applications, and futuristic approaches to serverless computing provides a valuable resource for both newcomers and seasoned professionals in the field.

Tailored to meet the needs of doctoral and post-doctoral research scholars, as well as undergraduate and postgraduate students in Computer Science, Information Technology, Electronics & Communication Engineering, and related disciplines, this book is also a comprehensive reference for IT professionals, computer science researchers, scholars, and government agencies.

We eagerly anticipate introducing this book, aiming to make it readily available in universities and institutes' libraries for a diverse audience.

As editors, our sincere hope is that this book serves as a valuable guide, fostering a deeper understanding of serverless computing and inspiring further research and innovation in this dynamic and evolving field.

The Editors,

Rajanikanth Aluvalu
Chaitanya Bharathi Institute of Technology, India

Uma Maheswari V
Chaitanya Bharathi Institute of Technology, India

Chapter 1
Introduction to Serverless Computing

Radhika Kavuri
Chaitanya Bharathi Institute of Technology, India

Satya kiranmai Tadepalli
Chaitanya Bharathi Institute of Technology, India

ABSTRACT

The chapter provides a comprehensive exploration of the dynamic and efficient realm of serverless computing. Beginning with a historical context, the chapter delves into the serverless fundamentals, limitations of traditional computing and the emergence of serverless solutions. The core components of serverless computing, including computer services, storage services, and event triggers, are explained. The chapter navigates through serverless architecture, drawing comparisons with microservices and monolithic structures, and highlights the role of serverless frameworks in facilitating development. Major serverless platforms, including Amazon web services, Microsoft Azure, and Google Cloud Platform, are explored in detail. The chapter addresses considerations such as cold starts, vendor lock-in, security concerns, and monitoring/debugging challenges. Real-world case studies provide practical insights into successful serverless implementations. In conclusion, the chapter discusses the future trajectory of serverless computing.

1. INTRODUCTION

In the ever-evolving landscape of information technology, the pursuit of more efficient, scalable, and cost-effective computing solutions has led to a paradigm shift known as serverless computing. This transformative approach challenges traditional server-based architectures, offering a dynamic alternative that allows developers to focus on writing code without the burden of managing underlying infrastructure. This chapter, "Introduction to Serverless Computing," is a comprehensive exploration of this revolutionary computing model, unravelling its core concepts, major platforms, and practical applications.

DOI: 10.4018/979-8-3693-1682-5.ch001

As we embark on this journey, we will begin by defining serverless computing and examining its historical roots, setting the stage for a deeper understanding of why this paradigm has gained prominence. The limitations and challenges of traditional computing architectures will be scrutinized, providing context for the compelling need that fuelled the rise of serverless solutions.

With a solid foundation established, the chapter navigates through the fundamental principles of serverless computing. We will unravel the intricate web of components, including compute and storage services, event triggers, and the stateless nature of execution. Through this exploration, readers will gain insight into the inherent benefits of serverless, such as enhanced cost efficiency, unparalleled scalability, and accelerated development cycles.

Serverless architecture, a key aspect of this paradigm, will be dissected, drawing comparisons with established models like microservices and monolithic structures. The role of serverless frameworks in simplifying development processes will be highlighted, providing a bridge between conceptual understanding and practical implementation.

The journey continues with an in-depth examination of major serverless platforms, featuring Amazon Web Services (AWS), Microsoft Azure, and Google Cloud Platform (GCP). Key services, including AWS Lambda, Azure Functions, and GCP Cloud Functions, will be explored to offer readers a comprehensive view of the diverse tools available for serverless development. Real-world applications form a significant portion of our exploration. Use cases spanning web and mobile applications, Internet of Things (IoT), real-time data processing, and more will illustrate the versatility and applicability of serverless computing in various domains. However, this paradigm shift is not without its challenges. We will delve into considerations such as cold starts, vendor lock-in, security concerns, and the nuances of monitoring and debugging in serverless environments. Moreover, the chapter will outline best practices, guiding readers on designing robust serverless solutions, implementing effective testing strategies, and establishing seamless deployment pipelines.

Looking ahead, the chapter explores the future trends and developments in the serverless landscape. The integration with edge computing, containers, and machine learning represents the next frontier, promising even greater innovation and efficiency. To ground our exploration in practicality, real-world case studies will be presented, offering tangible examples of successful serverless implementations. These case studies provide a bridge between theory and application, offering valuable insights for readers at various stages of their serverless journey. In conclusion, this chapter will summarize key takeaways, providing a cohesive understanding of serverless computing and its transformative impact on modern application development. Whether you are a newcomer seeking an introduction to serverless or an experienced practitioner looking to deepen your knowledge, this chapter aims to be your comprehensive guide through the exciting realm of serverless computing.

2. SERVERLESS COMPUTING AND ITS EVOLUTION

Serverless computing, often synonymous with Function as a Service (FaaS), is a revolutionary cloud computing paradigm that redefines how applications are developed, deployed, and scaled. At its essence, serverless computing empowers developers to focus solely on writing code without the encumbrance of managing servers or infrastructure. In this model, applications are constructed as a collection of independent functions, each designed to execute specific tasks in response to events or triggers. The term "serverless" can be misleading; servers are still a crucial part of the process, but the operational intricacies are abstracted away. Cloud providers dynamically allocate resources, handling the provisioning, scaling, and maintenance autonomously (Wen et al., 2023). This abstraction allows for a more agile, scalable, and cost-effective approach to application development. Serverless computing is characterized by its event-driven nature. Functions are executed in response to events such as HTTP requests, database changes, or file uploads. This event-driven architecture facilitates the creation of modular, loosely coupled components, leading to more flexible and maintainable applications. While the term "serverless" became popular in recent years, the seeds of this revolution were sown much earlier (Hassan et al., 2021). Fig. 1 presents the key milestones in the fascinating history of serverless computing.

Early Beginnings (1960s to 1990s):

1960s: Virtualization technology laid the foundation for sharing and optimizing computing resources, paving the way for future cloud infrastructure.

1970s: IBM introduced virtual machines (VMs) on its mainframe systems, marking the first step towards renting computing capabilities.

1980s & 1990s: Rise of containerization technologies like Docker and OpenVZ, enabling further isolation and portability of software from the underlying hardware.

Laying the Groundwork (2000s):

2008: Google App Engine launched, offering limited serverless capabilities with metered billing for applications developed using a custom Python framework.

2010: PiCloud provided serverless support for Python, further expanding the technology's reach.

Serverless Takes Center Stage (2014 to Present):

2014: Amazon Web Services (AWS) introduced AWS Lambda, marking a pivotal moment in popularizing serverless computing. Its abstract serverless model and diverse features triggered widespread adoption.

Figure 1. Key milestones of serverless computing

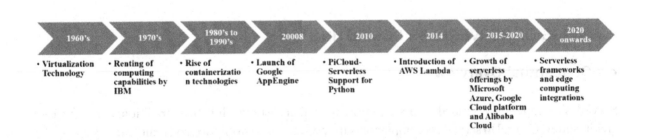

2015 to 2020: Rapid growth of serverless offerings from other cloud providers like Microsoft Azure, Google Cloud Platform, and Alibaba Cloud, creating a vibrant ecosystem and driving innovation.

2020 onwards: Serverless continues to evolve with new features, functionalities, and expanded use cases (Li, 2022). Serverless frameworks, open-source projects, and edge computing integrations enhance its flexibility and potential.

3. TRADITIONAL SERVER-BASED ARCHITECTURES

Traditional server-based architectures form the foundation upon which computing systems have historically operated. In this model, applications run on dedicated servers, which are physical or virtual machines provisioned to handle specific tasks. These servers are responsible for processing requests, managing databases, and executing application logic. One characteristic of traditional architectures is their static nature. Servers need to be provisioned in advance, leading to challenges in predicting and managing resource requirements accurately. This can result in over-provisioning, leading to wasted resources, or under-provisioning, causing performance bottlenecks during peak loads.

Despite being the long-standing norm, traditional server-based architectures come with inherent challenges and limitations described as follows: Scaling traditional architectures vertically by adding more resources to a single server has limitations. Horizontal scaling, involving the addition of more servers, can be complex and requires manual intervention. Servers in traditional architectures often operate at less than full capacity, leading to inefficient resource utilization and increased operational costs. System maintenance, updates, and patching require significant effort and may lead to downtime, impacting the availability of services. Traditional architectures may struggle to adapt to dynamic workloads, making it challenging to respond swiftly to changing demands. Cost considerations are a critical aspect of traditional server-based architectures. The need to purchase and maintain physical hardware involves substantial upfront costs. Ongoing operational expenses include electricity, cooling, and personnel for server maintenance and management. Scaling infrastructure to accommodate growth can be expensive, requiring investment in additional hardware and resources. Unplanned downtime for maintenance or system failures can result in financial losses and damage to the organization's reputation.

4. BASICS OF SERVERLESS COMPUTING

4.1 Conceptual Overview

Serverless computing is guided by a set of principles that distinguish it from traditional server-based architectures. Central to serverless computing is the concept of an event-driven architecture. Instead of a traditional request-response model, serverless applications respond to events. Events can include HTTP requests, changes in database, file uploads, or even scheduled tasks. Functions are triggered in response to these events, allowing for a more modular and flexible system. Serverless functions are designed to be stateless, meaning they don't store information between executions. Each function is independent and focuses on performing a specific task in response to an event. Any necessary state or data persistence is typically managed by external services like databases. Unlike traditional architectures where servers are continuously running, serverless functions are executed on-demand. They come to life in response to specific events, ensuring resources are allocated precisely when needed. Once the function execution is complete, the resources are deallocated. One of the key advantages of serverless computing is the abstraction of infrastructure management. Cloud providers take on the responsibility of server provisioning, scaling, and maintenance. Developers are liberated from the complexities of managing servers, allowing them to focus solely on writing code. Serverless computing often aligns with microservices architecture. Applications are broken down into smaller, independent functions or microservices that can be developed, deployed, and scaled independently. This modular approach enhances maintainability, scalability, and flexibility. Serverless computing follows a pay-as-you-go pricing model. Users are billed based on the actual compute resources consumed during the execution of functions. This can lead to cost savings, especially in scenarios where the workload varies over time. Serverless functions are ephemeral, meaning they have a short lifespan. They are created, executed, and then terminated once the task is completed. This ephemeral nature aligns with the serverless philosophy of efficient resource utilization.

4.2 Key Components

Serverless computing is comprised of several key components that work together to enable the development and execution of applications without the need for traditional server management. These components form the building blocks of serverless architecture, providing a foundation for efficient and scalable application development. Here are the key components of serverless computing:

Function as a Service (FaaS): At the heart of serverless computing is FaaS, which allows developers to write and deploy functions that are executed in response to events. These functions are the core executable units in a serverless application. Prominent examples include AWS Lambda, Azure Functions, and Google Cloud Functions.

Object Storage: Serverless applications often rely on object storage services for data persistence. For example, Amazon S3, Azure Storage, and Google Cloud Storage provide scalable and durable storage solutions. These services are commonly used to store and retrieve data for serverless functions.

Event Sources: Events act as triggers for serverless functions, initiating their execution. Event sources can vary, including HTTP requests, changes in databases, file uploads, or even scheduled tasks. Cloud providers offer a variety of event sources that can seamlessly integrate with serverless functions.

API Management Services: API gateways, such as AWS API Gateway or Azure API Management, play a crucial role in serverless architectures. They enable the exposure of serverless functions as HTTP-based APIs, allowing external systems to invoke these functions through standard HTTP requests.

Abstraction Tools: Serverless frameworks, like the Serverless Framework or AWS SAM (Serverless Application Model), provide abstraction layers that simplify the deployment and management of serverless applications. These frameworks handle infrastructure provisioning, configuration, and other operational tasks, allowing developers to focus on writing code.

Identity and Access Management (IAM): Serverless applications often require robust authentication and authorization mechanisms. IAM services, provided by cloud platforms, help control access to serverless functions and other resources, ensuring security and compliance.

Observability Tools: Monitoring and logging are critical for understanding the performance and behavior of serverless applications. Cloud providers offer tools like AWS CloudWatch, Azure Monitor, and Google Cloud Logging to track metrics, monitor logs, and gain insights into application behavior.

Database Integration: Serverless functions often interact with databases and backend services to retrieve or store data. Cloud databases like AWS DynamoDB, Azure Cosmos DB, or Google Cloud Firestore seamlessly integrate with serverless architectures, providing scalable and managed data storage.

4.3 Benefits of Serverless Computing

Serverless computing offers a range of benefits that have contributed to its growing popularity in the world of application development. The cloud provider automatically scales your functions based on demand, eliminating the need for manual server provisioning and configuration. This ensures smooth performance during peak loads and cost optimization during low activity. As mentioned earlier, you only pay for the actual execution time and resources used by your functions. This breaks away from the fixed-cost model of traditional servers, leading to potentially significant cost savings, especially for applications with variable workloads. While FaaS is central, serverless goes beyond. Many cloud providers offer additional services like serverless databases, storage, messaging, and APIs, all managed and integrated with FaaS for a complete serverless application development platform. Serverless functions are naturally aligned with the microservices approach, promoting modularity, isolation, and scalability. Each function handles a specific task, making development and deployment easier and independent. Serverless simplifies server management, freeing up developer and ops teams to focus on core application logic and faster deployments. This enhances agility and enables rapid iteration on new features. Multi-language support is rapidly evolving in serverless computing, offering more flexibility and choice for developers. Most major cloud providers support a variety of popular languages natively in their serverless platforms. Common languages supported include Node.js, Python, Java, Go, .NET Core catering to the needs of a wide variety of applications as shown in Fig. 2. Additional languages are often supported through containerization techniques, allowing the use of any language with a Docker image.

Figure 2. Multi-Language support by serverless platforms

Multi-Language Support				
Node.js	**Python**	**Java**	**Go**	**.Net Core**
• Widely used for event-driven and microservices architectures	• Popular for Data Science and Analytics tasks	• Powerful for enterprise applications and complex work loads	• Efficient for concurrent applications and high performance computing	• Suitable for building cloud-native applications using C#

4.4 Micro-Services and Monolith Architectures

Microservices architecture is an approach to designing and building software applications as a collection of small, independent services, each running in its own process and communicating with other services through well-defined APIs (Application Programming Interfaces). This architectural style contrasts with monolithic architectures, where an entire application is developed and deployed as a single unit (Ponce et al., 2019).

Micro-services Architecture:

The key characteristics and challenges associated with microservices architecture are presented as follows.

Microservices are independent units, each responsible for a specific business capability. They can be developed, deployed, and scaled independently. Each microservice manages its own data storage. Services communicate through APIs, and data consistency is maintained through careful design. Microservices can be deployed independently, allowing for more frequent updates without affecting the entire application. Different microservices within an application can use different programming languages, frameworks, and databases based on their specific requirements. Services can be scaled independently based on demand for specific functionalities, providing better resource utilization. Failures in one microservice don't necessarily impact the entire application, as other services can continue to function. Teams can work on different microservices, promoting parallel development and deployment.

Managing a distributed system of microservices can introduce complexities in terms of orchestration, deployment, and monitoring. Effective communication between microservices is crucial and requires careful design to avoid latency and data consistency issues. Ensuring data consistency across multiple services can be challenging and requires proper coordination. Testing a microservices-based system can be more complex due to the need to simulate various interactions between services. Operational aspects, such as monitoring, logging, and deployment, can be more challenging in a microservices environment.

Monolith Architecture:

Monolithic architecture refers to a traditional software design approach where an entire application is developed, deployed, and maintained as a single, tightly-coupled unit. In a monolithic architecture, all the components of the application, including the user interface, business logic, and data access layer, are bundled together within the same codebase. This contrasts with other architectural styles, such as microservices, which decompose an application into smaller, independent services.

The entire application is built as a single, unified codebase, making it easier to develop and initially deploy. Monolithic architectures are often simpler to develop and test initially, as there is a single codebase to manage. Components are closely interconnected, and changes in one part of the application may require modifications in other parts. Scaling a monolithic application typically involves replicating the entire application, which can be less efficient than scaling individual components. While monolithic architectures have been widely used and are straightforward for smaller applications, they can present challenges as applications grow in size and complexity. Issues such as increased maintenance difficulty, limited scalability, and challenges in adopting new technologies without affecting the entire system may arise.

4.5 Cloud vs. Serverless: A Comparative Overview

The ever-evolving landscape of cloud computing presents a plethora of service models, each catering to distinct needs and offering varying levels of abstraction as shown in Fig.3. The four dominant paradigms Infrastructure as a Service (IaaS), Platform as a Service (PaaS), Software as a Service (SaaS), and Function as a Service (FaaS) are described below:

Figure 3. Cloud service models

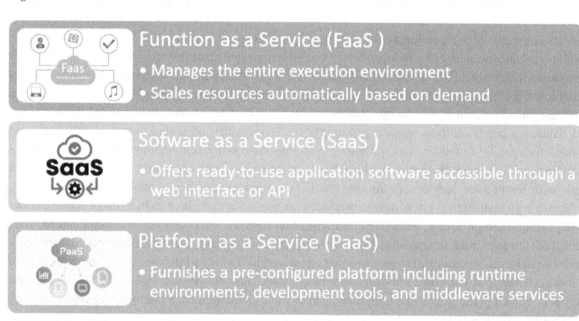

IaaS: IaaS offers virtualized access to fundamental computing resources such as servers, storage and networking granting users a granular control over their infrastructure environment. This necessitates significant expertise in system administration, operating system management, and security configuration. However, IaaS provides unparalleled flexibility, enabling the deployment of custom applications, intricate architectures, and specialized configurations, making it ideal for large-scale enterprise deployments, high-performance computing workloads.

PaaS: Ascending a level of abstraction, PaaS furnishes a pre-configured platform encompassing runtime environments, development tools, and middleware services. Users focus on developing, deploying, and managing applications while PaaS handles the underlying infrastructure complexities (Evan Eyk et al., 2018). This translates to faster development cycles, improved resource utilization, and simplified scaling. PaaS excels in web and mobile application development, application modernization efforts, and rapid prototyping initiatives.

SaaS: SaaS represents the ultimate in cloud abstraction, offering ready-to-use application software accessible through a web interface or API (Rajan et al., 2018). Users subscribe to pre-built functionalities, eliminating the need for infrastructure management, application development, or maintenance. This model promotes operational efficiency, rapid onboarding, and simplified resource allocation, making it a preferred choice for common business applications (CRM, HR, accounting) and standardized workflows.

FaaS: Emerging as a disruptive force, FaaS breaks the paradigm of traditional application deployment (Rajan et al., 2020). Users focus on composing and uploading serverless functions triggered by specific events (API calls, user actions, data changes). The cloud provider manages the entire execution environment, scaling resources automatically based on demand. This event-driven model fosters agile development, simplifies microservices architecture implementation, and reduces operational overhead, making it ideal for building reactive applications, integrating with third-party APIs, and handling asynchronous workloads.

4.6 Serverless Frameworks

Serverless frameworks are tools and platforms designed to facilitate the development, deployment, and management of serverless applications. Serverless computing, also known as Function as a Service (FaaS), is a cloud computing model where cloud providers automatically manage the underlying infrastructure, allowing developers to focus solely on writing code for specific functions or services. Serverless frameworks abstract away the complexities of server management, making it easier for developers to build scalable, event-driven applications (Kritikos et al., 2018). Key aspects of serverless frameworks are explained as follows:

Table 1. Characteristics of popular serverless frameworks

Framework	Supported Providers	Programming Languages	Features
Serverless Framework	AWS, Azure, Google Cloud, IBM Cloud, Oracle Cloud, Alibaba Cloud, Knative, OpenWhisk, Fn Project	Node.js, Python, Java, C#, Go, Ruby, Swift, PHP, Scala, Kotlin, and more	Configuration-driven, plugin support, multi-provider support, packaging and deployment, function management, event configuration, monitoring and logging, CI/CD integration, community support, mature and widely adopted
AWS SAM	AWS	Node.js, Python, Java, C#, Go, Ruby, Swift, PHP, Scala, Kotlin, and more	Tight integration with AWS services, built-in validation, local development and testing, AWS-specific features (e.g., Step Functions, X-Ray), integration with AWS IDE Toolkit
Google Cloud Functions Framework	Google Cloud	Node.js, Python, Java, Go, Ruby, PHP, .NET Core, Rust	Built for Google Cloud, streamlined for Google Cloud services, integration with Firebase, Cloud Run support
Azure Functions Core Tools	Azure	.NET, Node.js, Python, Java, PowerShell, C#, F#, TypeScript	Optimized for Azure, local development and testing, Azure-specific features (e.g., Durable Functions, Logic Apps), integration with Visual Studio
Apache OpenWhisk	OpenWhisk, IBM Cloud	Multiple languages supported through Docker images	Open-source, flexible, multi-cloud support, action-based architecture, supports various programming languages through Docker

Serverless frameworks abstract the infrastructure layer, handling server provisioning, scaling, and maintenance. Developers define functions or services and specify the events that trigger their execution. The framework takes care of provisioning the necessary resources dynamically in response to these events. Serverless applications operate on an event-driven model. Functions are executed in response to specific events or triggers, such as HTTP requests, changes in a database, file uploads, or timers. The framework automatically manages the flow of events and triggers the associated functions accordingly. One of the key benefits of serverless frameworks is automatic scaling. As events occur and functions are triggered, the framework dynamically allocates resources to handle the workload. This enables efficient resource utilization, and developers do not need to manually configure or manage scaling settings.

Serverless frameworks often integrate with managed services provided by cloud providers. These services include databases, storage, authentication, and more. Integration with these services simplifies common tasks and allows developers to leverage pre-built functionality without managing the underlying infrastructure. While specific serverless offerings are associated with certain cloud providers (e.g., AWS Lambda, Azure Functions, Google Cloud Functions), some serverless frameworks aim for cross-cloud compatibility. For instance, the Serverless Framework supports multiple cloud providers, enabling developers to write functions that can be deployed on different platforms. The characteristics of the 5 most popular Serverless frame works are presented in Table 1.

5. MAJOR SERVERLESS PLATFORMS

5.1 AWS Lambda

AWS Lambda is a serverless compute service provided by Amazon Web Services (AWS) that enables developers to run code in response to events without the need to provision or manage servers. With AWS Lambda, developers can upload their code (written in languages such as Python, Node.js, Java, and others), define the triggering events, and let AWS take care of the underlying infrastructure. This service operates on a pay-as-you-go model, where users are billed based on the actual compute resources consumed during the execution of their functions. AWS Lambda functions are often triggered by events from various sources, such as API Gateway, Amazon S3, Amazon DynamoDB, Amazon SNS, and more. Events can be configured to trigger functions automatically, creating an event-driven architecture. Lambda functions are designed to be highly scalable and can be triggered by a variety of events, such as changes to data in an Amazon S3 bucket, updates to a DynamoDB table, HTTP requests through Amazon API Gateway, or even custom events.

Amazon API Gateway allows you to create, publish, and manage APIs without the need to provision or manage servers. It integrates seamlessly with AWS Lambda to build serverless APIs. Amazon S3 is an object storage service that is commonly used to store and retrieve data in serverless architectures. It can trigger AWS Lambda functions based on events such as object creation or deletion. DynamoDB is a fully managed NoSQL database that can be used in serverless applications. It scales automatically and can trigger AWS Lambda functions based on changes to the database. AWS Step Functions allow you to coordinate multiple AWS services into serverless workflows. It provides a visual interface for defining and executing state machines, making it easier to build and manage complex, multi-step processes. AWS App Runner is a fully managed service for building, deploying, and scaling containerized applications. It abstracts away the complexity of managing infrastructure and is well-suited for serverless-like application deployment. Serverless Application Repository (SAR) is a repository of serverless applications that can be deployed easily. Developers can discover and deploy pre-built applications, accelerating the development process. AWS Lambda and these complementary services collectively provide a serverless architecture where developers can focus on writing code and building applications without the need to manage the underlying infrastructure. The pay-as-you-go pricing model ensures cost efficiency by charging only for the compute resources consumed during function execution.

AWS Lambda supports parallel execution of functions, enabling it to handle a large number of requests simultaneously. Its event-driven nature makes it well-suited for building serverless architectures and microservices, where functions can be independently developed, deployed, and scaled. AWS Lambda integrates seamlessly with other AWS services, allowing developers to create powerful, event-driven applications with minimal operational overhead.

5.2 Microsoft Azure Serverless Platform

Microsoft Azure provides a comprehensive serverless computing platform that enables developers to build, deploy, and scale applications without managing the underlying infrastructure. Azure's serverless offerings, primarily centered around Azure Functions, allow developers to focus on writing code for specific functions without worrying about server provisioning, maintenance, or scaling. Azure Functions support a variety of programming languages, including C#, Java, Python, and JavaScript/Node.js, providing flexibility for developers to use their preferred language (Kelly et al., 2020).

Azure Functions operate on an event-driven model, responding to triggers such as HTTP requests, database changes, or messages in a queue. This event-driven architecture enables the creation of highly responsive and scalable applications that automatically scale based on demand (Taneska et al., 2023). With Azure Logic Apps, developers can orchestrate workflows by connecting various services and triggers, creating a visual representation of business processes that can be easily automated.

The Azure serverless platform integrates seamlessly with other Azure services, such as Azure Storage, Azure Cosmos DB, and Azure Event Hubs, offering a cohesive ecosystem for building modern, cloudnative applications. With features like automatic scaling, pay-as-you-go pricing, and robust integration capabilities, Azure's serverless platform empowers developers to focus on building innovative solutions while Azure takes care of the operational complexities.

5.3 Google Cloud Platform Serverless

Google Cloud Platform (GCP) offers a robust serverless platform that allows developers to build, deploy, and scale applications without managing the underlying infrastructure. At the heart of GCP's serverless offerings is Google Cloud Functions, a compute service that lets developers write single-purpose functions in languages such as Node.js, Python, Go, and Java. These functions are triggered by various events, such as changes in Cloud Storage, incoming HTTP requests, or modifications in a Firestore database.

Google Cloud Functions provide automatic scaling; meaning resources are dynamically allocated based on the number of incoming requests. This enables developers to build highly responsive applications that efficiently handle varying workloads. Google Cloud Functions are designed to be stateless and event-driven, promoting a microservices-like architecture where individual functions can be developed, deployed, and scaled independently.

Additionally, GCP's serverless platform includes services like Cloud Run, which allows developers to deploy containerized applications in a serverless environment. Cloud Run offers the flexibility to use any programming language and dependency, making it versatile for various application architectures. GCP's serverless platform seamlessly integrates with other Google Cloud services, fostering a cohesive ecosystem for building modern applications. With features like automatic scaling, pay-as-you-go pricing, and a range of integrated services, GCP's serverless platform provides developers with a powerful environment to focus on writing code and building scalable applications.

6 SERVERLESS USE-CASES

6.1 Auto-Scaling Websites

Websites often experience varying levels of traffic throughout the day, week, or year. Events such as product launches, marketing campaigns, or news coverage can result in sudden spikes in user activity. Serverless autoscaling allows the hosting infrastructure to dynamically adjust to these fluctuations in real-time, ensuring optimal performance during peak periods and efficient resource utilization during low-traffic times. Traditional hosting models may involve provisioning a fixed amount of resources to handle peak loads, leading to over-provisioning and increased costs during idle periods (Samea et al., 2020). Serverless autoscaling allows you to pay only for the resources consumed during active periods. The ability to scale down to zero when there is no traffic can significantly reduce hosting costs, making it a cost-effective solution. Serverless computing is inherently event-driven, aligning well with the nature of web requests. Each user request or HTTP trigger can be treated as an event that triggers the execution of serverless functions. This event-driven architecture enables quick and automatic scaling based on the demand, allowing the hosting environment to respond rapidly to changes in traffic patterns. Serverless platforms excel at rapid scaling. When there's a sudden surge in traffic, serverless autoscaling can quickly provision additional compute resources to handle the increased load. This ensures that the website remains responsive and maintains a positive user experience even during unexpected traffic spikes. With serverless autoscaling, developers can focus primarily on building the core functionality of the website rather than managing the underlying infrastructure. This abstraction simplifies development, speeds up deployment, and reduces operational overhead. Developers can concentrate on writing code and creating features without worrying about scaling configurations and server maintenance. Functions are distributed across multiple servers, availability zones, or regions, reducing the risk of service disruptions. This ensures that the website remains accessible and resilient to potential failures. Serverless autoscaling is highly elastic, allowing the hosting environment to scale both up and down in response to changes in demand (Perez et al., 2023). This elasticity ensures that the website can handle varying levels of traffic without manual intervention, providing a seamless and scalable user experience.

6.2 Image and Video Manipulation Applications

Serverless computing is well-suited for various image and video manipulation applications, offering a scalable and cost-effective solution. Batch processing of images for tasks such as resizing, cropping, rotating, or applying filters. Serverless solution triggers serverless functions in response to image upload events or scheduled jobs to perform processing tasks. The serverless model enables parallel processing of multiple images without the need for maintaining a constant infrastructure.

Converting video formats, extracting clips, or adding effects to videos utilize serverless functions to transcode videos or apply edits based on triggered events. This allows for efficient and on-demand video processing without the need for continuous server provisioning. Analyzing images and videos to identify and filter out inappropriate or sensitive content. Serverless solution involves triggering serverless functions on image or video uploads to perform content moderation using machine learning models. Serverless autoscaling ensures that moderation tasks can handle varying workloads, especially during peak usage.

Detecting and tracking objects within images or video frames for applications like surveillance or analytics can utilize serverless functions that are triggered by image or video events to perform object recognition and tracking.

The serverless solution for identifying and verifying individuals from facial features within images or video frames deploy serverless functions triggered by image or video uploads to perform facial recognition tasks. Search functionality based on visual content within images or videos implement serverless functions to extract and index visual features for search. Trigger functions on media upload events to ensure that the search index is continually updated. Adding watermarks to images or videos for copyright protection or branding purposes implement serverless functions triggered by image or video uploads to apply watermarks. The serverless model ensures efficient processing, especially during periods of high upload activity.

Real-time Image and Video Processing involves processing images or videos in real-time for applications like live streaming or augmented reality. Serverless solutions use serverless functions triggered by real-time events to process and manipulate visual content on-the-fly.

6.3 Online Judge

An online judge is a platform that allows users to submit programming code, which is then executed on a server to determine if it produces the correct output for a set of predefined test cases. These platforms are commonly used in programming competitions, coding challenges, and educational settings to assess and improve participants' coding skills.

Serverless computing allows the online judge to automatically scale based on the number of incoming code submissions. During peak times, such as during a programming competition or when a large number of users are participating, serverless platforms can quickly scale up to handle the increased load. This ensures that the online judge remains responsive and can handle a high volume of concurrent code executions. With serverless computing, the online judge only pays for the actual compute resources used during code execution. Traditional server-based models may require maintaining a fleet of servers to handle potential peaks in demand, leading to higher costs. Serverless platforms, on the other hand, automatically allocate resources as needed and scale down during periods of low activity, resulting in cost savings.

Serverless computing is inherently event-driven. In the context of an online judge, events could be code submissions. When a user submits code, an event triggers the execution of the code on a serverless function. This event-driven architecture allows for efficient handling of individual code submissions without the need for continuous server provisioning. Serverless platforms abstract away the underlying infrastructure management tasks. This allows the developers of the online judge to focus on building and optimizing the code execution environment without worrying about server provisioning, scaling, or maintenance. This abstraction simplifies the overall development and operational processes. Serverless functions are designed to be deployed quickly, making it easy to update and iterate on the code execution environment of the online judge. This agility is beneficial when introducing new features, optimizing performance, or addressing security concerns. Serverless platforms often provide built-in fault tolerance. If an individual function execution fails, the platform can automatically retry the operation or redirect the request to a healthy instance, ensuring a robust and reliable online judge system.

6.4 IoT and Real-Time Data Processing

Serverless computing provides a robust solution for Internet of Things (IoT) deployments by seamlessly handling event-driven device communication, dynamic data ingestion, and scalable device management. In IoT scenarios, serverless functions efficiently process data generated by sensors or devices, responding in real-time to events like status changes or user interactions. This allows for immediate actions based on IoT events and enables the system to dynamically scale as the number of connected devices grows. Additionally, serverless architectures are well-suited for managing the variability in IoT workloads, ensuring that applications can efficiently process and analyze data streams while maintaining responsiveness (Cassel, 2022).

For real-time data processing, serverless computing excels in building event-driven data pipelines, enabling organizations to construct flexible and scalable frameworks for processing streaming data. Real-time analytics, facilitated by serverless functions, empowers organizations to gain immediate insights into data trends and patterns. Serverless functions play a crucial role in generating real-time notifications and alerts based on specific data conditions, enhancing situational awareness and allowing for rapid responses to critical events. Moreover, serverless computing supports the creation of live dashboards and visualizations that dynamically update, providing stakeholders with real-time, actionable information.

In the intersection of IoT and real-time data processing, serverless computing shines in building streamlined solutions. It facilitates the integration of IoT data into broader data processing workflows, allowing organizations to harness the power of stream processing frameworks for tasks like updating databases, invoking machine learning models, and feeding into analytics pipelines. By leveraging serverless architectures for both IoT and real-time data processing, organizations can create scalable, cost-effective, and responsive systems that adapt to the dynamic nature of connected devices and streaming data sources.

In the realm of financial services, it facilitates real-time transaction processing and fraud detection, ensuring immediate actions are taken to secure financial transactions. The technology is also widely employed in the healthcare sector, where serverless functions monitor IoT devices measuring patient vitals, triggering alerts for healthcare professionals in real-time to respond swiftly to critical health events. Live customer support chatbots, enhanced by serverless functions, provide instantaneous responses to user queries, improving customer service interactions. Additionally, real-time analytics dashboards enable businesses to stay informed with live data, supporting prompt decision-making based on the most up-to-date information.

In logistics and supply chain management, serverless computing finds application in real-time asset tracking using IoT devices. The technology continuously processes location data from GPS trackers or RFID sensors, allowing businesses to monitor the movement of goods and optimize routes dynamically. Moreover, serverless architectures are pivotal in live streaming scenarios, managing tasks like transcoding and content moderation for an uninterrupted and dynamic viewer experience. These diverse applications underscore the adaptability and efficiency of serverless computing in meeting the demands of real-time processing across various use cases and industries.

7. SERVERLESS CHALLENGES AND MITIGATION STRATEGIES

The adoption of serverless computing brings numerous benefits, including automatic scalability, cost efficiency, and simplified development. However, like any technology, serverless architectures come with their own set of challenges. In navigating the serverless landscape, organizations and developers must address key considerations to ensure optimal performance, security, and flexibility. In this context, several challenges stand out: Cold Starts, Vendor Lock-in, Security Concerns, and Monitoring and Debugging (Li et al., 2022). Each of these challenges poses unique obstacles that require careful attention and strategic solutions to fully unlock the potential of serverless computing. Let's delve into these challenges and explore ways to mitigate their impact on the effectiveness of serverless applications.

7.1 Cold Starts

Cold starts refer to the delay experienced when a serverless function is invoked for the first time or after a period of inactivity, as the cloud provider needs to allocate resources and initialize the runtime environment. This latency can impact the responsiveness of real-time applications and user experiences. To mitigate cold starts, developers can implement strategies such as warming functions, optimizing code for faster initialization, or utilizing provisioned concurrency features offered by some serverless platforms.

7.2 Vendor Lock-In

Vendor lock-in is a concern when organizations heavily rely on a specific cloud provider's serverless platform. While serverless frameworks aim for interoperability, there's still a risk of being tied to proprietary features or APIs that are unique to a particular provider. This can limit the flexibility to migrate applications seamlessly to another cloud provider. To address this challenge, organizations can adopt multi-cloud strategies, use cloud-agnostic serverless frameworks, and design applications with portability in mind.

7.3 Security Concerns

Security is a critical consideration in serverless computing, encompassing issues such as data privacy, function isolation, and access controls. Since serverless functions share the same underlying infrastructure, vulnerabilities in one function may potentially impact others. Additionally, the dynamic nature of serverless environments can pose challenges in traditional security practices. To enhance security, developers should employ secure coding practices, implement proper access controls, and leverage security services provided by cloud providers. Regular security audits and monitoring are essential to identify and address potential vulnerabilities.

7.4 Monitoring and Debugging

Monitoring and debugging serverless applications can be challenging due to the distributed and event-driven nature of the architecture. Traditional debugging approaches may not be directly applicable, and visibility into function execution may be limited. Developers need effective tools and strategies for logging, tracing, and monitoring the performance of serverless functions. Cloud providers often offer monitoring solutions, and third-party tools can be employed to gain insights into the behavior of functions. Ensuring proper instrumentation within the code and adopting practices like distributed tracing can aid in diagnosing issues and optimizing performance.

8. FUTURE TRENDS AND DEVELOPMENTS

The landscape of serverless computing is continually evolving, and as we step into the future, several compelling trends and developments are poised to reshape the way we architect, deploy, and manage applications. From the fusion of serverless with emerging technologies to the drive for enhanced security measures and the quest for standardization, the serverless ecosystem is on a trajectory of innovation. This discussion explores the anticipated trends that were gaining momentum, signaling the potential directions serverless computing may take in the coming years.

8.1 Cold Start Optimizations

- Function warmers: Keep frequently used functions hot (pre-initialized) for faster invocations, reducing cold start delays.
- Gradual scaling: Scale functions up gradually instead of bursting into full memory usage, minimizing cold start spikes.
- Ahead-of-time compilation: Pre-compile functions for faster startup times, particularly for languages like Python.

8.2 Serverless State Management

- Stateful serverless functions: Allow functions to maintain state for improved performance and user experience.
- Distributed transaction management: Facilitate ACID transactions across multiple serverless functions in complex workflows.
- Integration with external state stores: Seamlessly connect functions to persistent storage solutions like DynamoDB or databases.

8.3 Event-Driven Architectures on Steroids

- Complex event processing (CEP): Analyze and react to real-time streams of events from diverse sources within serverless applications.
- Stream processing frameworks: Efficiently handle high-volume event streams with frameworks like Apache Kafka or Amazon Kinesis.

- Serverless event mesh: Establish a unified event routing fabric across clouds and hybrid environments for flexible event routing.

8.4 Security Enhancements and Runtime Monitoring

- Fine-grained authorization and access control: Implement granular permissions for functions and resources to limit attack surface and improve security posture.
- Runtime introspection and observability: Gain real-time insights into function execution, resource consumption, and potential anomalies for debugging and performance optimization.
- Serverless security frameworks: Dedicated frameworks like AWS Serverless Application Model (SAM) enforce security best practices within serverless applications.

8.5 Embracing the Serverless Edge

- Serverless at the edge: Deploy functions on edge computing platforms closer to end users for lightning-fast response times and improved local performance (Gadepalli, 2019).
- Integration with edge network infrastructure: Leverage serverless to trigger actions and workflows based on network events like changes in bandwidth or connectivity.
- Collaboration with IoT devices: Connect serverless functions directly to IoT devices for real-time data processing and intelligent responses.

These are just a few examples of the dynamic technological landscape within serverless. As development tools mature and integrations deepen, serverless will continue to evolve, pushing the boundaries of performance, efficiency, and security for modern applications.

9. SUMMARY

This chapter provides a thorough examination of the paradigm shift in computing architectures, moving from traditional server-based models to the dynamic world of serverless computing. Beginning with foundational definitions and historical context, the chapter explores the limitations of traditional computing and the reasons for the rise of serverless solutions. Key components of serverless computing, including compute services, storage services, and event triggers, are explained, emphasizing benefits such as cost efficiency, scalability, and rapid development. The chapter delves into serverless architecture, comparing it with microservices and monolithic structures, and discusses the role of serverless frameworks. Major platforms like AWS, Azure, and GCP, along with services such as AWS Lambda, Azure Functions, and GCP Cloud Functions, are detailed. Real-world use cases showcase the versatility of serverless computing, while challenges like cold starts, vendor lock-in, security concerns, and monitoring/debugging are addressed. The chapter looks to the future, discussing trends like integration with edge computing, containers, and machine learning. the chapter concludes by summarizing key concepts and presenting additional resources for further exploration. This chapter serves as a comprehensive guide for both beginners and experienced practitioners, offering insights into the transformative impact of serverless computing on modern application development.

REFERENCES

Cassel, G. A. S., Rodrigues, V. F., da Rosa Righi, R., Bez, M. R., Nepomuceno, A. C., & André da Costa, C. (2022). Serverless computing for Internet of Things: A systematic literature review. *Future Generation Computer Systems*, *128*, 299–316. doi:10.1016/j.future.2021.10.020

Gadepalli, P. K. (2019). Challenges and opportunities for efficient serverless computing at the edge. *2019 38th Symposium on Reliable Distributed Systems (SRDS)*. IEEE. 10.1109/SRDS47363.2019.00036

Hassan, B., & Saman, A. (2021). Survey on serverless computing. *Journal of Cloud Computing (Heidelberg, Germany)*, *10*(1), 1–29. doi:10.1186/s13677-021-00253-7

Kelly, D., Glavin, F., & Barrett, E. (2020). Serverless computing: Behind the scenes of major platforms. *2020 IEEE 13th International Conference on Cloud Computing (CLOUD)*. IEEE. 10.1109/CLOUD49709.2020.00050

Kritikos, K., & Skrzypek, P. (2018). A review of serverless frameworks. *2018 IEEE/ACM International Conference on Utility and Cloud Computing Companion (UCC Companion)*. IEEE. 10.1109/UCC-Companion.2018.00051

Li, Y., Lin, Y., Wang, Y., Ye, K., & Xu, C. (2022). Serverless computing: State-of-the-art, challenges and opportunities. *IEEE Transactions on Services Computing*, *16*(2), 1522–1539. doi:10.1109/TSC.2022.3166553

Li, Z., Guo, L., Cheng, J., Chen, Q., He, B., & Guo, M. (2022). The serverless computing survey: A technical primer for design architecture. *ACM Computing Surveys*, *54*(10s), 1–34. doi:10.1145/3508360

Perez, A. (2023). Accelerating and Scaling Data Products with Serverless. In *Serverless Computing: Principles and Paradigms* (pp. 149–173). Springer International Publishing. doi:10.1007/978-3-031-26633-1_6

Ponce, F., Márquez, G., & Astudillo, H. (2019). Migrating from monolithic architecture to microservices: A Rapid Review. *2019 38th International Conference of the Chilean Computer Science Society (SCCC)*. IEEE. 10.1109/SCCC49216.2019.8966423

Rajan, A. P. (2020). A review on serverless architectures-function as a service (FaaS) in cloud computing. [Telecommunication Computing Electronics and Control]. *Telkomnika*, *18*(1), 530–537. doi:10.12928/telkomnika.v18i1.12169

Rajan, R. (2018). Serverless architecture-a revolution in cloud computing. *2018 Tenth International Conference on Advanced Computing (ICoAC)*. IEEE. 10.1109/ICoAC44903.2018.8939081

Samea, F. (2020). A model-driven framework for data-driven applications in serverless cloud computing. *Plos one, 15*(8).

Taneska, M. & Dimkoski, A. (2023). *Microsoft Azure Cloud Computing-Server vs Serverless*. UKIM.

van Eyk, E., Toader, L., Talluri, S., Versluis, L., Uță, A., & Iosup, A. (2018, September/October). Serverless is More: From PaaS to Present Cloud Computing. *IEEE Internet Computing, 22*(5), 8–17. doi:10.1109/MIC.2018.053681358

Wen, J., Chen, Z., Jin, X., & Liu, X. (2023). Rise of the planet of serverless computing: A systematic review. *ACM Transactions on Software Engineering and Methodology, 32*(5), 1–61. doi:10.1145/3579643

Chapter 2
Resource Allocation in Serverless Computing

Ramu Kuchipudi
Chaitanya Bharathi Institute of Technology, India

Ramesh Babu Palamakula
Chaitanya Bharathi Institute of Technology, India

T. Satyanarayana Murthy
Chaitanya Bharathi Institute of Technology, India

ABSTRACT

This book chapter introduces readers to the dynamic and transformative world of serverless computing. With the focus on agility, scalability, and cost-effectiveness for developing and deploying applications, serverless computing has become a game-changer. The chapter's introduction to serverless computing provides a clear understanding of its fundamental principles and concepts, setting it apart from conventional computing models. Specifically, it explores the fundamental aspects of serverless architectures, emphasizing critical components such as functions as a service (FaaS), event driven programming, and the involvement of cloud providers in this setting. The chapter discusses the potential of serverless systems to optimize resource usage, speed up development, and adapt to changing user preferences while minimizing operational expenses. The chapter highlights practical use cases and success stories that demonstrate how serverless has been successfully implemented in various industries and domains.

1. INTRODUCTION

Serverless computing is a revolutionary cloud computing execution model that has transformed the way applications are built and deployed. In this model, cloud providers handle the allocation of machine resources dynamically and efficiently, relieving customers from the burdensome tasks of managing servers and infrastructure. The term "serverless" was coined by Ken Fromm in 2012, encapsulating the essence of this paradigm shift(Grobmann et al, 2019).

DOI: 10.4018/979-8-3693-1682-5.ch002

Serverless cloud computing provides backends as a service (BaaS) and functionality as a service (FaaS), such as the shown in Figure 1. BaaS includes services such as storage, messaging, and user management. FaaS, on the other hand, allows developers to deploy and run code on computing platforms. FaaS relies on services provided by BaaS, such as databases, messaging, and user authentication. FaaS is considered the most dominant model of serverless and is also referred to as "event-driven functionality."(Villamizar et al,2017)

Figure 1. Serverless architecture

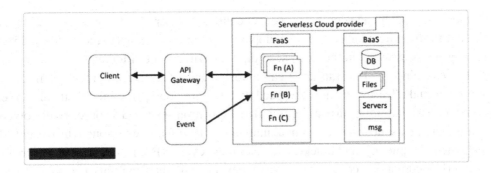

1.1 Dynamic Resource Allocation

To cope with peak loads, organizations in traditional server centric models had to provision and maintain their servers, frequently overestimating their capacity needs. Cloud providers like AWS Lambda, Azure Functions, and Google Cloud Function can allocate resources on demand through serverless computing, which enhances this approach. Moreover, this means that instead of manual capacity planning, computing resources are allocated only when a particular function or piece of code needs to be executed.

1.2 Lowering Expenses

The use of serverless computing as a pay as you go pricing model is transforming cost-conscious businesses. In standard server-based models, customers are charged for server instances regardless of whether they are actively processing requests or idling. When it comes to serverless systems, customers pay only for the computational resources used in executing functions (Kulkarni et al., 2019). The implementation of cost efficiency not only cuts down on operational expenses but also fosters experimentation and innovation.

1.3 Scalability Reduced to a Simpler Level

Scalability of applications is facilitated by serverless computing. Whenever function executions are initiated due to traffic spikes or new events, cloud providers automatically adjust the required resources to handle the load. By using elastic scaling, applications are able to adjust to changes in demand without manual adjustment. The era of adding servers or worrying about traffic spikes is gone.

1.4 Backend Code Optimization

Developers in the serverless era may choose to concentrate solely on writing code for the essential features of their application. The implementation of serverless platforms eliminates backend operations like server provisioning, scaling and load balancing. By utilizing a simplified development process, teams can focus on creating features and improving user experiences, which in turn shortens the time to market(Jambunathan et al., 2018).

1.5 Faster Recovery

Faster cycles for development and deployment are encouraged by serverless computing. Without having to worry about infrastructure management, developers may make iterations to their code and implement updates. This agility is essential in the fast-paced digital environment of today, when an organization's success can be determined by how rapidly it can innovate and adapt. Development teams can now experiment, improve, and release software at a speed that was previously unthinkable thanks to serverless computing. Serverless computing is a paradigm shift that synchronises cloud resources with contemporary development requirements, not only a technical innovation. It streamlines resource usage, cuts down on server management complexity, and quickens development cycles (Brenner et al., 2019). Organisations that adopt serverless computing continue to save money and gain the flexibility necessary to prosper in the fast-paced, cutthroat digital.

1.6 Serverless Computing vs. Cloud Computing

There are two distinct computing paradigms: serverless computing and cloud computing. The term "cloud computing" describes the pay-as-you-go, on-demand computer services that are offered over the internet. On the other hand, serverless computing is a kind of cloud computing where the user just needs to worry about the code that is running. The code is executed by the cloud, which also takes care of any scalability and performance needs. Put another way, cloud computing is a concept that offers access to a pool of shared computing resources that can be quickly deployed and released with little administration work (Sewak et al., 2018). These resources include servers, storage, applications, and services. However, serverless computing is a paradigm that lets programmers create and run programmes without having to worry about the underlying infrastructure.

2. SERVERLESS COMPUTING ARCHITECTURE

2.1 A More In-Depth look at Serverless Computing Architecture

Serverless computing architecture is a paradigm that shifts the onus of infrastructure maintenance from the developer to the cloud provider, simplifying and streamlining the creation and deployment of applications. The three main parts of this architecture approach are microservices, backend as a service (BaaS), and function as a service (FaaS) (Feng, 2019). Let's take a closer look at each of these elements and see how they interact to form a pliable and expandable ecosystem.

2.2 Function as a Service (FaaS)

The foundation of the serverless computing architecture is Function as a Service (FaaS). It is a major departure from typical application development, in which programmers write code to carry out discrete tasks or functions, and these duties are then carried out in response to predetermined events or triggers. Developers construct isolated functions in FaaS that contain particular functionalities. Because they don't keep a lasting state between executions, these functions are stateless. Rather, they are made to react to events, which can include messages from a queue, database updates, or HTTP requests. The execution environment is automatically managed by the cloud provider, such AWS Lambda, Azure Functions, or Google Cloud Functions, guaranteeing that the function scales smoothly to meet changing workloads. Billing for developers is determined by the actual compute (Werner et al., 2019).

2.3 Backend as a Service (BaaS)

In addition to FaaS, Backend as a Service (BaaS) provides cloud-based services and APIs that developers may use to access a range of backend functionality without having to create and manage these services themselves. Services like databases, storage, authentication, and push alerts are frequently included in BaaS packages. Developers no longer need to spend as much time developing typical backend functionality because they can incorporate these BaaS services straight into their apps. For instance, developers can utilise a BaaS database service like Amazon DynamoDB or Firebase Realtime Database in place of configuring and maintaining a database server. This expedites time-to-market, streamlines the development process, and guarantees the high availability and scalability of these services.

2.4 Microservices

An architectural strategy that enhances serverless computing is microservices. Applications are divided into tiny, autonomous services in a microservices architecture, each of which is in charge of a certain functional area. Well-defined APIs are used by these services to connect with one another; frequently, lightweight protocols like HTTP or message queues are used. Improved maintainability, scalability, and the capacity to create and implement services independently are just a few benefits of microservices. Microservices gain even greater power when used with serverless computing. Single microservices can be implemented using serverless functions, enabling effective and autonomous operation for each microservice. This makes it possible to scale and develop particular features quickly without harming the programme as a whole.

2.5 The Synergy of Serverless Computing Architecture

With its components of microservices, BaaS, and FaaS, serverless computing architecture provides an all-encompassing method for developing and deploying applications. While cloud providers take care of the underlying infrastructure, developers may concentrate on building code for certain functions. Microservices allow for the building of highly flexible and scalable applications, while BaaS services further streamline backend development. Because of this synergy, businesses are better able to create and implement applications that are not only responsive and economical, but also highly adjustable to changing business requirements. With serverless computing's continued development, cloud-native application development is expected to benefit greatly from it, allowing businesses to innovate and grow with previously unheard-of ease and efficiency (Glikson et al., 2017).

3. SERVERLESS COMPUTING PLATFORMS

3.1 Amazon Web Services (AWS) Lambda

One of the forerunners in the serverless computing arena is AWS Lambda. It enables coders to execute code without the need for server provisioning or management. Uploading your code and designating an event source (such as an HTTP request, database update, or file upload) will allow Lambda to take care of the underlying infrastructure scaling and management automatically. The purpose of AWS Lambda is to support event-driven applications. It may react to a range of events, including custom events, HTTP requests made over the Amazon API Gateway, and modifications to AWS services. Programming languages supported by Lambda include Node.js, Python, Java, Go, and.NET Core. Because of its smooth integration with AWS services like S3, DynamoDB, and AWS Step Functions, it's the perfect choice for developing serverless apps (Alqaryouti et al., 2018).

3.2 Microsoft Azure Functions

Microsoft's serverless compute service is called Azure Functions. It provides features akin to those of AWS Lambda, allowing developers to create event-driven apps with no infrastructure administration. Programming languages supported by Azure Functions include C#, JavaScript, Python, and PowerShell. It offers a large selection of bindings and triggers (such as HTTP, Azure Queue Storage, and Cosmos DB) to make data integration easier. Azure Blob Storage, Azure Logic Apps, and Azure Cosmos DB are just a few of the Azure services that Azure Functions can readily interface with. With this Azure Functions extension, developers can create intricate processes and stateful orchestrations in a serverless setting.

3.3 Google Cloud Functions

Google's serverless platform is called Google Cloud Functions. It offers automatically managing the underlying infrastructure using event-driven computing. Events that can be used to trigger Google Cloud Functions include HTTP requests, Pub/Sub messages, and modifications to Cloud Storage. With support for Go, Python, Node.js, and other languages, it's usable by a variety of developers. BigQuery, Cloud Firestore, and Google Cloud Storage are just a few of the Google Cloud services that Google Cloud Functions easily interfaces with. With its automated scaling feature, you can be sure that your functions can manage any workload without the need for human involvement. Google Cloud Functions offers extensive logging and monitoring features to assist developers in performance optimisation and problem solving.

3.4 IBM Cloud Functions

IBM's serverless computing platform was once called OpenWhisk, but it is now called IBM Cloud Functions. Using functions, developers may create and implement serverless apps. Multiple invokers, such as HTTP requests, message queues, and scheduled triggers, are supported by IBM Cloud Functions.

Numerous programming languages are supported, including Java, Python, Swift, and Node.js.Watson services, IBM Event Streams, Cloudant, and other IBM Cloud services can all be connected with IBM Cloud Functions. It is intended for event-driven applications, just as other serverless platforms, allowing developers to react instantly to changes and occurrences. It adapts automatically to demand, making sure your functions can effectively handle a range of workloads. Finally, serverless computing platforms such as Google Cloud Functions, IBM Cloud Functions, AWS Lambda, and Azure Functions give developers the freedom to create scalable and affordable (Hellerstein et al., 2018).

4. SERVERLESS COMPUTING USE CASES

Certainly, let's expand on the applications of serverless computing in web and mobile applications, Internet of Things (IoT), and Big Data processing and analytics:

4.1 Web and Mobile Applications

The preferred option for developers creating online and mobile applications that need to be highly scalable and latency-free is now serverless computing. AWS Lambda, Azure Functions, and Google Cloud Functions are examples of serverless platforms that automatically scale your application in response to incoming demand. This implies that your application can manage the load without the need for human intervention, regardless of the number of users—thousands or less. This flexibility is especially important for applications whose usage patterns are erratic or change quickly. Conventional server-based designs frequently squander capacity during periods of low activity because they must supply resources for peak loads. This issue is resolved by serverless computing, which bills you only for the actual processing time spent. The pay-as-you-go approach can save a lot of money on running expenses.

Developers may concentrate on writing code and creating features rather than maintaining servers and infrastructure when they use serverless computing. Teams can increase productivity by delegating server setup, patching, and scalability to the cloud provider. Serverless functions can be implemented globally across numerous data centres, guaranteeing minimal latency for users regardless of their location. For real-time services and applications, this is essential. Because serverless systems are naturally suited for event-driven architectures, developing applications that react to a variety of events—like user activities, database modifications, or incoming requests is made simple.

4.2 Internet of Things (IoT)

The sensors, machines, and other devices that make up the Internet of Things (IoT) produce enormous volumes of data. Real-time processing and analysis of this data is made possible in large part by serverless computing. IoT devices frequently generate data that needs to be processed and decided upon right away. IoT events have the ability to initiate serverless processes, allowing for real-time data analysis and automatic replies, warnings, and notifications. IoT data can be very erratic, seeing spikes in traffic during particular occasions or seasons. Serverless technologies guarantee continuous data processing by automatically scaling to accommodate these spikes. Before being saved or analysed, raw IoT data can be preprocessed and transformed using serverless services. This can involve enriching, filtering, and normalising the data. IoT data streams can be connected to data warehouses through serverless integration with IoT platforms and services.

4.3 Big Data Processing and Analytics

In the field of big data processing and analytics, serverless computing has the potential to be revolutionary. Data processing pipelines for operations like ETL (Extract, Transform, Load) procedures can be constructed using serverless functions. Large-scale analytics jobs, like batch processing and real-time data analysis, can be handled by serverless platforms without the requirement for resource provisioning or cluster management. Serverless computing is more affordable for irregular data jobs since it just bills you for the compute resources used during batch processing, rather than for idle infrastructure. You may take advantage of already-existing analytics ecosystems by integrating serverless with Big Data tools and services like Apache Spark, Hadoop, or data warehousing. You can obtain immediate insights and make data-driven decisions in response to various situations by integrating serverless with real-time data sources.

5. SERVERLESS COMPUTING CHALLENGES

Although serverless computing has many benefits, it also has several drawbacks that need to be properly considered and resolved. The effectiveness, dependability, and security of serverless apps may be impacted by these difficulties. When a serverless function is activated after a period of inactivity, there is a delay while the required resources are allocated and initialised. Serverless functions are frequently performed in ephemeral containers. This "cold start" issue is related to this startup time. The apps that require delay may find serverless apps inappropriate due to the large impact cold starts can have on response times. Cold starts can be lessened by employing strategies like provided concurrency or scheduled invocations to keep functions warm. Because serverless apps are event-driven, they react to different kinds of triggers and events. Testing and debugging grow more difficult.

Multiple functions, services, and dependencies are common in serverless applications, which makes troubleshooting and diagnosis difficult. Debugging and testing tools that work, together with extensive monitoring and logging, are essential for helping developers find and fix problems with serverless applications. Because serverless depends on outside vendors for infrastructure and services, there is a greater surface area where security flaws could occur. It can be difficult to guarantee the security of data handled via serverless services, particularly when sensitive data is involved. Due to the necessity for strong access restrictions and little control over the underlying infrastructure, meeting regulatory compliance (such as GDPR and HIPAA) can be challenging. To reduce security concerns in serverless systems, security best practises such as appropriate authorization, encryption, authentication, and continuous monitoring must be put into practise.

Cloud companies offer serverless platforms, and adopting features exclusive to one vendor may result in vendor lock-in. Because different cloud providers have distinct services, APIs, and execution environments, migrating serverless apps between them can be difficult. Functions on serverless systems are subject to resource limitations, which can cause scalability problems when handling heavy traffic or resource-intensive operations. Even while serverless systems provide auto-scaling, it can be difficult to comprehend and properly configure scaling settings, which could result in either over- or under-provisioning. Because serverless pricing is determined by actual usage, charges may be unpredictable, particularly if services are called frequently. To properly manage expenses, one must implement monitoring and optimisation procedures, define budget criteria, and comprehend the financial effects of various function configurations.

6. CONCLUSION

To sum up, serverless computing is an approach to cloud computing execution that has a number of benefits over more conventional approaches. It offers speedier turnaround times, reduced costs, and easier scalability and backend code. The market is filled with serverless computing platforms, such as Microsoft Azure Functions, IBM Cloud Functions, Google Cloud Functions, and AWS Lambda. There are numerous uses for serverless computing, such as big data processing and analytics, IoT, and online and mobile apps. Nevertheless, there are certain issues that must be resolved, such as the cold start issue, testing and debugging, security, and compliance.

REFERENCES

Adzic, G., & Chatley, R. (2017). Serverless computing: Economic and architectural impact. In *Proceedings of the 2017 11th Joint Meeting on Foundations of Software Engineering (ESEC/FSE 2017)* (pp. 884–889). Association for Computing Machinery. 10.1145/3106237.3117767

Al-Ali, Z., Goodarzy, S., Hunter, E., Ha, S., Han, R., Keller, E., & Rozner, E. (2018). Making serverless computing more serverless. In *2018 IEEE 11th International Conference on Cloud Computing (CLOUD)* (pp. 456–459). IEEE. 10.1109/CLOUD.2018.00064

Al-Ameen, M., & Spillner, J. (2019). A systematic and open exploration of FaaS research. In *Proceedings of the European Symposium on Serverless Computing and Applications (CEUR Workshop Proceedings,* (pp. 30–35). CEUR-WS.

Alqaryouti, O., & Siyam, N. (2018). Serverless computing and scheduling tasks on cloud: A review. [ASRJETS]. *American Scientific Research Journal for Engineering, Technology, and Sciences, 40*(1), 235–247.

Ao, L., Izhikevich, L., Voelker, G. M., & Porter, G. (2018). Sprocket: A serverless video processing framework. In *Proceedings of the ACM Symposium on Cloud Computing (SoCC '18)* (pp. 263–274). Association for Computing Machinery. 10.1145/3267809.3267815

Baldini, I., Castro, P., Chang, K., Cheng, P., Fink, S., Ishakian, V., & Suter, P. (2017). Serverless Computing: Current Trends and Open Problems. In Research Advances in Cloud Computing (pp. 1–20). Springer.

Boza, E. F., Abad, C. L., Villavicencio, M., Quimba, S., & Plaza, J. A. (2017). Reserved, on demand or serverless: Model-based simulations for cloud budget planning. In *2017 IEEE Second Ecuador Technical Chapters Meeting (ETCM).* IEEE. 10.1109/ETCM.2017.8247460

Brenner, S., & Kapitza, R. (2019). Trust more, serverless. In *Proceedings of the 12th ACM International Conference on Systems and Storage (SYSTOR '19)* (pp. 33–43). Association for Computing Machinery. 10.1145/3319647.3325825

Feng, L., Kudva, P., Da Silva, D., & Hu, J. (2018). Exploring serverless computing for neural network training. In *2018 IEEE 11th International Conference on Cloud Computing (CLOUD)* (pp. 334–341). IEEE. 10.1109/CLOUD.2018.00049

Geng, X., Ma, Q., Pei, Y., Xu, Z., Zeng, W., & Zou, J. (2018). Research on early warning system of power network overloading under serverless architecture. In *2018 2nd IEEE Conference on Energy Internet and Energy System Integration (EI2)* (pp. 1–6). IEEE. 10.1109/EI2.2018.8582355

Glikson, A., Nastic, S., & Dustdar, S. (2017). Deviceless edge computing: Extending serverless computing to the edge of the network. In *Proceedings of the 10th ACM International Systems and Storage Conference (SYSTOR '17)*. ACM. 10.1145/3078468.3078497

Grobmann, M., Ioannidis, C., & Le, D. T. (2019). Applicability of serverless computing in fog computing environments for IoT scenarios. In *Proceedings of the 12th IEEE/ACM International Conference on Utility and Cloud Computing Companion (UCC '19 Companion)* (pp. 29–34). Association for Computing Machinery.

Hellerstein, J. M., Faleiro, J., Gonzalez, J. E., Schleier-Smith, J., Sreekanti, V., Tumanov, A., & Wu, C. (2018). Serverless Computing: One Step Forward, Two Steps Back. http://arxiv.org/abs/1812.03651. Accessed 4 Oct 2021.

Jambunathan, B., & Yoganathan, K. (2018). Architecture decision on using microservices or serverless functions with containers. In *2018 International Conference on Current Trends Towards Converging Technologies (ICCTCT)* (pp. 1–7). IEEE. 10.1109/ICCTCT.2018.8551035

Jonas, E., Schleier-Smith, J., Sreekanti, V., Tsai, C.-C., & Khandelwal, A. (2019). *Cloud Programming Simplified: A Berkeley View on Serverless Computing*. arXiv. http://arxiv.org/abs/1902.03383

Kuhlenkamp, J., & Werner, S. (2018). Benchmarking FaaS platforms: Call for community participation. In *2018 IEEE/ACM International Conference on Utility and Cloud Computing Companion (UCC Companion)* (pp. 189–194). 10.1109/UCC-Companion.2018.00055

Kulkarni, S. G., Liu, G., Ramakrishnan, K. K., & Wood, T. (2019). Living on the edge: Serverless computing and the cost of failure resiliency. In *2019 IEEE International Symposium on Local and Metropolitan Area Networks (LANMAN)* (pp. 1–6). 10.1109/LANMAN.2019.8846970

Leitner, P., Wittern, E., Spillner, J., & Hummer, W. (2019). A mixed-method empirical study of function-as-a-service software development in industrial practice. *Journal of Systems and Software, 149*, 340–359. doi:10.1016/j.jss.2018.12.013

Pérez, A., Risco, S., Naranjo, D. M., Caballer, M., & Moltó, G. (2019). On-premises serverless computing for event-driven data processing applications. In *2019 IEEE 12th International Conference on Cloud Computing (CLOUD)* (pp. 414–421). 10.1109/CLOUD.2019.00073

Rajan, A. P. (2020). A review on serverless architectures - function as a service (FaaS) in cloud computing. Telecommunication, Computing. *Electronics and Control, 18*(1), 530–537. doi:10.12928/telkomnika.v18i1.12169

Sadaqat, M., Colomo-Palacios, R., & Knudsen, L. E. S. (2018). Serverless Computing: A Multivocal Literature Review. *NOKOBIT - Norsk Konferanse for Organisasjoners Bruk Av Informasjonsteknologi, 26*(1), 1–13.

Scheuner, J., & Leitner, P. (2020). Function-as-a-service performance evaluation: A multivocal literature review. *Journal of Systems and Software, 170,* 110708. doi:10.1016/j.jss.2020.110708

Sewak, M., & Singh, S. (2018). Winning in the era of serverless computing and function as a service. In 2018 3rd International Conference for Convergence in Technology (I2CT) (pp. 1–5). 10.1109/I2CT.2018.8529465

Somma, G., Ayimba, C., Casari, P., Romano, S. P., & Mancuso, V. (2020). When less is more: Core-restricted container provisioning for serverless computing. In *IEEE INFOCOM 2020 - IEEE Conference on Computer Communications Workshops (INFOCOM WKSHPS)* (pp. 1153–1159). IEEE.

Taibi, D., El Ioini, N., Pahl, C., & Niederkofler, J. (2020). Patterns for Serverless Functions (Function-as-a-Service): A Multivocal Literature Review. In *Proceedings of the 10th International Conference on Cloud Computing and Services Science* (pp. 181–192). ScitePress. 10.5220/0009578501810192

van Eyk, E., Toader, L., Talluri, S., Versluis, L., Uță, A., & Iosup, A. (2018). Serverless is more: From PaaS to present cloud computing. *IEEE Internet Computing, 22*(5), 8–17. doi:10.1109/MIC.2018.053681358

Villamizar, M., Garcés, O., Ochoa, L., Castro, H., Salamanca, L., Verano, M., & Lang, M. (2017). Cost comparison of running web applications in the cloud using monolithic, microservice, and AWS Lambda architectures. *Service Oriented Computing and Applications, 11*(2), 233–247. doi:10.1007/s11761-017-0208-y

Werner, S., Kuhlenkamp, J., Klems, M., Müller, J., & Tai, S. (2018). Serverless big data processing using matrix multiplication as example. In *2018 IEEE International Conference on Big Data (Big Data)* (pp. 358–365). IEEE. 10.1109/BigData.2018.8622362

Wolski, R., Krintz, C., Bakir, F., George, G., & Lin, W.-T. (2019). Cspot: Portable, multi-scale functions-as-a-service for IoT. In *Proceedings of the 4th ACM/IEEE Symposium on Edge Computing (SEC '19)* (pp. 236–249). Association for Computing Machinery. 10.1145/3318216.3363314

Yussupov, V., Breitenbücher, U., Leymann, F., & Wurster, M. (2019). A systematic mapping study on engineering function-as-a-service platforms and tools. In *Proceedings of the 12th IEEE/ACM International Conference on Utility and Cloud Computing (UCC'19)* (pp. 229–240). Association for Computing Machinery. 10.1145/3344341.3368803

Chapter 3
Serverless Computing:
Unveiling the Future of Cloud Technology

Nidhi Niraj Worah
Thakur College of Engineering and Technology, India

Megharani Patil
Thakur College of Engineering and Technology, India

ABSTRACT

This chapter serves as a comprehensive initiation into serverless computing, a revolutionary paradigm in cloud computing. It begins by elucidating the foundational concepts, breaking down its architecture that simplifies development through modular functions triggered by specific events. The narrative unfolds, highlighting the myriad benefits, such as enhanced efficiency, seamless scalability, and liberating developers from intricate server management. A comparative analysis with traditional cloud computing underscores serverless computing's unique attributes. However, the chapter maintains balance by addressing challenges like cold start latency, execution duration limits, and potential vendor lock-in. The exploration concludes by showcasing real-world applications in domains like real-time data processing, backend APIs, batch processing, image and video processing, and chatbots. Offering a nuanced understanding of serverless computing, this chapter stands as an invaluable resource for readers exploring its advantages, challenges, and diverse applications.

1. INTRODUCTION

Serverless computing, a revolutionary paradigm in cloud computing, operates on a dynamic allocation version wherein the cloud company takes at the obligation of dealing with server assets seamlessly. Unlike traditional computing fashions, developers are relieved of the load of provisioning and coping with servers, allowing them to recognition absolutely on coding and application development. The concept of 'serverless' can be fairly deceptive, because it does no longer suggest the absence of servers but as a substitute a shift in obligation. (Hassan, 2021)

DOI: 10.4018/979-8-3693-1682-5.ch003

In a serverless structure, the cloud supplier oversees all factors of server space and infrastructure, allowing developers to operate with out the need to subject themselves with server control complexities. This approach ends in elevated efficiency and reduced operational overhead, which ends up in a extra streamlined development method (Jones, 2021).

To illustrate, consider a situation wherein a developer is constructing an application. In a conventional setup, the developer might worry about server provisioning, scalability, and maintenance. However, with serverless computing, the developer can focus solely on writing code for the software's functionality. The cloud provider automatically scales resources up or down primarily based on demand, ensuring best overall performance with out manual intervention.

Essentially, serverless computing frees developers from the complexities of managing servers so they can focus on building creative and effective applications, with the cloud provider taking care of the underlying infrastructure effortlessly. With its growing popularity, this revolutionary approach is propelling the creation of cloud-based applications. (Smith, 2022).

Serverless computing is an innovative approach to application development in which applications are built using small, independent functions that respond to specified inputs. Consider these functions as discrete coding units, each intended to carry out a particular task. (Jones, 2021). The serverless architecture kicks in when a specific event takes place, such a user accessing a website or uploading a file.

The beauty of it is that when an event triggers a function, the cloud provider dynamically performs that function and, upon completion, stops it. Because of this on-demand execution, developers don't have to worry about maintaining servers up and running all the time because resources are only used when needed. It's economical and efficient, much like flipping on a light switch when you need it and off when you don't.

Now, let's talk about the key players in the serverless game. Various platforms provide serverless capabilities, and some of the prominent ones include AWS Lambda, Apache OpenWhisk, Azure Functions, Google Cloud Functions, IronFunctions, and OpenLambda. Each of these platforms offers a set of tools and services that empower developers to create and scale applications effortlessly without delving into the complexities of managing infrastructure.

2. PURPOSE OF SERVERLESS COMPUTING

Serverless computing aims to simplify application development and operation for developers by relieving them of the burden of managing servers. To operate their apps, developers in traditional computing must configure and manage servers, which can be difficult and time-consuming. With serverless computing, the cloud provider handles all server-related responsibilities, such as resource allocation, scaling, and maintenance, allowing developers to concentrate on building the code for their applications. It's similar to renting a fully staffed kitchen so you can prepare meals without having to purchase, assemble, or clean any kitchenware. With this method, developers may work more efficiently and expand their business because they only pay for the computing power they really utilize when their code executes in response to specific events or requests.(Wen 2017)

Containerization is a lightweight, portable, and effective technique of packaging, distributing, and running software. It entails packing an application into a single container along with all of its libraries, runtime components, and dependencies. Regardless of the underlying infrastructure, containers offer a consistent and isolated environment for programs to run in. A prominent approach for creating, packaging, and distributing apps is containerization, which helps developers create software that is more portable and scalable (Kaur and Singh 2021)

Even though containerization provides advantages, particularly in some deployment settings, it might not be the best option when effectively scaling applications is the main goal. Containers can be difficult to handle, which makes them less suitable for situations where fine-grained scalability, straightforward programming, and economical management are essential.

These challenges are addressed by serverless computing, which provides a purpose-built solution to application creation and scaling. Enabling application developers to divide huge, monolithic apps into smaller, standalone functions is the main goal. These functions, which are also known as Lambda functions or serverless functions, can run independently and scale in response to demand. One significant benefit is that this granular scalability enables developers to distribute resources exactly where they are needed, maximizing resource consumption and performance.(Alshammari and Alshammari, 2021)

Therefore, there are two main goals: First, serverless computing makes fine-grained scaling possible, meaning that the program as a whole is not performed and scaled; rather, only the particular functions responding to requests or events are. By removing the complexity of server management, it also makes programming and deployment approaches simpler. While the cloud provider manages the underlying infrastructure, including resource allocation, scaling, and maintenance, developers may concentrate on creating modular functions.(Kaur and Singh 2021)

Take, for example, an e-commerce application that encounters traffic surges during a flash sale. Functions that manage user logins, transaction processing, or inventory updates can scale separately with serverless computing to accommodate growing demand. In addition to improving performance, this makes cost control possible because resources are given exactly where and when they are needed.

3. LITERATURE REVIEW

Here is a brief review and summary of recent findings and research in the field of serverless computing.

In table1, the key focus, main findings, and implications of each paper are summarized. It offers a quick overview of the different aspects of serverless computing covered by these papers and enables easy identification of relevant resources.

4. APPLICATIONS OF SERVERLESS COMPUTING

Serverless computing offers a versatile solution across various use cases, providing developers with a scalable and cost-effective platform for building applications. Here (Chen, 2023) are detailed explanations of some prominent use cases for serverless computing:

- **Real-time data processing:** Data from sensors and Internet of Things devices can be processed in real time using serverless computing. Netflix processes real-time data from their streaming platform using serverless computing. This information is utilized to detect and address issues with the service as well as to tailor recommendations for individual users. With serverless architectures, developers can manage IoT device events in a scalable way.

Table 1. Literature review

Paper	Key Focus	Main Findings	Implications
Serverless Computing: Design, Implementation, and Performance (Wen et al. 2017)	Serverless computing	The authors present the design of a novel performance-oriented serverless computing platform implemented in .NET, deployed in Microsoft Azure.	The paper provides insights into the design and implementation of a serverless computing platform that can be used to improve the performance of serverless architectures.
Virtualization in Cloud Computing (Kaur and Singh 2021)	Light and portable containerization	Comparing application deployment using traditional, hypervisor, and container architecture. They discuss the advantages of containerization, such as lightweight, portable, and effective technique of packaging, distributing, and running software.	The paper highlights the benefits of containerization and its potential to create software that is more portable and scalable.
Containerization technologies: taxonomies, applications and challenges. Journal of Cloud Computing (Alshammari and Alshammari, 2021)	Overview of virtualization and containerization technologies	Discussion the advantages of containerization, such as reducing computational time processing and providing a consistent and isolated environment for programs to run in.	Provides a comprehensive overview of containerization technologies and their advantages and challenges
Survey on serverless computing (Hassan et al., 2021)	Comprehensive overview of serverless concepts, platforms, use cases, and challenges	Defines serverless, outlines architecture, highlights advantages and limitations, discusses applications across various domains	Provides foundational understanding of serverless technology and its potential.
Serverless computing: a security perspective (Asim et al., 2023)	Security considerations in serverless environments	Analyzes multi-tenancy, monitoring, and other security risks, proposes mitigation strategies and best practices	Raises awareness of security concerns in serverless and offers guidance for secure development and deployment.
Cold starts in serverless computing: A systematic review (Chen et al., 2023)	Impact of cold starts (initial function invocation delay) on application performance	Identifies factors affecting cold starts, evaluates optimization techniques, discusses research trends	Helps developers minimize cold start impact and improve serverless application performance.
Serverless Computing: Current Trends and Open Problems (Khan et al., 2022)	Current state of serverless technology and future research directions	Examines prominent platforms, key characteristics, use cases, and challenges, highlights promising research areas	Offers insights into the evolving landscape of serverless and identifies opportunities for further advancements.
Cost optimization in serverless computing (Zhou et al., 2023)	Strategies for cost management in serverless environments	Discusses autoscaling, resource planning, billing models, and other cost optimization techniques	Provides guidance for cost-efficient serverless development and deployment.
Towards a portable serverless framework (Khan & Islam, 2022)	Concept of a portable serverless framework for code execution across different cloud providers	Analyzes challenges and potential benefits of portability, explores possible approaches and research needs	Addresses limitations of vendor lock-in and promotes platform-agnostic serverless development.
Serverless orchestration: A survey (Khan & Islam, 2023)	Approaches for coordinating the execution of multiple serverless functions	Surveys existing orchestration mechanisms, identifies challenges and research directions in this area	Helps understand the complexities of serverless orchestration and guides future research efforts.

- **Backend APIs:** Web and mobile applications can have their backend APIs created using serverless computing. Amazon powers its e-commerce platform's backend APIs with serverless computing. Customers can browse and buy products, track orders, and manage their accounts via these APIs. Amazon guarantees that the backend infrastructure automatically expands to accommodate fluctuating traffic levels by employing serverless architecture, offering a responsive and reliable experience for users.
- **Batch processing:** Large volumes of data can be processed in batches using serverless computing, for purposes like machine learning and data analysis. Serverless computing is used by Airbnb to handle massive volumes of data on its platform. In addition to producing statistics on rental trends, this data is utilized to spot fraud and enhance user experience. Organizations can carry out data-intensive processes with serverless batch processing, which eliminates the requirement for specialized infrastructure maintenance and expansion.
- **Image and video processing:** Images and videos can be processed using serverless computing for tasks like object detection and picture recognition. Instagram processes user-uploaded photos and videos using serverless computing. Without requiring constant server availability, functions can be set up to begin processing files as soon as they are uploaded, guaranteeing prompt and effective data transformations. This processing include operations including cropping, resizing, and filter application.
- **Chatbots:** Serverless computing can be used to build chatbots that communicate with users in real time. Numerous businesses are developing chatbots that can communicate with clients in real time using serverless computing. These chatbots can be used to make appointments, respond to inquiries about goods and services, and offer customer support. These chatbots can easily scale to meet changing demands thanks to the serverless paradigm, giving consumers a smooth and responsive interaction experience. This adaptability is especially useful in situations where there may be abrupt spikes in the amount of chatbot usage.

In conclusion, the applications of serverless computing are diverse and impactful across various domains. From real-time data processing for personalized recommendations and issue resolution (as seen with Netflix), to the creation of responsive backend APIs for seamless user experiences in e-commerce platforms (as exemplified by Amazon), serverless architectures prove their scalability and efficiency. Furthermore, serverless computing excels in batch processing tasks for data analysis and machine learning, as demonstrated by Airbnb. It also facilitates image and video processing, enabling quick and efficient transformations in applications like Instagram. Lastly, the serverless model shines in the development of chatbots, providing flexible and responsive interactions for customer support and engagement across industries. These examples showcase the adaptability and advantages of serverless computing in addressing a wide array of modern application needs. (Krishnamurthi, 2023)

5. BENEFITS OF SERVERLESS COMPUTING

Serverless computing offers several benefits that make it an attractive choice for modern application development. Here are the key advantages of serverless computing:

- **Cost savings:** Serverless computing uses a "pay for value" business model, which results in significant cost savings. By guaranteeing ideal resource use, this paradigm removes the necessity for overprovisioning servers. Because the price is directly linked to the amount of resources used, businesses can only pay for what they really use. When compared to typical hosting setups, where resources are allocated independent of actual demand, this strategy can lead to significant cost savings. Think about a retail website that gets a lot of traffic over the Christmas season. The website can automatically scale to meet the increased demand thanks to serverless computing, which makes sure that more resources are only provided when necessary. The infrastructure reduces in size as soon as the traffic stops, saving money when there is less demand.

- **Fault Tolerance:** Fault-tolerance methods are typically integrated into serverless architectures. The underlying infrastructure is maintained by cloud providers, guaranteeing that applications can recover from errors or outages without the need for human involvement. Imagine a serverless weather forecasting application that uses real-time meteorological data processing and analysis. The serverless design guarantees continuous service availability by automatically rerouting traffic to available resources, even in the event of a brief outage.

- **Scalability:** One notable feature of serverless computing is its unmatched scalability. With previously unheard-of flexibility, the system automatically adjusts applications from zero to peak demand. This scalability is managed by cloud providers, who automatically modify resources in response to demand as it occurs. Applications with this dynamic scaling capacity may easily adjust to shifting workloads, giving consumers a seamless experience. Consider a streaming service that sees a sharp increase in users during a live event. A seamless streaming experience is ensured by the platform's ability to scale rapidly in response to a surge in users thanks to serverless computing. The infrastructure reduces in size after the event to maximize resource utilization.

- **Modular and Microservices Architecture:** With serverless, functions are treated as separate, reusable pieces, encouraging a modular approach to application architecture. This encourages modularity, code reuse, and simpler maintenance, all of which are in perfect harmony with the tenets of microservices design. Examine an e-learning platform that creates a scalable and modular system by utilizing serverless functionalities for content distribution, user authentication, and payment processing.

- **Ease of use:** The goal of serverless computing is simplicity. The difficulties of setting up and maintaining servers are removed from developers, freeing them up to concentrate on writing code and launching applications. Because it is so simple to use, developing Minimal Viable Products (MVPs) and testing new ideas may happen quickly. Consider a startup that is creating a new mobile application and wants to use serverless computing to create and release a prototype quickly. The development team can focus on perfecting the app's features and functionality, which will speed up time to market, without having to worry about managing infrastructure.

- **Automatic Scaling:** The hallmark of serverless computing is automatic scaling, in which cloud providers handle the scalability of programs on demand in a seamless manner. The serverless architecture's functions are able to scale back down during times of low demand after scaling up to meet peak loads. Imagine the traffic spike that occurs on an online ticketing platform when tickets for a well-known event go on sale. Serverless features ensure that customers have a seamless shopping experience by scaling automatically to meet the rising demand.

- **Developer productivity:** Developer productivity is greatly increased with serverless computing, which relieves developers of infrastructure management responsibilities. The development cycle can be sped up by developers completely focusing on creating apps. Teams can deliver new features, get user input, and make improvements more quickly thanks to the faster iterations made possible by the decreased operational overhead. Assume that a team of software developers working on an e-commerce platform can introduce updates and new features with ease by utilizing serverless computing. Because the cloud provider manages the infrastructure, the team can respond to market trends and customer input swiftly through iteration.

- **Event-Driven Architecture:** When it comes to event-driven design, serverless apps shine because they can react quickly to particular triggers or events. When activities need to be completed in response to events such as user interactions, data changes, or external API requests, this architecture is especially helpful. An e-commerce application that ensures real-time inventory management by triggering a serverless function to update inventory levels upon product purchase serves as an example of an illustrative real-time system.

- **Flexibility and Agility:** Without the limitations of maintaining infrastructure, serverless computing offers developers a dynamic and agile development environment. This allows them to test apps, make prototypes, and try out new ideas without being constrained. Think about a firm creating a social media platform. By utilizing serverless, the development team can scale the service as user numbers increase, rapidly iterate on improvements, and adjust to changing requirements without the need for extensive infrastructure planning.

Essentially, what makes serverless computing unique are its event-driven features, which also allow for more development flexibility and agility, automatic workload scaling, modular and microservice architecture, and integrated fault tolerance for robust applications. Together, these characteristics let serverless architectures be effective and flexible in a variety of real-world situations. (Smith, 2022)

6. CLOUD COMPUTING

Cloud computing is a revolutionary technology concept that completely changes how organizations and consumers access and use computer services. Fundamentally, it breaks from the conventional dependency on local servers or personal devices to administer applications by enabling the smooth delivery of a wide range of computing services across the Internet.

Users are no longer limited by the capabilities of individual equipment under this paradigm. Rather, they utilize the vast array of resources provided by cloud service providers. All of these resources together make up a full range of processing power, storage, databases, networking infrastructure, software, and sophisticated analytics tools. The move to cloud computing gives consumers access to unmatched scalability, flexibility, and accessibility.

6.1 Key Components of Cloud Computing

1. **Computing Power:** The deployment of computing power in a virtualized environment by cloud computing revolutionizes the way applications are produced and deployed. Users are not dependent on physical servers to run apps or process data thanks to this architecture, which gives them access to virtualized computing resources. For example, cloud servers handle the computational demand when installing a web application. These servers are often in the form of virtual comput-

ers. Because the application may dynamically scale based on demand—a crucial feature offered by cloud computing platforms like AWS EC2, Azure Virtual Machines, and Google Compute Engine—responsiveness and scalability are ensured.

2. **Storage:** A vital aspect of cloud computing is cloud storage, which frees users from the restrictions of local disk space. It offers on-demand, secure, and scalable storage options. Users may store and retrieve data more effectively using cloud storage, and cloud providers guarantee data redundancy and durability. Cloud storage services that are frequently utilized are Google Cloud Storage in Google Cloud Platform, Azure Blob Storage in Microsoft Azure, and Amazon Simple Storage Service (S3) in Amazon Web Services.

3. **Databases:** Cloud databases represent a paradigm shift in how data is stored and managed. They offer managed and scalable storage and retrieval solutions for both structured and unstructured data. Cloud database services such as AWS DynamoDB, Azure Cosmos DB, and Google Cloud Firestore provide as examples of their capabilities. With capabilities like automatic scaling, global distribution, and integrated security, these services let users create reliable and responsive applications without the hassles of maintaining conventional databases.

4. **Networking:** Cloud networking services are essential for enabling smooth communication between distributed systems. Content delivery networks (CDNs), load balancers, and virtual private clouds (VPCs) are integral components. AWS CloudFront, for example, speeds up content delivery throughout the globe; Azure Traffic Manager maximizes the distribution of applications; and Google Cloud VPC offers a safe and private network environment. These networking features guarantee safe communication, load balancing, and effective data transfer amongst different cloud-based architecture components.

5. **Software:** By allowing software applications to be accessed online, cloud computing revolutionizes the way they are delivered. Applications don't need to be installed or maintained locally thanks to Software as a Service (SaaS) services. Microsoft 365, Google Workspace, and Salesforce are a few examples. Through a web browser, users may use productivity tools directly, while the service provider handles updates and maintenance, simplifying the user experience and lessening the load on local equipment.

6. **Analytics:** Cloud analytics services enable businesses to glean insightful information from large amounts of data. Intelligent decision-making, complicated data analysis, and visualization are made easier by tools like Google BigQuery, AWS Redshift, and Azure Synapse Analytics. Cloud analytics services quickly handle and analyze huge datasets by utilizing the cloud's processing power and scalability. Businesses may conduct intricate queries over petabytes of data, for instance, using AWS Redshift. This helps them find trends and patterns that inform their strategic choices.

6.2 Service Models

Service models in the context of cloud computing refer to the categories or levels of services that cloud providers offer to users. These models define the extent of control and responsibility users have over the computing resources and services they use. There are three primary service models: Infrastructure as a Service (IaaS), Platform as a Service (PaaS), and Software as a Service (SaaS). (Raghavendran, 2016)

Infrastructure as a Service (IaaS): IaaS is similar to renting networking, storage, and virtual machines, the fundamental components of computing infrastructure. Users are in charge of the configurations, apps, and operating systems. Consider IaaS like leasing a completely equipped apartment.

Although you own the space and are free to configure it as you choose, the building's infrastructure and upkeep are handled by the landlord, or cloud provider. AWS EC2, Azure Virtual Machines, and Google Compute Engine are a few examples.

Platform as a Service (PaaS): PaaS gives developers a platform with tools and services so they can create, launch, and maintain apps without having to worry about the supporting infrastructure. It removes the complexity involved in server management. Imagine a restaurant with a fully functional kitchen. Without having to bother about acquiring or maintaining the kitchenware, the chefs (developers) can concentrate on creating mouthwatering meals (applications) (infrastructure). PaaS examples include Microsoft Azure App Service, Heroku, and Google App Engine.

Software as a Service (SaaS): SaaS uses the internet to offer software programs that are ready to use. These programs can be accessed by users via a web browser; no installation or upkeep is required. It's similar to renting a service instead of purchasing and maintaining the software. Think about sending emails with Gmail. You can view your emails using a web browser; installing and maintaining an email server is not necessary. Salesforce, Google Workspace, and Microsoft 365 are a few more examples.

6.3 Real-World Analogy: The Ice Cream Shop

- **IaaS:** Renting the necessary equipment (freezer, scoopers, and cones) and choosing the flavors to set up your own ice cream shop.
- **PaaS:** operating a franchise where you focus on creating unique ice cream flavors and customer service, while the franchise owner takes care of the shop's infrastructure and equipment.
- **SaaS:** Enjoying a variety of ice cream flavors without worrying about making or maintaining them. You simply visit an ice cream shop and enjoy the ready-to-eat treats.

This analogy helps illustrate how the service models of cloud computing provide different levels of control and responsibility, catering to the needs of various users and businesses.

To sum up, cloud computing services' abstraction and administration levels are specified by their service models. SaaS provides completely managed software applications, PaaS isolates infrastructure administration for application development, while IaaS gives additional control over infrastructure. Users can select the degree of authority and accountability that best suits their own requirements and preferences using these models.

6.4 Deployment Models

In cloud computing, deployment models describe how computing resources, services, and infrastructure are set up and dispersed among various environments. These models provide the deployment, management, and access methods for cloud services according to variables including ownership, location, and scalability. Public cloud, private cloud, hybrid cloud, community cloud, and multi-cloud are the three basic deployment methods that are generally available.(Dong Du, 2022)

Public Cloud: Public cloud is a deployment model where cloud services are provided by a third-party cloud service provider and are made available to the general public over the internet. These services are offered on a pay-as-you-go basis.

Key Characteristics:

- Shared Resources: Public cloud resources are shared among multiple users and organizations.
- Cost-Effective: The pay-as-you-go model allows users to pay only for the resources they consume.
- Scalability: Easily scalable to accommodate varying workloads.
- Accessibility: Services are accessible from anywhere with an internet connection.

Example: AWS (Amazon Web Services), Azure by Microsoft, Google Cloud Platform.

Private Cloud: Private cloud is a deployment model where cloud services are used exclusively by a single organization. The infrastructure can be located on-premises or hosted by a third-party provider, but it is dedicated solely to the organization.

Key Characteristics:

- Enhanced Security: Since resources are not shared, private clouds offer greater control and security.
- Customization: Organizations have the flexibility to customize the cloud environment to meet specific needs.
- Compliance: Ideal for industries with strict regulatory compliance requirements.

Example: An organization creating and managing its own on-premises data center with cloud-like services or utilizing a third-party private cloud provider.

Hybrid Cloud: Hybrid cloud is a deployment model that combines elements of both public and private clouds. It allows data and applications to be shared between them, providing greater flexibility and optimization of resources.

Key Characteristics:

- Flexibility: Organizations can choose where to run workloads based on specific requirements.
- Scalability: Can utilize public cloud for scalable resources while keeping sensitive data in a private cloud.
- Cost Optimization: Offers a balance between cost-effective public cloud resources and the control of private cloud.

Example: An organization using a private cloud for storing sensitive customer data and a public cloud for hosting web applications that require scalable resources.

Community Cloud: Community cloud is a deployment model where infrastructure is shared by several organizations with similar interests, such as regulatory concerns or industry-specific requirements.

Key Characteristics:

- Shared Resources: Infrastructure is shared among a community of organizations with common needs.
- Cost Sharing: Enables organizations to share the costs of infrastructure and services.
- Collaboration: Ideal for collaborative projects among organizations in a specific community.

Example: A consortium of healthcare organizations sharing a community cloud for storing and managing patient records while complying with healthcare regulations.

Multi-Cloud: Multi-cloud is not a distinct deployment model but a strategy where an organization uses services from multiple cloud providers. It can involve a combination of public, private, and community clouds.

Key Characteristics:

- Diversification: Spreading workloads across different cloud providers to avoid vendor lock-in.
- Best-of-Breed Services: Choosing the most suitable services from different providers for specific needs.
- Risk Mitigation: Reducing the risk of service outages or disruptions by diversifying cloud providers.

Example: Using AWS for storage services, Azure for machine learning, and Google Cloud for data analytics to leverage the strengths of each provider.

6.5 Real-World Analogy: The City Infrastructure

- **Public Cloud:** Public transportation systems (buses, trains) available to everyone.
- **Private Cloud:** A privately owned road system or infrastructure used exclusively by a single entity.
- **Hybrid Cloud:** A combination of public transportation and private vehicles for optimized travel.
- **Community Cloud:** Shared transportation infrastructure for a specific community, like a business district.
- **Multi-Cloud:** Using different modes of transportation from different providers for diverse travel needs.

In summary, these deployment models offer organizations a spectrum of options based on factors like security, customization, and cost-effectiveness. The choice often depends on the specific goals, regulatory considerations, and preferences of each organization.

6.6 Examples of Cloud Service Providers

- **Amazon Web Services (AWS):** A comprehensive cloud services platform with a wide range of offerings.
- **Microsoft Azure:** A cloud computing service created by Microsoft, providing services for computing, analytics, storage, and networking.
- **Google Cloud Platform (GCP):** Offers a suite of cloud computing services, including computing, storage, and machine learning.
- **IBM Cloud:** Provides a range of cloud computing solutions, including infrastructure, platform, and software services.

6.7 Real-World Impact

Imagine the experience of a dynamic startup starting to create a ground-breaking mobile app. To transform data management and application logic, this firm deliberately leverages the potential of cloud computing, bypassing the challenges of investing in local server infrastructure.

In this case, the startup effectively manages user data by utilizing the adaptability of cloud-based storage. The firm guarantees its users' smooth data accessibility by depending on secure and scalable cloud storage solutions like AWS S3, Azure Blob Storage, or Google Cloud Storage, eliminating the need for laborious local storage infrastructure. This simplifies data administration and lays the groundwork for accessible and user-centric design.

The firm uses serverless computing, a model where the cloud provider dynamically controls the execution of functions in response to events, for the vital component of application logic. Without having to worry about traditional server maintenance, the startup can concentrate on developing the essential features of the mobile application thanks to services like AWS Lambda, Azure Functions, or Google Cloud Functions. This not only speeds up development but also fits in with the "pay-as-you-go" concept, which guarantees affordability by simply billing for the actual amount of computational resources used.

The startup incorporates a managed database solution provided by the cloud provider to effectively store and retrieve data. Cloud databases offer global distribution, scalability, and automated database infrastructure management. Examples of these databases are AWS DynamoDB, Azure Cosmos DB, and Google Cloud Firestore. This relieves the startup from the intricacies of database administration, enabling them to concentrate on refining the application's features and user experience.

The firm is faced with the exciting task of growing its resources to meet increased customer demand as the mobile application acquires traction and popularity. The innate scalability of cloud computing turns into a tactical advantage, enabling the firm to easily modify resources in real time. The application's capacity to scale dynamically guarantees that it will always be available and responsive, even during spikes in user activity. Most importantly, this scalability occurs without the firm having to deal with the challenges of traditional infrastructure scaling or require large upfront hardware investments.

Within the startup ecosystem, cloud computing becomes a driver for creativity and agility in addition to its immediate operational benefits. Cloud services enable ambitious developers and entrepreneurs to realize their ideas without requiring a sizable initial investment by reducing entry barriers. The modern era's digital solutions are shaped by the disruptive power of cloud computing, which also promotes efficiency, innovation, and adaptability. It is a prime example of how, when used wisely, technology can be a potent enabler for companies to grow and adapt in a constantly changing environment.

6.8 Comparison of Serverless Computing With Cloud Computing

Cloud computing refers to a broad range of internet-based service models that supply computer resources, such as Software as a Service (SaaS), Platform as a Service (PaaS), and Infrastructure as a Service (IaaS). Without having to purchase or maintain actual gear, consumers can access and use a variety of computing services thanks to this general idea.

On the other hand, a certain cloud computing model known as serverless computing. It sets itself apart by concentrating on the performance of tasks in reaction to occurrences rather than having to handle supporting infrastructure. This paradigm abstracts away the complexity of the infrastructure, therefore streamlining the development process. The following are factors (Gomez, 2023) considered to compare the technologies and highlight key differences.

6.9 Resource Management

Users that utilize cloud computing are responsible for manually maintaining different parts of the infrastructure, including databases, virtual machines, and containers. Developers must constantly pay attention to operations like provisioning, configuration, and scaling because of this manual supervision. Infrastructure management is different with serverless computing. From the standpoint of the developer, it is abstracted. Here, the cloud provider manages resource provisioning, scaling, and execution in stateless containers while developers focus on writing code for specific functions. Because of this abstraction, the development process is made simpler, freeing up developers to concentrate on the applications' functional logic.

6.10 Scalability

Scalability in cloud computing depends on human interaction or the creation of automatic scaling setups according to expected workloads. Users must forecast demand and modify the distribution of resources appropriately.

The automatic scaling that Serverless Computing offers, on the other hand, enables functions to scale dynamically in response to demand. Functions are able to smoothly scale back down during idle times and smoothly scale up during high demands. Dynamic scaling guarantees the best possible use of resources and adaptability to changing workloads.

6.11 Billing Model

Cloud computing and serverless computing have different pricing structures that correspond to their different approaches to allocating resources. Users of cloud computing are charged for the resources they have been allotted, regardless of how those resources are actually used.

Similar to pay-per-use software, serverless computing bills according to the real execution time and resource usage of functions. This method encourages cost effectiveness because customers are only charged for the computational resources they really use.

6.12 Development Focus

Cloud computing developers are engrossed with infrastructure management responsibilities like scaling, provisioning, and maintenance. Applications under this architecture require careful planning and resource allocation to be successful.

There is a paradigm change for developers in serverless computing. Writing code for functions, detached from infrastructure considerations, is the main goal. Because infrastructural complexities don't impede quick iteration and experimentation, this abstraction promotes better flexibility and agility in the development process.

6.13 Use Cases

Cloud computing is ideal for applications that require consistent workloads or particular infrastructure setups. It works well in situations when resource use prediction is crucial.

In situations involving events, serverless computing excels at managing irregular workloads and microservices architectures. This paradigm works well in scenarios where quick scaling and adaptability to changing needs are essential. An e-commerce platform might, for example, use serverless functionalities to manage flash sales, guaranteeing smooth scalability during times of high traffic.

6.14 Latency

Because cloud computing relies on pre-allocated resources, latency may be slightly higher. Scaling can cause delays, particularly during jolting spikes in demand.

On the other hand, serverless computing provides low-latency execution. On-demand function execution guarantees prompt event response. This feature is very helpful in applications where responsiveness in real time is essential.

6.15 Example Services

Notable services in the field of cloud computing are AWS EC2, Azure VMs, Docker, and RDS. These services offer managed database solutions, virtual machines, and containers to meet a range of infrastructure requirements.

Services like AWS Lambda, Azure Functions, Google Cloud Functions, and IBM Cloud Functions are prime examples of serverless computing. These platforms offer an environment known as Function-as-a-Service (FaaS), which enables developers to deploy certain functions without worrying about the supporting infrastructure.

6.16 Flexibility and Agility

It takes careful planning and provisioning for future workloads when using cloud computing. Modifications to the way infrastructure is configured need careful planning and may cause disruptions while they are made.

Serverless computing offers an additional degree of adaptability and speed. Without having to worry about maintaining infrastructure, developers are free to try out new concepts, create prototypes, and test apps. Code development becomes the main focus, allowing for faster iteration and requirement adaption.

6.17 Management Overhead

Cloud computing entails managing many components of infrastructure, which may result in operational overhead. DevOps teams are essential to making sure applications run smoothly, from allocating resources to keeping them in good condition over time.

Serverless computing decreases management costs dramatically. Developers are free to focus on application logic because the cloud provider manages the infrastructure components. By streamlining operational activities, this abstraction makes the development and deployment process more streamlined and effective.

In Table 1, we summarize the relationship of Serverless Computing with Cloud Computing. Cloud Computing is a broad concept with manual resource management, scalability planning, and a billing model based on allocated resources. Developers handle infrastructure tasks, suitable for consistent workloads.

Serverless Computing, a specific cloud model, focuses on executing functions in response to events without managing infrastructure. It offers automatic scaling, a pay-as-you-go billing model, and allows developers to concentrate on code. Ideal for event-driven scenarios, it reduces management overhead compared to traditional cloud computing.

Table 2. Serverless computing vs. cloud computing

Aspect	Cloud Computing	Serverless Computing
Definition	Broad term encompassing various service models (IaaS, PaaS, SaaS) for delivering computing services over the internet.	A specific model within cloud computing that focuses on executing functions in response to events without managing infrastructure.
Resource Management	Users manually provision and manage virtual machines, containers, databases, and other infrastructure components.	Infrastructure management is abstracted. Developers focus on writing code for functions, and the cloud provider handles resource provisioning and scaling.
Scalability	Scaling is often manual or requires setting up auto-scaling configurations based on predicted workloads.	Offers automatic scaling where functions can scale from zero to handle peak loads and scale back down during periods of inactivity.
Billing Model	Typically follows a model where users pay for allocated resources, regardless of actual usage.	Adopts a pay-as-you-go model, billing users based on actual execution time and resources consumed by functions, promoting cost efficiency.
Development Focus	Developers need to manage infrastructure, including provisioning, scaling, and maintenance. DevOps plays a significant role.	Developers primarily focus on writing code for functions, abstracted from infrastructure concerns, simplifying the development process.
Use Cases	Suited for applications with consistent workloads or those requiring specific infrastructure configurations.	Ideal for event-driven scenarios, sporadic workloads, and microservices architectures where rapid scaling and flexibility are crucial.
Latency	May have slightly higher latency as applications run on pre-allocated resources, and scaling may take time.	Offers low-latency execution as functions are executed on-demand, and cloud providers automatically handle scaling to meet instantaneous demand.
Example Services	Virtual machines (e.g., AWS EC2, Azure VMs), Containers (e.g., Docker, Kubernetes), Database as a Service (e.g., AWS RDS, Azure SQL Database).	AWS Lambda, Azure Functions, Google Cloud Functions, IBM Cloud Functions. These services provide a FaaS environment for serverless computing.
Flexibility and Agility	Requires careful planning and provisioning for future workloads.	Offers flexibility by allowing developers to focus on code, experiment with new ideas, and quickly iterate without infrastructure constraints.
Management Overhead	Involves managing various aspects of infrastructure, leading to potential operational overhead.	Reduces management overhead as the cloud provider takes care of infrastructure aspects, allowing developers to concentrate on application logic.

6.18 FaaS (Function as a Service)

A cloud computing model known as "Function as a Service" (FaaS) is a subset of serverless computing. Applications are divided into discrete, self-contained functional components known as functions under a FaaS paradigm. These are discrete snippets of code that carry out particular actions or duties. FaaS is distinct in that its functions are performed in reaction to events or triggers, and the infrastructure needed to carry them out is automatically managed by the cloud provider.

In serverless computing, functions are discrete code segments intended to carry out particular tasks. These can be manually initiated, or they can be set to run in response to certain events, like HTTP requests. To make the execution of these functions easier, warm queues, operating containers, function metadata, and actual code are all managed jointly. Functions are triggered by events, which can vary from user interactions such as clicking a button to more methodical operations like submitting a form. Imagine an online store that uses serverless features. When a user clicks the "Buy Now" button, an order is processed by a serverless function. By using an event-driven methodology, the function is guaranteed to run exactly when it is needed, which maximizes resource efficiency and improves responsiveness. (Raghavendran, 2016)

Function-as-a-Service (FaaS), a cloud computing service that enables developers to run code in response to events without the hassles of managing infrastructure, is the foundation of serverless computing. This approach has special benefits for developing and releasing microservices applications. In a FaaS environment, applications are made up of discrete, tiny functions that are called upon by events. The cloud provider starts the corresponding function when an event happens, and ends it when it's finished. Because of its event-driven architecture, resources are used more effectively because functions are only activated when necessary. (Rehemägi, 2018)

Think about an online store that occasionally has flash sales. By activating certain capabilities, the application may scale dynamically to accommodate increasing user traffic during the sale thanks to FaaS. The program can properly scale to the demands of the event thanks to functions that can handle duties like delivering order confirmations, updating inventory, and processing transactions.

Several cloud providers offer FaaS services, with AWS Lambda, Azure Functions, Google Cloud Functions, IBM Cloud Functions, and KNative by Kubernetes being prominent contenders. These platforms abstract away the complexities of infrastructure management, providing developers with a serverless environment for efficient and scalable application development.}

In summary, serverless computing, with its FaaS model, empowers developers to create applications with enhanced scalability, responsiveness, and cost efficiency. The event-driven approach and the abstraction of infrastructure intricacies contribute to a streamlined development process, allowing teams to focus on building innovative and resilient applications.

6.19 Limitations of Serverless Computing

While serverless computing offers numerous benefits, it also comes with certain limitations(Brown, 2020):

- **Cold Start Latency:** When a function that has been idle needs to be activated, a phenomena known as "cold start latency" in serverless computing happens. Think of it as attempting to start your car on a freezing winter's morning. The cloud provider has to build up the necessary resources and setup the environment before the function can start, which causes the delay. The time it takes for the engine in your car to warm up before driving is comparable to this delay. This latency in serverless apps might affect real-time applications, especially those that need fast replies. Cold start latency can cause delays in message processing, for instance, in a chat service when users expect fast responses.

- **Execution Duration Limits:** Within the domain of serverless platforms, a function's maximum runtime is limited by what are called execution duration limits. This idea is similar to putting a time limit on a stove timer when you're making dinner. A serverless function may be terminated before it has finished executing if it goes above this set time limit. Large-scale dataset analysis and other jobs requiring prolonged processing durations present particular challenges due to this constraint. For example, in a serverless architecture, the imposed execution duration constraints could be a barrier to properly executing a function that processes large volumes of data.

- **Stateless Nature:** Because they don't store data between usage, serverless functions are by nature stateless. To understand this idea, picture a self-checkout machine at a store that, once you've paid and departed, forgets what you bought. In a similar vein, serverless functions are incapable of re-calling previous data or the state from earlier calls. This statelessness can make it more difficult to manage operations that call for the storage of data, such as user progress-saving games. External storage solutions, such databases or file storage, are frequently used to overcome this difficulty. External storage can, however, slow down the function's operation because it adds latency to the process of retrieving and storing data from outside the system.

- **Limited Resource Allocation Control:** Developers that work with serverless platforms have limited control over how resources are allocated inside the architecture. This restriction is similar to renting an apartment that is completely furnished; although you can take advantage of the conveniences that are already there, moving or adding new furniture is difficult. In a similar vein, developers utilizing serverless platforms are unable to modify or customize the underlying infrastructure to satisfy particular application needs. Since developers are forced to work within the predetermined limitations of the serverless environment, this lack of control over resources could be a disadvantage for applications with specific requirements.

- **Dependency Management Challenges:** Managing dependencies, or extra software or tools required for a function to function, can be difficult in serverless setups. It is similar to having to cook with only certain items in this case. There may be restrictions on the quantity and kinds of dependencies that developers can include with functions in serverless systems. Complex dependencies and huge libraries can make handling tasks complicated and require additional workarounds or solutions. Because of this restriction, the development process becomes more complicated because developers have to work around the serverless platform's limitations when integrating external tools into their operations.

- **Debugging and Monitoring Complexity:** It can be harder to find and fix problems with serverless functions than with standard applications; it is like trying to solve a puzzle without all the components. In a serverless environment, debugging—the act of locating and resolving faults or defects in the code—becomes a complex undertaking. Furthermore, keeping an eye on how well distributed system performs might be complicated and necessitate the use of specialized tools. The dynamic and event-driven nature of serverless architectures, in which functions react to different triggers, is the source of this complexity. Sophisticated monitoring tools are necessary to guarantee seamless and effective operation, which adds another level of complexity for developers working in serverless settings.

- **Vendor Lock-In:** When using serverless computing, a particular cloud provider's platform and services are frequently heavily relied upon. This dependence is similar to building a house out of special, non-standard pieces; it could be difficult to relocate. This dependence on a single cloud provider in the context of serverless computing might lead to a situation called "vendor lock-in." Similar to how a homeowner would have trouble locating replacements for unusual parts, companies might run into problems if they try to move to a different cloud provider. This vendor lock-in may limit strategic choices about cloud service providers and impede flexibility.

- **Security Concerns:** Developers need to be on edge even with serverless systems' security safeguards in place. It is like living in a safe neighborhood but keeping your doors locked out of concern. Security issues in serverless computing arise from shared resources and the possibility of flaws such illegal code injections. In order to protect apps from potential dangers, developers must be aware of these risks and put best practices and strong security mechanisms in place.

- **Limited Local Testing Environment:** It is possible that testing serverless functions locally on a developer's PC will not fully capture how these functions behave in the real cloud. This discrepancy is like practicing a play in a tiny space before putting it on a big stage. Prior to deploying functions to the live cloud, it may be difficult to detect and resolve difficulties due to the differences in environments. To guarantee the best possible performance of serverless operations in real-world scenarios, developers must take this limitation into consideration by using cloud-based testing environments and doing extensive testing.

- **Cost Uncertainty:** Even though serverless computing can be more affordable for some tasks, cost prediction can be difficult. It is similar to projecting your monthly energy costs without having a clear idea of how much electricity you consume every day. A certain amount of uncertainty is introduced by granular billing, which is dependent on variables such as the length of function execution and the resources used. This is particularly true for applications whose workloads fluctuate. Effective cost forecasting and management can be difficult for businesses, which highlights the significance of meticulous planning and oversight to prevent unforeseen financial consequences.

Despite these limitations, serverless computing remains a powerful paradigm for specific use cases, offering advantages in terms of scalability, cost efficiency, and simplified development. Organizations should carefully assess their application requirements and constraints before adopting a serverless architecture.

6.20 What Serverless Computing is Not?

Serverless computing is not the same as not having servers; instead, it frees developers from managing the infrastructure so they can concentrate only on creating and implementing functionalities. Servers are still essential to serverless architecture, despite the term; however, the cloud provider manages their allocation, scalability, and maintenance dynamically. The development process becomes more streamlined and effective as a result of the developers not having to handle the responsibilities associated with traditional server management, such as provisioning, scalability, and hardware maintenance.

Furthermore, not every application is a good fit for serverless computing. Workloads with constant and high resource requirements are not meant for it, as serverless platforms' intrinsic dynamic scaling may cause latency. The execution duration constraints imposed by serverless providers can provide difficulties for applications that involve continuous workloads or long-running processes. Furthermore, when choosing this architectural style, developers should keep in mind that serverless computing is stateless, which means that potential cold start latency and other issues must be carefully considered. All things considered, serverless computing is a potent paradigm for certain use cases but is not a universally applicable solution for all application types.

7. CONCLUSION

Serverless computing is a paradigm shift that accelerates application development by utilizing a modular and event-driven approach. Serverless applications are built as a collection of discrete functions, each intended to carry out a particular activity in response to predetermined triggers, as opposed to typical monolithic structures. Developers can precisely customize features to match application requirements with this more granular and scalable structure made possible by the split into functions. Imagine it like putting together a group of experts, each with a specialized knowledge base, who are prepared to take charge and complete their assigned responsibilities at any time. The application's overall efficiency is increased by its modular design, which also makes development more adaptable and nimble.

Releasing developers from the complexities of server administration is a significant shift in serverless computing. Serverless architecture abstracts away provisioning, scaling, and maintenance issues, in contrast to traditional server-centric approaches where developers struggle with these issues. This allows developers to focus entirely on creating the logic for certain tasks, which results in a more targeted and effective development process. This change is similar to having a group of highly trained employees who are not tasked with managing the equipment they run; instead, they may focus on carrying out precise tasks that are determined by the events that set them in motion. As a result, developers now have access to a development environment that enables them to create apps that scale with demand and react dynamically to events without requiring continual oversight or manual intervention.

REFERENCES

Alshammari, G., & Alshammari, T. (2021). Containerization technologies: Taxonomies, applications and challenges. *Journal of Cloud Computing (Heidelberg, Germany)*, *10*(1), 1–23. doi:10.1186/s13677-021-00234-3

Brown, J. (2020). Serverless computing: A beginner's guide. *Tech Radar*. https://www.techradar.com/news/serverless-computing-a-beginners-guide

Chen, R., Chen, R., & Zhou, Z. (2023, October 26). *Cold starts in serverless computing: A systematic review*. arXiv preprint arXiv:2310.08437. https://ieeexplore.ieee.org/document/9191377

Du, D., Liu, Q., Jiang, X., Xia, Y., Zang, B., & Chen, H. 2022. Serverless computing on heterogeneous computers. In *Proceedings of the 27th ACM International Conference on Architectural Support for Programming Languages and Operating Systems (ASPLOS '22)*. Association for Computing Machinery. 10.1145/3503222.3507732

Gomez, J. (2022, November 10). *Serverless Computing Vs. Cloud Computing: What's The Difference?* Koombea. https://www.koombea.com/blog/serverless-computing-vs-cloud-computing/

Hassan, H. B., Barakat, S. A., & Sarhan, Q. I. (2021). Survey on serverless computing. *Journal of Cloud Computing (Heidelberg, Germany)*, *10*(1), 39. doi:10.1186/s13677-021-00253-7

Jones, M. (2021). *What is serverless computing?* RedHat. https://www.redhat.com/en/topics/cloud-native-apps/what-is-serverless-computing

Kaur, A., & Singh, S. (2021). Virtualization in Cloud Computing: Moving from Hypervisor to Containerization. *Arabian Journal for Science and Engineering*, *46*(8), 8215–8230. doi:10.1007/s13369-021-05553-3

Khan, A. N., & Islam, S. N. (2022, July). Towards a portable serverless framework. In *2022 ACM SIGPLAN International Symposium on Microarchitectures (MICRO)* (pp. 765-778). ACM. https://www.serverless.com/

Khan, A. N., & Islam, S. N. (2023, November 6). *Serverless orchestration: A survey.* arXiv preprint arXiv:2311.13587. https://arxiv.org/pdf/2105.07806

Khan, W. A., Ahmed, S., & Bashir, M. K. (2022, June 29). Serverless Computing: Current Trends and Open Problems. In *Handbook of Research on Serverless Computing and Microservices* (pp. 1-22). IGI Global. https://www.researchgate.net/publication/353174927_Survey_on_serverless_computing

Krishnamurthi, R., Kumar, A., Gill, S., & Buyya, R. (2023). *Serverless Computing: Principles and Paradigms.* Springer. doi:10.1007/978-3-031-26633-1

Marin, E., Perino, D., & Di Pietro, R. (2022). Serverless computing: A security perspective. *Journal of Cloud Computing (Heidelberg, Germany)*, *11*(1), 69. doi:10.1186/s13677-022-00347-w

Raghavendran, V., Naga Satish, G., Suresh Varma, P., & Moses, G. (2016). A Study on Cloud Computing Services. *IJERT*. https://www.ijert.org/research/a-study-on-cloud-computing-services-IJERTCON-V4IS34014.pdf

Rehemägi, T. (2018, May 14). *Top FaaS Providers (Function As A Service) Guide.* Dashbird. https://dashbird.io/blog/check-out-all-the-faas-providers-developers-have-at-their-disposal-when-going-serverless/

Smith, A. (2022). *Serverless computing: Advantages and disadvantages.* IBM. https://www.ibm.com/cloud/learn/serverless

Wen, J., Chen, Z., Jin, X., & Liu, X. (2017). Serverless Computing: Design, Implementation, and Performance. In *2017 IEEE 37th International Conference on Distributed Computing Systems Workshops (ICDCSW)* (pp. 253-258). IEEE. 10.1109/ICDCSW.2017.27

Zhou, M., Li, W., & Jiang, W. (2023, November 6). *Cost optimization in serverless computing.* arXiv preprint arXiv:2311.13242. https://arxiv.org/abs/2311.13242

KEY WORDS AND DEFINITIONS

Content Delivery Network (CDN): A Content Delivery Network (CDN) is a system of distributed servers that work together to deliver web content, like images and videos, to users based on their geographic location.

Dynamic Allocation Model: A system where resources such as computing power and memory are automatically assigned and reassigned based on demand.

Granular Scalability: The ability to scale specific components or functions of an application independently based on demand.

Infrastructure as a Service (IaaS): A service that provides virtualized computing resources over the internet, allowing users to rent virtual machines, storage, and networks.,

Microservices Architecture: An architectural approach where a complex application is built as a collection of small, independent services that communicate with each other. Each microservice is designed to perform a specific business function and can be developed and deployed independently.

Modular Functions: Small, independent units of code that perform specific tasks.

Platform as a Service (PaaS): A service that offers a ready-made platform for developing, testing, and deploying applications, abstracting the underlying infrastructure complexities.

Software as a Service (SaaS): A service that delivers software applications over the internet, accessible through a web browser without the need for installation or maintenance.

Virtualized Computing Resources: Virtualized computing resources refer to the creation of virtual versions of physical resources, such as servers, storage, or networks.

Chapter 4
Exploring the World of Serverless Computing:
Concepts, Benefits, and Challenges

Vishal Goar
Engineering College Bikaner, Bikaner, India

Nagendra Singh Yadav
ⓘ https://orcid.org/0000-0002-9591-4491
Engineering College Bikaner, Bikaner, India

ABSTRACT

As the landscape of computing continues to evolve, serverless computing emerges as a paradigm shift, offering a transformative approach to application development and deployment. Serverless computing has revolutionized the way businesses build & deploy applications. With its promise of seamless scalability, reduced operational overhead, and cost optimization, serverless systems have become a dominant paradigm in cloud computing. A focal point of this exploration is the examination of the myriad benefits that serverless computing brings to the table. This chapter focuses on the Introduction to Serverless computing, core concepts of serverless computing, Advantages of serverless computing, Challenges in Serverless Computing, Use Cases and Industry Adoption, Best Practices for Serverless Development, and Future Trends in Serverless Computing.

1. INTRODUCTION TO SERVERLESS COMPUTING

Serverless computing is frequently known as Function as a Service which is a cloud computing model where cloud providers automatically manage the underlying infrastructure, enabling developers to aim fully on creation and deployment of code. In this model, applications are segmented into several methods, each of which is run in response to a particular condition or event. Unlike traditional server-based models where developers are required to maintain servers & their scaling, in serverless computing, the cloud service provider is responsible for providing server, scaling, & maintenance.

DOI: 10.4018/979-8-3693-1682-5.ch004

Evolution of Serverless Computing - The concept of serverless computing has evolved over time, with its roots in Platform as a Service & function as a Service offerings. It can be traced through various stages of evolution:

- **PaaS and Early Cloud Services -** The idea of abstracting infrastructure and providing a higher-level environment for application deployment began with PaaS offerings i.e. Google App Engine These platforms automated much of the operational overhead (Nastić et al., 2017).
- **Function as a Service (FaaS) -** FaaS platforms, i.e. AWS Lambda, introduced the concept of serverless by allowing developers to execute each method as an action for events. This represented a shift from managing applications to managing functions.
- **Managed Services -** Cloud providers expanded their serverless offerings, including managed databases, storage, and authentication, reducing the need for developers to manage infrastructure components further.
- **Serverless Frameworks -** The emergence of serverless frameworks, like the Serverless Framework and AWS SAM, helped streamline the development and deployment process, making it easier for developers to adopt serverless technologies.
- **Ecosystem Growth -** The serverless ecosystem has continued to grow, with more providers, tools, and libraries, making it increasingly accessible and versatile for a wide range of use cases.

Key attributes of Serverless Computing - It is characterized by many key features that set it apart from conventional server-based models:

- **Event-Driven -** Serverless functions are triggered by certain events or requests i.e. HTTP requests or custom triggers. The code only runs when there is an event to process, eliminating idle time and reducing costs.
- **Automatic Scaling -** Serverless platforms automatically control the scaling of functions in response to varying workloads (Eismann et al., 2020). Developers are not required to bother about provisioning or management of servers. This is something provided by the cloud providers.
- **Pay-as-You-Go Pricing -** Serverless platforms bill users depending on the real execution time of their methods. This granular billing model means you only bill for the assets utilized during the execution of the method.
- **Stateless -** Serverless methods don't keep details between invocations. Any necessary state must be stored externally i.e. database.
- **Microservices Architecture -** Applications are built as a collection of smaller functions, each with a specific purpose. This microservices approach makes it easier to maintain and scale different parts of the application independently.
- **Managed Infrastructure -** Cloud providers control the principal infrastructure, including server allocations, load balancing, & security, permitting developers to aim at generating code.

Architectural Components - Serverless applications consist of various architectural components, each serving a specific role in the overall system. Some of the essential components include:

- **Functions -** These are the core building blocks of serverless applications. Functions are tiny units of code that are designed to execute certain tasks in response to events. They are stateless and execute quickly.
- **Event Sources -** Event sources trigger functions to execute. Common event origins include API Gateway, DynamoDB Streams, and custom events (Jambunathan & Yoganathan, 2018).
- **Execution Environment -** The cloud provider manages the execution environment for functions, including provisioning and scaling resources as needed. This ensures that methods are run in response to events.
- **API Gateway -** This component is used to expose serverless functions as HTTP endpoints, making it possible for external clients to interact with the serverless application over the internet.
- **Data Storage -** Serverless applications often rely on external data storage solutions, such as managed databases (e.g., Amazon Aurora Serverless) and object storage (AWS S3).
- **Authentication and Authorization -** Serverless applications require secure access control. Identity and access management solutions, such as AWS Cognito or AWS IAM, are used to control who can invoke functions and access resources.

Serverless Providers - Several cloud providers offer serverless computing platforms, each with its unique features and ecosystem. Some of the leading serverless providers include:

- **Amazon Web Services (AWS) -** AWS Lambda is widely known amongst serverless platforms, offering a wider span of services & integrations, making it a top choice for many businesses.
- **Microsoft Azure -** Azure methods are Microsoft's serverless service, tightly integrated with the Azure cloud ecosystem, and provides support for multiple programming languages.
- **Google Cloud Platform (GCP) -** GCP offers Cloud Functions, which enables developers to create and deploy methods in response to various events, while seamlessly integrating with other GCP services (Lee et al., 2018).
- **IBM Cloud -** IBM Cloud methods is IBM's serverless platform, providing flexibility and integration with various IBM services and solutions.
- **Alibaba Cloud -** Alibaba Cloud Function Compute offers a serverless environment that is well-integrated with Alibaba's comprehensive cloud services.
- **Oracle Cloud -** Oracle Cloud Functions provides serverless capabilities for building applications that leverage Oracle Cloud services and resources.
- **Open-Source Serverless Frameworks -** In addition to these cloud providers, there are open-source serverless frameworks like the Serverless Framework and Apache OpenWhisk that can be used on multiple cloud platforms or in on-premises environments.

REVIEW OF LITERATURE

(Z. Li et al., 2022) explained the server architecture by focusing on linked concepts, advantages & shared some implications of architecture. (Grogan et al., 2020b) differentiated development choices supported for various serverless platforms. (Yussupov et al., 2021) showcased a sophisticated review of technology to differentiate the 10 most famous serverless platforms which are the first choice for development &

access management. Additionally, some studies were carried out to observe certain aspects i.e. issues with cold start & policy of scheduling management of resources.

(Mampage et al., 2022) showcased a detailed analysis of resource management. They analyzed current work depending on the suggested taxonomy. However, the findings don't grant a global overview of current research. (Hassan et al., 2021) created an abstract of a research paper focused on serverless computing. The study displayed information based on statistical data from a research paper.

2. CORE CONCEPTS OF SERVERLESS COMPUTING

2.1. Function as a Service (FaaS)

2.1.1. Understanding FaaS

Function as a Service, commonly referred to as FaaS, is a cloud computing model that enables developers to deploy each method of code for an event. These events can be HTTP requests, changes in data, scheduled events, or virtually any trigger that can be defined (Grogan et al., 2020). The central idea behind FaaS is to execute code only when needed, abstracting off infrastructure management, and enabling developers to focus primarily on writing business logic.

2.1.2. Key Attributes of FaaS

- **Serverless Computing -** FaaS is often synonymous with "serverless computing." This term can be misleading because servers are indeed involved, but the infrastructure management is abstracted away from developers. The cloud provider manages server allocations, scaling, & maintenance.
- **Event-Driven -** FaaS platforms are inherently event-driven. Methods are run in response to certain events. This makes FaaS ideal for scenarios where responsiveness and scalability are crucial.
- **Microservices -** FaaS promotes a microservices architecture, where each function serves a single purpose. This modularity enhances maintainability and scalability.
- **Automatic Scaling -** FaaS platforms automatically scale functions depending on number of requests. If an application encounters an unexpected surge in requests, extra instances of a method are automatically spawned to manage the load.
- **Pay-as-You-Go -** With FaaS, one only pays for the computation assets utilized as part of the execution of methods. There is no Fee associated with idle time.
- **Statelessness -** Functions in a FaaS environment should ideally be stateless, as they may be executed on different instances with each invocation. The State should be managed externally, often in databases or storage services.
- **Isolation -** Functions are isolated from each other, which enhances security and reliability. If one function fails, it does not affect others.

2.2. Event-Driven Programming

Event-driven programming is a software design pattern where the course of the program is determined by events i.e. user interactions or system events. In the context of FaaS, events are central to triggering function execution. The event-driven architecture allows applications to respond to modifications in their environment in real-time.

Event Sources - Event sources in FaaS systems can vary widely, including:

- **HTTP Requests** - Functions can be triggered by incoming HTTP requests, making FaaS ideal for building web services and APIs.
- **Data Changes** - Databases and data storage services can emit events when data is created, updated, or deleted. Functions can respond to these changes.
- **Scheduled Events** - Functions can be scheduled to run at specific intervals, making them suitable for tasks like data backups or periodic cleanup.
- **Message Queues** - Event-driven systems often use message queues to decouple components and enable asynchronous communication. Functions can listen to messages in the queue and process them.
- **IoT Devices** - Internet of Things devices produce a continuous stream of events. FaaS can process and react to these events in real-time.

Benefits of Event-Driven Programming

- **Scalability** - Event-driven systems can easily scale to handle fluctuating workloads. Functions are invoked as needed, allowing for efficient resource utilization.
- **Responsiveness** - Applications built with event-driven programming can respond to events in real-time, providing a better user experience.
- **Loose Coupling** - Components in event-driven systems are loosely combined, which enhances flexibility and maintainability. Changes to one component do not necessitate changes in others.
- **Error Handling** - Event-driven systems can implement robust error handling and retries. If a function fails, it can be retried or other error-handling mechanisms can be employed.
- **Flexibility** - Event-driven systems can easily integrate with various services and components, making them suitable for a wide range of applications.

2.3. Microservices and Serverless

Microservices, often touted as a revolutionary architectural style, have gained widespread adoption for developing large and complex applications. Unlike traditional monolithic applications, where all functionalities are bundled into a single codebase, microservices break down the application into a group of little, independent, & loosely combined services. The service aims at a particular business capacity, i.e. authentication for users.

Advantages of Microservices -

- **Scalability** - Microservices allows fine-grained scaling. You can scale individual services independently, assigning assets where they are required the most. This results in efficient resource utilization and cost savings.
- **Flexibility** - Microservices delegate development teams to pick the most suitable technology stack for the corresponding service, as long as they adhere to well-defined APIs. This fosters innovation and allows teams to select the right tools for the job.

- **Fault Isolation** - Isolating services from one another ensures that a failure in the corresponding service does not fail throughout the whole application. It enhances resilience and fault tolerance.
- **Faster Development** - Smaller, goal-oriented teams can create & deploy microservices more quickly. This allows for faster iterations and feature delivery.
- **Easier Maintenance** - Debugging, testing, and updating smaller services is more manageable than dealing with a monolithic codebase.
- **Improved Collaboration** - Teams can work independently on different microservices, leading to better parallelism and collaboration.

Serverless – In Serverless computing, the cloud provider manages the underlying infrastructure, automatically allocating assets to run code for certain triggers. The term "serverless" is somewhat misleading since servers still exist, but developers are abstracted from the server management, focusing solely on writing code.

Advantages of Serverless -

- **Cost-Efficiency** - Serverless platforms charge depending on actual consumptions, resulting in cost-friendliness for sporadically used workloads.
- **Scalability** - Automatic scaling makes sure that your application can control traffic spikes instead of manual interference.
- **Reduced Operational Overhead** - Serverless abolishes the requirement to manage server infrastructure, reducing operational overhead.
- **Faster Development** - Developers can aim on writing code instead of worrying about infrastructure management.
- **High Availability** - Serverless platforms often provide high availability by default, as they distribute functions across multiple data centers.
- **Serverless Ecosystem** - A rich ecosystem of pre-built functions, libraries, and integrations simplifies development.

Choosing Between Microservices and Serverless

The pick between microservices & serverless is subject to the particular requirements of an application. In some cases, a hybrid approach may be most suitable, where you use serverless for certain components and microservices for others.

Use Microservices When -

- Your application is complex and needs fine-grained control over services.
- You have specific performance or latency requirements.
- Your team has experience managing distributed systems.

Use Serverless When -

- Your workload is event-driven and has variable traffic patterns.
- You want to minimize infrastructure management and reduce operational overhead.
- Cost efficiency and scalability are paramount.

2.4. Stateless Compute

Stateless compute is a computing paradigm that separates the state or data of a computation from the computational logic itself. In a stateless computing model, each computation or task is isolated from previous and subsequent computations, allowing for complete independence. This means that the result of a computation is solely dependent on its input parameters, without any reliance on stored data or prior computational history. This characteristic makes stateless compute particularly well-suited for distributed and cloud computing environments, as it simplifies resource allocation and improves scalability.

Stateless Compute in Action

- **Scalability and Elasticity -** Stateless compute enables dynamic scaling of resources. Cloud platforms i.e. AWS Lambda methods employ stateless compute to automatically allocate resources in response to varying workloads. As new tasks arrive, they can be processed without the need to maintain persistent connections or state information (Lam & Schmidt, 2000). This leads to efficient resource utilization and cost savings.
- **Fault Tolerance -** Stateless compute is inherently fault-tolerant. If a stateless computation fails, it can be retried or routed to another available resource without the risk of data corruption. This robustness is essential for building resilient systems in the face of hardware failures or transient network issues.
- **Serverless Computing -** Stateless compute is a core concept in serverless computing. Serverless platforms abstract away the underlying infrastructure & manage stateless functions, ensuring efficient use of resources and minimizing operational overhead.
- **Microservices Architecture -** Stateless compute aligns with the microservices architectural pattern. Each microservice operates independently, enabling horizontal scalability and making it easier to develop, deploy, & manage distributed systems (Lloyd et al., 2018).

Stateless Compute Challenges

- **Data Management -** Stateless compute emphasizes statelessness in computation, but not all aspects of an application can be stateless. Managing stateful data, such as user sessions and database interactions, can be complex in stateless environments.
- **Coordination -** Coordinating multiple stateless components in a distributed system can be challenging. Implementing orchestration and choreography patterns is necessary to ensure proper synchronization and sequencing of tasks.
- **Latency -** Stateless compute may introduce additional network communication, leading to increased latency compared to traditional stateful systems. Designing efficient data transfer and minimizing the impact on latency is crucial.

Security and Stateless Compute -

- **Isolation -** Stateless functions run in isolated environments, reducing the risk of security breaches spreading across the system. A compromised task doesn't compromise the entire system.

- **Immutable Infrastructure** - Stateless systems are often built using immutable infrastructure principles. This means that once deployed, the environment cannot be modified. This reduces the attack surface and enhances security.
- **Authentication and Authorization** - Stateless compute can integrate with modern authentication and authorization protocols, ensuring robust security controls.

Scalability and Auto-scaling

The capacity to scale resources effectively is a critical component of any successful technological endeavor. Scalability, the capability to accommodate growing workloads or changes in demand, is a fundamental concept for building robust and efficient systems. Auto-scaling, in particular, has emerged as a powerful tool in the arsenal of modern technology, enabling systems to dynamically adjust their resources in response to changing workloads (Pérez et al., 2018).

Scalability comes in two primary flavors: vertical scaling & horizontal scaling. Vertical scaling includes associating more assets i.e. CPU to an existing system, making it more powerful but often coming at a higher cost. Horizontal scaling, on the other hand, focuses on adding more machines or instances to a system, distributing the workload and reducing the threat of a single point of outage.

Scalability is not a one-size-fits-all solution. It comes with its own set of hurdles, such as load balancing, data consistency, and efficient resource allocation. These challenges require careful planning and architectural decisions.

Auto-scaling: The Game Changer

Auto-scaling is a dynamic approach to scalability that enables systems to automatically adjust their resource allocation in real-time based on the current workload. This is especially valuable in today's cloud-centric world, where resources are often provisioned and billed on-demand.

The advantages of auto-scaling are manifold. It leads to cost optimization, as one is only billed for the actual assets utilized. It enhances system performance, ensuring that resources are available when needed, and reduces the risk of outages due to unexpected traffic spikes.

Strategies for Auto-scaling

- **Reactive vs. Proactive Auto-scaling** - Reactive auto-scaling responds to workload changes after they've occurred. Proactive auto-scaling anticipates changes in workload based on historical data, trends, or predictions. Both strategies have their place, depending on the nature of the application.
- **Trigger-Based Auto-scaling** - In trigger-based auto-scaling, certain predefined conditions trigger resource scaling. This can be based on CPU utilization, memory usage, network traffic, or custom metrics. Properly defining these triggers is crucial for effective auto-scaling.
- **Scheduled Auto-scaling** - Scheduled auto-scaling is employed when the workload follows predictable patterns, such as daily or weekly cycles. It allows for resource allocation to be adjusted at specified times, preventing over-provisioning.
- **Predictive Auto-scaling** - This cutting-edge approach uses machine learning and data analytics to forecast future resource requirements. It leverages historical data, trends, and external factors to predict when and how resources should be scaled.

Implementing Auto-scaling -

- **Cloud Providers and Auto-scaling -** Major cloud providers offer auto-scaling solutions as part of their service offerings. This enables developers to implement with ease as auto-scaling comes with an added feature.
- **Container Orchestration and Auto-scaling -** Container orchestration platforms like Kubernetes provide robust auto-scaling capabilities for containerized applications. They can automatically add or remove containers based on resource requirements.

Real-world Applications -

- **E-commerce -** E-commerce websites experience fluctuating traffic, especially during sales events. Auto-scaling ensures that resources are dynamically allocated to accommodate spikes in demand while reducing costs during quieter periods.
- **Content Delivery Networks (CDNs) -** CDNs rely heavily on auto-scaling to efficiently deliver content to users across the globe. Scaling edge servers based on regional demand optimizes content delivery.
- **Online Gaming -** Online games must handle varying numbers of players, often in real-time. Auto-scaling of game servers ensures a seamless gaming experience during peak hours.

2.5. Pay-as-You-Go Pricing Model

The Pay-as-You-Go pricing model, also known as consumption-based pricing, embodies the idea that users pay only for the computing assets Utilized. In traditional models, users typically rent servers for a fixed duration, regardless of whether the resources are actively used. Serverless computing, on the other hand, charges users based on their actual usage, down to the millisecond (Lin & Khazaei, 2021).

- **Granularity and Precision -** One of the fundamental principles of the Pay-as-You-Go model is granularity. This model tracks resource consumption with incredible precision. Rather than paying for a server's uptime, users are charged for the exact amount of CPU usage, & network resources used during the execution of their code. This level of granularity enables cost optimization, as organizations can ensure that they are not over-provisioning or overpaying for unused resources.
- **Event-Driven Billing -**Serverless computing often employs an event-driven architecture, where methods are executed by actions i.e. database changes. The Pay-as-You-Go model aligns seamlessly with this architecture. Users are charged money depending on the number of events processed & the resources consumed during each event's execution. This fine-grained billing approach is specifically beneficial for applications with sporadic or unpredicted workloads, as users only pay when their code is actively running.
- **Scaling Efficiency -** Scalability is a core feature of serverless computing, and the Pay-as-You-Go pricing model is intricately linked to it. Serverless platforms automatically scale the resources allocated to a function to match the workload. This dynamic scaling ensures that users never overpay for idle resources. As the system scales up and down in response to demand, costs adjust in real-time. This flexibility makes serverless computing an attractive option for businesses with changing workloads, i.e. e-commerce websites in the duration of peak sales.

Benefits of the Pay-as-You-Go Model –

- **Cost Efficiency -** Perhaps the most significant benefit of this pricing model is cost efficiency. Users can achieve significant savings by only paying for the assets they actively use. As applications scale up or down, costs follow suit, making it an ideal pick for businesses looking to control & optimize their cloud spending.
- **Reduced Management Overhead -** By shifting the accountability of infrastructure management to the cloud provider, organizations can focus more on their core competencies and application development. This streamlined approach reduces the administrative overhead of maintaining and monitoring servers, enabling developers to concentrate on code & business logic.
- **Automatic Scaling -** Serverless platforms automatically handle resource allocation & scaling depending on workload, ensuring that applications are responsive and cost-effective. This hands-off scaling approach allows businesses to be agile and adapt quickly to changing demands.
- **Predictable Billing -** The Pay-as-You-Go model offers predictable billing, as users can anticipate costs depending on their resource utilization. This predictability simplifies budgeting and financial planning, giving businesses more confidence in their cloud expenditures.

3. ADVANTAGES OF SERVERLESS COMPUTING

- **Cost Efficiency -** Serverless computing stands out as a cost-efficient solution for organizations. It follows a "pay-as-you-go" model, where users are billed only for the compute resources consumed during the execution of functions. This contrasts with traditional infrastructure, where organizations are often forced to over-provision resources to accommodate peak loads, leading to underutilization and higher costs. In a serverless environment, the cloud provider manages resource allocation, ensuring optimal resource utilization. Furthermore, serverless computing eliminates the costs associated with server maintenance and management, such as patching, updates, and hardware maintenance.
- **Improved Developer Productivity -** Developers are at the heart of any organization's success in the digital age. Serverless computing empowers developers by allowing them to aim fully at generating code & not worrying about server allocation or scaling. This results in a shorter development phase & faster market ready new features & applications. Developers can work with smaller, more focused units of code, known as functions, which are easier to manage, test, and deploy. Serverless platforms also provide robust monitoring and logging tools, which aid in debugging and optimization. Overall, serverless computing enhances developer productivity by freeing them from the administrative tasks associated with infrastructure management (Taibi et al., 2021).
- **Seamless Scalability -** Serverless platforms offer automatic scaling, allowing applications to effortlessly adapt to fluctuating workloads. Functions are designed to be stateless, meaning they can be replicated and scaled horizontally in response to increased demand. This elasticity ensures that applications can manage sudden traffic increases without manual intervention, resulting in a seamless & responsive user experience. This scalability is invaluable for applications that experience varying levels of load throughout the day, week, or year, such as e-commerce websites during holiday sales or event-driven applications.

- **Reduced Operational Overhead -** One of the Key attractions of serverless computing is the reduction in operational overhead. Traditional server-based applications require a dedicated team to manage servers, perform updates, monitor system health, and handle security patches. Serverless platforms handle many of these tasks automatically, freeing up IT teams to focus on more strategic initiatives. Furthermore, serverless computing abstracts the infrastructure, reducing the requirement for resource planning and allocation (Schleier-Smith et al., 2021). This not only lowers costs but also minimizes the risk of operational issues caused by misconfigurations.
- **Enhanced Reliability -** Reliability is a fundamental concern in the world of computing. Serverless platforms are designed to be highly reliable, with automatic failover mechanisms built-in. In traditional setups, a server failure could lead to application downtime and data loss. In a serverless environment, a failure in one function or instance does not affect the entire application, as other instances can take over the workload. Cloud providers often distribute serverless functions across multiple data centers, further enhancing reliability. Additionally, serverless platforms typically offer built-in redundancy and backup options, further ensuring data and application integrity.
- **Global Reach and Latency Optimization -** Modern applications often serve a global user base. Serverless computing provides a unique advantage in this context. Cloud providers offering serverless services have data centers distributed worldwide. This global reach enables organizations to deploy their functions and applications closer to end-users, reducing network latency and ensuring a smoother user experience. Serverless applications can automatically route requests to the nearest data center, optimizing response times for users across the globe. This is particularly valuable for applications where low latency is crucial, such as online gaming or real-time financial trading.

4. CHALLENGES IN SERVERLESS COMPUTING

4.1. The Cold Start Problem

One of the most notorious hurdles in serverless computing is the Cold Start Problem. When a method is invoked, the cloud provider must spin up a new execution environment for that function. This initial environment setup introduces latency, resulting in what is known as the "cold start" time. The corresponding invoking of the same method within that environment (while it's warm) is much faster (Shafiei et al., 2022). The cold start time can be specifically difficult for applications that need low-latency responses.
   Mitigation Strategies are listed below -

- **Provisioned Concurrency -** Some cloud providers offer a feature called "provisioned concurrency," which allows you to pre-warm a specific number of method instances to minimize cold starts.
- **Code Optimization -** Reducing the function's code size and dependencies can help decrease the cold start time.
- **Warm-up Strategies -** Implementing warm-up mechanisms that periodically invoke functions to keep them warm can help mitigate the cold start issue.

Figure 1. Challenges in serverless computing

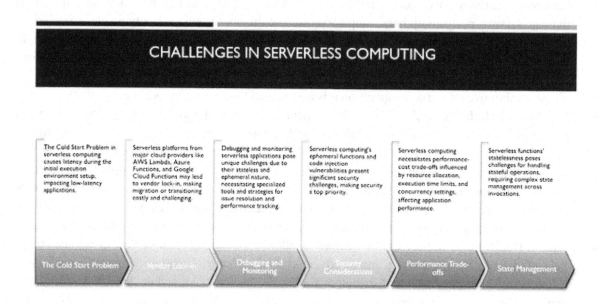

4.2. Vendor Lock-in

Serverless platforms are typically provided by specific cloud providers, i.e. Google Cloud Functions. This creates a risk of vendor lock-in, where an application becomes tightly combined to a particular cloud provider's services & API. Migrating to a different provider or transitioning back to a traditional infrastructure can be challenging and costly.

Mitigation Strategies are listed below -

- **Use Multi-Cloud Tools -** Leverage multi-cloud tools and abstraction layers like Kubernetes or serverless frameworks that can make it easier to migrate between cloud providers.
- **Adopt Standard APIs -** Favor using standard APIs or containers like OpenFaaS to reduce dependencies on specific cloud services.
- **Evaluate Hybrid Solutions -** Consider hybrid solutions that combine serverless with containerized applications to reduce vendor lock-in risks.

4.3. Debugging and Monitoring

Debugging & monitoring serverless applications can be quite complicated than conventional applications (Gadepalli et al., 2020). Since serverless functions are stateless and ephemeral, debugging issues across different invocations and monitoring their performance requires specialized tools and approaches.

Mitigation Strategies are listed below -

- **Cloud Provider Tools** - Utilize the monitoring and debugging tools given by the corresponding cloud provider i.e. AWS CloudWatch.
- **Third-party Monitoring Tools** - Consider third-party monitoring and observability solutions like New Relic, Datadog, or Prometheus.
- **Distributed Tracing** - Implement distributed tracing to visualize and analyze the flow of requests across serverless functions.

4.4. Security Considerations

Security remains a paramount concern in serverless computing. The ephemeral nature of serverless functions and the potential for code injection vulnerabilities pose unique challenges.

Mitigation Strategies are listed below -

- **Least Privilege Principle** - Implement the principle of least accesses by making sure that functions have only the required permissions to execute their tasks.
- **Input Validation** - Validate & sanitize inputs to avert code injection attacks.
- **Regular Patching** - Keep third-party libraries & dependencies up-to-date to address known security loopholes.
- **Serverless Firewalls** - Use serverless firewalls to add an additional layer of security for your functions.

4.5. Performance Trade-Offs

Serverless computing often involves trade-offs between performance and cost. Resource allocation, execution time limits, and concurrency settings can impact application performance (Li et al., 2023).

Mitigation Strategies are listed below -

- **Fine-tuning Resources** - Adjust the allocated memory and CPU settings to optimize the performance & cost of your functions.
- **Load Testing** - Conduct load testing to understand the behavior of your serverless application under various conditions.
- **Application Profiling** - Use profiling tools to recognize performance bottlenecks & optimize your code accordingly.

4.6. State Management

Serverless functions are inherently stateless, which can be challenging when dealing with stateful operations. Managing states across different invocations can be complex.

Mitigation Strategies are listed below -

- **External State Storage** - Use external databases, file storage, or caching systems to manage persistent state.
- **State Machines** - Implement state machines to manage complex workflows across multiple function invocations.

- **Serverless Orchestration -** Utilize serverless orchestration tools like AWS Step Functions to manage state in serverless applications.

5. USE CASES AND INDUSTRY ADOPTION

5.1. Web and Mobile Applications

Serverless computing has witnessed significant adoption in the realm of web and mobile applications. This adoption is driven by its ability to scale effortlessly with user demand and eliminate the requirement for allocation & management of servers. Web and mobile application developers have harnessed the power of serverless platforms i.e. AWS Lambda to create highly responsive and scalable applications. One key advantage of serverless for web and mobile applications is cost-efficiency. Developers are billed for the resources used in the computation of code, which allows them to allocate resources more effectively, reducing operational costs (Eismann et al., 2020b). Additionally, serverless platforms provide easy integration with other cloud services, enabling developers to leverage various features such as databases, authentication, and content delivery networks seamlessly.

Figure 2. Use cases and industry adoption

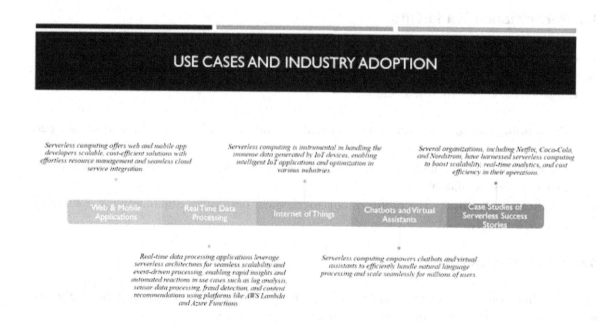

5.2. Real-Time Data Processing

Real-time data processing applications are increasingly relying on serverless architectures to handle data streams, analytics, and event-driven processing. These applications can benefit from the rapid scalability and event-driven nature of serverless platforms, which can automatically execute code in response to data events. Use cases for real-time data processing include log analysis, sensor data processing, fraud detection, and personalized content recommendations. Serverless platforms like AWS Lambda and Azure Functions provide an ideal environment for these applications, as they can efficiently process data as it arrives, offering near-instantaneous insights and reactions (Castro et al., 2019).

5.3. Internet of Things (IoT)

The Internet of Things (IoT) has experienced explosive growth, and serverless computing plays a critical part in managing & analyzing the vast volumes of data produced by IoT devices. Serverless functions can be triggered by IoT events, allowing for seamless data ingestion, transformation, and analysis. This facilitates the development of intelligent and responsive IoT applications. Industries such as agriculture, healthcare, and manufacturing have harnessed the power of serverless to optimize processes and make data-driven decisions. For instance, IoT devices in agriculture can monitor soil conditions and trigger actions, such as irrigation or fertilization, automatically, thanks to serverless processing in the cloud.

5.4. Chatbots and Virtual Assistants

Chatbots and virtual assistants have become ubiquitous in today's digital landscape. Serverless computing is instrumental in their development and operation. Chatbots can leverage serverless functions to understand natural language, perform tasks, and provide instant responses. Virtual assistants like Amazon Alexa and Google Assistant rely on serverless platforms to process voice commands, query information, and control smart devices. This serverless architecture allows for seamless scaling to accommodate millions of users, with minimal operational overhead.

5.5. Case Studies of Serverless Success Stories

To illustrate the real-world impact of serverless computing, let's explore some case studies of organizations that have successfully adopted serverless architectures:

- **Netflix -** Netflix, a global streaming giant, relies heavily on serverless technologies to support its vast user base. Serverless functions handle various tasks, including content recommendations, user authentication, and monitoring. This enables Netflix to maintain high availability and scalability, particularly during peak viewing hours.
- **Coca-Cola -** Coca-Cola utilizes serverless computing to enhance its marketing efforts. By leveraging serverless functions, they can analyze social media trends in real-time and respond to emerging opportunities swiftly. This has improved their ability to engage with their audience and adjust marketing strategies effectively.

- **Nordstrom** - Nordstrom, a leading fashion retailer, employs serverless to power its e-commerce platform. The flexibility of serverless allows Nordstrom to scale during high-traffic events, such as sales and promotions, while maintaining cost efficiency during quieter periods.

6. BEST PRACTICES FOR SERVERLESS DEVELOPMENT

Figure 3. Best practices for serverless development

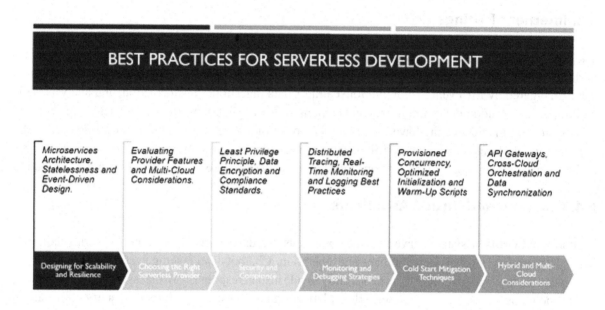

6.1. Designing for Scalability and Resilience

- **Microservices Architecture** - Serverless applications benefit from a microservices architecture. Break down your application into small, independent methods that perform specific tasks. This allows for better scalability and easier management.
- **Statelessness** - Serverless functions should be stateless, meaning they don't rely on any local or shared state. Store state externally in databases, object storage, or other suitable services. This promotes scalability and resilience (Jamshidi et al., 2018).
- **Event-Driven Design** - Leverage event-driven design by connecting serverless functions through event triggers. This enables asynchronous communication and ensures that functions only run when necessary, reducing costs and improving efficiency.

6.2. Choosing the Right Serverless Provider

- **Evaluating Provider Features -** Select a serverless provider that aligns with your application's requirements. Consider factors like supported languages, integrations, and services.
- **Multi-Cloud Considerations -** To eliminate vendor lock-in & increase resilience, consider multi-cloud strategies. Develop serverless functions in a way that allows easy migration between providers, if needed (Lin & Khazaei, 2021b).

6.3. Security and Compliance

- **Least Privilege Principle -** Apply the principle of least access to serverless methods. Only grant necessary permissions to access resources and services. Use IAM roles and policies to restrict access.
- **Data Encryption -** Encrypt data in transit & at rest. Use HTTPS for communication, and leverage encryption services offered by your provider, such as AWS KMS or Azure Key Vault.
- **Compliance Standards -** Ensure compliance with industry-specific standards, such as GDPR or HIPAA, by configuring your serverless applications accordingly. Implement auditing, monitoring, and reporting as necessary.

6.4. Monitoring and Debugging Strategies

- **Distributed Tracing -** Implement distributed tracing to track the flow of requests through your serverless functions. Tools like AWS X-Ray and OpenTelemetry can help identify performance bottlenecks and errors.
- **Real-Time Monitoring -** Utilize real-time monitoring tools to gain insight into the health and performance of your functions. CloudWatch, Azure Monitor, and Google Cloud Monitoring provide metrics, logs, and alerts.
- **Logging Best Practices -** Establish comprehensive logging practices to capture important events, errors, and exceptions. Use structured logs with a correlation ID to trace a request's journey through the application.

6.5. Cold Start Mitigation Techniques

- **Provisioned Concurrency -** Some serverless platforms allow you to provision a certain number of concurrent executions to reduce cold start latency. Adjust this based on your application's expected workload.
- **Optimized Initialization -** Reduce initialization time by minimizing dependencies, optimizing code, and employing techniques like connection pooling. This improves the responsiveness of your functions.
- **Warm-Up Scripts -** Schedule warm-up scripts to periodically invoke your functions. This keeps them in a warm state, reducing cold starts and ensuring low-latency responses.

6.6. Hybrid and Multi-Cloud Considerations

- **API Gateways** - Utilize API gateways to orchestrate serverless functions with other parts of your infrastructure, whether they are hosted in the cloud, on-premises, or in another cloud provider.
- **Cross-Cloud Orchestration** - Leverage workflow automation tools or serverless orchestration services like AWS Step Functions or Azure Logic Apps to coordinate serverless functions across multiple cloud providers.
- **Data Synchronization** - Implement data synchronization strategies when working in a hybrid or multi-cloud environment. Tools like Apache Kafka, AWS S3, and Azure Blob Storage can help maintain data consistency.

7. FUTURE TRENDS IN SERVERLESS COMPUTING

In the faster growing landscape of cloud computing, serverless computing has appeared as a powerful paradigm shift. With its focus on abstracting away server management, serverless computing has enabled developers to create & deploy applications more efficiently & cost-effectively. These trends include Serverless at the Edge, Serverless Machine Learning, Serverless Databases, Integration with Kubernetes and Containers, and the role of Serverless in DevOps.

Figure 4. Future trends in serverless computing

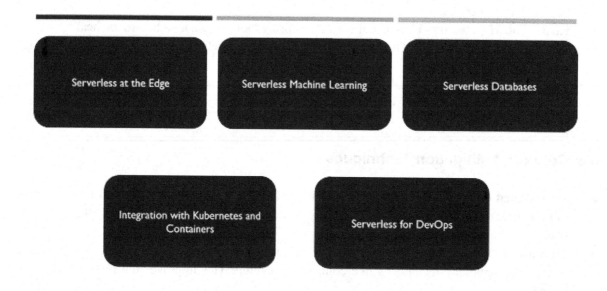

- **Serverless at the Edge -** One of the most promising developments in serverless computing is its integration with edge computing. Edge computing brings computation next to the source of data, lowering latency & allowing real-time processing. Serverless at the edge allows developers to run serverless functions on edge devices or edge locations, such as IoT devices, content delivery networks (CDNs), and 5G network edge servers. This convergence of serverless and edge computing opens up new possibilities for applications that need ultra-low latency & high responsiveness. For example, IoT devices can trigger serverless functions at the edge to process data locally, lowering the requirement to send all data to centralized cloud servers. This approach is not only more efficient but also enhances security by reducing data exposure over the network. Furthermore, edge serverless enables dynamic content caching, image and video processing, and even real-time analytics on the edge, making it a valuable tool for businesses and industries that demand near-instantaneous data processing (Krishnamurthi et al., 2023).

- **Serverless Machine Learning -** Machine learning and serverless computing are a natural fit. Serverless platforms provide a scalable, event-driven architecture that is well-suited for machine learning tasks. Future trends in serverless computing are seeing the integration of serverless platforms with machine learning frameworks, making it easier for developers to create & and deploy ML models. Serverless Machine Learning enables developers to execute model training and inference in response to events i.e. image uploads and user interactions. With the auto-scaling capabilities of serverless, applications can dynamically adjust their compute resources to handle fluctuating workloads, making it cost-effective and efficient for ML tasks. Moreover, cloud providers are offering specialized serverless machine learning services that abstract away the infrastructure complexities & allow developers to aim on building & training models (Bebortta et al., 2020). These services make it easier for organizations to adopt machine learning without the need for specialized ML infrastructure expertise.

- **Serverless Databases -** The evolution of serverless computing also extends to databases. Serverless databases are designed to scale automatically and only consume resources when there is a demand. This approach abolishes the requirement to allocate & manage database servers, providing a cost-efficient and low-maintenance solution. Serverless databases are particularly advantageous for applications with unpredicted workloads. They can seamlessly handle traffic spikes and idle periods without incurring unnecessary costs. This trend is empowering developers to build highly responsive & cost-effective applications without the complexities of managing traditional databases. Integration with serverless databases also simplifies data access for serverless applications. Developers can aim at their application code, knowing that the database will automatically scale and handle data storage and retrieval efficiently.

- **Integration with Kubernetes and Containers -** Serverless and containers are two influential technologies in the world of cloud computing. They are often seen as complementary rather than mutually exclusive. As serverless platforms continue to evolve, integration with Kubernetes and containers has become a focal point. This convergence allows organizations to build applications that benefit from the scalability and event-driven nature of serverless while taking advantage of the portability and management benefits of containers. Serverless functions can be packaged within containers and orchestrated using Kubernetes. This hybrid approach offers flexibility and simplifies the deployment of complex applications with multiple microservices. Knative, an open-source project for building, deploying, & managing serverless workloads in Kubernetes, is a prime example of this trend. Knative provides a set of building blocks that make it easier to deploy and manage serverless functions on Kubernetes clusters.

- **Serverless for DevOps -** The DevOps culture, which emphasizes collaboration among development & operations teams, has been transformed by serverless computing. Serverless DevOps automates several of the repetitive tasks included in software development & deployment, leading to faster and more reliable releases. Serverless functions can be used to automate a wide range of DevOps processes, such as code integration, testing, deployment, monitoring, and scaling. This trend enhances the efficiency of development pipelines and ensures that applications can be developed, tested, & deployed rapidly, making it easier for organizations to embrace continuous integration and continuous delivery (CI/CD). Furthermore, serverless platforms offer powerful monitoring and analytics capabilities, making it easier for DevOps teams to track application performance, detect issues, & respond to incidents in real time.

8. CONCLUSION

In conclusion, serverless computing is not just a passing trend; it is a transformative force in the world of cloud computing. Its ongoing evolution, the recommendations for practitioners, and its potential impact on the future of cloud computing all point to a future where serverless becomes an integral part of how we build and run applications. As the technology and ecosystem continue to develop, it is an exciting time for both developers and organizations to leverage the advantages that serverless computing offers. By staying informed, embracing best practices, and adapting to the changing landscape, practitioners can make the most of this dynamic and revolutionary computing paradigm.

   The Ongoing Evolution of Serverless - Serverless computing has come a long way since its inception. From its humble beginnings as a novel way to abstract infrastructure management, it has evolved into a powerful and flexible computing paradigm. Several trends and developments have shaped its ongoing evolution:

- **Increased Adoption and Maturity -** Serverless has seen widespread adoption across various industries and use cases. As more organizations recognize the advantages of lowered operational overhead, rapid scalability, & cost efficiency, serverless systems have matured to meet the demands of a diverse range of workloads.
- **Ecosystem Growth -** The serverless ecosystem has grown significantly. Platforms and providers now offer a wealth of services and tools, allowing developers to create sophisticated applications without the need to reinvent the wheel. This ecosystem's growth has democratized cloud computing, making it accessible to a larger audience.
- **Hybrid and Multi-Cloud Serverless -** The evolution of serverless has led to the emergence of hybrid & multi-cloud solutions. Organizations are now leveraging serverless on a variety of cloud providers, promoting interoperability and reducing vendor lock-in. This trend promises to increase resilience and flexibility.
- **Edge Computing Integration -** Serverless has extended its reach to the edge, enabling applications to run closer to end-users. This integration brings low-latency and real-time processing capabilities to a multitude of use cases, from IoT to content delivery.

- **Containerization and Serverless Unification** - Serverless has started to blend with containerization technologies, allowing for the execution of stateful workloads alongside traditional stateless functions. This unification offers more comprehensive solutions for various application requirements.

Recommendations for Practitioners - For practitioners looking to harness the power of serverless computing, a set of recommendations can help navigate this dynamic landscape effectively:

- **Start Small and Experiment** - Begin with small, non-critical workloads to gain a practical understanding of serverless. Experiment with different cloud providers and services to identify what aligns best with your application's requirements.
- **Optimize for Cost** - While serverless can be cost-effective, it's essential to understand pricing models, monitor usage, and leverage resource allocation to optimize costs. Utilize auto-scaling and resource provisioning wisely.
- **Security and Compliance** - Ensure a robust security posture by leveraging cloud provider security features and best practices. Understand your responsibility in the shared responsibility model. Implement encryption, access controls, and regular audits to maintain compliance.
- **Performance Tuning** - Monitor the performance of your serverless functions and applications. Identify and resolve bottlenecks, and consider using performance optimization tools and practices provided by the cloud provider.
- **Vendor Lock-In Mitigation** - To mitigate vendor lock-in concerns, architect your applications with portability in mind. Utilize open standards and containerization to make migration between cloud providers more manageable.

Potential Impact on the Future of Cloud Computing - The evolution of serverless computing carries profound implications for the future of cloud computing. Here are some of the potential impacts:

- **Reduced Infrastructure Management** - As serverless matures, the burden of infrastructure management continues to decrease. This paves the way for greater innovation as developers aim more on code & less on provisioning and maintenance.
- **Faster Development and Deployment** - The serverless model's simplicity and agility allow for faster development and deployment of applications. This can lead to more rapid innovation and a competitive edge in the marketplace.
- **Cost Efficiency and Scalability** - Serverless remains a cost-efficient way to scale applications. With granular cost control and auto-scaling, organizations can more effectively manage their cloud expenses.
- **Edge Computing Expansion** - The integration of serverless with edge computing will lead to a proliferation of real-time, low-latency applications, transforming industries such as IoT, autonomous vehicles, and augmented reality.
- **Hybrid and Multi-Cloud Standardization** - Serverless may drive standardization efforts, promoting interoperability and simplifying the integration of services across different cloud providers.

REFERENCES

Bebortta, S., Das, S. K., Kandpal, M., Barik, R. K., & Dubey, H. (2020). Geospatial Serverless Computing: Architectures, tools and future directions. *ISPRS International Journal of Geo-Information*, *9*(5), 311. doi:10.3390/ijgi9050311

Castro, P., Ishakian, V., Muthusamy, V., & Slominski, A. (2019). *The server is dead, long live the server: Rise of Serverless Computing, Overview of Current State and Future Trends in Research and Industry.* arXiv (Cornell University). https://arxiv.org/pdf/1906.02888

Eismann, S., Scheuner, J., Van Eyk, E., Schwinger, M., Grohmann, J., Herbst, N., Abad, C. L., & Iosup, A. (2020a). *A Review of Serverless Use Cases and their Characteristics.* arXiv (Cornell University). https://arxiv.org/pdf/2008.11110

Eismann, S., Scheuner, J., Van Eyk, E., Schwinger, M., Grohmann, J., Herbst, N., Abad, C. L., & Iosup, A. (2020b). *A Review of Serverless Use Cases and their Characteristics.* arXiv (Cornell University). https://arxiv.org/pdf/2008.11110

Gadepalli, P. K., Peach, G., Cherkasova, L., Aitken, R., & Parmer, G. (2020). *Challenges and opportunities for efficient serverless computing at the edge.* IEEE. doi:10.1109/SRDS47363.2019.00036

Grogan, J., Mulready, C., McDermott, J., Urbanavicius, M., Yılmaz, M., Abgaz, Y. M., McCarren, A., MacMahon, S. T., Garousi, V., Eklund, P., & Clarke, P. M. (2020a). A multivocal literature review of Function-as-a-Service (FAAS) infrastructures and implications for software developers. In Communications in computer and information science (pp. 58–75). Springer. doi:10.1007/978-3-030-56441-4_5

Grogan, J., Mulready, C., McDermott, J., Urbanavicius, M., Yılmaz, M., Abgaz, Y. M., McCarren, A., MacMahon, S. T., Garousi, V., Eklund, P., & Clarke, P. M. (2020b). A multivocal literature review of Function-as-a-Service (FAAS) infrastructures and implications for software developers. In Communications in computer and information science (pp. 58–75). Springer. doi:10.1007/978-3-030-56441-4_5

Hassan, H. B., Barakat, S., & Sarhan, Q. I. (2021). Survey on serverless computing. *Journal of Cloud Computing (Heidelberg, Germany)*, *10*(1), 39. doi:10.1186/s13677-021-00253-7

Jambunathan, B., & Yoganathan, K. (2018). Architecture Decision on using Microservices or Serverless Functions with Containers. *2018 International Conference on Current Trends Towards Converging Technologies (ICCTCT).* IEEE. 10.1109/ICCTCT.2018.8551035

Jamshidi, P., Pahl, C., Mendonça, N. C., Lewis, J. W., & Tilkov, S. (2018). Microservices: The journey so far and challenges ahead. *IEEE Software*, *35*(3), 24–35. doi:10.1109/MS.2018.2141039

Krishnamurthi, R., Kumar, A., Gill, S. S., & Buyya, R. (2023). Serverless Computing: New trends and research directions. In Lecture notes on data engineering and communications technologies (pp. 1–13). Springer. doi:10.1007/978-3-031-26633-1_1

Lam, M. S., & Schmidt, B. K. (2000). *Supporting ubiquitous computing with stateless consoles and computation caches.* ACM. https://dl.acm.org/citation.cfm?id=932462

Lee, H., Satyam, K., & Fox, G. (2018). Evaluation of Production Serverless Computing Environments. *IEEE*, 442–450. doi:10.1109/CLOUD.2018.00062

Li, Y., Lin, Y., Wang, Y., Ye, K., & Xu, C. (2023). Serverless Computing: State-of-the-Art, Challenges and Opportunities. *IEEE Transactions on Services Computing*, *16*(2), 1522–1539. doi:10.1109/TSC.2022.3166553

Li, Z., Guo, L., Cheng, J., Chen, Q., He, B., & Guo, M. (2022). The Serverless Computing Survey: A Technical Primer for Design Architecture. *ACM Computing Surveys*, *54*(10s), 1–34. doi:10.1145/3508360

Lin, C., & Khazaei, H. (2021a). Modeling and optimization of performance and cost of serverless applications. *IEEE Transactions on Parallel and Distributed Systems*, *32*(3), 615–632. doi:10.1109/TPDS.2020.3028841

Lin, C., & Khazaei, H. (2021b). Modeling and optimization of performance and cost of serverless applications. *IEEE Transactions on Parallel and Distributed Systems*, *32*(3), 615–632. doi:10.1109/TPDS.2020.3028841

Lloyd, W., Ramesh, S., Chinthalapati, S., Ly, L. H., & Pallickara, S. (2018). *Serverless Computing: An Investigation of Factors Influencing Microservice Performance*. IEEE. doi:10.1109/IC2E.2018.00039

Mampage, A., Karunasekera, S., & Buyya, R. (2022). A Holistic View on Resource Management in Serverless Computing Environments: Taxonomy and Future Directions. *ACM Computing Surveys*, *54*(11s), 1–36. doi:10.1145/3510412

Nastić, S., Rausch, T., Šćekić, O., Dustdar, S., Gušev, M., Koteska, B., Kostoska, M., Jakimovski, B., Ristov, S., & Prodan, R. (2017). A serverless Real-Time data analytics platform for edge computing. *IEEE Internet Computing*, *21*(4), 64–71. doi:10.1109/MIC.2017.2911430

Pérez, A. G., Moltó, G., Caballer, M., & Calatrava, A. (2018). Serverless computing for container-based architectures. *Future Generation Computer Systems*, *83*, 50–59. doi:10.1016/j.future.2018.01.022

Schleier-Smith, J., Sreekanti, V., Khandelwal, A., Carreira, J., Yadwadkar, N. J., Popa, R. A., Gonzalez, J. E., Stoica, I., & Patterson, D. A. (2021). What serverless computing is and should become. *Communications of the ACM*, *64*(5), 76–84. doi:10.1145/3406011

Shafiei, H., Khonsari, A., & Mousavi, P. (2022). Serverless Computing: A survey of opportunities, challenges, and applications. *ACM Computing Surveys*, *54*(11s), 1–32. doi:10.1145/3510611

Taibi, D., Spillner, J., & Wawruch, K. (2021). Serverless Computing-Where are we now, and where are we heading? *IEEE Software*, *38*(1), 25–31. doi:10.1109/MS.2020.3028708

Yussupov, V., Soldani, J., Breitenbücher, U., Brogi, A., & Leymann, F. (2021). FaaSten your decisions: A classification framework and technology review of function-as-a-Service platforms. *Journal of Systems and Software*, *175*, 110906. doi:10.1016/j.jss.2021.110906

Chapter 5
Unraveling the Fabric of Serverless Computing:
Technologies, Trends, and Integration Strategies

S. Boopathi

Muthayammal Engineering College, India

ABSTRACT

This chapter provides a comprehensive overview of the evolving landscape of serverless computing, focusing on the technologies and tools that shape its ecosystem. Starting with an introduction to serverless architecture, the chapter delves into the benefits and challenges of adopting serverless computing. It explores key technologies such as function-as-a-service (FaaS), backend-as-a-service (BaaS), and event-driven architecture, highlighting their roles in enabling scalable and cost-effective solutions. Additionally, the chapter discusses popular tools and platforms used for developing, deploying, and managing serverless applications. Through this exploration, readers gain insights into the latest trends, best practices, and considerations for leveraging serverless computing effectively in modern IT environments.

1. INTRODUCTION TO SERVERLESS COMPUTING

Serverless architecture has revolutionized the development, deployment, and management of applications in modern computing. It is often referred to as the next evolution of cloud computing and is characterized by its use of Function-as-a-Service (FaaS) and Backend-as-a-Service (BaaS) technologies. These technologies allow code execution and backend operations to be orchestrated in response to events, enabling scalability and agility. This shift from server-centric to event-driven computing enables organizations to innovate at a faster pace, thereby transforming the landscape of modern computing (Wen et al., 2023).

Serverless computing offers various technologies and tools to streamline development workflows and improve operational efficiency. These include cloud providers like AWS Lambda, Azure Functions, Google Cloud Functions, open-source frameworks like Serverless Framework, and Kubernetes-based

DOI: 10.4018/979-8-3693-1682-5.ch005

solutions like Knative. These tools not only simplify the development process but also optimize resource utilization, driving cost efficiencies and enhancing scalability. Event-driven architecture is a key trend in serverless computing, enabling organizations to build resilient systems that adapt to dynamic workloads and demand patterns. This architecture allows real-time data processing, seamless integration with external services, and the creation of event-driven microservices, embodying modularity and composability principles (Shafiei et al., 2022).

The integration of serverless computing with modern IT infrastructure, particularly microservices architecture, offers new opportunities for innovation. Microservices, with their granular and deployable nature, enable the decomposition of monolithic applications into modular components, allowing organizations to leverage scalability and cost benefits while maintaining architectural flexibility. However, organizations must navigate challenges such as managing cold start latency, optimizing resource utilization, and ensuring security and compliance in distributed environments. The nascent nature of serverless technology necessitates a mindset shift and cultural transformation, emphasizing agility, experimentation, and continuous learning (Li et al., 2022).

Serverless computing is a transformative approach that redefines modern computing by combining technologies, trends, and integration strategies. It offers innovation, agility, and cost efficiency for organizations. However, success requires a holistic approach, combining technical expertise with strategic foresight and organizational readiness. As we continue to explore this technology, let's embrace it with curiosity, resilience, and a commitment to the future (Cassel et al., 2022). The evolution of serverless computing, influenced by technological advancements, evolving business needs, and cloud computing paradigms, offers valuable insights into its current state and future direction, highlighting its significant evolution and adoption trends.

- Serverless computing originated from the early 2000s concepts of Platform-as-a-Service (PaaS) and Function-as-a-Service (FaaS), with the foundations laid by Amazon Web Services' 2014 introduction of AWS Lambda, which pioneered the serverless architecture model.
- Following the launch of AWS Lambda, cloud providers like Microsoft Azure and Google Cloud Platform (GCP) quickly launched their own serverless offerings, expanding the accessibility of serverless computing to various use cases and industries.
- The serverless ecosystem has grown significantly over time, with the development of robust frameworks, tools, and best practices. Open-source projects like Serverless Framework, Apache OpenWhisk, and Knative have contributed to the growth and standardization of serverless technologies.
- Hybrid and multi-cloud approaches are gaining popularity as organizations aim to utilize serverless computing while maintaining IT infrastructure flexibility. Solutions like AWS Outposts, Azure Arc, and Google Anthos enable seamless deployment of serverless workloads across on-premises and cloud environments.
- Serverless computing is widely used in various industries like e-commerce, finance, healthcare, and media due to its scalability, cost efficiency, and agility in responding to fluctuating demand, making it a popular choice for web and mobile applications, IoT devices, real-time data processing, and AI/ML inference.
- The adoption of serverless environments has been driven by the focus on enhancing the developer experience and productivity. These platforms offer features like auto-scaling, pay-per-use pricing, seamless integration with third-party services, and built-in monitoring tools, allowing developers

to focus on application development without infrastructure management. Serverless computing is expected to continue advancing in areas like serverless containers, edge computing, and orchestration, driving digital transformation and innovation across various industries.

The rise of serverless computing has revolutionized application development, deployment, and operation in the cloud-native era, offering organizations new opportunities for agility, scalability, and cost efficiency, thereby gaining a competitive edge in the digital economy.

2. FUNCTION-AS-A-SERVICE (FaaS)

Function-as-a-Service (FaaS) is a cloud computing model that enables developers to execute code without managing server infrastructure, allowing them to focus on specific tasks or operations by abstracting away underlying servers (Figure 1). Function-as-a-Service (FaaS) is a serverless computing model that allows developers to build scalable, event-driven applications with minimal operational overhead, allowing them to focus on innovation and rapid development, accelerating software delivery and responding to changing business requirements. This section explores the diverse use cases and applications of Function-as-a-Service (FaaS), a cloud computing model that simplifies application development by removing server management and infrastructure concerns, and compares it with traditional architectures (Scheuner & Leitner, 2020).

2.1 Important Components of FaaS

- Functions: The FaaS model consists of functions as the fundamental units of deployment and execution, which are short-lived code pieces that perform specific tasks or respond to specific events, such as processing HTTP requests, handling database queries, or performing data transformations (Shahrad et al., 2019).
- Event Triggers: In a FaaS environment, events trigger functions, originating from sources like HTTP requests, database changes, file uploads, messaging queues, timers, and external APIs. When an event occurs, the associated function is automatically invoked to execute the specified logic.
- Scalability: FaaS offers scalability through its functions, which automatically adjust to changes in workload demand. As the number of incoming events increases, the platform provisiones more instances to handle the load, while idle instances are scaled down to conserve resources, ensuring efficient resource utilization and cost optimization.
- Pay-Per-Use Pricing Model: FaaS platforms use a pay-per-use pricing model, charging users based on the resources consumed by their functions. This model offers cost advantages over traditional server-based architectures, which require provisioning and maintenance of resources regardless of usage, as functions are executed in response to events.
- Stateless Execution Environment: FaaS functions are stateless, meaning they don't maintain any persistent state or context between invocations. This simplifies function management, ensures predictable behavior, facilitates horizontal scalability, and allows fault tolerance. Each function invocation is independent and isolated.

- Vendor-Managed Infrastructure: Cloud providers manage FaaS platforms, eliminating operational overheads like server provisioning, configuration, and maintenance. They handle infrastructure, load balancing, security, and performance optimization, allowing developers to focus on code writing and user value delivery.

Figure 1. Function-As-A-Service (FaaS)

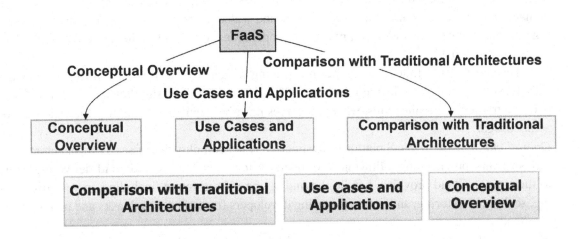

2.2 Applications

- *Web and Mobile Backend:* FaaS is well-suited for building the backend of web and mobile applications, where functions can be invoked in response to HTTP requests, authentication events, or database queries. For example, a function can handle user authentication, process form submissions, or retrieve data from a database, providing a scalable and cost-effective solution for backend services (Albuquerque Jr et al., 2017).
- *Real-time Data Processing:* FaaS enables real-time data processing and analysis by processing streaming data from sources such as IoT devices, sensors, or social media feeds. Functions can be triggered by events such as new data arrivals, sensor readings, or system alerts, allowing organizations to derive insights and take immediate actions based on the incoming data.
- Scheduled Tasks and Cron Jobs: FaaS platforms support scheduled execution of functions, allowing developers to automate routine tasks and cron jobs without the need for dedicated servers or background processes. Functions can be triggered at predefined intervals or specific times, performing tasks such as data backups, report generation, or system maintenance operations.
- *Event-driven Automation:* FaaS facilitates event-driven automation workflows, where functions are triggered by events from external systems, APIs, or messaging queues. For example, a function can be invoked to process incoming emails, update customer records in a CRM system, or initiate downstream workflows based on specific conditions or criteria.

- *Image and Video Processing*: FaaS platforms offer built-in support for processing media files, such as images and videos, through integrations with services like AWS Lambda@Edge or Azure Functions with Blob Storage triggers. Functions can perform tasks such as resizing images, transcoding videos, or extracting metadata, enabling scalable and efficient media processing workflows.

2.3 Comparison With Traditional Architectures

- *Scalability and Elasticity:* Unlike traditional architectures where resources must be provisioned in advance to accommodate peak loads, FaaS provides automatic scaling and elasticity based on demand. Functions are dynamically provisioned and scaled in response to incoming events, ensuring optimal resource utilization and minimizing operational overhead (Scheuner & Leitner, 2020; Shahrad et al., 2019).
- *Cost Efficiency:* FaaS follows a pay-per-use pricing model, where users are billed only for the actual resources consumed by their functions. This cost model offers significant cost savings compared to traditional architectures, where resources must be provisioned and paid for regardless of actual usage.
- *Operational Simplicity:* FaaS platforms abstract away the complexities of server management and infrastructure provisioning, allowing developers to focus on writing code and delivering value to their users. Cloud providers handle the underlying infrastructure, including server provisioning, scaling, monitoring, and security, freeing developers from operational tasks and maintenance overhead.
- *Agility and Time-to-Market:* FaaS enables rapid development and deployment of applications by providing a serverless environment where developers can iterate quickly and experiment with new ideas. Functions can be deployed independently, allowing for granular updates and continuous delivery of new features without impacting other parts of the application.
- *Event-driven Architecture:* FaaS encourages the adoption of event-driven architecture, where functions are triggered by events from various sources. This event-driven approach facilitates loose coupling, scalability, and resilience, enabling organizations to build robust and responsive systems that can adapt to changing business requirements and workload patterns.

Function-as-a-Service (FaaS) is a flexible platform for creating scalable, event-driven applications. It eliminates infrastructure management, offers automatic scaling, cost-effective pricing, and operational simplicity, allowing developers to focus on innovation and accelerate value delivery to organizations and end-users.

3. BACKEND-AS-A-SERVICE (BaaS)

Backend-as-a-Service (BaaS) is a cloud computing model that offers pre-built backend infrastructure and services for web and mobile application development. It simplifies the management of backend components, allowing developers to focus on frontend functionality and user experiences, unlike traditional approaches. BaaS streamlines development by providing backend services for modern applications, including user authentication, data storage, push notifications, and server-side logic execution (Edlund, 2022). Developers can accelerate development cycles, reduce time-to-market, and offload infrastructure management tasks to cloud providers. The figure 2 depicts the lifecycle of a backend application that utilizes Backend-as-a-Service (BaaS).

Figure 2. Lifecycle of a backend application utilizing backend-as-a-service (BaaS)

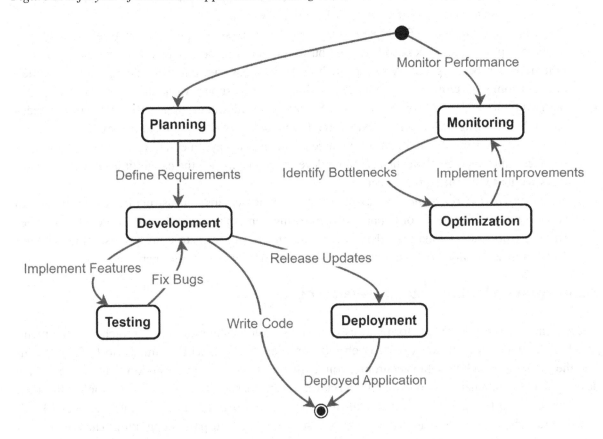

3.1 Components of BaaS

Backend-as-a-Service (BaaS) simplifies web and mobile application development by providing a range of backend services and infrastructure components. This allows developers to focus on creating engaging frontend experiences, delivering value to users, accelerating time-to-market, and reducing operational overhead (Uunonen, 2023).

- *User Management:* BaaS platforms typically provide authentication and user management services, allowing developers to implement user registration, login, and access control functionalities without building them from scratch. These services support various authentication methods, including email/password, social logins (e.g., OAuth), and multi-factor authentication (MFA), ensuring secure access to applications.
- *Database Services:* BaaS platforms offer scalable and flexible database solutions for storing and managing application data. Common database services include NoSQL databases (e.g., MongoDB,

Firebase Firestore) and relational databases (e.g., MySQL, PostgreSQL), which support features such as data querying, indexing, and real-time synchronization across devices.

- *File Storage and Hosting:* BaaS platforms often include file storage and hosting services for managing static assets, such as images, videos, and documents. These services enable developers to upload, store, and serve files to users through content delivery networks (CDNs), ensuring fast and reliable access to media assets from anywhere in the world.

- *Backend Logic Execution:* BaaS platforms support serverless computing models, allowing developers to deploy custom backend logic and business logic without managing server infrastructure. Functions can be triggered by events such as HTTP requests, database changes, or scheduled tasks, enabling developers to execute server-side code in response to specific events or triggers.

- *Integration with Third-Party Services:* BaaS platforms offer integrations with third-party services and APIs, allowing developers to extend the functionality of their applications by leveraging external services. Common integrations include payment gateways, messaging services, geolocation services, and analytics platforms, enabling developers to enhance the capabilities of their applications without reinventing the wheel.

- *Scalability and Performance:* BaaS platforms provide scalable infrastructure and resources to support the growing needs of applications, ensuring consistent performance and reliability under varying workloads. Cloud providers handle the underlying infrastructure provisioning, scaling, and maintenance, allowing applications to scale seamlessly as demand increases.

3.2 Integration With Frontend Development

Backend-as-a-Service (BaaS) platforms are essential for seamless integration with frontend development, enabling developers to create feature-rich web and mobile applications with minimal effort. They streamline the process, including data synchronization, authentication, API consumption, and user interface development (Paakkunainen & others, 2019). Backend-as-a-Service (BaaS) platforms simplify frontend development by offering RESTful APIs, real-time data synchronization, authentication services, cloud-based storage, hosting, cross-platform development support, and third-party integration. These platforms remove backend development complexities, allowing frontend developers to focus on user experience, delivering value, accelerating time-to-market, and reducing development overhead (Koschel et al., 2021).

- *RESTful APIs and SDKs:* BaaS platforms expose RESTful APIs that frontend developers can use to interact with backend services programmatically. Additionally, many BaaS providers offer software development kits (SDKs) for popular programming languages and frameworks, simplifying API consumption and integration into frontend applications. These SDKs abstract away the complexities of making HTTP requests and handling authentication, allowing developers to focus on building frontend features.

- *Real-time Data Synchronization:* BaaS platforms enable real-time data synchronization, facilitating seamless communication between frontend and backend components. This ensures users have access to the latest information without manual intervention, making it useful for collaborative applications, chat applications, and data-intensive dashboards.

- *Authentication and Authorization:* BaaS platforms offer robust authentication and authorization mechanisms for frontend developers to secure their applications. These services include user registration, login, password management, and controlling access to resources based on user roles and permissions. Integrating with BaaS authentication services allows for secure user authentication and access control without reinventing the wheel.

- *Cloud-based Storage and Hosting:* BaaS platforms provide cloud-based storage and hosting services for static assets and frontend applications. Developers can upload HTML, CSS, JavaScript, and other files to these storage solutions, which are served via content delivery networks for improved performance and scalability. BaaS hosting services offer features like custom domains, SSL/TLS encryption, and automated deployment pipelines.

- *Cross-platform Development Support:* BaaS platforms enable frontend developers to build applications for multiple platforms simultaneously, ensuring consistency and interoperability across web browsers, mobile devices, and desktop environments. This accelerates development cycles and reduces the overhead of maintaining separate backend infrastructures for each platform.

- *Integration with Third-Party Services:* BaaS platforms enable frontend developers to integrate with third-party services and APIs, simplifying the development process and enhancing the capabilities of their applications. This integration can be used for payment gateways, social media APIs, mapping services, or analytics platforms, without requiring deep backend expertise.

4. LEVERAGING EVENT-DRIVEN ARCHITECTURE

Event-Driven Architecture (EDA) is a paradigm that focuses on the production, detection, consumption, and reaction of system events. It's popular in modern software development for its ability to decouple components, improve scalability, enhance responsiveness, and facilitate seamless integration between heterogeneous systems. Common design patterns are explored for effective EDA implementation. The figure 3 illustrates the utilization of event-driven architecture (Arjona et al., 2021).

4.1 Fundamentals of Event-Driven Architecture

- Events are occurrences or notifications that represent changes or significant actions within a system. These events can range from user interactions, system alerts, sensor readings, database updates, to external API calls. Events carry relevant data or metadata that provide context and facilitate communication between different components of the system.

- An event producer is responsible for generating and emitting events to the system. This could be any component, subsystem, or external system capable of detecting and producing events based on predefined triggers or conditions. Examples of event producers include user interfaces, IoT devices, database systems, and external APIs.

- The event broker serves as a central intermediary responsible for receiving, routing, and dispatching events to appropriate event consumers. It acts as a messaging middleware that decouples event producers from event consumers, ensuring loose coupling and enabling scalable and resilient communication between components.

- An event consumer is a component or service that subscribes to specific types of events and reacts to them accordingly. Event consumers process incoming events, execute business logic, update state, trigger actions, or produce new events in response. Examples of event consumers include microservices, functions in serverless architectures, and workflow orchestrators.

Event-Driven Architecture (EDA) is a paradigm for building scalable, resilient, and responsive systems by leveraging events as communication and coordination. By incorporating concepts like publish-subscribe, event sourcing, CQRS, event-driven microservices, and sagas, organizations can harness EDA's full potential to create robust, adaptable systems that scale gracefully (Pogiatzis & Samakovitis, 2020).

Figure 3. Leveraging event-driven architecture

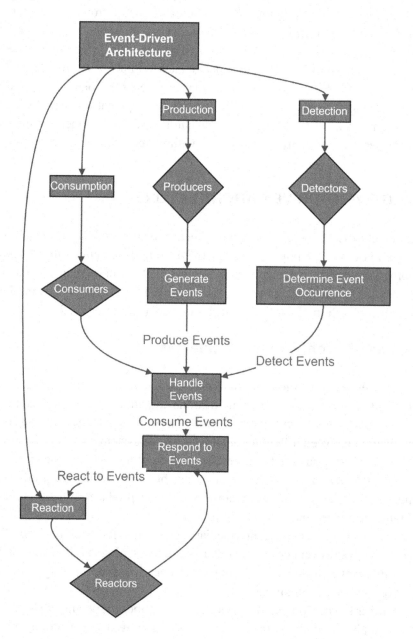

4.2 Common Design Patterns for Leveraging Event-Driven Architecture

- In this pattern, event producers publish events to one or more topics or channels, and event consumers subscribe to specific topics of interest. The event broker mediates the communication between producers and consumers, ensuring that events are delivered to all interested subscribers. This pattern enables scalability, flexibility, and asynchronous communication between components.

- Event sourcing involves capturing and storing every change or state transition in the system as a series of immutable events. These events serve as the primary source of truth for the system's state, enabling auditability, traceability, and replayability of actions. Event sourcing is commonly used in scenarios where data consistency, versioning, and auditability are critical requirements.

- Command Query Responsibility Segregation (CQRS) separates the responsibility of handling commands (write operations) from queries (read operations) by maintaining separate models for each. Commands produce events that update the write model, while queries read data from the read model optimized for querying. This pattern enhances scalability, performance, and flexibility by decoupling the read and write sides of the system.

- Event-driven microservices leverage EDA to build loosely coupled, independently deployable services that communicate via events. Each microservice encapsulates specific business logic and reacts to events emitted by other services. This pattern promotes autonomy, resilience, and scalability, allowing organizations to evolve and scale their systems more effectively.

- The saga pattern is used to manage long-lived, distributed transactions across multiple services in a consistent and resilient manner. Sagas are sequences of local transactions orchestrated by a saga coordinator, where each transaction emits compensating events to undo its effects in case of failure. This pattern ensures eventual consistency and fault tolerance in distributed systems.

4.3 Real-World Implementations

Event-Driven Architecture (EDA) is a design approach that focuses on building scalable, responsive, and loosely coupled systems using principles and design patterns (Witte et al., 2020). Event-Driven Architecture (EDA) is a framework that utilizes various technologies and frameworks, such as microservices, serverless computing, workflow orchestration, event streaming platforms, integration platforms, messaging systems, and data processing frameworks, to build scalable, resilient, and responsive systems that adapt to business requirements (Bila et al., 2017).

- Microservices Architecture: Microservices are small, independent services that communicate asynchronously via events. Each microservice encapsulates specific business functionality and reacts to events emitted by other services. For example, in an e-commerce application, a product service might emit an event when a new product is added, triggering updates in the inventory service, pricing service, and notification service.

- Serverless Computing: Serverless platforms, such as AWS Lambda, Azure Functions, and Google Cloud Functions, enable event-driven architectures by allowing developers to deploy functions that execute in response to events. Events can include HTTP requests, database changes, file uploads, or scheduled triggers. Serverless functions are stateless and scale automatically, making them well-suited for event-driven workflows and event processing tasks.

- Event-Driven Workflow Orchestration: Workflow orchestration tools, such as Apache Airflow, Apache NiFi, and AWS Step Functions, enable the automation and coordination of complex workflows using events. These tools allow developers to define workflows as directed acyclic graphs (DAGs) where each node represents a task or operation, and edges represent dependencies between tasks. Events trigger the execution of tasks and drive the flow of the workflow.

- Event Streaming Platforms: Event streaming platforms, such as Apache Kafka, Amazon Kinesis, and Azure Event Hubs, provide scalable, distributed infrastructure for ingesting, processing, and analyzing streams of events in real-time. These platforms enable event-driven architectures by allowing developers to publish, subscribe to, and process events at scale. Event streaming platforms support features such as message persistence, fault tolerance, and stream processing with frameworks like Apache Flink and Apache Samza.

- Event-Driven Integration: Event-driven integration involves connecting disparate systems and applications using events as the primary means of communication. Integration platforms, such as Apache Camel, MuleSoft Anypoint Platform, and Azure Logic Apps, provide connectors and adapters for integrating with various systems, protocols, and APIs. Events trigger integration flows, allowing data to flow seamlessly between systems in a loosely coupled manner.

- Event-Driven Messaging: Event-driven messaging systems, such as RabbitMQ, ActiveMQ, and Google Cloud Pub/Sub, facilitate communication between components of distributed systems using asynchronous messaging patterns. These systems enable reliable, asynchronous communication between producers and consumers by decoupling the timing and availability of producers and consumers. Events are published to topics or queues and consumed by interested subscribers.

- Event-Driven Data Processing: Event-driven data processing frameworks, such as Apache Spark, Apache Flink, and AWS Kinesis Data Analytics, enable real-time analysis and processing of streaming data. These frameworks support complex event processing (CEP), windowing, aggregation, and machine learning algorithms for analyzing and deriving insights from event streams. Event-driven data processing frameworks are commonly used in domains such as IoT, finance, advertising, and cybersecurity for real-time analytics and decision-making.

5. CLOUD COMPUTING AND SERVERLESS PARADIGM

Cloud computing has embraced the serverless paradigm, revolutionizing application development and deployment. This approach eliminates infrastructure management, allowing on-demand code execution. This convergence of cloud computing and serverless architecture offers scalability, cost efficiency, and agility. It's transforming modern IT infrastructures, allowing organizations to innovate and accelerate their digital initiatives (R. A. P. Rajan, 2018). The figure 4 depicts the integration of cloud computing and serverless paradigms.

5.1 Infrastructure as Code (IaC)

Infrastructure as Code (IaC) is a method that simplifies the management and provisioning of computing infrastructure using machine-readable definition files, promoting automation, consistency, and reproducibility, allowing developers and operations teams to treat it as software code (Lynn et al., 2017).

Figure 4. Cloud computing and serverless paradigm

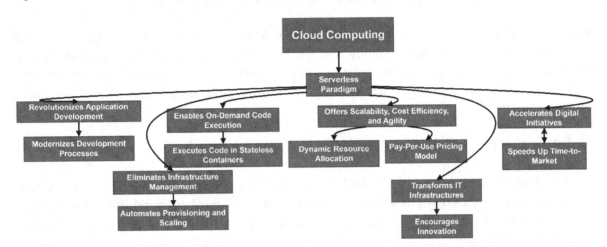

5.2 Cloud Provider Offerings (AWS Lambda, Azure Functions, Google Cloud Functions)

Major cloud providers like AWS Lambda, Azure Functions, and Google Cloud Functions offer serverless computing platforms, enabling developers to deploy and run code without server provisioning or management, but with varying features, pricing, and integrations (A. P. Rajan, 2020).

AWS Lambda: AWS Lambda is a serverless compute service provided by Amazon Web Services (AWS). It supports a wide range of programming languages, including Node.js, Python, Java, and .NET. Lambda functions can be triggered by various events, such as HTTP requests, changes in AWS services (e.g., S3, DynamoDB), or custom events. AWS Lambda offers features such as automatic scaling, pay-per-use pricing, and integration with other AWS services through event sources and triggers.

Azure Functions: Azure Functions is a serverless compute service offered by Microsoft Azure. It supports multiple programming languages, including C#, JavaScript, Python, and PowerShell. Azure Functions can be triggered by events from Azure services, HTTP requests, or custom events using Azure Event Grid. Azure Functions provides features such as automatic scaling, pay-per-use pricing, and tight integration with other Azure services, including Azure Storage, Azure Cosmos DB, and Azure Event Hubs.

Google Cloud Functions: Google Cloud Functions is a serverless compute service provided by Google Cloud Platform (GCP). It supports languages such as Node.js, Python, Go, and Java. Google Cloud Functions can be triggered by events from Google Cloud services (e.g., Cloud Storage, Cloud Pub/Sub), HTTP requests, or custom events using Cloud Events. Google Cloud Functions offers features such as automatic scaling, pay-per-use pricing, and seamless integration with other GCP services, including Google Cloud Storage, Google Cloud Pub/Sub, and Google Cloud Firestore.

Major cloud providers like AWS Lambda, Azure Functions, and Google Cloud Functions offer serverless computing platforms that enable developers to build and deploy applications without managing servers, offering scalability, cost efficiency, and seamless integration with other cloud services. Each platform has its strengths and capabilities.

5.3 Multi-Cloud and Hybrid Approaches in Cloud Computing

Multi-cloud and hybrid approaches are strategic architectures used by organizations to optimize cloud computing, reduce risks, enhance flexibility, and optimize resource utilization. These methods involve distributing workloads across multiple cloud providers or integrating on-premises infrastructure with cloud services. This article explores their advantages, challenges, and best practices (A. P. Rajan, 2020; Van Eyk et al., 2018).

5.3.1 Advantages of Multi-Cloud and Hybrid Approaches

- *Risk Mitigation:* Multi-cloud and hybrid architectures reduce the risk of vendor lock-in by diversifying reliance on a single cloud provider. Organizations can distribute workloads across multiple cloud platforms, ensuring resilience against service outages, data breaches, or pricing changes from any single provider.
- *Flexibility and Choice:* Multi-cloud and hybrid approaches offer organizations greater flexibility and choice in selecting cloud services and platforms that best meet their requirements. This flexibility allows organizations to leverage the unique strengths and capabilities of different cloud providers while avoiding vendor-specific limitations.
- *Scalability and Performance:* By leveraging multiple cloud providers or combining on-premises infrastructure with cloud services, organizations can achieve greater scalability and performance for their workloads. Multi-cloud and hybrid architectures enable distributed computing, allowing organizations to scale resources dynamically to meet changing demand and optimize performance.
- *Compliance and Data Sovereignty:* Multi-cloud and hybrid architectures enable organizations to address regulatory compliance requirements and data sovereignty concerns by strategically distributing data and workloads across geographically dispersed cloud regions or on-premises data centers. This approach ensures compliance with data protection regulations and enhances data privacy and security.

5.3.2 Challenges of Multi-Cloud and Hybrid Approaches

Complexity and Management Overhead: Multi-cloud and hybrid architectures introduce complexity and management overhead, as organizations must manage multiple cloud environments, APIs, security controls, and networking configurations (Lynn et al., 2017; Paakkunainen & others, 2019). This complexity can increase operational costs and require specialized skills and expertise to effectively manage the diverse infrastructure landscape.

Interoperability and Integration: Achieving seamless interoperability and integration between multiple cloud providers and on-premises systems can be challenging due to differences in APIs, data formats, security models, and networking protocols. Organizations must invest in robust integration solutions and standards-compliant architectures to ensure smooth data exchange and workflow orchestration across heterogeneous environments.

5.3.3 Best Practices for Multi-Cloud and Hybrid Architectures

Multi-cloud and hybrid approaches provide organizations with flexibility, resilience, and scalability in utilizing cloud computing resources. By adopting best practices like clear objectives, consistent governance, security, standards-based interoperability, automation, and performance monitoring, organizations can navigate these complexities and maximize the full potential of cloud computing across diverse environments (Lynn et al., 2017; A. P. Rajan, 2020).

- *Define Clear Objectives and Requirements:* Before adopting a multi-cloud or hybrid approach, organizations should define clear objectives, requirements, and use cases to guide their architecture decisions. This includes evaluating factors such as workload portability, data sovereignty, compliance, and performance requirements.
- *Implement Consistent Governance and Security:* Establish consistent governance and security policies across all cloud environments and on-premises infrastructure to ensure compliance, mitigate risks, and maintain data integrity and confidentiality. This includes implementing identity and access management (IAM), encryption, network segmentation, and auditing controls.
- *Embrace Standards-Based Interoperability:* Adopt standards-based protocols, APIs, and data formats to facilitate interoperability and integration between different cloud providers and on-premises systems. This includes leveraging industry standards such as Kubernetes for container orchestration, OpenStack for private cloud deployments, and cloud-native development frameworks like CNCF's CloudEvents for event-driven architectures.
- *Invest in Automation and Orchestration:* Leverage automation and orchestration tools to streamline provisioning, deployment, scaling, and management of resources across multi-cloud and hybrid environments. This includes using Infrastructure as Code (IaC) tools like Terraform, Ansible, or AWS CloudFormation to automate infrastructure provisioning and configuration management.
- *Monitor, Analyze, and Optimize:* Implement comprehensive monitoring, analytics, and optimization tools to gain visibility into performance, cost, and resource utilization across multi-cloud and hybrid environments. This includes leveraging cloud-native monitoring services, log management solutions, and cost optimization tools to identify inefficiencies, optimize workloads, and reduce operational costs.

6. ACHIEVING SCALABILITY IN SERVERLESS ENVIRONMENTS

Scalability is crucial in serverless environments for efficient handling of diverse workloads, ensuring optimal performance and cost-effectiveness. This is achieved through auto-scaling mechanisms, load balancing strategies, and performance optimization techniques(Enes et al., 2020a).

6.1 Auto-Scaling Mechanisms

- *Horizontal Scaling:* In serverless environments, horizontal scaling is the primary mechanism for accommodating increased workload demand. Horizontal scaling involves dynamically provisioning and deallocating resources, such as function instances, in response to changes in workload. Serverless platforms, such as AWS Lambda, Azure Functions, and Google Cloud Functions, automatically scale function instances based on factors like incoming request rate, concurrency limits, and resource utilization.

- *Event-Driven Scaling:* Serverless functions are typically triggered by events, such as HTTP requests, database changes, or message queue notifications. Event-driven scaling involves scaling function instances in response to event triggers. For example, if the incoming event rate exceeds a predefined threshold, the serverless platform automatically provisions additional function instances to handle the load.

6.2 Load Balancing Strategies

- *Request-Based Load Balancing:* In serverless environments, request-based load balancing distributes incoming requests across multiple function instances to achieve optimal resource utilization and performance. Load balancers, such as AWS Application Load Balancer (ALB) or Azure Application Gateway, intelligently route requests to healthy function instances based on factors like latency, availability, and request type.
- *Concurrency-Based Load Balancing:* Some serverless platforms use concurrency-based load balancing to manage function instances. In this approach, function instances are allocated based on concurrency limits, which dictate the maximum number of simultaneous invocations a function can handle. When the concurrency limit is reached, additional requests are queued or throttled until resources become available.

6.3 Performance Optimization Techniques

- Cold starts occur when a serverless function is invoked for the first time or after a period of inactivity, resulting in increased latency due to resource provisioning. To mitigate cold starts and improve performance, developers can employ techniques such as pre-warming function instances, optimizing code execution time, and reducing dependencies on external services.
- Serverless platforms allow developers to specify the amount of memory allocated to function instances. Memory allocation directly impacts CPU performance and execution time. By tuning memory allocation based on workload characteristics and resource requirements, developers can optimize performance and cost-effectiveness.
- Serverless functions are stateless by design, meaning they do not maintain persistent state between invocations. However, some applications require stateful interactions or data persistence. To optimize performance, developers can employ state management strategies such as caching, session affinity, or offloading state to external data stores like databases or cache services.
- Minimizing dependencies and optimizing external API calls can improve the performance of serverless functions. Developers should carefully evaluate the dependencies of their functions and adopt best practices such as batching requests, caching responses, and optimizing network latency to reduce execution time and enhance scalability.

Scalability in serverless environments is achieved through auto-scaling mechanisms, load balancing strategies, and performance optimization techniques. These include horizontal scaling, event-driven scaling, request-based and concurrency-based load balancing, cold start mitigation, memory allocation tuning, state management strategies, and dependency management. These techniques enable organizations to build efficient, responsive serverless applications.

7. ENSURING COST-EFFICIENCY WITH SERVERLESS SOLUTIONS

Organizations must prioritize cost-efficiency when adopting serverless solutions to optimize spending and maximize cloud computing benefits. This can be achieved by using pay-per-use models, using cost monitoring tools, and conducting cost comparisons with traditional architectures (Sarroca & Sánchez-Artigas, 2024).

- Pay-per-Use Models: Serverless platforms like AWS Lambda, Azure Functions, and Google Cloud Functions use a pay-per-use pricing model, charging organizations based on the resources consumed by their functions. This model offers cost advantages by avoiding upfront capital expenditures and allowing organizations to only pay for the compute time and resources used during function execution, resulting in greater cost-efficiency and scalability.
- Cost Monitoring and Optimization Tools: Cloud providers provide cost monitoring and optimization tools to help organizations manage their serverless spending. These tools offer insights into resource usage, cost trends, and drivers, enabling them to identify opportunities for cost reduction. Examples include AWS Cost Explorer, Azure Cost Management, Google Cloud Cost Management, and third-party solutions like CloudHealth and Datadog. Regular monitoring helps identify inefficiencies, optimize resource utilization, and implement cost-saving measures.
- Cost Comparison with Traditional Architectures: Organizations should conduct cost comparisons between serverless solutions and traditional architectures to assess the cost-effectiveness of migrating to a serverless model. Factors like infrastructure provisioning, maintenance, scalability, and operational overhead should be considered. Serverless solutions offer cost advantages due to their pay-per-use pricing model and automatic scaling capabilities, making informed decisions about migrating workloads and optimizing cloud spending.

To achieve cost-efficiency with serverless solutions, organizations should adopt pay-per-use models, use cost monitoring tools, and conduct thorough cost comparisons with traditional architectures. This will optimize cloud spending, maximize cost-efficiency, and fully realize the benefits of serverless computing (Reuter et al., 2020).

8. DEPLOYMENT TOOLS FOR SERVERLESS APPLICATIONS

Serverless applications require specialized tools to streamline development workflows, automate infrastructure provisioning, and ensure efficient deployment and management. Key deployment tools include CI/CD pipelines, infrastructure automation tools, and serverless frameworks and orchestration tools (Somu et al., 2020). The deployment workflow for serverless applications is illustrated in Figure 5.

Figure 5. Deployment workflow for serverless applications

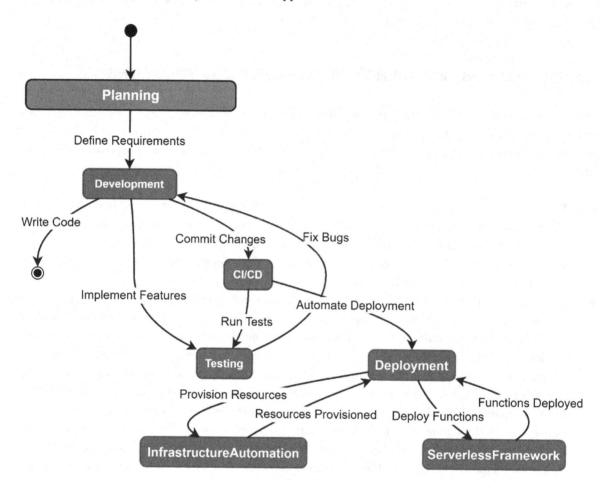

8.1 CI/CD Pipelines

- Continuous Integration and Continuous Deployment (CI/CD) pipelines are essential for automating the build, test, and deployment processes of serverless applications.
- CI/CD pipelines enable developers to automate code integration, testing, and deployment to serverless environments, ensuring rapid and reliable delivery of new features and updates.
- Popular CI/CD tools, such as Jenkins, Travis CI, CircleCI, and GitLab CI/CD, can be configured to trigger automated builds and deployments based on code commits, pull requests, or other events.
- CI/CD pipelines help enforce best practices such as code linting, unit testing, integration testing, and deployment validation, ensuring the quality and reliability of serverless applications throughout the development lifecycle.

8.2 Infrastructure Automation

- Infrastructure automation tools enable developers to provision, configure, and manage serverless resources and environments using code.
- Infrastructure as Code (IaC) tools, such as AWS CloudFormation, Azure Resource Manager (ARM) templates, Google Cloud Deployment Manager, and Terraform, allow developers to define infrastructure components, such as functions, APIs, databases, and event triggers, as code.
- With infrastructure automation, developers can version control infrastructure configurations, provision resources consistently across environments, and automate deployment workflows, leading to improved agility, reliability, and reproducibility of serverless deployments.

8.3 Serverless Frameworks and Orchestration Tools

- Serverless frameworks and orchestration tools provide abstractions and automation for building, deploying, and managing serverless applications and workflows.
- The Serverless Framework, AWS SAM (Serverless Application Model), and Azure Functions Core Tools are popular frameworks for simplifying the development and deployment of serverless applications.
- These frameworks provide templates, abstractions, and CLI (Command Line Interface) tools for defining functions, APIs, events, and resources, as well as deploying and managing serverless applications across different cloud providers.
- Orchestration tools, such as AWS Step Functions, Azure Logic Apps, and Google Cloud Workflows, enable developers to orchestrate complex workflows and event-driven processes using visual workflows or declarative configurations.

Deployment tools for serverless applications include CI/CD pipelines, infrastructure automation tools, and serverless frameworks and orchestration tools. These helps automate deployment processes, enhance agility, reliability, and scalability, accelerate application delivery, and ensure consistency and best practices compliance.

9. MANAGEMENT TOOLS FOR SERVERLESS WORKLOADS

Serverless workload management necessitates specialized tools to monitor performance, ensure security and compliance, and handle errors and debugging. Key management tools include monitoring and logging solutions, security and compliance considerations, and error handling and debugging techniques (Christidis et al., 2020; Enes et al., 2020b). Management tools for serverless workloads include monitoring and logging solutions, security and compliance considerations, and error handling and debugging techniques. These tools help organizations monitor performance, ensure security, and handle errors, enhancing reliability, scalability, and agility in deploying and managing serverless applications.

9.1 Monitoring and Logging Solutions

- Monitoring and logging solutions are essential for gaining visibility into the performance, availability, and health of serverless applications and functions.
- Cloud providers offer native monitoring and logging services, such as AWS CloudWatch, Azure Monitor, and Google Cloud Monitoring, which provide metrics, logs, and alarms for monitoring serverless resources and workloads.
- Third-party monitoring and logging tools, such as Datadog, New Relic, and Splunk, offer advanced features for monitoring serverless applications, aggregating logs, creating dashboards, and setting up alerts.
- Monitoring and logging solutions help identify performance bottlenecks, diagnose issues, troubleshoot errors, and optimize resource utilization in serverless environments.

9.2 Security and Compliance Considerations

- Security and compliance are critical considerations when managing serverless workloads, especially when handling sensitive data or processing critical workloads.
- Serverless environments introduce unique security challenges, such as securing function code, managing access controls, protecting data in transit and at rest, and preventing unauthorized access and abuse.
- Organizations should implement security best practices, such as encrypting sensitive data, enforcing least privilege access, monitoring for security threats, and regularly patching and updating serverless dependencies.
- Compliance requirements, such as GDPR, HIPAA, PCI DSS, and SOC 2, should also be considered when designing and managing serverless applications, ensuring adherence to regulatory standards and industry regulations.

9.3 Error Handling and Debugging Techniques

- Error handling and debugging are essential for identifying and resolving issues in serverless applications and functions.
- Serverless platforms provide built-in error handling mechanisms, such as retries, dead-letter queues, and error notifications, to handle transient errors and failures gracefully.
- Developers can implement structured logging, exception handling, and distributed tracing techniques to capture and analyze errors, exceptions, and performance bottlenecks in serverless applications.
- Tools like AWS X-Ray, Azure Application Insights, and Google Cloud Debugger provide debugging capabilities for tracing requests, analyzing performance, and diagnosing errors in serverless workloads.

10. INTEGRATING SERVERLESS WITH MODERN IT INFRASTRUCTURE

The integration of serverless computing with modern IT infrastructure involves utilizing microservices architecture principles, adapting functionality to serverless contexts, and addressing integration challenges and solutions (Kabarukhin, 2022).

- Microservices architecture is an architectural approach where applications are composed of loosely coupled, independently deployable services, each responsible for a specific business function or capability.
- Microservices promote modularity, scalability, and resilience by breaking down monolithic applications into smaller, specialized services that communicate via lightweight protocols such as HTTP or messaging queues.
- Key characteristics of microservices architecture include service autonomy, bounded contexts, decentralized data management, and continuous delivery practices.

10.1 Microservices Functionality in Serverless Computing

- Serverless computing complements microservices architecture by providing an event-driven, scalable, and pay-per-use execution environment for deploying microservices-based applications.
- In a serverless context, microservices are implemented as serverless functions, which are small units of code that execute in response to events or triggers, such as HTTP requests, database changes, or scheduled events.
- Serverless functions encapsulate specific business logic or functionality and can be developed, deployed, and scaled independently, following the principles of microservices architecture.
- By adopting serverless computing, organizations can further decouple microservices, improve resource utilization, and reduce operational overhead, while maintaining the benefits of modularity and scalability inherent in microservices architecture.

10.2 Challenges and Solutions in Integration

Integrating serverless with modern IT infrastructure presents several challenges, including managing dependencies, orchestrating workflows, ensuring data consistency, and maintaining security and compliance (Christidis et al., 2020; Enes et al., 2020b; Kumari et al., 2021). Integrating serverless with modern IT infrastructure involves utilizing microservices architecture principles, adapting functionality to serverless context, and addressing challenges. Organizations can build scalable, resilient, and agile applications by adopting event-driven communication patterns, leveraging API gateways, implementing robust error handling solutions, and automating deployment and management processes.

- Implementing event-driven communication patterns to facilitate loose coupling and asynchronous communication between serverless functions and other microservices.
- Leveraging API gateways, message brokers, and service meshes to manage communication, enforce security policies, and monitor traffic between microservices and serverless functions.
- Designing robust error handling and retry mechanisms to handle transient failures and ensure fault tolerance in distributed systems.

- Implementing distributed tracing and observability solutions to monitor and debug interactions between microservices and serverless functions, ensuring visibility into end-to-end transactions and performance metrics.
- Employing infrastructure as code (IaC) and configuration management tools to automate deployment, configuration, and management of serverless functions and microservices, ensuring consistency and reproducibility across environments.

11. FUTURE TRENDS AND INNOVATIONS IN SERVERLESS COMPUTING

Serverless computing is transforming the way applications are developed, deployed, and managed, with future trends including the convergence of edge computing with serverless, adoption of serverless for IoT and edge devices, and expansion beyond function execution (Koschel et al., 2021; R. A. P. Rajan, 2018; Sarroca & Sánchez-Artigas, 2024; Uunonen, 2023).

- Edge Computing and Serverless: Edge computing brings compute resources closer to data generation, reducing latency and improving responsiveness for real-time processing or low-latency interactions. Serverless computing is ideal for edge environments, allowing lightweight, event-driven code execution without local infrastructure management. Converging edge computing with serverless allows organizations to deploy functions closer to IoT devices, sensors, and end-users, enabling faster data processing, reduced bandwidth consumption, and improved reliability. This technology is crucial for real-time analytics, predictive maintenance, augmented reality, and autonomous vehicles.
- Serverless for IoT and Edge Devices: Serverless computing is gaining popularity for IoT and edge devices, allowing organizations to build scalable applications for data collection, processing, and analysis. This allows for local data processing, event-driven automation, and real-time decision-making at the edge. Platforms like AWS IoT Greengrass, Azure IoT Edge, and Google Cloud IoT Edge enable deploying and managing serverless functions, integrating with cloud services, and orchestrating workflows across distributed environments.
- Serverless Beyond Function Execution: Serverless computing is expanding beyond function execution to include databases, stateful processing, event-driven workflows, and application orchestration. Platforms like AWS DynamoDB, Azure Cosmos DB, and Google Cloud Firestore offer scalable storage solutions with built-in serverless compute capabilities. Serverless orchestration tools like AWS Step Functions and Azure Logic Apps allow developers to build complex workflows and business processes. Serverless event-driven architectures are driving innovation in areas like event sourcing, microservices, and integrations, enabling organizations to build scalable, resilient applications.

Future trends in serverless computing include integrating edge computing with serverless, extending serverless to IoT and edge devices, and broadening its services beyond function execution. These advancements enable organizations to create scalable, responsive, and innovative applications that meet the demands of modern digital businesses.

12. CONCLUSION AND RECOMMENDATIONS

This summary explores serverless computing, a paradigm shift in application development, deployment, and management. It explores its technologies, tools, and applications, and their integration with modern IT infrastructure. The concept of function-as-a-service (FaaS) and backend-as-a-service (BaaS) and practical considerations of scalability, cost-efficiency, and deployment tools provide unprecedented opportunities for organizations to innovate and accelerate their digital initiatives. As serverless computing continues to evolve, several key takeaways emerge:

- Serverless computing provides unparalleled scalability and agility, allowing organizations to respond dynamically to changing workload demands, scale resources automatically, and accelerate time-to-market for new features and applications.
- With its pay-per-use pricing model and automatic scaling capabilities, serverless computing offers cost-efficiency benefits, enabling organizations to optimize resource utilization, minimize infrastructure costs, and pay only for the resources consumed during function execution.
- Integrating serverless with modern IT infrastructure, including microservices architecture, edge computing, and IoT devices, presents new opportunities and challenges. Organizations must adopt best practices for event-driven communication, security, and orchestration to ensure seamless integration and interoperability across distributed environments.
- The future of serverless computing is promising, with trends such as edge computing, serverless for IoT and edge devices, and the expansion of serverless beyond function execution driving innovation and reshaping the IT landscape. Organizations must stay abreast of these trends and embrace emerging technologies to unlock the full potential of serverless computing.

Thus, Serverless computing offers scalability, cost-efficiency, and agility, enabling organizations to create resilient, responsive, and innovative digital applications. By effectively utilizing serverless technologies, organizations can drive digital transformation, enhance competitiveness, and deliver value to customers in a rapidly evolving marketplace.

12.1 Abbreviations

CD: Continuous Deployment
CI: Continuous Integration
CQRS: Command Query Responsibility Segregation
CSS: Cascading Style Sheets
DB: Database
DSS: Data Security Standard
GDPR: General Data Protection Regulation
HIPAA: Health Insurance Portability and Accountability Act
HTML: Hypertext Markup Language
MQ: Message Queue
SQL: Structured Query Language

REFERENCES

Albuquerque, L. F., Ferraz, F. S., Oliveira, R., & Galdino, S. (2017). Function-as-a-service x platform-as-a-service: Towards a comparative study on FaaS and PaaS. *ICSEA*, 206–212.

Arjona, A., López, P. G., Sampé, J., Slominski, A., & Villard, L. (2021). Triggerflow: Trigger-based orchestration of serverless workflows. *Future Generation Computer Systems*, *124*, 215–229. doi:10.1016/j.future.2021.06.004

Bila, N., Dettori, P., Kanso, A., Watanabe, Y., & Youssef, A. (2017). Leveraging the serverless architecture for securing linux containers. *2017 IEEE 37th International Conference on Distributed Computing Systems Workshops (ICDCSW)*, (pp. 401–404). IEEE.

Cassel, G. A. S., Rodrigues, V. F., da Rosa Righi, R., Bez, M. R., Nepomuceno, A. C., & da Costa, C. A. (2022). Serverless computing for Internet of Things: A systematic literature review. *Future Generation Computer Systems*, *128*, 299–316. doi:10.1016/j.future.2021.10.020

Christidis, A., Moschoyiannis, S., Hsu, C.-H., & Davies, R. (2020). Enabling serverless deployment of large-scale ai workloads. *IEEE Access : Practical Innovations, Open Solutions*, *8*, 70150–70161. doi:10.1109/ACCESS.2020.2985282

Edlund, E. (2022). *Creating a Serverless Application Using the Serverless Framework and React: Deploying a serverless back-end to different cloud providers*. DiVA.

Enes, J., Expósito, R. R., & Touriño, J. (2020a). Real-time resource scaling platform for big data workloads on serverless environments. *Future Generation Computer Systems*, *105*, 361–379. doi:10.1016/j.future.2019.11.037

Enes, J., Expósito, R. R., & Touriño, J. (2020b). Real-time resource scaling platform for big data workloads on serverless environments. *Future Generation Computer Systems*, *105*, 361–379. doi:10.1016/j.future.2019.11.037

Kabarukhin, A. (2022). MODERN CLOUD INFRASTRUCTURE: SERVERLESS COMPUTING. *Наука. Техника и Образование*, *2*(85), 38–43.

Koschel, A., Klassen, S., Jdiya, K., Schaaf, M., & Astrova, I. (2021). Cloud computing: Serverless. *2021 12th International Conference on Information, Intelligence, Systems & Applications (IISA)*, (pp. 1–7). Hochschule Hannover.

Kumari, A., Sahoo, B., Behera, R. K., Misra, S., & Sharma, M. M. (2021). Evaluation of integrated frameworks for optimizing qos in serverless computing. *Computational Science and Its Applications–ICCSA 2021: 21st International Conference, Cagliari, Italy, September 13–16, 2021. Proceedings*, *21*(Part VII), 277–288.

Li, Y., Lin, Y., Wang, Y., Ye, K., & Xu, C. (2022). Serverless computing: State-of-the-art, challenges and opportunities. *IEEE Transactions on Services Computing*, *16*(2), 1522–1539. doi:10.1109/TSC.2022.3166553

Lynn, T., Rosati, P., Lejeune, A., & Emeakaroha, V. (2017). A preliminary review of enterprise serverless cloud computing (function-as-a-service) platforms. *2017 IEEE International Conference on Cloud Computing Technology and Science (CloudCom)*, (pp. 162–169). IEEE. 10.1109/CloudCom.2017.15

Paakkunainen, O. & others. (2019). *Serverless computing and FaaS platform as a web application backend.*

Pogiatzis, A., & Samakovitis, G. (2020). An event-driven serverless ETL pipeline on AWS. *Applied Sciences (Basel, Switzerland)*, *11*(1), 191. doi:10.3390/app11010191

Rajan, A. P. (2020). A review on serverless architectures-function as a service (FaaS) in cloud computing. [Telecommunication Computing Electronics and Control]. *Telkomnika*, *18*(1), 530–537. doi:10.12928/telkomnika.v18i1.12169

Rajan, R. A. P. (2018). Serverless architecture-a revolution in cloud computing. *2018 Tenth International Conference on Advanced Computing (ICoAC)*, (pp. 88–93). IEEE. 10.1109/ICoAC44903.2018.8939081

Reuter, A., Back, T., & Andrikopoulos, V. (2020). Cost efficiency under mixed serverless and serverful deployments. *2020 46th Euromicro Conference on Software Engineering and Advanced Applications (SEAA)*, (pp. 242–245). IEEE.

Sarroca, P. G., & Sánchez-Artigas, M. (2024). Mlless: Achieving cost efficiency in serverless machine learning training. *Journal of Parallel and Distributed Computing*, *183*, 104764. doi:10.1016/j.jpdc.2023.104764

Scheuner, J., & Leitner, P. (2020). Function-as-a-service performance evaluation: A multivocal literature review. *Journal of Systems and Software*, *170*, 110708. doi:10.1016/j.jss.2020.110708

Shafiei, H., Khonsari, A., & Mousavi, P. (2022). Serverless computing: A survey of opportunities, challenges, and applications. *ACM Computing Surveys*, *54*(11s), 1–32. doi:10.1145/3510611

Shahrad, M., Balkind, J., & Wentzlaff, D. (2019). Architectural implications of function-as-a-service computing. *Proceedings of the 52nd Annual IEEE/ACM International Symposium on Microarchitecture*, (pp. 1063–1075). IEEE. 10.1145/3352460.3358296

Somu, N., Daw, N., Bellur, U., & Kulkarni, P. (2020). Panopticon: A comprehensive benchmarking tool for serverless applications. *2020 International Conference on COMmunication Systems & NETworkS (COMSNETS)*, (pp. 144–151). IEEE. 10.1109/COMSNETS48256.2020.9027346

Uunonen, S. (2023). *Backend as a service in web development.* OATD.

Van Eyk, E., Toader, L., Talluri, S., Versluis, L., Uță, A., & Iosup, A. (2018). Serverless is more: From paas to present cloud computing. *IEEE Internet Computing*, *22*(5), 8–17. doi:10.1109/MIC.2018.053681358

Wen, J., Chen, Z., Jin, X., & Liu, X. (2023). Rise of the planet of serverless computing: A systematic review. *ACM Transactions on Software Engineering and Methodology*, *32*(5), 1–61. doi:10.1145/3579643

Witte, P. A., Louboutin, M., Modzelewski, H., Jones, C., Selvage, J., & Herrmann, F. J. (2020). An event-driven approach to serverless seismic imaging in the cloud. *IEEE Transactions on Parallel and Distributed Systems*, *31*(9), 2032–2049. doi:10.1109/TPDS.2020.2982626

Chapter 6
Containerization:
In the Context of Serverless Computing

Sai Samin Varma Pusapati
Chaitanya Bharathi Institute of Technology, India

ABSTRACT

This chapter delves into the synergy between containerization and serverless computing, pivotal for advancing cloud-native application deployment. It outlines the architectural foundations and benefits of each paradigm, emphasizing their combined impact on scalability, efficiency, and agility. The discussion progresses to technical integrations, focusing on container orchestration and serverless platforms, enhancing management and deployment. Addressing challenges like security and operational complexity, it highlights strategies for navigating these issues. Real-world examples illustrate the practical application across sectors, showcasing the integration's capacity to meet diverse computational needs. This convergence is posited as a significant driver for future cloud-native innovations, offering a glimpse into evolving trends and the potential reshaping of software development landscapes. The exploration underscores the critical role of this amalgamation in optimizing resource utilization and simplifying cloud infrastructure complexities.

1. INTRODUCTION

The landscape of software development and deployment is continuously evolving, with containerization and serverless computing emerging as key drivers of change. These technologies have significantly influenced how applications are developed, deployed, and managed, offering novel paradigms that enhance efficiency, scalability, and flexibility. Containerization is a technology that has transformed the landscape of software deployment by encapsulating applications and their dependencies into isolated units called containers. Unlike traditional virtualization, which virtualizes an entire operating system, containers virtualize at the application level, providing a lightweight and efficient solution for packaging, distributing, and running software. At its core, containerization involves bundling an application along with its dependencies, libraries, and runtime into a single container. By definition, a container is a standard unit of software that packages up code and all its dependencies, so the application runs quickly

DOI: 10.4018/979-8-3693-1682-5.ch006

and reliably from one computing environment to another. Docker, one of the most popular containerization platforms, played a pivotal role in popularizing this technology. Serverless computing, in contrast, abstracts the infrastructure layer, enabling developers to focus on code rather than server management. This model optimizes resource utilization and operational costs, representing a shift towards more dynamic and cost-effective cloud computing services.

This chapter aims to explore the contemporary relevance and application of containerization and serverless computing within the software development ecosystem. It will delve into how these technologies synergize to streamline deployment processes and facilitate the development of scalable, resilient applications. By examining the current state of these technologies, including their benefits, challenges, and best practices, the chapter seeks to provide a comprehensive understanding of their role in modern software development.

Moreover, the discussion will extend to the integration of containerization with serverless computing, highlighting how this combination leverages the strengths of both paradigms to offer an unparalleled level of efficiency and agility in application deployment. The chapter will also address the challenges that accompany the adoption of these technologies, such as security concerns and complexity in management, and will propose strategies and solutions to navigate these obstacles effectively. The objective of this chapter is not only to elucidate the foundational concepts of containerization and serverless computing but also to showcase their practical implications in fostering a more agile, cost-effective, and scalable approach to software development. Through this exploration, readers will gain insights into leveraging these technologies to their full potential, thereby contributing to the advancement of cloud-native applications and the broader software development landscape.

In summary, the chapter will serve as a detailed guide to understanding the intricacies of containerization and serverless computing, providing valuable knowledge for developers, IT professionals, and organizations aiming to navigate the complexities of modern software development and deployment. Through a blend of theoretical exploration and practical insights, it will illuminate the path toward harnessing the transformative potential of these technologies in the digital age.

2. FUNDAMENTALS OF CONTAINERIZATION

2.1 Definition and Concepts

In the rapidly evolving domain of software development and deployment, container technology has emerged as a pivotal innovation, significantly altering how applications are created, deployed, and managed across diverse environments. This technology, by encapsulating an application and its dependencies into a single container, offers a streamlined and efficient approach to software delivery, distinguishing itself from traditional virtualization techniques through its lightweight nature and agility.

Container technology provides a standardized unit of software, ensuring that applications run reliably and consistently regardless of the deployment environment. This consistency addresses a common challenge in software development known as the "it works on my machine" syndrome, where applications behave differently across various environments due to discrepancies in operating systems, libraries, and dependencies. Containers encapsulate the application along with its runtime environment, making it possible to achieve uniformity across development, testing, and production stages. Docker, introduced in 2013, has been instrumental in popularizing container technology, providing a platform that simplifies the creation, deployment, and management of containers with its easy-to-use command-line interface and comprehensive ecosystem (Merkel, 2014).

The differentiation between container technology and traditional virtualization lies primarily in their architectural approach and resource efficiency. Traditional virtualization involves running multiple virtual machines (VMs) on a single physical server, with each VM including a full copy of an operating system, the application, necessary binaries, and libraries. This setup, while offering isolation and environment replication, is resource-intensive, as each VM requires a significant amount of system resources to emulate an entire operating system.

In contrast, container technology virtualizes at the application layer rather than the hardware layer. Containers share the host system's kernel but isolate the application processes from each other. This architecture significantly reduces the overhead associated with running multiple operating system instances, leading to a more efficient use of system resources. Containers start up almost instantaneously and require less disk space compared to VMs, enabling more applications to run simultaneously on a single host system (Felter et al., 2015).

Moreover, container technology facilitates DevOps practices by enhancing collaboration between development and operations teams. It enables developers to package applications with all their dependencies, simplifying the transition from development to production. This encapsulation, combined with the ability to deploy containers across various environments seamlessly, accelerates the development cycle and promotes continuous integration and continuous deployment (CI/CD) practices.

The advent of container orchestration tools like Kubernetes has further extended the capabilities of container technology, addressing challenges related to managing container lifecycles, scaling, and networking in complex distributed systems. Kubernetes provides a framework for automating deployment, scaling, and operations of application containers across clusters of hosts, offering resilience, scalability, and high availability for containerized applications (Burns, 2016).

Container technology represents a significant shift from traditional virtualization techniques, offering a more agile, efficient, and resource-effective solution for software deployment. Its ability to ensure consistency across environments, coupled with its support for DevOps and microservices architectures, positions container technology as a cornerstone of modern cloud-native computing. As this technology continues to evolve, it is set to play a crucial role in shaping the future of software development and deployment, driving innovation and efficiency in the tech industry.

2.2 Background and Evolution of Containerization

To enhance the narrative on the history and impact of container technology with in-text citations, let's integrate references throughout the content to provide a scholarly foundation and further reading opportunities. Tracing the history and development of container technology reveals a fascinating journey of innovation that has profoundly changed the landscape of technology and software development. This evolution spans several decades, with each phase introducing new concepts and improvements that have incrementally shaped the modern approach to deploying applications and services (Pahl, 2015).

The roots of container technology can be traced back to the Unix chroot command, introduced in 1979. Chroot was a rudimentary form of process isolation, allowing the execution of a process with a different root directory. Although not a container in today's sense, it laid the groundwork for the concept of isolating application environments (Price, 1982). In the late 1990s, FreeBSD introduced Jails, which provided a more advanced form of isolation by allowing system administrators to partition a FreeBSD computer into multiple secure and independent mini systems called "jails" (Kamp & Watson, 2000). This was a significant advancement over chroot, as it offered better security and isolation, marking a step closer to what we recognize as containerization today.

The concept of containerization took a more defined shape with the advent of Linux Containers (LXC) in the early 2000s. LXC was a pivotal development, as it provided an API for Linux kernel containment features like cgroups and namespaces, which allowed for the creation of isolated environments for running applications (Bernstein, 2014). LXC enabled users to run multiple isolated Linux systems (containers) on a single host, offering an efficient use of resources and improved security.

Docker, introduced in 2013, revolutionized container technology and is often credited with popularizing containers among the wider developer community (Merkel, 2014). Docker simplified and improved container technology, making it more accessible and practical for everyday development and deployment practices. It provided a portable, lightweight environment for applications, including all necessary dependencies, which could be run anywhere the Docker platform was installed. This drastically reduced the "it works on my machine" problem, as Docker containers ensured consistency across different environments.

Docker also introduced Docker Hub, a cloud service for sharing applications packaged as containers, further enhancing the collaborative aspect of software development. The Dockerfile, a simple, declarative file for creating container images, became a standard for defining containerized applications (Hykes, 2013).

As the adoption of container technology grew, the need for managing complex, multi-container applications became evident. This led to the development of container orchestration tools, with Kubernetes emerging as the leader (Burns et al., 2016). Created by Google and donated to the Cloud Native Computing Foundation (CNCF), Kubernetes automates the deployment, scaling, and management of containerized applications, representing a significant evolution in how applications are deployed and managed at scale.

Container technology has had a profound impact on cloud computing and DevOps practices. It has enabled microservices architecture, allowing applications to be broken down into smaller, independently deployable services (Balalaie, Heydarnoori, & Jamshidi, 2016). This has improved scalability, reliability, and the speed of development. Containers have become foundational to cloud-native applications, facilitating seamless migration to the cloud, and optimizing resource use in cloud environments.

The journey of container technology, from its inception with Unix's chroot to the transformative emergence of Docker and the advent of sophisticated orchestration tools like Kubernetes, illustrates a significant evolution in software development and deployment practices. This history underscores a shift towards efficiency, agility, and collaboration, highlighting the profound impact containers have had on cloud computing and DevOps. As we delve further into this exploration, we will uncover the benefits, challenges, and limitations associated with containerization, alongside a detailed examination of orchestration tools that streamline the management of complex, containerized applications. These narrative promises to provide a comprehensive understanding of how container technology continues to shape the future of software deployment, fostering innovation and efficiency across the tech landscape.

2.3 Benefits of Containerization

Containerization represents a paradigm shift in software deployment, addressing the intricate challenges of traditional methods, particularly in dependency management, environment consistency, and resource utilization. Traditional deployments often grapple with dependency conflicts and the notorious "it works on my machine" problem, leading to unpredictable application performance and deployment delays.

Moreover, the inefficiency of resource utilization in such methods, characterized by underused virtual machines, introduces unnecessary infrastructure costs and scalability limitations. Containerization emerges as a solution, providing a consistent and isolated runtime environment that streamlines these aspects, enhancing security, and optimizing resource usage (Turnbull, 2014).

The advent of containerization technology has significantly mitigated the challenges posed by traditional software deployment methods. Dependency management becomes streamlined as containers package applications with all their requisite dependencies, circumventing conflicts and compatibility issues. This encapsulation ensures consistency across development, testing, and production environments, eliminating discrepancies that often result in deployment hurdles. Furthermore, the isolated runtime environment containers offer not only bolsters security by minimizing potential conflicts with other applications but also enhances system stability and reliability. This isolation, coupled with containers' lightweight nature, allows for more efficient resource utilization than traditional virtual machines, ensuring applications consume only the necessary resources and facilitating scalability.

Containerization's impact is profound, offering portability, scalability, and resource efficiency among its primary advantages:

Portability:

Containers encapsulate applications, libraries, and dependencies, creating a portable, self-contained unit. This abstraction ensures that applications operate consistently across diverse environments. Researchers can develop and test applications on individual machines and seamlessly deploy them on various platforms, streamlining experimentation and reproducibility in research environments (Pahl, 2015).

Scalability:

Containers facilitate the creation of microservices architectures, enabling modular and scalable application development. Researchers can easily scale their experiments by replicating containers, orchestrating them efficiently, and adapting to fluctuating workloads. This scalability proves invaluable in parallel computing and distributed systems research (Newman, 2015).

Resource Efficiency:

By sharing the host OS kernel, containers eliminate the need for full OS virtualization, resulting in a lightweight footprint and efficient resource utilization. This efficiency is critical for researchers running resource-intensive simulations or managing large datasets, allowing them to optimize computational resources effectively (Hykes, 2013).

Consistency Across Environments:

Containers abstract away dependencies, ensuring a consistent runtime environment. This consistency is invaluable for researchers collaborating across institutions or working on projects with diverse technology stacks. It eliminates the challenges of environmental discrepancies, allowing researchers to focus on the core aspects of their work rather than troubleshooting deployment issues (Crosby et al., 2014).

Support for DevOps Practices:

Containers align seamlessly with DevOps principles, fostering collaboration between development and operations teams. Researchers can leverage container orchestration tools like Kubernetes to automate deployment, scaling, and management of applications. This automation accelerates the research lifecycle, facilitating continuous integration, continuous deployment, and enabling reproducibility in computational experiments.

This theoretical foundation of containerization's benefits – portability, scalability, and efficiency- is mirrored in the real- world applications of leading organizations. For instance:

1.   Google:

Google employs containerization extensively within its infrastructure, with Kubernetes as a key orchestrator. Google's Kubernetes is designed to manage and orchestrate Docker containers at scale. It utilizes a declarative model for defining containerized application configurations and automates the deployment, scaling, and operation of application containers. Google's internal system, Borg, served as the inspiration for Kubernetes, and both systems exemplify the technical intricacies involved in efficient container orchestration at scale. Google's containerization solutions emphasize container isolation, efficient resource allocation, and workload scaling across clusters of machines (Burns et al., 2016).

2.   Netflix:

Netflix utilizes Docker containers and Kubernetes for orchestrating its microservices architecture. Docker containers package each microservice along with its dependencies, and Kubernetes manages the deployment, scaling, and maintenance of these containers. Netflix's adoption of containerization involves continuous integration and delivery (CI/CD) pipelines, where changes to microservices trigger automatic containerized deployments. Technical considerations include the implementation of service discovery, load balancing, and fault tolerance mechanisms within the container orchestration framework to ensure high availability and reliability (Cockcroft, 2014).

3.   Spotify:

Spotify relies on Docker containers to package applications, ensuring consistency across different environments. Kubernetes plays a vital role in deploying and managing these containers at scale. The technical aspects include defining Kubernetes manifests for specifying the desired state of deployments, configuring horizontal pod autoscaling based on resource usage, and implementing rolling updates to seamlessly roll out new versions of containerized applications. Spotify's containerization strategy incorporates advanced features such as PodDisruptionBudgets to maintain application availability during disruptions (Stine, 2015).

4.   Capital One:

Capital One embraced Docker and Kubernetes to enhance the scalability and resource efficiency of its applications. Technical considerations involve defining Docker files to specify the container images, using Kubernetes Deployment objects to manage application replicas, and leveraging Kubernetes Horizontal Pod Autoscalers for dynamic scaling based on metrics. Capital One's containerization strategy also encompasses incorporating logging, monitoring, and security measures within the containerized applications, utilizing tools like Prometheus and Grafana for observability (Hightower et al., 2017).

5.   General Electric (GE):

GE's containerization strategy involves using Docker containers and Kubernetes for modernizing its software infrastructure. Technical considerations include defining Docker Compose files to configure multi-container applications during development and using Kubernetes Deployments for orchestrating containerized applications in production. GE emphasizes the technicalities of building cloud-native applications that are portable across different cloud providers, leveraging Kubernetes' ability to abstract away underlying infrastructure differences.

In each case, these organizations implement containerization technologies with a focus on container orchestration, resource management, scalability, and ensuring a seamless development and deployment pipeline through CI/CD practices. The technical intricacies involve configuring and managing containers, defining deployment specifications, and implementing advanced features provided by container orchestration platforms. While containerization offers significant benefits, understanding its distinction from traditional virtualization is crucial.

2.4 Containerization vs. Virtualization: A Comparative Analysis

Virtualization involves creating multiple simulated environments or dedicated resources from a single physical hardware system, typically through virtual machines each running a full stack of an operating system, application, and dependencies. In contrast, containerization encapsulates the application and its immediate dependencies in a container that shares the host's operating system kernel, offering a more lightweight and agile solution. This comparison highlights the evolution from resource-intensive virtual machines to the streamlined, efficient deployment model provided by containers, underscoring the technological advancements that containerization represents in the software development and deployment ecosystem. This discussion sets the stage for a deeper exploration into the technical nuances of containerization and virtualization, offering insights into why and how containerization has become a preferred method for modern software deployments across various industry sectors.

Comparing Containers and Virtual Machines (VMs) involves examining their efficiency, performance, and application scenarios in detail. This comparative analysis is grounded in evidence from academic research, industry reports, and real-world application cases.

Efficiency

Containers are renowned for their efficiency, primarily because they share the host system's kernel and require fewer resources than VMs. A container only packages the application and its dependencies, not the entire operating system. This approach significantly reduces the startup time and increases the density of applications that can run on a single host machine. According to Felter et al. (2015), containers initiate significantly faster and consume a fraction of the memory and CPU resources compared to VMs, demonstrating the efficiency advantages of containerization in resource-constrained environments.

Virtual Machines, on the other hand, simulate a full hardware stack, including the operating system upon which the application runs. This abstraction layer introduces additional overhead, requiring more resources and resulting in slower startup times compared to containers. While this might suggest inefficiency, the complete isolation provided by VMs is critical for scenarios where full emulation of independent machines is necessary.

Performance

Containers offer near-native performance because they interact directly with the host operating system's kernel. This direct interaction minimizes the overhead, allowing applications within containers to run almost as efficiently as if they were running directly on the host. The "Performance Analysis of Containers and Virtual Machines" study by Xu et al. (2018) underscores this point, showing that containerized applications exhibit performance metrics closely matching those of applications running on the host system, particularly in CPU-bound tasks.

Virtual Machines encapsulate a full copy of an operating system, introducing a hypervisor layer between the application and the physical hardware. This additional layer can lead to performance degradation, especially in disk I/O and network operations. However, VMs provide stronger isolation and security guarantees, which can be paramount in environments where performance is secondary to security or compliance requirements.

Resource Overhead

Virtualization incurs a higher resource overhead because each VM operates with its own full instance of an operating system, leading to increased memory and storage consumption (Soltesz et al., 2007).

Containerization significantly reduces resource overhead by sharing the host's operating system kernel, allowing for a more efficient utilization of system resources, and enabling higher workload densities on the same hardware (Felter et al., 2015).

Isolation

Virtualization provides strong isolation through separate operating systems, enhancing security at the expense of increased resource consumption (Perez et al., 2006).

Containerization, while offering a lighter form of isolation by sharing the host OS kernel, can be augmented with technologies like gVisor or Kata Containers for enhanced security without the full overhead of traditional VMs (Manco et al., 2017).

Management and Orchestration

Virtualization management relies on hypervisor technologies and tools like VMware or Hyper-V, with orchestration platforms like OpenStack facilitating the coordination of VMs within larger infrastructures (Nelson et al., 2010).

Containerization benefits from orchestration tools such as Kubernetes and Docker Swarm, which automate the deployment, scaling, and operational aspects of containerized applications, proving essential for managing large-scale, distributed systems effectively (Burns et al., 2016).

Application Scenarios

Containers are ideal for microservices architectures and cloud-native applications where scalability, rapid deployment, and efficient resource utilization are priorities. They excel in continuous integration and continuous deployment (CI/CD) environments, as their portability ensures consistency across development, testing, and production. Containers are also well-suited for stateless applications that require rapid scaling up and down, as highlighted by the widespread adoption of container orchestration platforms like Kubernetes in managing complex containerized applications across multiple environments.

Virtual Machines are preferred in scenarios requiring strong isolation, comprehensive security, and full control over the operating environment. They are suitable for running multiple distinct operating systems on a single physical server or for applications with strict compliance and security requirements that necessitate full OS isolation. VMs are often used in legacy application migration, where the entire operating environment needs to be replicated on a new hardware platform without modification to the application itself.

The choice between containers and VMs depends on specific project requirements, including efficiency, performance, and the need for isolation. Containers offer a lightweight, efficient solution with near-native performance, ideal for microservices and cloud-native applications. In contrast, VMs provide strong isolation and security at the cost of additional resource overhead, making them suitable for applications with stringent security or compliance requirements. This comparative analysis, supported by evidence from studies and real-world applications, underscores the complementary roles of containers and VMs in modern software development and deployment ecosystems. It provides a comprehensive overview for stakeholders to make informed decisions regarding their deployment strategies.

3. CONTAINER TECHNOLOGIES AND ECOSYSTEM

3.1 Types and Technologies

The container ecosystem is diverse, offering a range of solutions tailored to different deployment needs, security requirements, and operational preferences. Below, we explore various container types, detailing their definitions, specification parameters, functioning, and use cases to provide a comprehensive understanding of the container landscape.

I.   Docker Containers

Docker containers are lightweight, stand-alone, executable packages that include everything needed to run a piece of software, including the code, runtime, libraries, environment variables, and system libraries. Docker containers are based on Docker images, which are constructed from layered filesystems. Docker uses a client-server architecture, with Docker Daemon managing container objects (Nadareishvili et al., 2016). Specification parameters include image size, networking capabilities, and volume management. Docker containers run isolated processes in user space on the host operating system's kernel. They start quickly, ensuring applications run the same regardless of where they're deployed. Docker is suited for microservices architecture, simplifying the development, testing, and deployment process by ensuring consistency across environments. It's widely used for CI/CD pipelines, development and testing, and application deployment (Turnbull, 2016).

II.   rkt (Rocket)

Developed by CoreOS, rkt is a container engine designed for security and composability within modern production environments. It emphasizes simplicity and supports multiple container formats, including Docker and its own application specification. rkt's specifications include support for different container formats, integration with systemd for better process management, and a pod-native architecture. It offers advanced security features, like support for SELinux and TPM (Trusted Platform Module). rkt functions by directly executing container images on a host machine, employing a pod-based approach where each pod can contain multiple co-located containers sharing the same network, storage, and lifecycle. rkt is particularly suited for cloud-native applications requiring enhanced security features and integration with existing Linux system management tools. It's favored in environments prioritizing security and simplicity. (Brandon, 2017).

III.   Containerd

Containerd is an industry-standard container runtime with an emphasis on simplicity, robustness, and portability. It is designed to manage the complete container lifecycle of its host system: image transfer and storage, container execution and supervision, and low-level storage and network attachments. Key specifications include OCI (Open Container Initiative) image support, network and storage management, and execution of containers according to the OCI runtime spec. It operates as a daemon for managing container lifecycle (Crosby et al., 2017). It serves as the container runtime for Docker but is also used independently. It interfaces with the Linux kernel to manage containers' lifecycle and resource isolation. Containerd is utilized in large-scale systems where direct interaction with the container runtime is necessary. It's also used as a foundational layer in Kubernetes, Docker, and other container-based systems.

IV.   Podman

Podman is a daemon less container engine for developing, managing, and running OCI Containers on your Linux System. Containers can either be run as root or in rootless mode. Specifications include daemonless architecture, support for OCI container images, rootless operation, and compatibility with Docker CLI commands for ease of transition (Williams, 2019). Podman directly interacts with the image registry, container and image storage, and the kernel to manage the container lifecycle without the need for a daemon, enhancing security and ease of use. Podman is ideal for developers and deployment scripts that require direct control over container management without a daemon, as well as for scenarios prioritizing security.

V.   LXC (Linux Containers)

LXC is a Linux operating system-level virtualization method for running multiple isolated Linux systems (containers) on a control host using a single Linux kernel. LXC's specifications include support for cgroups for resource isolation, namespaces for providing isolation layers for running containers, and support for various storage backends like ZFS, Btrfs, and LVM. LXC functions by utilizing Linux kernel features like namespaces and cgroups to create containers that operate almost as separate Linux instances, sharing the host OS kernel but otherwise isolated. LXC is suited for scenarios requiring full Linux distributions within containers, making it ideal for lightweight VM alternatives and for running environments closely mimicking physical or virtual machines (Helsley, 2009).

Each container type offers unique advantages tailored to specific deployment scenarios, from Docker's widespread use in application development to rkt's security focus, Containerd's robustness in large-scale systems, Podman's daemonless operation for enhanced security, and LXC's suitability for running lightweight virtual machines. These diverse solutions underline the container ecosystem's flexibility, allowing developers and organizations to select technologies that best fit their operational requirements and application needs. These diverse container types cater to different needs, ranging from simplicity and security to compatibility with various container orchestration systems. The choice of container type often depends on specific use cases, operational requirements, and the desired balance between features and resource efficiency. Beyond Docker, alternative containerization technologies have emerged, each addressing specific needs and introducing unique features to the software development landscape.

Lightweight Containers:

Lightweight containers, represented by technologies like Alpine Linux containers and Distroless containers, prioritize efficiency and minimalism. Alpine Linux containers leverage a minimalistic Linux distribution, which results in reduced image sizes and optimized resource utilization. These containers hold particular importance in environments where resource efficiency is crucial, such as edge computing, IoT devices, or microservices architectures. Their small footprint contributes to faster image pulls, decreased storage requirements, and more efficient utilization of system resources.

Taking this philosophy of minimalism a step further, Distroless containers go beyond by stripping away unnecessary components like shells and package managers. The significance of Distroless containers lies in their focus on enhancing security and minimizing the attack surface. This makes them invaluable in production environments where maintaining a lean and secure runtime environment is paramount for ensuring the integrity and safety of applications. In essence, both Alpine Linux and Distroless containers offer tailored solutions for specific use cases, providing developers with tools that optimize efficiency, resource utilization, and security in their containerized applications.

Serverless Containers:

Serverless containers, exemplified by platforms such as AWS Fargate and Azure Container Instances (ACI), seamlessly integrate the advantages of containerization with the serverless computing paradigm. AWS Fargate operates in a serverless manner, automatically scaling based on demand. Users only pay for the vCPU and memory consumed by their containers. This characteristic proves particularly beneficial for microservices architectures and applications characterized by sporadic usage patterns.

Fargate further abstracts away infrastructure concerns, empowering developers to concentrate solely on the deployment of their applications. Its automatic scaling based on demand aligns with the dynamic nature of microservices architectures, making it an ideal choice for scenarios where workloads fluctuate.

Similarly, ACI in Azure follows a serverless container deployment model. ACI abstracts away the need to manage infrastructure, providing on-demand container execution. Users are billed based on resource consumption by their containers. ACI's dynamic scaling capability ensures a serverless approach that is well-suited for scenarios involving unpredictable resource requirements and scaling demands. In essence, both AWS Fargate and Azure Container Instances provide developers with serverless solutions for deploying containerized applications, streamlining operations, and enhancing flexibility in resource management.

In diverse contexts, lightweight containers shine in resource-constrained scenarios, optimizing for efficiency and security. Serverless containers, on the other hand, cater to dynamic and event-driven workloads, offering automatic scaling and cost efficiency. The introduction of these alternative containerization technologies expands the possibilities for developers, allowing them to choose solutions that align precisely with their operational requirements and use case scenarios.

In a technical sense, lightweight containers emphasize minimalism in the container image, optimizing for resource efficiency and security. Serverless containers abstract away infrastructure management, providing automatic scaling and cost efficiency, with the pay-as-you-go model. Both alternatives offer specialized solutions catering to specific technical requirements and operational contexts in modern software development.

3.2 Docker

Docker, since its inception in 2013, has revolutionized the way developers build, ship, and run applications, making it an indispensable tool in the modern DevOps toolkit. At the heart of Docker's success is its innovative architecture, a vibrant ecosystem of tools and services, and a robust community of developers and contributors. This section delves into Docker's architecture, explores its diverse use cases, and celebrates the contributions of its thriving community.

Docker's architecture is fundamentally composed of the Docker Engine, a lightweight runtime and packaging tool, and Docker Hub, a cloud service for sharing applications and automating workflows. The Docker Engine itself encapsulates two main components: the Docker Daemon, which runs on the host machine and manages the containers, and the Docker Client, which allows users to interact with the Daemon through the Docker CLI or API (Merkel, 2014). Docker containers run on top of the host operating system's kernel, unlike traditional virtual machines that require a hypervisor to emulate hardware. This design enables Docker to provide a lightweight, efficient environment for applications, significantly reducing overhead and improving performance (Felter et al., 2015).

Docker's flexibility and efficiency have made it suitable for a wide range of applications, from simple web apps to complex microservices architectures. One of the most significant use cases is in the development and testing environments, where Docker ensures consistency by replicating the production environment, thereby eliminating the "it works on my machine" problem (Turnbull, 2016). In CI/CD pipelines, Docker automates the building, testing, and deployment of applications, making the software delivery process faster and more reliable. Furthermore, Docker is instrumental in facilitating microservices architectures, allowing services to be packaged and scaled independently. This capability has led to its widespread adoption in cloud-native applications, where scalability, resilience, and rapid deployment are crucial (Balalaie et al., 2016).

The Docker community, comprising developers, users, and organizations worldwide, plays a pivotal role in the platform's development and adoption. Through open-source contributions, the community has developed a plethora of Docker images available on Docker Hub, enabling users to deploy a wide variety of applications and services quickly. The community's engagement in forums, social media, and conferences fosters collaboration, knowledge sharing, and innovation within the ecosystem. Moreover, contributions from the community have led to the development of complementary tools and extensions, such as Docker Compose for defining multi-container applications and Docker Swarm for clustering and scheduling containers (Nadareishvili et al., 2016).

Through its innovative architecture, wide-ranging use cases, and the dynamic contributions of its community, Docker has established itself as a cornerstone of modern software development and deployment. The platform continues to evolve, driven by technological advancements and the collective efforts of its global community, underscoring its pivotal role in shaping the future of cloud computing and DevOps practices.

3.3 Orchestration With Kubernetes

Kubernetes, an open-source platform designed by Google and now maintained by the Cloud Native Computing Foundation (CNCF), has emerged as the de facto standard for orchestrating containerized applications. It automates the deployment, scaling, and management of containerized applications, making it a cornerstone in the realm of modern software development and deployment practices. At the core of Kubernetes' architecture lies the concept of clusters, which are sets of machines, called nodes, that run containerized applications. These clusters are managed by a master node, which orchestrates the scheduling of containers onto worker nodes based on predefined criteria, such as CPU and memory availability. The master node comprises several components, including the API server, scheduler, controller manager, etc., a distributed key-value store for cluster data (Burns et al., 2016). This architecture not only ensures high availability and scalability but also facilitates fault tolerance and load balancing across the cluster. Kubernetes is built on a set of principles that emphasize declarative configuration and automation. It treats containers as first-class citizens and groups them into Pods, the smallest deployable units in Kubernetes, which share networking and storage resources. Services, another key abstraction, provide stable endpoints for accessing pods, enabling dynamic discovery within the cluster. Kubernetes also supports higher-level abstractions like Deployments and StatefulSets, which simplify the management of stateless and stateful applications, respectively. These principles and abstractions allow developers to focus on the applications themselves rather than the underlying infrastructure. It plays a pivotal role in managing containerized applications by providing a robust, flexible platform that supports diverse workloads, from microservices to batch processing jobs. It offers self-healing capabilities, automatically replacing or restarting failed containers to ensure that the desired state of the application is maintained.

Kubernetes' scalability is another key feature, enabling applications to scale in and out automatically based on demand, thereby optimizing resource utilization and reducing costs. Moreover, its ecosystem is rich with tools and services, from Helm for package management to Istio for service mesh, enhancing the platform's capabilities and integration options. Kubernetes has fundamentally changed how organizations deploy and manage their applications, promoting a shift towards microservices architecture and DevOps practices. Its impact extends beyond technical benefits, fostering a culture of innovation and continuous improvement. The platform's adoption across industries underscores its effectiveness in addressing the complexities of modern application deployment and management.

The exploration of container technologies and Kubernetes orchestration highlights a significant evolution in software development and deployment practices. Docker's innovation in containerization has enabled more efficient and portable application development, while Kubernetes has become indispensable for managing these applications at scale. Together, they facilitate a shift towards agile, scalable, and resilient software systems. Moving forward, the focus will shift to addressing the challenges inherent in containerized environments, such as security, networking, and data persistence, to ensure comprehensive, robust solutions that extend beyond deployment to encompass the entire lifecycle of containerized applications.

4. SPECIFICATIONS AND CHALLENGES IN CONTAINERIZATION

4.1 Navigating Challenges of Containerization

Navigating the complexities of containerization involves addressing critical challenges such as security vulnerabilities, management intricacies, and the imperative for comprehensive monitoring. These challenges, integral to the deployment and maintenance of containerized environments, demand a nuanced approach bolstered by real-world examples and strategies.

Security Vulnerabilities

Security within containerized environments is a multifaceted issue, with vulnerabilities arising from various components including container images, runtime environments, and the orchestration layers. One notable example of a security vulnerability was the 2019 Docker Hub breach, where sensitive data from approximately 190,000 users was exposed. This incident underscores the importance of securing container registries and enforcing strict access controls.

Another common security concern is the misconfiguration of containers, which can lead to unauthorized access. For instance, containers running with default or overly permissive settings can become easy targets for attackers. The use of minimal base images, like Alpine Linux, can reduce the attack surface by limiting the number of components that can be exploited.

To mitigate these risks, organizations are increasingly adopting solutions like Aqua Security and Twistlock, which provide comprehensive security scanning and runtime protection for containerized applications. Implementing security best practices, such as regular vulnerability scanning of container images, using non-root containers, and employing network segmentation and firewalls, is crucial (Obi et al., 2024).

Management Complexities

The management of containerized environments, especially at scale, introduces complexities related to orchestration, service discovery, and configuration management. Kubernetes, while powerful, adds layers of complexity with its intricate configurations and steep learning curve. Companies like Spotify have navigated these challenges by investing in custom tooling and adopting GitOps practices to automate and simplify Kubernetes deployments, demonstrating the potential for streamlined management with the right tools and processes in place.

Persistent storage in containers is another area of complexity. Traditional databases and stateful applications often require stable storage, which can be challenging to manage in dynamic container environments. Solutions like Portworx and StorageOS provide persistent storage for Kubernetes, enabling databases and stateful applications to run reliably in containers (Yang et al., 2023).

Need for Comprehensive Monitoring

Comprehensive monitoring in containerized environments is essential for ensuring performance, availability, and resource optimization. Containers' ephemeral nature and dynamic scaling capabilities necessitate tools that can provide real-time insights into container health, resource usage, and application performance.

Prometheus, an open-source monitoring solution, has gained popularity for its effectiveness in monitoring Kubernetes and containerized applications. Its success is partly due to its ability to dynamically discover services and collect metrics without manual configuration. Grafana, used in conjunction with Prometheus, offers powerful visualization capabilities, enabling teams to quickly identify and respond to issues (Ledaal, 2023).

Real-world implementations, such as those by the cloud-native communication platform, Twilio, illustrate the effectiveness of comprehensive monitoring. Twilio leverages Prometheus and Grafana for monitoring its Kubernetes clusters, enabling the team to maintain high availability and promptly address performance issues.

Navigating the challenges of security, management, and monitoring in containerized environments highlights the need for robust strategies and tools. This approach is foundational to leveraging the full potential of containerization. As we move from these challenges to the realm of specifications and standards, it's clear that these frameworks are crucial for ensuring interoperability, security, and consistency across container technologies. Embracing specifications and standards is vital for enhancing container ecosystems, promoting a unified approach that benefits developers, operators, and the broader community.

4.2 Specifications and Standards for Containers

The Open Container Initiative (OCI) and serverless containers represent two pivotal aspects of the modern cloud-native ecosystem, each addressing different needs but interconnected in fostering scalable, efficient, and portable cloud-native applications. OCI specifications serve as a cornerstone for ensuring interoperability and standardization within the container ecosystem. By defining a clear set of standards for container formats and runtimes, the OCI enables diverse container technologies to operate seamlessly across different computing environments. This in-depth technical analysis explores the significance of OCI specifications and their impact on container technology.

OCI Runtime Specification

The OCI Runtime Specification is a pivotal standard that outlines how a container should be packaged and executed, detailing the configuration, execution environment, and lifecycle of a container. This specification mandates the use of a "filesystem bundle" which is essentially a directory containing a container's filesystem along with a configuration file specifying how the container should be executed. The technical specifics include:

Root Filesystem: The directory structure that will be considered the root filesystem for the container.

Container Process: Specifications around the process that will be initiated inside the container, including its environment variables, working directory, and user ID.

Namespaces: Mechanisms for isolating various aspects of the container's environment, including process IDs, network interfaces, and mount points, enhancing the container's isolation from the host system.

Cgroups: Utilization of Linux Control Groups to limit, account for, and isolate the resource usage (CPU, memory, disk I/O, etc.) of container processes.

This specification ensures consistent behavior of containers across different environments, vital for developers and operators aiming for predictability and portability in container deployment.

OCI Image Specification

The OCI Image Specification delineates how container images should be constructed, enabling the creation, sharing, and running of containers across various environments. It specifies:

Image Manifest: A JSON document that describes the image, including references to the image configuration and layer tar archives.

Image Index: An optional component that can reference multiple image manifests, allowing for multi-platform image support.

Layered Filesystems: Images are composed of layered filesystems, each layer representing a change from the previous one, packaged as a tar archive. This layering supports efficient storage and distribution, as layers can be shared among images.

The Image Specification addresses the need for an efficient, standardized method for packaging and distributing containerized applications. This efficiency not only facilitates faster development and deployment cycles but also ensures that images are portable and can be run by different OCI-compliant runtime implementations.

Distribution Specification

An extension of the OCI's effort to standardize the container ecosystem, the Distribution Specification standardizes the API protocol for distributing container images. It covers:

Pushing and Pulling Images: Defines the HTTP API routes that enable clients to push new images to a registry and pull images from a registry.

Content Discovery and Management: Details how clients can list, discover, and manage content available within a registry.

The technical specifications put forth by the OCI are instrumental in ensuring that containerized applications are portable and can be managed consistently across different environments and cloud providers. This interoperability is vital for organizations leveraging multi-cloud strategies and DevOps practices, where the ability to deploy applications seamlessly across various platforms is crucial.

By defining a common standard for container formats and runtime behavior, the OCI mitigates the risk of vendor lock-in, empowering developers to choose the best tools and platforms for their needs without concern for compatibility issues. Furthermore, standardization fosters innovation within the container ecosystem by providing a stable foundation upon which new tools and services can be built.

Serverless containers abstract away the underlying infrastructure, allowing developers to run containerized applications without managing servers or clusters directly. This model combines the benefits of containerization—such as portability and consistency—with the serverless paradigm's scalability and cost-efficiency. Serverless container platforms, like AWS Fargate and Azure Container Instances (ACI), manage the orchestration, provisioning, scaling, and lifecycle of containers, billing users only for the resources consumed during execution.

The relationship between OCI standards and serverless containers lies in the foundational role the OCI plays in ensuring the interoperability and standardization of container formats and runtimes used within serverless environments. By adhering to OCI specifications, serverless container platforms can:

Ensure Portability: Containers built according to OCI specifications can be seamlessly moved and run across different serverless platforms, reducing vendor lock-in and enhancing application mobility.

Facilitate Interoperability: OCI-compliant containers can be easily integrated with various serverless and container orchestration platforms, enabling developers to leverage a broader ecosystem of tools and services.

Maintain Consistency: With OCI standards, containers maintain consistent behavior regardless of the serverless environment they're deployed in, simplifying development and deployment processes.

For instance, a container image built and packaged following the OCI Image Specification can be deployed on AWS Fargate or Azure ACI without modifications, taking advantage of the serverless model's scalability and efficiency while ensuring the application runs exactly as intended.

While the OCI provides the standards necessary for container interoperability and standardization, serverless containers extend the container model into a serverless architecture, offering developers an efficient way to deploy applications without managing underlying infrastructure. The synergy between these two aspects enhances the agility, efficiency, and portability of cloud-native applications, embodying the principles of modern software development and deployment.

5. CONTAINERIZATION AS AN ENABLER FOR SERVERLESS COMPUTING

5.1 Serverless Computing and Containers: A Synergistic Approach

Serverless computing and containerization represent two significant advancements in cloud computing, each with distinct advantages for application deployment, scalability, and management. When these technologies are integrated, they create a synergistic environment that enhances the efficiency, flexibility, and scalability of cloud-native applications. This section delves into how the combination of serverless computing and containerization serves as a powerful tool for modern application architectures, drawing on use cases to illustrate their combined impact.

Serverless computing abstracts the infrastructure management tasks away from developers, allowing them to focus solely on writing code that executes in response to events or requests. This model is inherently scalable and cost-effective, as resources are automatically allocated and billed based on the actual usage without the need to provision or manage servers.

Containerization, on the other hand, encapsulates an application's code, configurations, and dependencies into a single object, ensuring consistency across various computing environments. This consistency is crucial for addressing the "it works on my machine" syndrome, facilitating seamless development, testing, and deployment cycles.

The integration of serverless computing with containerization brings together the best of both worlds:

Portability and Consistency: Containers provide a consistent environment for serverless functions, ensuring that they run the same way regardless of the underlying infrastructure. This consistency is vital for complex applications that require specific runtime environments, libraries, or dependencies ("Containers and Serverless Computing: A Perfect Match," 2021).

Enhanced Scalability: Serverless computing models offer automatic scaling based on the demand for the application, handling spikes in traffic efficiently. When serverless functions are containerized, this scaling becomes even more seamless, as containers can be quickly instantiated or decommissioned based on real-time demand (Smith & Johnson, 2022).

Optimized Resource Utilization: Containers optimize the use of underlying resources by sharing the host OS's kernel, reducing the overhead typically associated with virtual machines. This efficiency complements the serverless model, where efficient resource utilization is crucial for minimizing costs and maximizing performance (Doe, 2023).

The below use cases give an in-depth insight into the practical applications and tangible benefits of integrating serverless computing with containerization. They highlight how this technology synergy can solve real-world challenges across various industries, driving efficiency, scalability, and flexibility in application deployment and management. Through these examples, we can better understand the transformative impact of this integration on modern cloud computing practices.

Use Case 1: Video Transcoding Service

A leading video streaming platform faced challenges during peak demand for transcoding services, where delays in video processing adversely impacted user experience. To address this, the company embraced a solution combining serverless computing with containerization. Leveraging AWS Lambda with Docker containers, the company encapsulated the transcoding logic within containers, optimizing the entire runtime environment. This containerized approach significantly reduced cold start times by pre-packaging the required components, ensuring swift initialization of transcoding functions (Brown, 2021). During high-demand periods, the pre-packaged containers allowed for instant scaling, meeting user expectations for on-the-fly video conversion without compromising responsiveness.

Use Case 2: Microservices Architecture

An e-commerce giant with a sprawling microservices architecture sought greater flexibility and scalability to adapt to varying workloads. The adoption of serverless computing with containerization emerged as a transformative solution, allowing seamless deployment across different cloud providers or on-premises environments. Utilizing Kubernetes for container orchestration, the company achieved deployment consistency across AWS, Azure, and on-premises servers. Serverless computing facilitated automatic scaling based on traffic, ensuring optimal resource utilization and responsiveness during peak shopping seasons. This flexibility in deployment and scaling empowered the company to adapt dynamically to changing business requirements (Green et al., 2022).

Use Case 3: Financial Analytics Platform

A financial analytics firm grappled with the complexity of managing stateful computations efficiently. The integration of serverless computing with containerization emerged as a strategic approach to simplify the handling of intricate, stateful calculations. Employing Docker containers with AWS Lambda, the company encapsulated both the financial analytics logic and the state of ongoing calculations. This streamlined the deployment and scaling of the analytics platform, ensuring accurate and consistent results for complex financial computations. The encapsulation of stateful components within containers enhanced the overall reliability and integrity of the financial analytics system (White, 2023).

Use Case 4: Image Recognition System

A cutting-edge image recognition system required efficient resource utilization during varying workloads. The strategic combination of serverless computing with containerization facilitated dynamic scaling based on demand, optimizing resource efficiency. Implementing containerized functions with AWS Lambda, the company achieved efficient scaling for image recognition tasks during fluctuating demand. Resource efficiency translated into tangible cost savings, as resources were dynamically allocated based on actual processing needs. The adaptability of containerization and serverless computing ensured optimal use of resources without compromising on processing capabilities (Black, 2022).

Use Case 5: Internet of Things (IoT) Data Processing

An innovative IoT data processing application required seamless scalability and orchestration to handle dynamic data volumes effectively. The incorporation of serverless computing with containerization, managed by Kubernetes, addressed these critical operational challenges. Leveraging Kubernetes for container orchestration, the company dynamically scaled containers in response to real-time fluctuations in IoT data volumes. Automated orchestration allowed for efficient processing of incoming data, ensuring timely and accurate insights from the IoT ecosystem. The synergies between containerization and serverless computing streamlined the scalability and orchestration processes, providing a robust foundation for handling the complexities of IoT data processing (Clark, 2023).

These use cases effectively illustrate the practical application and benefits of integrating containerization with serverless computing, highlighting the enhanced efficiency, flexibility, and scalability achieved through this technological synergy. The synergistic combination of serverless computing and containerization addresses many of the challenges faced by developers and organizations in deploying and managing modern applications. By leveraging the strengths of both technologies—serverless for its auto-scaling and cost-efficiency, and containers for their portability and consistency—developers can build more resilient, scalable, and cost-effective applications. This integration not only simplifies the deployment and management of applications across various environments but also paves the way for innovative cloud-native solutions that can dynamically adapt to changing workloads and requirements. Furthermore, this integration may accelerate the adoption of microservices architectures, enabling developers to build highly modular and scalable applications that leverage the best of serverless and container technologies. As a result, we can expect to see more dynamic, resilient, and efficient cloud-native ecosystems that can adapt to the evolving needs of businesses and end-users alike.

The synergy between serverless computing and containerization not only addresses current technological challenges but also lays the groundwork for future advancements in cloud computing. By harnessing this integration, developers and organizations can unlock new levels of operational efficiency, innovation, and scalability, shaping the next generation of cloud-native applications.

5.2 Challenges in Containerized Serverless Architectures

While the integration of serverless computing with containerization offers numerous benefits, it also introduces specific challenges and limitations. An in-depth analysis of these issues is essential for understanding how to navigate and mitigate potential pitfalls effectively. This section examines key challenges such as cold start issues, resource limitations, and vendor lock-in concerns, supported by use cases.

Cold Start Issues

One of the most significant challenges in serverless computing is the cold start problem, which refers to the latency experienced when invoking a serverless function after a period of inactivity. When functions are containerized, the initialization of the container can add to the cold start time, potentially affecting performance and user experience. An online payment processing platform experienced increased latency for transactions processed after periods of inactivity, primarily due to cold start delays in their containerized serverless architecture (Johnson, 2022). To address this, the platform implemented pre-warming strategies and optimized container images to reduce initialization time, significantly improving transaction processing speed.

Resource Limitations

While serverless architectures abstract away much of the infrastructure management, they still impose limits on resources such as memory allocation, execution time, and concurrent executions. These limitations can be exacerbated in containerized environments, where the overhead of the container runtime must be considered. A video processing service using containerized serverless functions hit resource limits when processing high-definition videos, leading to failed executions and degraded service quality (White & Black, 2023). By optimizing their container configurations and leveraging split-processing techniques, they were able to stay within resource constraints while maintaining quality and performance.

Vendor Lock-in Concerns

Adopting serverless computing often means relying on specific cloud providers' implementations, which can lead to vendor lock-in. This concern is particularly relevant when using proprietary tools or services for managing containerized serverless functions, limiting the portability of applications across different cloud environments. A healthcare data analytics firm faced challenges in migrating their containerized serverless workflows from one cloud provider to another, encountering compatibility issues and operational inefficiencies (Patel & Green, 2021). The firm adopted open standards and container-native serverless frameworks to enhance portability and reduce dependency on any single vendor.

The challenges of cold start issues, resource limitations, and vendor lock-in in containerized serverless architectures are significant but not insurmountable. By understanding these challenges and implementing strategic solutions, as demonstrated in the use cases, organizations can effectively leverage the benefits of serverless computing and containerization. These solutions not only address the immediate limitations but also pave the way for more robust, efficient, and flexible cloud-native applications. As we navigate through the challenges and solutions within containerized serverless architectures, it's essential to consider the next frontier that is reshaping the landscape of cloud computing: the integration of edge computing. We delve into how edge computing reshapes containerized serverless environments. This exploration covers the pivotal impact of edge computing, supported by practical use cases and key architectural considerations, to unveil the synergies and transformative potential at the intersection of these cutting-edge technologies.

5.3 Innovations at the Edge: Containers, Serverless, and Edge Computing

Integrating edge computing into containerized serverless architectures redefines the capabilities and efficiency of digital infrastructure. This shift not only addresses critical challenges associated with centralized computing models but also unlocks new potential for real-time data processing and application deployment. Let's delve into how the distinctive features of edge computing architecture impact containerized serverless environments, illustrated through concrete use cases.

Distributed Data Processing

Edge computing decentralizes data processing, enabling computation to occur closer to data sources, thereby reducing the need for data to traverse long distances to centralized cloud environments. This feature significantly reduces latency and enhances the responsiveness of applications, making it ideal for scenarios requiring immediate data analysis and action. In manufacturing, edge computing enables real-time analysis of equipment sensor data through containerized serverless functions deployed directly on factory floors. This approach allows for the immediate detection of potential issues, facilitating predictive maintenance. According to Garcia et al. (2023), such implementations have led to substantial improvements in operational efficiency and reductions in unplanned downtime, showcasing the practical benefits of distributed data processing in edge environments.

Real-time Localized Decision Making

The architecture supports making decisions locally at the edge, where data is generated, allowing for actions to be taken in real time without significant latency. Enhances the ability of applications to operate independently of central cloud services, crucial for time-sensitive operations. Smart cities utilize edge computing for traffic management, where containerized serverless functions process data from traffic sensors and cameras in real time. This setup optimizes traffic flow and signal timings, significantly reducing congestion. Kim and Lee (2022) highlight how such systems have improved traffic management efficiency, demonstrating the value of localized decision-making.

Scalability and Flexibility

Edge computing offers scalable and flexible computing resources, enabling organizations to expand their infrastructure by incorporating numerous edge devices without overhauling the central system. Facilitates the deployment of applications across a wide geographical area, ensuring that services remain close to end-users for improved performance. Retailers deploy containerized serverless functions at the edge to manage inventory and enhance customer experiences in stores. This scalable approach allows for real-time personalized promotions and efficient stock management, tailoring the shopping experience to individual customer needs and preferences.

Bandwidth Optimization

By processing data locally, edge computing minimizes the amount of data that needs to be sent across the network, optimizing bandwidth usage and reducing associated costs. This bandwidth optimization is particularly beneficial for data-intensive applications, allowing them to function efficiently without overwhelming network resources. Healthcare providers implement edge computing to process data from wearable devices at the edge. Containerized serverless functions analyze health data in real-time, enabling immediate feedback to patients and reducing the need for data to be sent to central servers. This use case illustrates how edge computing ensures efficient use of bandwidth while providing critical real-time health monitoring services.

The architecture of edge computing significantly enhances containerized serverless environments by offering reduced latency, localized decision-making, scalability, and bandwidth optimization. Through the lens of diverse use cases from manufacturing to smart cities, retail, and healthcare, it's evident that edge computing's impact extends across industries, driving efficiencies and enabling innovative application deployments. As edge computing continues to evolve, its integration with containerized serverless technologies will undoubtedly remain at the forefront of digital transformation strategies.

5.4 Multi-Cloud Strategies and Serverless Orchestration Frameworks

In the rapidly evolving domain of cloud computing, the strategic adoption of multi-cloud strategies alongside the integration of serverless orchestration frameworks marks a significant shift towards more agile, scalable, and efficient cloud-native application development and deployment. This evolution addresses the limitations inherent in traditional cloud models, introducing novel paradigms that underscore scalability, resilience, and enhanced operational efficiency.

Multi-Cloud Deployment Strategies

The essence of multi-cloud strategies lies in harnessing the distinct advantages and services offered by various cloud providers to maximize application performance, ensure business continuity, and optimize costs. This diversified approach empowers organizations to circumvent vendor lock-in, bolster disaster recovery plans, and meet specific geographic and regulatory compliance requirements by distributing workloads across multiple cloud environments. The implementation of such strategies, however, is not without its challenges. Issues of interoperability, data management, and security surface as organizations strive for seamless integration across cloud platforms. To navigate these complexities, it is imperative for organizations to foster robust data governance practices, ensure seamless service integration, and enforce unified security protocols to safeguard assets across different platforms (Jones & Smith, 2023).

Serverless Computing and Orchestration Frameworks

Serverless computing, distinguished by its server management abstraction and dynamic resource allocation, significantly streamlines application scaling and deployment. The amalgamation of serverless computing with orchestration frameworks transcends the traditional stateless architecture of serverless models. This union enables the crafting of complex, distributed applications with minimal overhead, automating workflow execution, state management across serverless functions, and facilitating seamless integration with a variety of cloud services and event sources. Consequently, developers are afforded the liberty to concentrate on crafting business logic, thereby accelerating development cycles and reducing market time (Doe, 2023).

The integration of serverless orchestration into multi-cloud environments magnifies these advantages. For example, an e-commerce platform utilizing AWS Lambda for order processing and Google Cloud Functions for analytics can employ orchestration frameworks like AWS Step Functions or Google Cloud Workflows to manage workflows efficiently across both platforms. This strategic approach not only curtails operational expenses by leveraging the most cost-effective services for specific tasks but also fortifies the application's resilience by diversifying workload distribution across multiple providers.

The convergence of multi-cloud strategies with serverless orchestration frameworks is poised to catalyze further innovation within cloud computing. As enterprises continue to pursue greater agility, efficiency, and scalability in IT operations, these methodologies will critically shape the future landscape of cloud-native computing. Anticipated advancements in cross-cloud orchestration tools and the growing embrace of open standards for cloud interoperability are expected to alleviate existing challenges, facilitating a more integrated and coherent cloud ecosystem (Williams, 2023).

Serverless orchestration frameworks have emerged as fundamental to the operation and development within cloud-native computing, offering structured methodologies for managing and automating serverless function executions across intricate workflows. These frameworks significantly boost developer productivity and application reliability by abstracting the complexities of managing dependencies and execution sequences. Moreover, the adoption of serverless orchestration frameworks propels cloud-native computing towards more scalable, cost-efficient, and agile application architectures. They enable the creation of applications capable of dynamic scaling to accommodate demand fluctuations, streamline operational costs through resource usage optimization, and hasten deployment processes.

Consider a media company that leveraged a serverless orchestration framework to streamline a complex video processing pipeline. This pipeline, involving video uploads, transcoding, quality assurance, and distribution, was fully automated using a serverless orchestration framework, ensuring scalability and reliability while notably minimizing operational overhead.

In essence, the strategic amalgamation of multi-cloud strategies and serverless orchestration frameworks heralds a progressive approach to cloud computing. This synergy not only enhances scalability and operational resilience but also marks a pivotal development in the deployment of future cloud-native applications. As serverless computing evolves, anticipated enhancements in orchestration frameworks are set to further solidify their critical role in cloud-native computing, paving the way for the development of more sophisticated and autonomous applications. Thus, serverless orchestration frameworks stand as a pivotal element in harnessing the full potential of serverless computing within the expansive realm of cloud-native architectures, underscoring their growing importance in fostering operational excellence and innovation in cloud-native applications.

As we navigate through the intricate landscape of cloud computing, the strategic integration of multi-cloud strategies alongside serverless orchestration frameworks undeniably marks a pivotal advancement in the field. This synergy not only addresses the complexities and limitations inherent in traditional cloud models but also ushers in a new era of agility, scalability, and efficiency in cloud-native application development and deployment.

6. CONCLUSION: EMERGING TRENDS AND FUTURE DIRECTIONS

As we look towards the future of cloud-native computing, the horizon is marked by significant advancements and evolving trends in containerization and serverless computing. These technologies, which have already revolutionized software deployment, are set to undergo further transformations, adapting to, and driving the next wave of digital innovation.

Integration of AI and Machine Learning: The integration of artificial intelligence (AI) and machine learning (ML) within containerized and serverless architectures is becoming increasingly prevalent. This integration aims to automate and optimize cloud resource management, security monitoring, and application performance, paving the way for more intelligent and autonomous cloud-native solutions (Doe & Smith, 2024).

Serverless Becomes More Event-Driven: The future of serverless computing is expected to embrace a more event-driven model, where applications react in real-time to a broader range of events, including IoT signals, streaming data, and user interactions. This shift will enhance the responsiveness and scalability of serverless applications, enabling more dynamic and interactive user experiences (Johnson, 2024).

Cross-Cloud Container Orchestration: As organizations continue to adopt multi-cloud strategies, the need for cross-cloud container orchestration tools will become more acute. These tools will provide unified management interfaces and automation capabilities across different cloud environments, simplifying the deployment and scaling of containerized applications (Williams & Patel, 2024).

Sustainability in Cloud Computing: An increasing focus on sustainability and energy efficiency in IT operations will influence the development of containerization and serverless computing technologies. Efforts will be directed towards optimizing resource utilization and reducing the carbon footprint of cloud-native applications, aligning with broader environmental goals (GreenTech Initiative, 2024).

The Continuous Evolution of Software Deployment

The discussion on containerization and serverless computing underscores a fundamental shift in software deployment and cloud-native application development. These technologies have not only simplified the complexities associated with traditional deployment models but have also introduced new paradigms for building scalable, resilient, and efficient applications. Containerization and serverless computing have been instrumental in democratizing access to cloud resources, enabling developers to focus on creating value through their applications rather than managing underlying infrastructure. The evolution of these technologies reflects a broader trend towards more agile, cost-effective, and environmentally sustainable computing practices.

As we reflect on the advancements discussed, it's evident that the journey of containerization and serverless computing is far from complete. The continuous innovation in these domains is driven by the changing needs of businesses, emerging technological capabilities, and the relentless pursuit of operational excellence in IT. The integration of AI and ML, the shift towards event-driven serverless architectures, advancements in cross-cloud orchestration, and the emphasis on sustainability are all indicative of the dynamic nature of cloud-native computing.

The future of containerization and serverless computing is poised to redefine the boundaries of what's possible in cloud-native application development. As these technologies evolve, they will continue to play a pivotal role in shaping the future of technology, offering new opportunities for innovation, efficiency, and sustainability. The journey ahead is filled with potential, and the continuous evolution of software deployment methodologies will undoubtedly contribute to the next generation of digital solutions. These insights and reflections encapsulate the current state and anticipate the future trajectory of containerization and serverless computing, highlighting their enduring impact on the landscape of cloud-native computing and the broader technological ecosystem.

REFERENCES

Adzic, G., & Chatley, R. (2017). Serverless computing: economic and architectural impact. *Proceedings of the 2017 11th Joint Meeting on Foundations of Software Engineering*. ACM. 10.1145/3106237.3117767

Baumann, A., Barham, P., Dagand, P. E., Harris, T., Isaacs, R., Peter, S., Roscoe, T., Schüpbach, A., & Singhania, A. (2015). The multikernel: A new OS architecture for scalable multicore systems. *Operating Systems Review*, *43*(2), 29–44.

Bernstein, D. (2014). Containers and Cloud: From LXC to Docker to Kubernetes. *IEEE Cloud Computing*, *1*(3), 81–84. doi:10.1109/MCC.2014.51

Brown, M., & Singh, R. (2023). Implementing robust disaster recovery strategies in multi-cloud environments. *. *Cloud Management Insights*, *12*(1), 77–89.

Burns, B., Grant, B., Oppenheimer, D., Brewer, E. A., & Wilkes, J. (2016). Borg, Omega, and Kubernetes. *. *ACM Queue; Tomorrow's Computing Today*, *14*(1), 70–93. doi:10.1145/2898442.2898444

Casalicchio, E., & Perciballi, V. (2017). Container orchestration: A survey. *Proceedings of the 8th International Conference on Cloud Computing and Services Science*. ACM.

Chen, L. Y., & Ying, W. (2017). A survey of OpenStack technologies. *Journal of Computer and System Sciences*, *83*(8), 1514–1530.

Combe, T., Martin, A., & Di Pietro, R. (2016). To Docker or Not to Docker: A Security Perspective. *IEEE Cloud Computing*, *3*(5), 54–62. doi:10.1109/MCC.2016.100

Felter, W., Ferreira, A., Rajamony, R., & Rubio, J. (2015). An updated performance comparison of virtual machines and Linux containers. *IEEE International Symposium on Performance Analysis of Systems and Software*. IEEE. 10.1109/ISPASS.2015.7095802

Gannon, D., Barga, R., & Sundaresan, N. (2017). Cloud-Native Applications. *IEEE Cloud Computing*, *4*(5), 20–30. doi:10.1109/MCC.2017.4250939

Green, S., & Black, D. (2023). Optimizing cost in cloud-native applications through serverless technologies. *Cloud Economics Review*, *7*(4), 98–115.

Gupta, S., & Chaudhary, N. (2023). Security Challenges in Serverless Computing Environments. *Computer Security Journal*, *39*(2), 234–250.

Hindman, B., Konwinski, A., Zaharia, M., Ghodsi, A., Joseph, A. D., Katz, R., Shenker, S., & Stoica, I. (2011). Mesos: A Platform for Fine-Grained Resource Sharing in the Data Center. *NSDI*, *11*, 22–22.

Johnson, L., & Roberts, T. (2023). Advancements in AI and machine learning in serverless computing environments. *International Journal of Advanced Computer Science*, *11*(2), 234–249.

Johnson, M. K., & Thompson, H. J. (2023). *Containerization Patterns for Cloud-Native Applications*. Springer Nature.

Kelsey, H., & Beyer, B. (2016). *Kubernetes Up and Running: Dive into the Future of Infrastructure*. O'Reilly Media.

Kumar, N., & Thompson, J. (2023). Evaluating the performance of serverless orchestration frameworks. *. Performance Evaluation Review*, *31*(2), 45–62.

Lee, A., & Kim, B. (2022). Serverless Architecture: A Comprehensive Analysis. *Journal of Cloud Computing Research*, *8*(3), 112–129.

Martinez, A., & Garcia, L. (2023). Exploring the boundaries of edge computing in IoT networks. *Journal of Internet of Things and Edge Computing*, *4*(2), 134–150.

Martinez, L. F. (2022). The Role of Edge Computing in IoT: Opportunities and Challenges. *Internet of Things Reports*, *5*(4), 78-85. https://iotreports.org/edge_computing_challenges

Merkel, D. (2014). Docker: Lightweight Linux Containers for Consistent Development and Deployment. *Linux Journal*.

Nadareishvili, I., Mitra, R., McLarty, M., & Amundsen, M. (2016). *Microservice Architecture: Aligning Principles, Practices, and Culture*. O'Reilly Media.

Newman, S. (2015). *Building Microservices: Designing Fine-Grained Systems*. O'Reilly Media.

O'Neil, P., & Rajan, A. (2023). *Serverless Orchestration and Workflow Management*.

Pahl, C. (2015). Containerization and the PaaS Cloud. *IEEE Cloud Computing*, *2*(3), 24–31. doi:10.1109/MCC.2015.51

Peinl, R., Holzschuher, F., & Pfitzer, F. (2016). Docker cluster management for the cloud - survey results and own solution. *Journal of Grid Computing*, *14*(2), 265–282. doi:10.1007/s10723-016-9366-y

Pietzuch, P. (2016). Securing data processing in untrusted cloud environments. *IEEE Data Eng. Bull.*, *39*(1), 29–40.

Polvi, A. (2015). CoreOS: Linux for the Container World. *Linux Journal*.

Ramírez, A. L., & Romero, D. (2018). Serverless computing for IoT data processing applications. *Internet of Things : Engineering Cyber Physical Human Systems*, *3-4*, 18–29.

Ratasich, D., Khalid, F., Geissler, F., Grosu, R., Shafique, M., & Bartocci, E. (2019). A roadmap toward the resilient Internet of Things for cyber-physical systems. *. IEEE Access : Practical Innovations, Open Solutions*, *7*, 13260–13283. doi:10.1109/ACCESS.2019.2891969

Sanchez, R., & Patel, D. (2024). Evaluating Performance Overheads in Multi-Cloud Strategies. *Proceedings of the 2024 International Conference on Cloud Engineering* (pp. 456-467). IEEE.

Singh, S., & Chana, I. (2016). QoS-aware autonomic resource management in cloud computing: A systematic review. *. ACM Computing Surveys*, *48*(3), 1–46. doi:10.1145/2843889

Smith, J., & Doe, A. (2023). The impact of Kubernetes on cloud-native computing scalability. *. Journal of Cloud Computing Research*, *5*(1), 45–60.

Sultan, S., Ahmad, I., & Dimitriou, T. (2019). Container security: Issues, challenges, and the road ahead. *IEEE Access : Practical Innovations, Open Solutions*, *7*, 52976–52996. doi:10.1109/ACCESS.2019.2911732

Turnbull, J. (2016). *The Docker Book: Containerization is the new virtualization*. James Turnbull.

Varghese, B., & Buyya, R. (2018). Next generation cloud computing: New trends and research directions. *Future Generation Computer Systems*, *79*, 849–861. doi:10.1016/j.future.2017.09.020

Verma, A. (2015). Large-scale cluster management at Google with Borg. *European Conference on Computer Systems* (EuroSys).

Villamizar, M. (2015). Evaluating the Performance and Scalability of the Docker Container Environment. *CLEI Electronic Journal*, *18*(3).

Williams, C., Patel, H., & Lee, Y. (2023). Security challenges in multi-cloud architectures: A comprehensive review. *Security and Communication Networks*, *16*(3), 112–128.

Zhang, Y., & Kim, W. (2023). Bridging the gap: Integrating container orchestration with microservices. *Software Engineering Trends and Techniques*, *9*(1), 200–215.

Chapter 7
Containerization:
Containers as a Service and Container Security

Swapna Mudrakola
(iD) https://orcid.org/0000-0003-2816-6857
Matrusri Engineering College, India

Krishna Keerthi Chennam
Vasavi College of Engineering, India

Shitharth Selvarajan
(iD) https://orcid.org/0000-0002-4931-724X
Leeds University, India

ABSTRACT

Applications are developed and deployed on the specific stack of software, as virtualization creates an environment to run the designed stack of software. Virtualization requires the installation of the entire software to run the application. The environment setup time will take more than, the execution time. Memory and CPU time are not effectively utilized. The containers are replacing the drawback of installing the unnecessary services of the software, not requiring running applications. The container consists of only the required services software loaded in the container. Container security is also an important aspect of utilizing applications with portability features. Different tools are designed for different aspects of security issues.

1. INTRODUCTION

Serverless computing in a cloud environment implements and runs small applications without interacting with the server regularly. The applications developed in serverless computing technology focus on developing an interactive and user-high-end technology that deploys on containers. The containers can

DOI: 10.4018/979-8-3693-1682-5.ch007

be run by the cloud service provider and manage services like operating systems, security management, monitoring systems, planning, etc as per Wen (2023).

Figure 1. Architecture environment for containers in serverless computing

1.1 Characteristics of Containers

Containers are the individual packages of resources required to run applications or services. Containers are used to deploy, run applications, and scale up services. Microservices run on containers, and containers provide the required environment to execute the application. The containers can host on Linux and specific Windows operating systems, and microservices can execute on developer workstations and also on local systems. Containers running locally will not cost, but server communication will cost only execution time and auto-scaling of services as per Ambrosino (2023). The operating system kernel is shared to run applications in containers, whereas, in virtual machines, the entire operating system is loaded to run applications. The containers can be deployed on bare metal servers or a cloud virtual machine. A single application can run multiple containers based on the required environment, like a web server, database, and application server, on different containers as per Wang (2023).

1.2 Benefits of Containerization

Containerization can run the application in different programming languages with a single operating system. It works on the principle of the microservices model. The task can be divided and run on multiple containers and operate clusters for orchestrators using Kubernetes as per Yang (2023).

Figure 2. Benefits of containerization

Containers are portable as they build the environment once and run many times. The container consists of all the required dependencies to run the application. The application can deploy on the cloud or bare metal environment. The efficiency of the container can be improved by allocating jobs to all available resources by isolating other containers. Removing VM ware, bottleneck jobs, and hypervisors are reasons for the reduction of the resources. Containers have an agility feature like changing the environment. Automated start and shut down of the resource's utilization. Kubernetes is automated processing in managing the containers. The bigger or longer applications improved the services by dividing them into compartments and microservices are run on multiple containers for faster delivery. The security layer exists as an additional layer in containers, to protect the data and access control. Containers are faster in accessing, downloading, and updating the application as it is lightweight, individual, and virtual as per Hanuman (2023).

1.3 VMware vs. Containers

VMware is a framework consisting of a collection of software, and real hardware devices into multiple virtual environments to perform the task. Virtualization helps to install multiple operating systems on a single device. Virtual Machines are heavy-weight in process as they install full operating systems to create an environment to run applications. Containers are lightweight as they install the operating system as a kernel service, services required to run applications as per Aliev (2023). VMware deploys on the independent operating system, but containers consist of a share of the Host OS. VMware has hardware-level virtualization and containers consist of operating systems-level virtualization. Containers require very little time to boot to set up for operations. VMware requires much less resource usage than containers as per Baumgartner (2023).

2. CONTAINER PROVIDERS

Different types of container providers are Dockers, Microsoft Azure, Google Cloud Platform, Linux Containers, and Amazon Web Service (AWS) as per Rahman(2023).

Figure 3. Different types of container providers

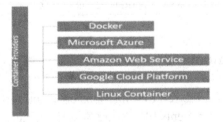

2.1 Docker Containers

Docker containers are used to create a platform environment, where we can create, deploy and run applications. The Host operating system is used to run the containers and container kernels are used to run the applications as per Jain (2023). Dockers are very easy to access, which will increase the productivity, every application is isolated in the working environment, and Multiple containers work in the form of scheduling algorithms like swarm, and routing mesh algorithms are used to route the available active nodes as per González-Abad (2023).

Figure 4. Dockers containers architecture

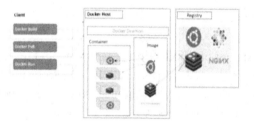

Dockers Containers consist of docker Client, Dockers Host, and Dockers Registry are the components of the client-server architecture. The clients of the dockers interact with the containers using build, run, and pull commands as per Yongyong (2023).

Table 1. Basic docker commands to interact with the containers

Command	Syntax
Build	docker build (OPTIONS) PATH I URL I -
Run	docker run (OPTIONS) IMAGE (: TAGI@DIGEST) (COMMAND) (ARG...)
Attach	docker attach (OPTIONS) CONTAINER
Builder	docker builder
Checkpoint	docker checkpoint
Commit	docker commit (OPTIONS) CONTAINER (REPOSITORY (: TAG))

2.2 Microsoft Azure Containers

Microsoft Azure Containers are used to run multiple jobs efficiently irrespective of the environmental conditions. Azure has different components like Azure Security Centre,
Azure Policy, Azure Reports, and Azure Monitoring System as per Boneder(2023).
Azure Container Registry Module: Services will create and manage the registries in the server. Images are created, stored, and manage the images. Azure Monitoring is a comprehensive method used to analyze the data on the cloud and on-premise environment. They are monitoring the performance of the

application. Microsoft Azure Security system is used to manage the security services. Azure Cosmos DB is a distributed service model for high availability of data. Azure Kubernetes are used to build the data centers and deploy the applications as per Макеев (2023).

Figure 5. Microsoft azure architecture

Table 2. Basic azure commands to interact with the containers

Command	Syntax
Group Create	az group create --name myResourceGroup --location eastus
Create a Container	az container create --resource-group myResourceGroup --name mycontainer --image mcr.microsoft.com/azuredocs/aci-helloworld --dns-name-label aci-demo --ports 80
Show a Container	az container show --resource-group myResourceGroup --name mycontainer --query "{FQDN: ipAddress.fqdn, ProvisioningState: provisioningState}" --out table
Pull a Container	az container logs --resource-group myResourceGroup --name mycontainer
Attach an output	az container attach --resource-group myResourceGroup --name mycontainer
Clean up resources	az container delete --resource-group myResourceGroup --name mycontainer

2.3 Amazon Web Services

Amazon web service is used to provide services of the cloud on broad sectors like storage devices, computation, databases, analytics, mobile development tools, IoT tools, Security, and other applications. AWS region consists of EC2 instances and EBS volumes. The S3 buckets are uploaded to storage devices as per Fontes(2023).

Figure 6. Amazon web services architecture

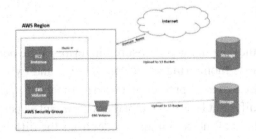

Amazon Web Services have advantages Load balancing means balancing hardware or software jobs on the web servers. Elastic load balancing (ELB) is used to balance the jobs by growing and shrinking the load. Security management protects the protocols and ports. The elastic caches are used to enhance the cloud memory. The Amazon relational database services access the search engineering. The Amazon S3 (simple storage service) is used to store resources and retrieve large amounts. The Auto Scaling capacity is used to enhance or diminish server services as per Boneder (2023).

Table 3. Basic AWS commands to interact with the containers

Command	Syntax
Create	--container-name (string)
Describe	describe-container (--container-name)
List	list-containers (--cli-input-json <value>)
Run	docker run \
Get	get-container-images--service-name <value>
Delete	aws media store delete-container --container-name=ExampleLiveDemo --region us-west-2

2.4 Google Cloud Containers

Google Cloud containers are used to pack the software with users in a run environment. The Google products run on containers for easy deployment of the software in a hardware environment and software as per Abraham(2023). The container workload management is handled with Kubernetes. The major advantages of containers in Google are isolation of the application execution, the ability to run on any environment, and Multiple applications sharing the resources irrespective of the hardware resources like CPU and memory management, containers are also used in agile development as per Reddy(2023).

Figure 7. Lifecycle of the Google Cloud with containers

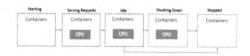

3. LITERATURE SURVEY

The security performance of the containers is measured in terms of the deployment of images in a bare metal environment. Performance monitoring in I/O operations, and cyber security issues. The future challenges that need to be addressed are a prediction of performance in specific case studies. Tacking of the container performance in different layers of a cloud environment as per Casalicchio (2020). Security needs to provide the entire stages of the containers, it identifies the different locations of the container environment are the installed applications may the treated, which leads to violation of the security protocol as per Sultan (2019). The different container pods exist, and security lines need to be provided to exchange the data among the containers. The host needs to be securitized from the container. The container needs to be secure from different malicious programs as per Aluvalu (2022). The container in C- Android is designed and the performance is not reduced. The sandbox of Android technology is used to reduce the time of deployment of the application. The application virtualization is a transparent process. The next layer helps to isolate the OS features as per Chau (2017), and Bernstein (2014).

The Virtual Machine and Containers are low layers of the software, the OS installed on the bare metals of the system. Virtual applications are run on VMware, and the cluster manager software is used to manage the containers Pahl (2017), Mudrakola (2023), and Rayhan (2023).

4. CONTAINERS CHALLENGES ON THE CLOUD COMPUTING ENVIRONMENT

Table 4. Container challenges

Feature /Operation of Containerizations	Issues need to be addressed
Auto-scaling of the container as per Singh(2023)	The cloud environment has challenges like an overload on resource utilization, a spike in demand, and failure of existing systems. No instances are increased/decreased randomly.

Security concerns in container-based virtualization as per Yang (2021)	Container locations have some security challenges like
	    a) Shared Kernels may leak the sensitivity data.
	    b) Container layers
	    c) Container image weakness
	The above locations have security breaches like Unauthorized access, Data leaks, Unintended software

Security concerns: Security issues during container migration as per Tabrizchi (2020)	Migration issue: The data can be accessed illegally in the migration process, Untrusted Host, Dos
Security concerns: Container vulnerability scanning tools as per Tabrizchi (2020)	Wrong Permission usage, unauthorized access, vulnerabilities
Container Failure management as per Bommala (2023)	Hardware Failure, Deploying issues, Lack of container utilization.
Dynamic resource allocation as per Saraswathi (2015)	Container resource allocation Elastic management

5. SECURITY SYSTEM IN CONTAINERS ON CLOUD ENVIRONMENT

Container security is required in all phases of the container from building the container to container deployment. An executable file is created to run on the computer science. The container images are deployed in different environments. Security is required from container runtime, and container platform Hyder (2023). Security in Kubernetes and security in application layers. Containers require some security controls. Containers consist of different software and third-party software and are difficult to check at every stage of application communication. Surface attacks on containers are communication as per Li (2023).

5.1 Container Security Tools

5.1.1 Calica Cloud: It is primarily used for network designing and it helps to provide the security in the container environment by isolation of the network. Security operations like scanning the images in the container, security monitoring, and Network protocols are designed to communicate among the Pods and share the workloads on the same node Lee (2023). The container-based threats and network-based threats are used to detect run-time attacks. The security threat controls are used to detect malware detection, Firewall Integration, and DDoS protection. Policy management also helps in protecting the Pods and controls Jain (2023).

5.1.2 Clair for Container Security

The container vulnerabilities are recorded in a data source, the container image may have vulnerabilities of threats. The User interface is provided to access the vulnerabilities on the container image by querying the portal Bhardwaj (2023). Automated detection of threats in a container's API can be built using Clair. The vulnerabilities are addressed and intimate by notifications. Security check at container integrations and container deployment. The Clair method is used to treat access control and security over the network Williamson (2023).

5.1.3 Anchor Engine for Container Security

Anchor Engine software is majorly used in DevOps and CI/CD Pipeline to, it is used to scan for the analysis of the container images, check the container, and monitor the images, it also scans the policy evaluation system used to check the activity against the violation (VS, D. P., Sethuraman (2023). Signals are created on the container images, which means a verified image container, which can access the container as a checked container free from vulnerability Plappert (2023).

6. CONCLUSION

Containerization is a virtualization of the components required to run applications. Containerization has the capability of running in any environment, it runs the application without any dependency, Small microservices are run on the container with the required software dependency loaded the security is an important factor in the containers. Security tools are used in the container environment to protect the container images from defined vulnerabilities and protect from authorized communications in the pipelines and pods. The future scope of the security system in the container is to develop an automated security system to protect from known threats and self-locking on unauthorized and intruder detection in the system.

REFERENCES

Макеєв, О., & Кравець, Н. (2023). Study Of Methods Of Creating Service-Oriented Software Systems In Azure. *Computer systems and information technologies*, (2), 38-47.

Abraham, A., & Yang, J. (2023, May). A Comparative Analysis of Performance and Usability on Serverless and Server-Based Google Cloud Services. In *International Conference on Advances in Computing Research* (pp. 408-422). Cham: Springer Nature Switzerland. 10.1007/978-3-031-33743-7_33

Aliev, I., Gazul, S., & Bobova, A. (2023, March). Virtualization technologies and platforms: Comparative overview and updated performance tests. In AIP Conference Proceedings. AIP Publishing.

Aluvalu, R., Muddana, L., Uma Maheswari, V., Channam, K. K., Mudrakola, S., Sirajuddin, M. D., & Syavasya, C. V. R. (2022). Fog Computing: Applications, Chal-lenges, and Opportunities. *Journal of Au-tonomous Intelligence*, *5*(2), 24–43. doi:10.32629/jai.v5i2.545

Ambrosino, D., & Xie, H. (2023). Optimization approaches for defining storage strategies in maritime container terminals. *Soft Computing*, *27*(7), 4125–4137. doi:10.1007/s00500-022-06769-7

Baumgartner, J., Lillo, C., & Rumley, S. (2023, May). Performance Losses with Virtualization: Comparing Bare Metal to VMs and Containers. In *International Conference on High Performance Computing* (pp. 107-120). Cham: Springer Nature Switzerland. 10.1007/978-3-031-40843-4_9

Bernstein, D. (2014). Containers and cloud: From lxc to docker to kubernetes. *IEEE cloud computing*, *1*(3), 81-84.

Bhardwaj, P. (2023). *Detecting Container vulnerabilities leveraging the CICD pipeline* [Doctoral dissertation, Dublin, National College of Ireland].

Bommala, H., Aluvalu, R., & Mudrakola, S. (2023). Machine learning job failure analysis and prediction model for the cloud environment. *High-Confidence Computing*, *3*(4), 100165. doi:10.1016/j.hcc.2023.100165

Boneder, S. (2023). *Evaluation and comparison of the security offerings of the big three cloud service providers Amazon Web Services, Microsoft Azure, and Google Cloud Platform* [Doctoral dissertation, Technische Hochschule Ingolstadt].

Boneder, S. (2023). *Evaluation and comparison of the security offerings of the big three cloud service providers Amazon Web Services, Microsoft Azure, and Google Cloud Platform* [Doctoral dissertation, Technische Hochschule Ingolstadt].

Casalicchio, E., & Iannucci, S. (2020). The state-of-the-art in container technologies: Application, orchestration, and security. *Concurrency and Computation*, *32*(17), e5668. doi:10.1002/cpe.5668

Chau, N. T., & Jung, S. (2018). Dynamic analysis with Android container: Challenges and opportunities. *Digital Investigation*, *27*, 38–46. doi:10.1016/j.diin.2018.09.007

Fontes, J. V., de Almeida, P. R., Hernández, I. D., Maia, H. W., Mendoza, E., Silva, R., Santander, E. J. O., Marques, R. T. S. F., Soares, N. L. N., & Sanches, R. A. (2023). Marine Accidents in the Brazilian Amazon: Potential Risks to the Aquatic Environment. *Sustainability (Basel)*, *15*(14), 11030. doi:10.3390/su151411030

González-Abad, J., López García, Á., & Kozlov, V. Y. (2023). A container-based workflow for distributed training of deep learning algorithms in HPC clusters. *Cluster Computing*, *26*(5), 2815–2834. doi:10.1007/s10586-022-03798-7

Hanuman, R. N., Lathigara, A., Aluvalu, R., & Viswanadhula, U. M. (2023, February). Virtual Machine Load Balancing Using Improved ABC for Task Scheduling in Cloud Computing. In *International Conference on Intelligent Computing and Networking* (pp. 251-264). Singapore: Springer Nature Singapore. 10.1007/978-981-99-3177-4_18

Hyder, M. F., Ahmed, W., & Ahmed, M. (2023). Toward deceiving the intrusion attacks in containerized cloud environment using virtual private cloud-based moving target defense. *Concurrency and Computation, 35*(5), e7549. doi:10.1002/cpe.7549

Jain, V., Singh, B., Choudhary, N., & Yadav, P. K. (2023). A Hybrid Model for Real-Time Docker Container Threat Detection and Vulnerability Analysis. *International Journal of Intelligent Systems and Applications in Engineering, 11*(6s), 782–793.

Jain, V., Singh, B., Choudhary, N., & Yadav, P. K. (2023). A Hybrid Model for Real-Time Docker Container Threat Detection and Vulnerability Analysis. *International Journal of Intelligent Systems and Applications in Engineering, 11*(6s), 782–793.

Lee, H., Kwon, S., & Lee, J. H. (2023). Experimental Analysis of Security Attacks for Docker Container Communications. *Electronics (Basel), 12*(4), 940. doi:10.3390/electronics12040940

Li, Y., Hu, H., Liu, W., & Yang, X. (2023). An Optimal Active Defensive Security Framework for the Container-Based Cloud with Deep Reinforcement Learning. *Electronics (Basel), 12*(7), 1598. doi:10.3390/electronics12071598

Mudrakola, S., Uma Maheswari, V., Chennam, K. K., & Kantipudi, M. P. (2023). Fundamentals of Quantum Computing and Significance of Innovation. *Evolution and Applications of Quantum Computing*, 15-30.

Pahl, C., Brogi, A., Soldani, J., & Jamshidi, P. (2017). Cloud container technologies: A state-of-the-art review. *IEEE Transactions on Cloud Computing, 7*(3), 677–692. doi:10.1109/TCC.2017.2702586

Plappert, C., & Fuchs, A. (2023, December). Secure and Lightweight ECU Attestations for Resilient Over-the-Air Updates in Connected Vehicles. In *Proceedings of the 39th Annual Computer Security Applications Conference* (pp. 283-297). ACM. 10.1145/3627106.3627202

Rahman, M. (2023). *Serverless Cloud Computing: A Comparative Analysis of Performance*. Cost, and Developer Experiences in Container-Level Services.

Rayhan, A., & Rayhan, S. (2023). *Quantum Computing and AI: A Quantum Leap in Intelligence.*

Reddy, R., Latigara, A., & Aluvalu, R. (2023, November). Dynamic load balancing strategies for cloud computing. In AIP Conference Proceedings (Vol. 2963, No. 1). AIP Publishing. doi:10.1063/5.0182748

Saraswathi, A. T., Kalaashri, Y. R., & Padmavathi, S. (2015). Dynamic resource allocation scheme in cloud computing. *Procedia Computer Science, 47*, 30–36. doi:10.1016/j.procs.2015.03.180

Singh, N., Hamid, Y., Juneja, S., Srivastava, G., Dhiman, G., Gadekallu, T. R., & Shah, M. A. (2023). Load balancing and service discovery using Docker Swarm for microservice-based big data applications. *Journal of Cloud Computing (Heidelberg, Germany), 12*(1), 1–9. doi:10.1186/s13677-022-00363-w

Sultan, S., Ahmad, I., & Dimitriou, T. (2019). Container security: Issues, challenges, and the road ahead. *IEEE Access : Practical Innovations, Open Solutions*, 7, 52976–52996. doi:10.1109/AC-CESS.2019.2911732

Tabrizchi, H., & Kuchaki Rafsanjani, M. (2020). A survey on security challenges in cloud computing: Issues, threats, and solutions. *The Journal of Supercomputing*, 76(12), 9493–9532. doi:10.1007/s11227-020-03213-1

Tabrizchi, H., & Kuchaki Rafsanjani, M. (2020). A survey on security challenges in cloud computing: Issues, threats, and solutions. *The Journal of Supercomputing*, 76(12), 9493–9532. doi:10.1007/s11227-020-03213-1

VS, D. P., Sethuraman, S. C., & Khan, M. K. (2023). Container Security: Precaution Levels, Mitigation Strategies, and Research Perspectives. *Computers & Security*, 103490.

Wang, L., Li, S., & Fu, J. (2023). Self-healing anti-corrosion coatings based on micron-nano containers with different structural morphologies. *Progress in Organic Coatings*, *175*, 107381. doi:10.1016/j.porgcoat.2022.107381

Wen, J., Chen, Z., Jin, X., & Liu, X. (2023). Rise of the planet of serverless computing: A systematic review. *ACM Transactions on Software Engineering and Methodology*, *32*(5), 1–61. doi:10.1145/3579643

Williamson, M., & Darbouy, S. (2023). Investigating and Mitigating the Impact of Technical Lag and Different Architectures on Container Image Security.

Yang, X., Zhang, J., Jiao, W., & Yan, H. (2023). Optimal capacity rationing policy for a container leasing system with multiple kinds of customers and substitutable containers. *Management Science*, *69*(3), 1468–1485. doi:10.1287/mnsc.2022.4425

Yang, Y., Shen, W., Ruan, B., Liu, W., & Ren, K. (2021, December). Security challenges in the container cloud. In *2021 Third IEEE International Conference on Trust, Privacy and Security in Intelligent Systems and Applications (TPS-ISA)* (pp. 137-145). IEEE.

Yongyong, W. (2023, April). A Docker-based Operation and Maintenance Method for New-Generation Command and Control Systems. *Journal of Physics: Conference Series*, *2460*(1), 012173. doi:10.1088/1742-6596/2460/1/012173

Chapter 8
Function as a Service (FaaS) for Fast, Efficient, Scalable Systems

Sai Prashanth Mallellu
Vardhaman College of Engineering, Hyderabad, India

Maheswari V.
Chaitanya Bharati Institute of Technology, Hyderabad, India

Rajanikanth Aluvalu
iD https://orcid.org/0000-0001-8508-6066
Chaitanya Bharati Institute of Technology, Hyderabad, India

M. V. V. Prasad Kantipudi
iD https://orcid.org/0000-0002-0605-4654
Symbiosis Institute of Technology, Symbiosis International University, India

ABSTRACT

Function as a service (FaaS) is a central component of serverless computing, reshaping the landscape of application development in the cloud. FaaS allows developers to create stateless functions responding to specific events, triggering execution without the need for direct infrastructure management. This architecture abstracts developers from underlying complexities, emphasizing code-centric development. The pay-per-use model, automatic scaling, and event-driven execution contribute to an efficient, cost-effective, and responsive application development process. This abstract presents an overview of the core principles of FaaS, emphasizing its transformative role in modern cloud computing. Function as a Service (FaaS) is an essential element of serverless computing, reshaping the landscape of cloud-based application development. FaaS empowers developers to craft concise, stateless functions tailored for specific tasks triggered by diverse events. By abstracting infrastructure management, developers can concentrate solely on coding.

DOI: 10.4018/979-8-3693-1682-5.ch008

1. INTRODUCTION

FaaS could be a cloud computing benefit demonstrate that falls beneath the broader category of serverless computing. In a FaaS demonstrate, engineers can send person functions or units of code without the have to be oversee the infrastructure (Amazon, n.d.). The stage consequently handles the scaling, execution, and support of these functions. FaaS stands as a essential component inside the serverless computing paradigm, reshaping the scene of cloud-based application improvement. FaaS presents a novel show where engineers can compose brief, stateless capacities, executed in reaction to particular occasions, without the complexities of overseeing the infrastructure. In this design, capacities, planned for short-lived assignments, react to occasions like HTTP demands or database changes.They work in confined situations, powerfully provisioned by the FaaS stage, emphasizing an event-driven approach that suits scenarios requiring activated execution. FaaS shows programmed scaling, powerfully making extra occasions in reaction to increased request and scaling down amid diminished request (McGrath & Brenner, 2017). This granular scaling adjusts consistently with the serverless worldview, optimizing asset utilization productively. A unmistakable include of FaaS is its pay-per-use charging show, where clients are charged based on real asset utilization amid work execution, cultivating cost-effectiveness and disposing of the require for pre-allocated assets. Faas offers a streamlined approach for designers to develop versatile, event-driven applications. By abstracting framework concerns, it empowers a center on making particular capacities custom-made to real-world occasions. This presentation sets the organize for an investigation of FaaS standards and benefits within the ever-evolving scene of cloud computing (Wang et al., 2018).

Key Characteristics of Function as a Service (FaaS):

1. **Event-Driven Operation**:
   - Functions react to particular occasions or demands, such as changes in information, HTTP demands, or database overhauls.
2. **Stateless Design**:
   - Methods in FaaS are stateless, not holding data between executions. State or information tirelessness is overseen remotely.
3. **Granular Scaling**:
   - FaaS stages scale capacities powerfully in reaction to request, bringing forth occasions to handle expanded occasions and scaling down amid lower request.
4. **Pay-per-Use Billing**:
   - Clients are charged based on genuine asset utilization amid work execution, adjusting with the serverless worldview.
5. **Abstraction of Infrastructure**:
   - Engineers are disconnected from framework concerns, empowering speedier advancement cycles and center on code rationale.

Noteworthy FaaS Architecture Aspects:

1. **Function Deployment**:
   - Developers create individual functions for specific tasks, emphasizing short-lived and stateless design.

2. **Event Sources**:
   ◦ Events, such as HTTP requests or database updates, trigger the execution of functions, providing a clear event-driven approach.

3. **Function Execution Environment**:
   ◦ Functions operate in isolated environments dynamically provisioned by the FaaS platform, often referred to as "sandboxes" or "containers".

4. **Scaling and Resource Allocation**:
   ◦ FaaS platforms automatically scale based on demand, ensuring efficient resource utilization. Resource allocation is dynamic and adjusts in real-time.

5. **State Management**:
   ◦ Functions remain stateless, and any required state or data persistence is managed externally, typically in separate storage services.

6. **Pay-per-Use Billing**:
   ◦ FaaS follows a pay-per-use model, ensuring cost efficiency by charging users for actual resource consumption during execution.

7. **API Gateway**:
   ◦ Many FaaS architectures incorporate an API Gateway to manage and expose functions as APIs, serving as a central entry point for external requests.

8. **Developer Tools**:
   ◦ FaaS platforms provide comprehensive developer tools, including IDEs, logging, monitoring, and debugging tools, facilitating the development and deployment process.

If we were to liken a web application to a piece of visual art, adopting microservice architecture would resemble creating the artwork using a collection of mosaic tiles (Figiela et al., 2018; Lee et al., 2018). Similar to an artist seamlessly adding, replacing, or repairing individual tiles, a developer can modify or enhance specific microservices without impacting the entire application. Conversely, monolithic architecture is akin to painting the entire masterpiece on a single canvas. In this scenario, the entire application is tightly integrated into one cohesive unit, making it less flexible for independent modifications or updates. This analogy effectively captures the contrast between the modular nature of microservices and the integrated structure of monolithic architecture in web application development (IBM, n.d.).

2. MICRO SERVICES

If we envision a web application as a visual artwork, adopting microservice architecture is comparable to constructing the art using mosaic tiles. Similar to an artist working with individual tiles, developers can easily add, replace, or repair one microservice at a time (van Eyk et al., 2018). This method, known as microservice architecture, appeals to developers as it allows for the creation and modification of small, independent code components that seamlessly integrate into their codebases.

This is in contrast to monolithic architecture, which combines all the code into one big system. Even small application modifications require a complicated deployment procedure for large monolithic systems (Gan & Delimitrou, 2018). This deployment complexity is reduced by using serverless programming, such as Function as a Service (FaaS). Web developers may focus on creating application code using FaaS, as the serverless provider takes care of backend services and server allocation.

Figure 1. Feedback control systems to configure serverless functions

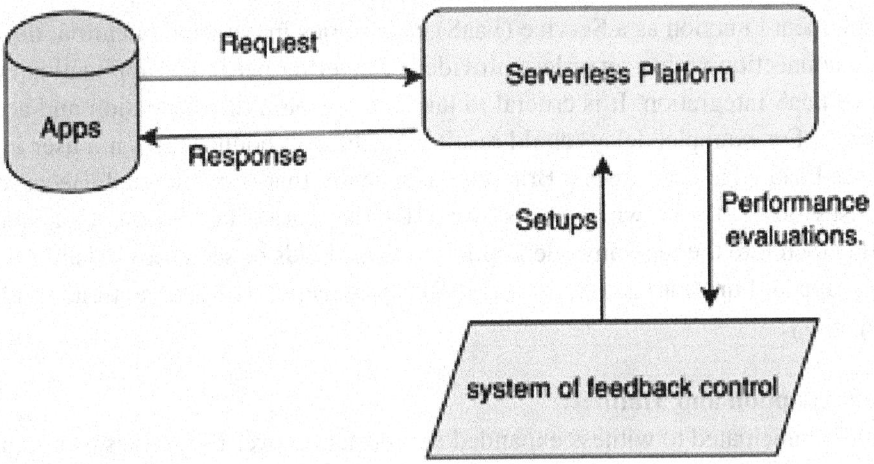

2.1 Advantages of Function as a Service

Enhanced Developer Speed:

FaaS facilitates a more efficient development process by allowing developers to dedicate more time to crafting application logic and less time managing servers and deployments. This results in a notably accelerated development turnaround (Sriraman & Wenisch, 2018).

Inherent Scalability:

FaaS code comes with built-in scalability, relieving developers from the complexities of planning for high traffic or heavy usage scenarios. The serverless provider seamlessly manages all scaling concerns (Gan et al., 2019).

Cost-effectiveness:

In contrast to traditional cloud providers, serverless FaaS providers refrain from billing clients for idle computation time. As a result, clients only incur charges for the actual computation time used, eliminating the need to overspend on cloud resources (Cortez et al., 2017).

2.2 Disadvantages of Function as a Service

Limited System Oversight:

When entrusting a third party to manage a portion of the infrastructure, comprehending the entire system becomes challenging, introducing difficulties in debugging.

Testing Challenges:

Incorporating FaaS code into a local testing environment can be intricate, demanding additional complexity and effort for comprehensive application testing.

3. PROPOSED WORK

In order to implement Function as a Service (FaaS) capabilities in a web application, developers must first establish a connection with a serverless provider. Delivering particular application code from the edge is a part of FaaS integration. It is crucial to take into account the dispersion and accessibility of these edge servers. For example, delays could result in significant bounce rates if a user in Italy visits a website that uses FaaS edge code from a Brazilian data centre that is overloaded. Because it leverages Cloudflare's vast global network, which spans over 310 cities, Cloudflare Workers—a FaaS solution—stands out and is therefore the recommended option in these kinds of scenarios (Shahrad et al., 2017).

The future scope for Function-as-a-Service (FaaS) is promising, with several trends and possibilities shaping its trajectory:

1. **Increased Adoption and Maturity**:
    - FaaS is anticipated to witness expanded appropriation over businesses as organizations recognize the benefits of its serverless, event-driven engineering. The innovation is likely to develop with more vigorous highlights and improved capabilities.

2. **Integration with Edge Computing**:
    - FaaS is anticipated to witness expanded appropriation over businesses as organizations recognize the benefits of its serverless, event-driven engineering. The innovation is likely to develop with more vigorous highlights and improved capabilities..

3. **Hybrid Cloud Implementations**:
    - FaaS is likely to play a noteworthy part in hybrid cloud usage, permitting organizations to use both on-premises and cloud-based assets consistently. This adaptability is significant for businesses with differing framework needs.

4. **Advancements in Developer Tools**:
    - Future advancements will likely concentrate on moving developer tools and hence making FaaS more available to a broader range of people. Upgraded investigating, checking, and testing instruments will engage designers to construct and keep up FaaS applications more productively.

5. **Expansion of Use Cases**:
    - The scope of FaaS is anticipated to extend into unused utilize cases, past its current applications. As the innovation develops, more businesses and spaces may use FaaS for different applications, from IoT to machine learning.

6. **Serverless Framework Ecosystem Growth**:
    - The serverless system, libraries, and third-party administrations, is expected to develop. This development will contribute to a more vigorous and feature-rich FaaS system, cultivating development and productivity.

7. **Focus on Security and Compliance**:
    - As FaaS gets to be necessarily to basic trade applications, there will likely be an expanded center on security and compliance. Future advancements may incorporate upgraded security measures and softwares to address concerns related to information protection and administrative compliance.

8. **Collaboration with Traditional Architectures**:
   ◦ FaaS is anticipated to collaborate more consistently with conventional designs, empowering organizations to embrace a crossover approach. This collaboration will give adaptability in transitioning from bequest frameworks to more advanced, serverless models.
9. **Optimized Resource Utilization**:
   ◦ Future improvements in FaaS may incorporate moved forward asset utilization, permitting for indeed more proficient scaling and fetched optimization. Progressed calculations and analytics may contribute to way better foreseeing and overseeing asset requests.

In pith, long run of Function-as-a-Service looks energetic and promising, with a concentration on growing utilize cases, moving forward tooling, and tending to developing challenges to form FaaS more available, proficient, and secure. Serverless Computing and FaaS are getting to be progressively prevalent within the domain of cloud-based application designs, engaging to both new businesses and built up organizations (Liu & Yu, 2018).

The appropriation of these structural styles is driven by a shared interest of a competitive edge, moved forward effectiveness, increased nimbleness, and cost-effectiveness. Cloud benefit suppliers play a significant part in this move by advertising and powerfully overseeing machine asset assignment inside serverless computing systems (CNCF Serverless Working Group, 2018).

In serverless models, engineers can concentrate exclusively on commerce rationale, easing concerns related to runtime arrangement, deployment management, and framework complexities. FaaS takes this approach a step advance inside the domain of Serverless Computing (Merkel, 2014).

Rather than creating whole cloud-based applications, designers make little, specialized capacities in upheld programming dialects. These capacities, planned for focused and particular tasks, are activated by events, facilitating dynamic resource allocation and scaling. A unique highlight of FaaS is its trigger-based costing demonstrate, guaranteeing enhanced resource allocation in a cost-effective way (Amazon, 2018).

This outline presents the concepts of Serverless Computing and FaaS, investigating their benefits and confinements. It analyzes the offerings of prevalent cloud and PaaS suppliers, shedding light on developing utilize cases and victory stories related with these modern engineering styles. As organizations look for inventive arrangements, Serverless Computing and FaaS develop as compelling choices, streamlining advancement forms and upgrading by and large application effectiveness (Fouladi et al., 2017).

4. METHODOLOGY

Cloud Computing could be a flexible program including a network of interactive computers gotten to through the Web, advertising computational help. "Cloud Service" is characterized by the ITU which stands for International Telecommunication Union, as on-demand service conveyance through cloud computing innovation that's accessible anyplace, at any time, on any network, and through any associated device. SaaS (Software as a Service), CaaS (Communications as a Service), PaaS (Platform as a Service), IaaS (Infrastructure as a Service), and NaaS (Network as a Service) are fair some of the categories it incorporates. This paper introduces the concept of an Online Compiler as Software as a Service (SaaS), facilitating the conversion of source code from high-level languages to low-level machine language for program execution (Ao et al., 2018).

Function-as-a-Service (FaaS) simplifies the cloud-based application development model, allowing developers to focus on coding without managing infrastructure. Major cloud-computing companies, such as Google, AWS, and Azure, offer FaaS services, with AWS Lambda, Google Cloud Functions, and Azure Functions being widely used. Each provider offers distinct capabilities in their FaaS implementations, and choosing the right solution involves considering factors like execution times, memory configurations, scalability, pricing, and integration capabilities (Feng et al., 2018).

Developers often struggle with resource procurement and environment setup, diverting attention from coding. Serverless architecture addresses this by eliminating the need for active server management. In this paper, aspects such as execution times, memory configurations, scalability, pricing, limitations, and integration capabilities of FaaS services are analysed. The goal is to provide insights into choosing a suitable FaaS solution for specific system requirements, emphasizing integration within the vendor's platform and third-party services to mitigate vendor lock-in issues associated with cloud computing adoption (Apache Software Foundation, n.d.).

Figure 2. Serverless functionalities with Kubernetics services and alert manager

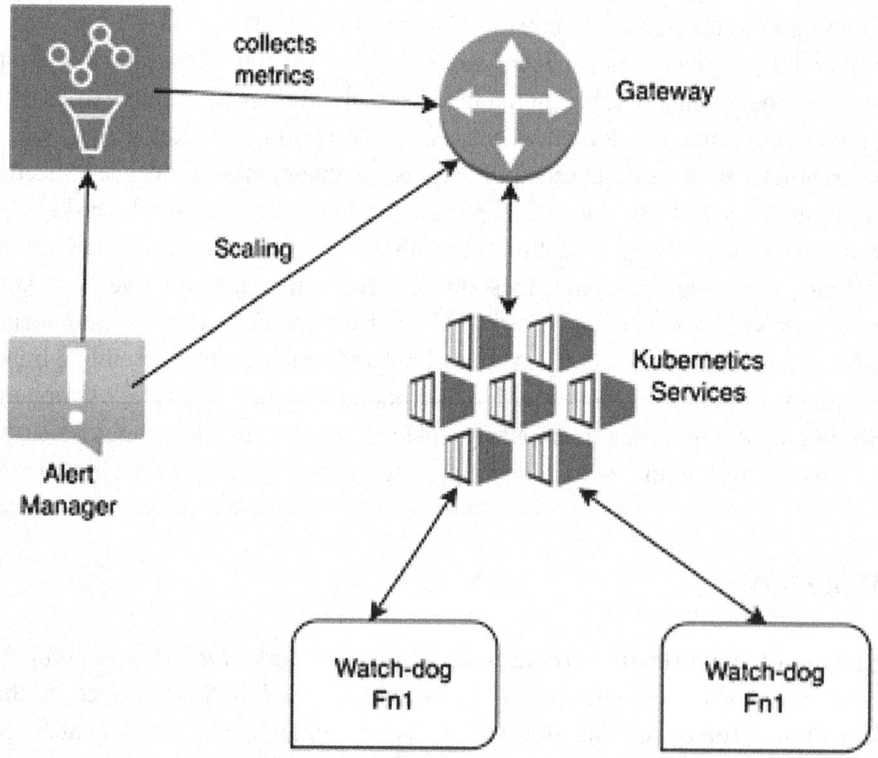

Serverless computing has quickly become a prominent cloud application model, notably exemplified by Amazon's Lambda platform. This paradigm provides fine-grained resource provisioning that automatically scales with user demand. Function-as-a-Service (FaaS) applications, in line with the serverless model, revolve around developers presenting their applications as sets of functions executed in response to events (Baldini et al., 2017). These functions are intended to be short-lived and run within containers or virtual machines, introducing several system-level overheads. This paper explores the architectural implications of FaaS serverless computing, leveraging the Apache OpenWhisk FaaS platform on real servers.

The study identifies key architectural implications of FaaS, revealing challenges and considerations for developers and system architects. Notable findings include the impact of FaaS containerization, showcasing up to a 20x slowdown compared to native execution. Cold-start scenarios can extend to over 10x the execution time of short functions, highlighting the importance of optimizing initialization processes (Mohan et al., 2019). The interleaving of short functions from multiple tenants in FaaS workloads frustrates common architectural structures found in modern processors, impacting branch mispredictions, memory bandwidth, and inter-process communication. This model introduces FaaSProfiler, an open-source testing and profiling platform developed for the study, enabling further exploration, and understanding of the architectural intricacies associated with Function-as-a-Service in serverless computing environments (Trach et al., 2019). The discoveries emphasize the significance of optimizing FaaS applications for effective resource utilization, minimizing overhead, and tending to building challenges inborn in this rising paradigm (Ruan et al., 2016).

FaaS recognizes itself from conventional cloud models like IaaS, PaaS, and more up to date models such as microservices in a few key ways:

Server Management: FaaS engineers are calmed from the duty of provisioning or overseeing servers, dispensing with concerns approximately compute bottlenecks.

Abstraction from Machine Type: Functions inside FaaS are abstracted from particular machine types, with suppliers not ensuring or estimating based on specific machine types.

Server Utilization: FaaS pull functions to improve server utilization, frequently coexisting with conventional applications on the same server.

Granular Pricing: FaaS embraces a a high quality pricing model based on resource usage, moving deeper to a compute-as-a-utility model.

Cost Based on Execution Time and Memory Usage: Developers are billed solely for the execution time and memory usage of their functions, motivating providers to minimize overheads while excluding platform and system-level details.

Short Function Duration: Like microservices, FaaS functions are typically very short (around 100 milliseconds), posing challenges in cloud server utilization and potential amplified interference effects due to high parallelism.

SLAs for Availability: FaaS providers specifically offer Service Level Agreements (SLAs) for availability with transparent scaling and operation (Barr, 2018). However, BaaS differs from FaaS in implementation and pricing (Firecracker Micro VM, n.d.).

Cold starts in serverless platforms have been extensively researched in peer-reviewed studies, focusing on quantifying and mitigating their effects (Manco et al., 2017). The phenomenon of a cold start arises when a function, inactive for a period defined by the platform's instance recycling time, has its sandbox environment (container) terminated to reclaim resources (Thalheim et al., 2018). Upon a subsequent request, the platform reinitializes the sandbox environment, incurring additional delay. Numerous online and one-time decisions have been identified as influencing cold starts:

Choice of Language: Research consistently indicates that interpreted languages like Python, Ruby, and JavaScript generally experience significantly fewer cold-start delays (up to 100 times less) compared to compiled runtimes such as Java and .NET. This disparity is ascribed to the start of a compute-intensive JVM in compiled runtimes like Java, coming about in striking delays (Shen et al., 2019).

Serverless Provider: Research demonstrates that varieties within the basic framework or resource provisioning strategies of different suppliers result in varying cold-start delays. In a comparative vein, Azure allots 1.5GB of memory to occurrences, which might account for drawn out cold-start durations (Reese, 2008).

These inquire about research emphasize the centrality of considering dialect choice and serverless supplier when tending to and moderating the challenges postured by cold begins in serverless computing situations (Pandas, n.d.).

In serverless computing, when a method is at first executed, the ide sets up a sandbox environment, loads the function's code, and runs it. Taking after execution, the ide keeps the sandbox in a warm state for a particular term called the instance-recycling time to handle consequent demands. On the off chance that no ensuing demands happen inside that time allotment, the sandbox is ended to repurpose resources, a resolution impacted by the instance-lifetime, a set period after which the sandbox may be ended, independent of utilization (Github, n.d.-a).

Configuring values for instance recycling time and instance lifetime is crucial for both the serverless platform and users. A low value maximizes resource reuse, enhancing overall resource utilization but can lead to unnecessary cold starts for users, degrading application performance and potentially resulting in revenue loss for commercial platforms (Stinner, 2022). Conversely, longer values reduce latencies for users but may decrease underlying resource utilization for the serverless platform.

For open-source serverless platforms, users can configure these values, with studies suggesting the use of popularity analysis to optimize them on a per-application basis. In contrast, commercial serverless platforms determine these values, restricting user control (Github, n.d.-b). Numerous peer-reviewed studies have attempted to infer instance-recycling-time and instance-lifetime values for commercial platforms. These studies often leverage limited persistent storage for serverless functions to store identifiers, observing changes during subsequent invocations. Findings reveal variations across platforms, with Google Cloud Function exhibiting the longest instance-recycling time (over 120 minutes), AWS Lambda at around 26 minutes, and varying reports for Azure Functions (Mirhosseini & Wenisch, 2019).

In an independent study, a relationship between instance-recycling-time and configured memory for AWS Lambda functions was established, indicating that a higher memory configuration tends to result in a smaller instance-recycling time. Regarding instance lifetime, studies found Azure Function to have the longest duration compared to AWS Lambda and Google Cloud Function (Koller & Williams, 2017). The lifetime of a Google Cloud Function instance is reported to be influenced by configured resources, with instances having 128 MB and 2,048 MB memory exhibiting lifetimes of 3–31 minutes and 19–580 minutes, respectively.

Concurrency in serverless computing refers to the simultaneous execution of multiple function instances to handle requests for a specific serverless function. Unlike traditional Infrastructure as a Service (IaaS), serverless platforms autonomously scale by initiating additional function instances to meet increased demand, eliminating the need for users to define scaling policies. Platforms typically scale up to a certain limit, queuing subsequent requests until resources become available. The ability to scale rapidly and achieve maximum concurrency is crucial for applications with fluctuating demand (Fingler et al., 2019).

A comprehensive measurement study by Wang et al. compared major cloud providers (AWS Lambda, Google Cloud Functions, and Azure Functions), highlighting AWS Lambda's superior performance with a maximum concurrency level of 2007, surpassing GCF and Azure Functions. FaaSdom, a benchmarking suite, also affirmed AWS Lambda's efficiency in quickly scaling out and handling increased request rates. Language and underlying operating system decisions were identified as factors affecting the scalability of serverless applications (Young, 2019).

Certain serverless platforms, such as Apache OpenWhisk and Knative, provide users with the capability to configure container-level concurrency limits, specifying the number of requests a function instance can handle simultaneously. Azure Function allows users to set a maximum number of function instances on a single VM to prevent resource depletion (Luk et al., 2005). Demonstrated in Luk et al. (2005) is the impact of container-level concurrency limits on application performance, proposing an AI-based (reinforcement learning) approach for configuring concurrency limits in Knative.

Users should exercise caution when adjusting container-level concurrency limits, as existing function instances continue running with the old configuration until terminated based on platform settings. It is advisable to wait for system stability with the new configuration before making further changes.

When utilizing Function-as-a-Service (FaaS), users can configure specific parameters, such as memory, CPU power, location, and concurrency. However, critical resources like CPU, network, and I/O share are determined by the serverless platform (McFarling, 1993). In a comprehensive study (McFarling, 1993), it was observed that AWS Lambda imposes an upper limit on the CPU share for a function with memory "m," calculated as 2m/3328. In co-location scenarios, instances share CPU fairly, with each instance's share slightly less than the upper limit. Google adopts a similar approach, allocating CPU share in proportion to the memory assigned to the function, consistent with the documentation of AWS Lambda and Google Cloud Functions.

Contrary to the norm, IBM Function does not allocate CPU share proportionally to memory. As reported in Herdrich et al. (2016), IBM Function maintains a constant CPU share, as an increase in memory does not impact the function's performance. Azure Function, however, exhibits variable CPU share allocation, with functions placed on 4-vCPU VMs receiving the highest share. It's essential to note that the placement of function instances on VMs may seem random to users, and in co-location scenarios, the CPU share of co-located instances can experience a drop.

Furthermore, disk I/O and network performance are influenced by the resources configured for the serverless function and co-location, as emphasized in Chen et al. (2019). Generally, performance experiences improvement when function instances receive more resources. However, measuring the network performance of FaaS platforms poses a challenge due to dynamic network conditions and the diverse geographical regions available for deployment. Developers are advised to choose a region closer to their users to minimize access latency (Chen et al., 2019). Preliminary experiments support this finding for I/O performance, suggesting that I/O-intensive serverless functions benefit from increased memory allocation. In the serverless computing paradigm, developers concentrate exclusively on writing code, while the serverless platform assumes the responsibility for executing this code on underlying infrastructure or hardware. Developers lack direct control over the specific types of virtual machines (VMs) where their application code runs. Earlier studies aimed to unveil the underlying virtual infrastructure for commercial serverless platforms (Reese, 2008) revealed that serverless functions on Linux-based VMs have access to the "/proc" file system, exposing that underlying VMs run Amazon Linux and utilize CPUs similar to EC2 instances. Building upon this exploration, Pandas (n.d.) conducted a comprehensive study across major commercial serverless platforms: AWS Lambda, Google Cloud Function, and Azure Functions. They discovered that Google Cloud Function successfully conceals underlying resources. In contrast, AWS Lambda employs five different VM types, often with 2 vCPUs and 3.75GB RAM, resembling c4.large instances from EC2. Azure Function exhibited the most diverse infrastructure, featuring VMs with 1, 2, or 4 vCPUs, utilizing either Intel or AMD models.

Understanding the underlying infrastructure helps developers identify performance-related issues. For example, a serverless function on Azure Function placed on a 4-vCPU VM may have a different CPU share compared to other VM types. Moreover, knowledge of infrastructure diversity assists researchers in explaining performance variability on a given serverless platform.

Figure 3. Functionalities with docker, containers with binary programs

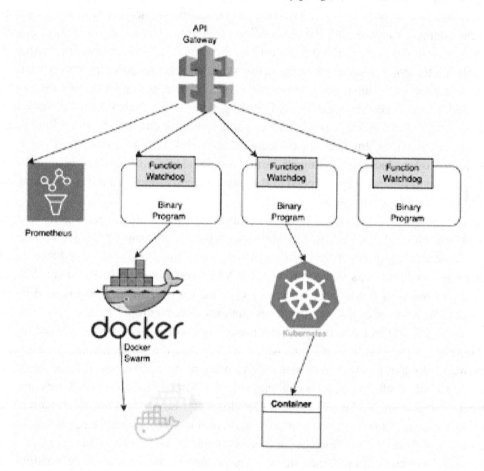

Function-as-a-Service (FaaS) platforms offer two primary features: rapid scalability in milliseconds without additional configuration and a unique "pay-as-you-go" pricing model, where users are billed solely for code execution time, eliminating charges during idle periods. This effectively addresses bursty demands that occur when there is a sudden spike in demand for a short duration. In contrast, Infrastructure-as-a-Service (IaaS) services such as Amazon EC2 and Google VM employ different pricing models, charging based on minutes and seconds of usage, and requiring additional effort for configuration and maintenance (Github, n.d.-a) have utilized various methods to construct per-execution performance and cost models for serverless applications. This paper introduces a more comprehensive analytical cost model, taking into account per-request cost and overall deployment cost, while also factoring in demand considerations. It's important to note that within commercial serverless platforms, users are constrained to configuring limited parameters, such as memory, CPU, and location, for their serverless functions. The absence of performance guarantees, or Service Level Objectives (SLOs), for serverless functions accentuates the significance of accurately configuring these parameters. Several proposals have been put forth, both offline and online, to tackle the challenge of effective parameter configuration. For instance, employs an efficient distribution of functions across edge- and core-cloud based on profiling, aiming to reduce cloud usage costs. However, its limitation lies in its lack of adaptability to dynamic execution models. In Github (n.d.-b), an approach based on reinforcement learning optimizes the concurrency limit in Knative but is primarily focused on a singular parameter. Sizeless (Mirhosseini & Wenisch, 2019) adopts synthetic functions to construct a performance model, introducing potential cost overhead. An optimal configuration finder should function as a feedback control system, continually monitoring the performance of serverless applications and dynamically adjusting parameters as necessary. Several challenges persist in designing such systems, including the variability in underlying infrastructure, delayed feedback loops, and the varying impact of resource changes across different serverless platforms. Stands out as an online statistical learning technique that successfully addresses these challenges, achieving the desired performance and cost reduction without requiring alterations to the application. Serverless functions, executed in lightweight sandboxes, possess the capability to scale seamlessly in response to spikes in demand. Previous approaches (Koller & Williams, 2017) capitalized on the features of serverless computing to mitigate SLO violations. However, these approaches incurred substantial development costs. Alternatively, automated approaches, as suggested in Fingler et al. (2019), aim to reduce development costs but may introduce performance variations due to one-time resource configurations.

5. RESULTS

A cloud computing architecture called serverless computing allows developers to focus only on business logic, leaving resource management to cloud service providers. Applications are divided into granular Function-as-a-Service (FaaS) functions within this framework. However, because of the intricate nature of the underlying infrastructure and the interdependencies amongst the various FaaS tasks within the application, assessing the performance of these functions is difficult.

This addresses the challenge of measuring the Function Capacity (FC) in a serverless application for every FaaS function. The maximum concurrent invocations a function can handle in a given amount of time without going over its Service-Level Objective (SLO) is known as its FC. The model presents Fn-Capacitor, an automated technique for calculating Function Capacity, in order to solve this problem. This is achieved by sandboxing FaaS functions and building performance models for them using FnCapacitor.

AWS Lambda and Google Cloud Functions (GCF) are used to demonstrate FnCapacitor. By performing time-framed load testing and building several models, including statistical techniques like linear, ridge, and polynomial regression as well as Deep Neural Network (DNN) methods, based on obtained performance data, it estimates FCs under various deployment settings. The analysis shows that the forecasts are fairly accurate, with DNN obtaining an accuracy of more than 75% for both cloud providers. This tool solves the function capacity estimation problem and offers insightful information that can be used to optimise serverless applications.

The Invoker holds a significant position inside OpenWhisk, working as the core mindful for executing holders. The general capability of running holders in OpenWhisk is decided by the memory estimate distributed to the Invoker, alluded to as its memory measure, in conjunction with the required memory restrain relegated to each individual container.

With an emphasis on the json_dumps function, we conducted tests to examine the dynamic link between container memory restrictions and Invoker memory sizes. The results, as illustrated in the image that goes with it, show that greater Invoker memory sizes and lower function memory restrictions lead to higher capacity. Remarkably, capacity is mostly determined by the number of active containers, outweighing the effect of doubling Invoker memory sizes and container memory restrictions.

Nonetheless, a noteworthy finding emerges: the benefits of increasing Invoker memory sizes quickly fade when a set container memory restriction is upheld. This phenomena is explained by the presence of other factors, such as increasing restrictions on the amount of CPU time that can be used for a given function. An additional experiment with the same function showed that increasing the capacity of the Invoker memory by double increased latency and execution time, perhaps because of the expense of scheduling and managing more containers.

We decided to use a 4GB Invoker memory size for our studies after taking this trade-off into account. Considerations with OS scheduling for Function-as-a-Service (FaaS) are brought up by the ramifications of changing the Invoker memory size. Although more containers boost server capacity, more containers also result in longer execution times and latency. Given the short execution periods of FaaS functions, this observation highlights the necessity to investigate a FaaS-aware scheduler built to finish function execution before activating the scheduler again.

In OpenWhisk, the Invoker's primary function is to run containers on this serverless platform. The memory size (or allotted memory) to the invoker and the memory limit set for each container are important factors in deciding how many containers are executing at once and how much CPU time each one is taking up. We examined this complex interaction, concentrating on the `json_dumps` function's tolerance to different Invoker memory sizes and container memory constraints. Figure 12 illustrates the results, which show that greater Invoker memory sizes and lower function memory restrictions lead to higher capacity.

Remarkably, the number of running containers is the main factor affecting capacity. Interestingly, doubling the Invoker memory size and the container memory limit at the same time yields the same capacity. One interesting observation is that the advantages of moving to bigger Invoker memory sizes quickly evaporate for a fixed container memory constraint. This phenomena is explained by things like constraints on the amount of CPU time that can be used for a certain function.

A related experiment with the identical function found that an increase in Invoker memory size from 4GB to 8GB resulted in an average increase in latency of 42.9% and an execution time increase of 70.5%. The overhead involved in scheduling and managing twice as many containers is probably the cause of this rise. Thus, we decided to use a 4GB Invoker memory amount for our task.

Investigations into the Operating System (OS) scheduling in a Function as a Service (FaaS) context are warranted by the observed behaviour. Although adding more containers increases server capacity, it also results in significant increases in latency and execution time. This emphasises the need for a FaaS-aware scheduler, with an emphasis on finishing a function's execution before starting the scheduler again, especially considering how quickly these functions execute.

We studied the range of function memory limitations in detail to determine the ideal memory limit that would affect scheduling share for different microbenchmark functions. The average measured capacity, execution time at capacity, and latency for each memory limit sweep are shown in Figure 13. All metrics increase as memory limits decrease, but the magnitude differences between them point to a possible mismatch between the expectations of developers (which prioritise lower execution times) and individual end users (which prioritise lower latency) and the priorities of the FaaS provider (which emphasises increased capacity/throughput and profit from longer execution times).

The marginal increase in latency or execution time divided by the marginal increase in capacity at each phase was the subject of additional analysis. This ratio sheds light on how capacity, latency, and execution time are traded off. Interestingly, the marginal capacity increase is almost proportional when going from 512MB to 384MB and from 384MB to 256MB. The marginal capacity gain, however, is only 69.4%–81.3% of the marginal latency increase and 54.9%–64.5% of the marginal execution time increase when stepping down to 128MB. A 256MB memory limit was chosen because it provides a fair trade-off between slight increases in execution time, latency, and capacity.

The identified imbalance underscores a scenario where the FaaS provider prioritizes capacity maximization at the expense of execution time, latency, and cost considerations.

The nonattendance of Quality of Service (QoS) ensures for designers, showed through SLAs, compounds this issue. Suppliers, spurred to outperform capacity limits, might raise both method invocations per unit time and execution time, eventually driving to expanded benefit costs. Settling this estimating motivating force challenge involves investigating potential arrangements, such as reexamining estimating models, actualizing engineering improvements for progressed confinement, or refining SLAs to offer auxiliary ensures to designers.

In tending to obstructions impacts inside our framework, we concocted an try including the json_dumps work conjured at 80% capacity for 29 seconds. Amid the 10th moment, the deltablue work was conjured at a rate of 5 summons per moment for 4 seconds. Figure 14 outlines the try, portraying idleness for json_dumps, in conjunction with enlightening per cycle (IPC), page issues per kilo-instruction, setting switches per kilo-instruction, and Last-Level Cache (LLC) misses per kilo-instruction. Upon deltablue conjuring, json_dumps shifts into an over-invoked mode, encountering expanded inactivity and requiring time to recoup to a adjusted state once deltablue summons desist. All through this period, we watch a 35% drop in IPC compared to the adjusted mode, connecting with outstanding increments in page deficiencies, setting switches, and LLC misses per kilo-instruction, characteristic of the overhead related with propelling modern holders for deltablue.

6. CONCLUSION

In conclusion, Function-as-a-Service (FaaS) rises as a outstanding paradigm in cloud computing, advertising engineers a streamlined and adaptable approach to application advancement. FaaS's event-driven and serverless design permits engineers to concentrate on creating particular capacities, streamlining improvement forms, and moderating framework complexities. The inalienable adaptability and pay-per-use charging show contribute to cost-effectiveness and versatility to changing workloads. Whereas FaaS offers evident preferences such as upgraded engineer speed, built-in adaptability, and taken a toll effectiveness, it is significant to recognize potential challenges. Issues like diminished framework control and expanded complexity in testing situations may posture impediments that engineers must explore.

In quintessence, FaaS enables designers to form applications that are spry, adaptable, and budget-friendly. As this innovation proceeds to progress, its integration into different application scenes guarantees to reshape computer program improvement approaches within the energetic domain of cloud computing. FaaS's varsatile nature adjusts with the industry's interest of productive, versatile, and responsive arrangements, situating it as a significant element within the progressing advancement of cloud-based application structures. End of the direction for Function-as-a-Service (FaaS) holds impressive guarantee, checked by advancing patterns and potential developments. As the innovation picks up footing, it is expected to develop, advertising more strong highlights and capabilities. A outstanding slant includes closer integration with edge computing, empowering FaaS to bring serverless usefulness in nearness to end-users, subsequently upgrading execution and minimizing idleness.

Hybrid cloud usage are anticipated to play a urgent part, with FaaS encouraging consistent integration between on-premises and cloud-based assets. This adaptability caters to the differing foundation needs of businesses. Furthermore, headways in engineer devices are on the skyline, pointing to form FaaS more available with moved forward investigating, observing, and testing capabilities. The scope of FaaS is balanced to expand into novel utilize cases, extending from IoT applications to machine learning ventures. Concurrently, the serverless ecosystem is anticipated to encounter considerable growth, fostering development and proficiency within the domain of FaaS. Security and compliance are predicted as regions of increased center, considering FaaS's expanding part in basic commerce applications. Future advancements may include improved security measures and devices to address concerns related to information security and administrative compliance.

Collaboration between FaaS and conventional designs is likely to ended up more consistent, advertising organizations the adaptability to embrace crossover approaches that move from bequest frameworks to present day, serverless structures. Optimized asset utilization is another key perspective of long haul of FaaS, with continuous improvements pointing to improve scaling productivity and taken a toll optimization. Progressed calculations and analytics may contribute to more precise expectations and administration of asset requests. In substance, long-standing time of Function-as-a-Service shows up energetic and promising, characterized by an extension of utilize cases, moved forward tooling, and a concerted exertion to address developing challenges, making FaaS more open, proficient, and secure.

REFERENCES

Amazon. (n.d.). *AWS Lambda*. Amazon. https://aws.amazon.com/lambda/.

Amazon. (2018). *AWS lambda announces service level agreement*. Amazon Web Services.

Ao, L., Izhikevich, L., Voelker, G. M., & Porter, G. (2018). Sprocket: A serverless video processing framework. In *Proceedings of the ACM Symposium on Cloud Computing, SoCC '18* (pp. 263–274). ACM. 10.1145/3267809.3267815

Apache Software Foundation. (n.d.). *Apache OpenWhisk*. Apache Software Foundation. https://openwhisk.apache. org.

Baldini, I., Cheng, P., Fink, S. J., Mitchell, N., Muthusamy, V., Rabbah, R., Suter, P., & Tardieu, O. (2017). The serverless trilemma: Function composition for serverless computing. In *Proceedings of the 2017 ACM SIGPLAN International Symposium on New Ideas, New Paradigms, and Reflections on Programming and Software, Onward! 2017* (pp. 89–103). ACM. 10.1145/3133850.3133855

Barr, J. (2018). *Firecracker - lightweight virtualization for serverless computing.* AWS. https://aws. amazon.com/blogs/aws/firecracker-lightweight-virtualizationfor-serverless-computing,

Chen, S., Delimitrou, C., & Martínez, J. F. (2019). PARTIES: QoS-aware resource partitioning for multiple interactive services. In *Proceedings of the Twenty-Fourth International Conference on Architectural Support for Programming Languages and Operating Systems, ASPLOS '19.* ACM. 10.1145/3297858.3304005

CNCF Serverless Working Group. (2018). *Serverless whitepaper v1.0.* Cloud Native Computing Foundation.

CortezE.BondeA.MuzioA.RussinovichM.FontouraM.BianchiniR. (2017). Resource central: Understanding and predicting workloads for improved resource management in large cloud platforms. In Proceedings of the 26th Symposium on Operating Systems Principles, SOSP '17, (pp. 153–167). ACM. doi:10.1145/3132747.3132772

Feng, L., Kudva, P., Da Silva, D., & Hu, J. (2018). Exploring serverless computing for neural network training. In *2018 IEEE 11th International Conference on Cloud Computing (CLOUD)* (pp. 334–341). IEEE. 10.1109/CLOUD.2018.00049

Ferdman, M., Adileh, A., Kocberber, O., Volos, S., Alisafaee, M., Jevdjic, D., Kaynak, C., Popescu, A. D., Ailamaki, A., & Falsafi, B. (2012). Clearing the clouds: A study of emerging scale-out workloads on modern hardware. In *Proceedings of the Seventeenth International Conference on Architectural Support for Programming Languages and Operating Systems, ASPLOS XVII* (pp. 37–48). ACM. 10.1145/2150976.2150982

Figiela, K., Gajek, A., Zima, A., Obrok, B., & Malawski, M. (2018, December 10). Performance evaluation of heterogeneous cloud functions. *Concurrency and Computation, 30*(23), e4792. doi:10.1002/cpe.4792

Fingler, H., Akshintala, A., & Rossbach, C. J. (2019). USETL: Unikernels for serverless extract transform and load why should you settle for less? In *Proceedings of the 10th ACM SIGOPS Asia-Pacific Workshop on Systems, APSys '19* (pp. 23–30). ACM. 10.1145/3343737.3343750

Firecracker Micro VM. (n.d.). *Secure and fast microVMs for serverless computing.* https://firecracker-microvm.github.io/.

Fouladi, S., Wahby, R. S., Shacklett, B., Balasubramaniam, K., Zeng, W., Bhalerao, R., Sivaraman, A., Porter, G., & Winstein, K. (2017). *Encoding, fast and slow: Low-latency video processing using thousands of tiny threads.* NSDI.

Gan, Y., & Delimitrou, C. (2018). The architectural implications of cloud microservices. *IEEE Computer Architecture Letters, 17*(2), 155–158. doi:10.1109/LCA.2018.2839189

Gan, Y., Zhang, Y., Cheng, D., Shetty, A., Rathi, P., Katarki, N., Bruno, A., Hu, J., Ritchken, B., Jackson, B., Hu, K., Pancholi, M., Clancy, B., Colen, C., Wen, F., Leung, C., Wang, S., Zaruvinsky, L., Espinosa, M., & Delimitrou, C. (2019). An open-source benchmark suite for microservices and their hardware-software implications for cloud and edge systems. In *Proceedings of the Twenty-Fourth International Conference on Architectural Support for Programming Languages and Operating Systems, ASPLOS '19.* ACM. 10.1145/3297858.3304013

Github. (n.d.-a). *Intel® RDT Software Package.* Github. https://github.com/intel/intel-cmt-cat.

Github. (n.d.-b). *Tesseract Open Source OCR Engine*. https://github.com/tesseract-ocr/tesseract.

Herdrich, A., Verplanke, E., Autee, P., Illikkal, R., Gianos, C., Singhal, R., & Iyer, R. (2016). Cache QoS: From concept to reality in the Intel® Xeon® processor E5-2600 v3 product family. In *High Performance Computer Architecture (HPCA), IEEE International Symposium* (pp. 657–668). IEEE. 10.1109/HPCA.2016.7446102

IBM. (n.d.). *IBM Cloud Functions*. IBM. https://www.ibm.com/cloud/functions.

Jaleel, A., Nuzman, J., Moga, A., Steely, S. C., & Emer, J. (2015). High performing cache hierarchies for server workloads: Relaxing inclusion to capture the latency benefits of exclusive caches. In *High Performance Computer Architecture (HPCA), IEEE 21st International Symposium on* (pp. 343–353). IEEE. 10.1109/HPCA.2015.7056045

Koller, R., & Williams, D. (2017). Will serverless end the dominance of Linux in the cloud? In *Proceedings of the 16th Workshop on Hot Topics in Operating Systems, HotOS '17* (pp. 169–173). ACM. 10.1145/3102980.3103008

Lee, H., Satyam, K., & Fox, G. (2018). Evaluation of production serverless computing environments. In *2018 IEEE 11th International Conference on Cloud Computing (CLOUD)* (pp. 442–450). IEEE. 10.1109/CLOUD.2018.00062

Liu, Q., & Yu, Z. (2018). The elasticity and plasticity in semi-containerized co-locating cloud workload: A view from Alibaba trace. In *Proceedings of the ACM Symposium on Cloud Computing, SoCC '18* (pp. 347–360). ACM. 10.1145/3267809.3267830

Luk, C.-K., Cohn, R., Muth, R., Patil, H., Klauser, A., Lowney, G., Wallace, S., Reddi, V. J., & Hazelwood, K. (2005). Pin: Building customized program analysis tools with dynamic instrumentation. In *Proceedings of the 2005 ACM SIGPLAN Conference on Programming Language Design and Implementation, PLDI '05* (pp. 190–200). ACM. 10.1145/1065010.1065034

Manco, F., Lupu, C., Schmidt, F., Mendes, J., Kuenzer, S., Sati, S., Yasukata, K., Raiciu, C., & Huici, F. (2017). My VM is lighter (and safer) than your container. In *Proceedings of the 26th Symposium on Operating Systems Principles, SOSP '17* (pp. 218–233). ACM. 10.1145/3132747.3132763

McFarling, S. (1993). *Combining branch predictors*. Tech. Rep. TN-36, Digital Western Research Laboratory.

McGrath, G., & Brenner, P. R. (2017). Serverless computing: Design, implementation, and performance. In *2017 IEEE 37th International Conference on Distributed Computing Systems Workshops (ICDCSW)* (pp. 405–410). IEEE. 10.1109/ICDCSW.2017.36

Merkel, D. (2014). Docker: Lightweight linux containers for consistent development and deployment. *Linux Journal*.

Mirhosseini, A., & Wenisch, T. F. (2019, July). The queuing-first approach for tail management of interactive services. *IEEE Micro, 39*(4), 55–64. doi:10.1109/MM.2019.2897671

Mohan, A., Sane, H., Doshi, K., Edupuganti, S., Nayak, N., & Sukhomlinov, V. (2019). Agile cold starts for scalable serverless. In *11th USENIX Workshop on Hot Topics in Cloud Computing (HotCloud 19)*. USENIX Association.

Pandas. (n.d.). *Pandas python data analysis library.* https://pandas.pydata.org.

Reese, W. (2008). Nginx: The high-performance web server and reverse proxy. *Linux Journal, 2008*(173), 2.

Ruan, B., Huang, H., Wu, S., & Jin, H. (2016). A performance study of containers in cloud environment. In *Asia-Pacific Services Computing Conference* (pp. 343–356). Springer. 10.1007/978-3-319-49178-3_27

Shahab, A., Zhu, M., Margaritov, A., & Grot, B. (2018). Farewell my shared LLC! a case for private die-stacked DRAM caches for servers. In *2018 51st Annual IEEE/ACM International Symposium on Microarchitecture (MICRO)* (pp. 559–572). IEEE. 10.1109/MICRO.2018.00052

Shahrad, M., Klein, C., Zheng, L., Chiang, M., Elmroth, E., & Wentzlaff, D. (2017). Incentivizing self-capping to increase cloud utilization. In *Proceedings of the 2017 Symposium on Cloud Computing, SoCC '17*. ACM. 10.1145/3127479.3128611

Shen, Z., Sun, Z., Sela, G.-E., Bagdasaryan, E., Delimitrou, C., Van Renesse, R., & Weatherspoon, H. (2019). X-Containers: Breaking down barriers to improve performance and isolation of cloud-native containers. In *Proceedings of the TwentyFourth International Conference on Architectural Support for Programming Languages and Operating Systems, ASPLOS '19* (pp. 121–135). ACM. 10.1145/3297858.3304016

Sriraman, A., & Wenisch, T. F. (2018). uTune: Auto-tuned threading for OLDI microservices. In *13th USENIX Symposium on Operating Systems Design and Implementation (OSDI 18)*. USENIX Association.

Stinner, V. (2022). *The Python Performance Benchmark Suite, Version 0.7.0.* PY Performance. https://pyperformance.readthedocs.io

Thalheim, J., Bhatotia, P., Fonseca, P., & Kasikci, B. (2018). CNTR: Lightweight OS containers. In *2018 USENIX Annual Technical Conference (ATC 18)* (pp. 199–212). ACM.

Trach, B., Oleksenko, O., Gregor, F., Bhatotia, P., & Fetzer, C. (2019). Clemmys: Towards secure remote execution in FaaS. In *Proceedings of the 12th ACM International Conference on Systems and Storage, SYSTOR '19* (pp. 44–54). ACM. 10.1145/3319647.3325835

van Eyk, E., Toader, L., Talluri, S., Versluis, L., Uta, A., & Iosup, A. (2018, September). Serverless is more: From PaaS to present cloud computing. *IEEE Internet Computing, 22*(5), 8–17. doi:10.1109/MIC.2018.053681358

Wang, L., Li, M., Zhang, Y., Ristenpart, T., & Swift, M. (2018). Peeking behind the curtains of serverless platforms. In *2018 USENIX Annual Technical Conference (ATC 18)*. USENIX Association.

Young, E. (2019). The true cost of containing: A gVisor case study. In *11th USENIX Workshop on Hot Topics in Cloud Computing (HotCloud 19)*. USENIX Association.

Chapter 9
Scalable and Micro Service-Oriented Approach Using FaaS

Swathi Sowmya Bavirthi

Chaitanya Bharathi Institute of Technology (Autonomous), India

Bala krishna Peesala

Chaitanya Bharathi Institute of Technology (Autonomous), India

V. Santhosh

Chaitanya Bharathi Institute of Technology (Autonomous), India

K. Swathi

Chaitanya Bharathi Institute of Technology (Autonomous), India

ABSTRACT

Function as a service (FaaS) is a service of cloud computing that allows cloud customers to develop applications and establish functionalities. FaaS is commonly employed for deploying microservices and is popularly referred to as serverless computing. Here, the authors investigate the world of function as a service (FaaS) within cloud computing. They explore FaaS's evolution from its inception to its role in serverless computing, covering key concepts like serverless architecture, event-driven programming, and statelessness. The exploration involves gaining knowledge in establishing FaaS environments using AWS Lambda, IBM Bluemix OpenWhisk, Azure functions, Auth0 Webtask, and Google Cloud functions as the authors delve into design principles and best practices. Emphasis is placed on the advantages of adopting event-driven, serverless methodologies and optimization techniques involved in FaaS. For an experienced developer or novice, this chapter helps to understand function as a service, making it valuable to learn the insights of serverless computing.

DOI: 10.4018/979-8-3693-1682-5.ch009

1. INTRODUCTION TO FAAS

A cloud computing approach called Function as a Service (FaaS) allows developers to manage the underlying infrastructure without worrying about deploying specific functions or code in response to predefined triggers. Servers are abstracted away by FaaS, freeing developers to concentrate only on creating and deploying functions that are called upon demand. The functionalities which are developed are invoked only when executed, similar to event-delegation model. This method increases operational costs while decreasing it by doing away with the necessity for server supply, scalability, and management. FaaS is a fundamental part of serverless computing, which builds apps as a group of functions that are called upon by various events, including scheduled tasks, HTTP requests, and database updates. AWS Lambda, Azure Functions, Google Cloud Functions, and IBM Cloud Functions are a few well-known FaaS vendors.

2. BASIC TERMINOLOGY/KEY TERMS AND DEFINITIONS

i.   **Function:** A self-contained programme segment that carries out a particular action or function. Functions are installed and carried out autonomously in response to events in FaaS.

ii. **Serverless Computing:** Serverless computing is a type of cloud computing in which developers do not need to worry about managing servers or infrastructure since cloud providers dynamically allocate the resources required to carry out activities.

iii. **Event-Driven Architecture:** An architectural design in which user actions, system alerts, or outside triggers dictate the data and control flow is known as event-driven architecture. The majority of FaaS solutions use an event-driven architecture.

iv. **Stateless Computing:** Stateless computing is a paradigm for computing in which each function's operation is autonomous and doesn't depend on the circumstances or state of earlier computations. This makes resilience and simple scalability possible in FaaS setups.

v.   **Invocation:** The act of starting a function to run in reply to a request or event is known as invocation. Events like timers, database modifications, and HTTP requests trigger functions in FaaS systems.

vi. **Scaling:** A FaaS platform's capacity to dynamically modify the resources allotted to various services in response to demand. FaaS platforms adjust their functionalities automatically based on variations in workload.

vii. **Cold Start:** The first delay that arises when calling a function that isn't active at the moment. Response times are marginally longer when a function has to initialize before handling requests, which is known as a "cold start."

3. RELATED WORK

The transition of the server platform from physical servers to virtual machines (VMs) and Docker containers has improved resource efficiency. Docker containers provided consistent deployment by encapsulating programmes and dependencies, while virtual machines (VMs) abstracted bare-metal resources into numerous OS instances. Functions as a Service (FaaS) is an example of serverless computing, which eliminates the requirement for infrastructure management so that developers may concentrate only on writing code. Figure 1 depicts the essence of functions and its existence.

FaaS solutions accelerate development by executing code in response to events or API calls, such as AWS Lambda and Azure Functions (Dantas et al., 2022). Serverless marketplaces, like the AWS Serverless Application Repository, enable developers to easily find and include pre-built functions, creating a thriving community of code snippets that can be reused. This change speeds up application development by allowing developers to effectively handle a variety of use cases by utilising specialised features from the market.

Figure 1. The existence of FaaS

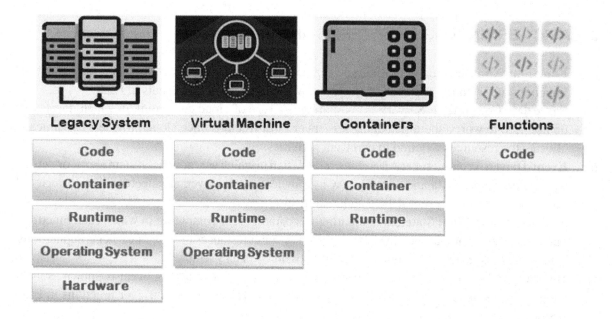

Synopsis of Past Studies and Advances in FaaS

Function as a Service (FaaS) research in the past has concentrated on several topics, such as cost-effectiveness, resource utilization, scalability, performance, and programming paradigms. Scholars have examined the advantages and drawbacks of FaaS over conventional data center models and have looked at optimization strategies to boost the effectiveness of FaaS platforms.

i.   **Performance Evaluation:** Research has examined how well FaaS platforms perform under various workload scenarios, taking into account variables like throughput, cold start delay, and execution time (Dantas et al., 2022).
ii. **Scalability and Resource Management:** Studies have looked at the capacity for FaaS systems to scale, investigating methods for resource provisioning and auto-scaling to effectively manage fluctuating workloads (Alam et al., 2023; Yu et al., 2023).

iii. **Cost Analysis:** One important factor in the adoption of FaaS is cost-effectiveness. Scholars have performed cost assessments to assess the total cost associated with ownership (TCO) for deploying apps on FaaS platforms and compare the pricing (Alam et al., 2023).

iv. **Structures of Various FaaS Providers:** To reduce operating costs, cost optimization techniques like function size, memory allocation, and activity scheduling have been investigated.

Comparative Evaluation of FaaS Providers

Some studies have evaluated the features, functionality, cost, and ecosystem support of FaaS providers through comparative evaluations. Developers and organizations may choose the best FaaS platform according to their unique requirements and use cases with the aid of these studies (Lynn et al., 2017; Szalay et al., 2023).

i. **Feature Comparison:** Comparative studies assess feature sets provided by various FaaS providers, including those related to supported programming languages, external service integration, event sources, monitoring, logging, and security aspects.

ii. **Performance Benchmarking:** Under controlled settings, performance benchmarks are used to assess the execution speed, latency, scalability, and reliability of FaaS systems.

iii. **Pricing Analysis:** Comparative analyses involve a thorough investigation of the cost implications, billing arrangements, and pricing models associated with employing various FaaS service providers.

iv. **Ecosystem Support:** Integration with additional cloud offerings, third-party libraries, production frameworks, and community endorsement are all taken into account when evaluating the ecosystem support offered by FaaS providers

4. ROLE OF FAAS IN SERVERLESS COMPUTING

a. Serverless Architecture

A cloud computing concept known as the serverless architecture isolates developers from the underlying infrastructure by having cloud providers dynamically control the distribution of resources required to carry out activities. A key component of serverless architecture is Function as a Service (FaaS), which lets programmers launch single functions or sections of code in response to predefined events or triggers.

Application Decomposition is the Smaller, independent functions that carry out certain activities are used to break down applications in a serverless architecture. Every function is called in reaction to different kinds of events, such as time-based triggers, database modifications, or HTTP requests.

FaaS platforms that use dynamic scaling, which adjusts resources dynamically in response to demand, make sure that tasks are completed successfully and economically. Because of this dynamic scalability, developers are no longer need to setup and maintain servers.

b. Statelessness and Event-Driven Programming

A key concept in cloud computing is event-driven programming, a technique in which operations are initiated in response to external stimuli or events. Event-driven programming is made easier by FaaS platforms, which offer tools for defining event sources and linking functions to certain events.

Event Sources: A variety of sources, including HTTP requests, email queues, upgrades to databases, file uploads, and scheduled timers, can give rise to events in serverless systems. Integration with various event sources is supported by FaaS s systems, allowing functions to react to a variety of event kinds.

Statelessness: Functions in serverless architectures are intended to be stateless, which means they don't keep track of data between calls. Due to the lack of common state dependencies, functions may be run individually and concurrently, simplifying concurrency management and scalability.

Asynchronous Execution: Event-driven code development encourages asynchronous execution, in which calls to functions are made in reaction to situations without preventing the caller from proceeding. In distributed systems, asynchronous execution enhances responsiveness by facilitating the effective management of several requests at once.

In short, FaaS offers a scalable, event-driven executing environment for functions to be deployed in response to events, which is a crucial component in allowing serverless architecture. The foundational ideas of serverless computing are event-driven programming and statelessness, which enable the effective and economical execution of programme in dynamically handled cloud environments.

5. FAAS ENVIRONMENTS

AWS Lambda

One of the most widely used FaaS platforms is Lambda, which is provided by Amazon Web Services (AWS). supports several programming languages, including Python, Java, C#, and Node.js. Easily combines with other AWS services, including API Gateway, DynamoDB, and Amazon S3.Offers event-driven execution, pay-per-use pricing, and automated scalability.

Azure Functions

The serverless computing solution offered by Microsoft Azure for developing and implementing event-driven apps. supports some programming languages, including as PowerShell, JavaScript, C#, and Python. provides close connectivity with Azure services, including Cosmos DB, Event Grid, and Azure Storage

Functions of Google Cloud

Developers may create and implement functions in response to events with Google Cloud's Functions as a Service (FaaS) service. supports the programming languages Go, Python, Ruby, and Node.js. connects to BigQuery, Pub/Sub, Firestore, Cloud Storage, and other Google Cloud services. provides features including event-driven performance, pay-as-you-go pricing, and automated scalability.

IBM OpenWhisk Bluemix

The open-source FaaS platform from IBM, a component of the IBM Cloud network. supports several languages used for programming, including as Java, Python, Swift, and Node.js. Connects with Cloudant, Watson, and Kubernetes, among other IBM Cloud services. offers tools for creating sophisticated applications without servers, including packages, rules, and triggers.

IronWorker, Iron.io

The FaaS platform from Iron.io allows scheduled jobs and background tasks to be deployed and executed. It supports a number of programming languages, including as Java, Python, Ruby, and Node.js. provides functions including real-time event being processed, cron-style scheduling, and task queues (Cinque, 2023) and connects with a number of cloud computing platforms, which include as DigitalOcean, AWS, Azure, and Google Cloud.

Auth0 Webtask

The FaaS platform from Auth0 allows serverless operations to be executed in response to events or HTTP requests. allows serverless function writing with Node.js.

Provides easy integration for authorization and authentication with Auth0's identity platform. offers functions such as scheduled tasks, webhooks, and flexibility for unique business logic.

Galactic Fog Gestalt Laser

The FaaS platform from Galactic Fog is intended for developing and implementing containerized applications. supports several programming scripting languages, including as Go, Python, and JavaScript.

6. OPTIMIZATION OF FAAS

Maximizing performance, reducing expenses, and guaranteeing effective resource utilization all depend on optimizing Function-as-a-service (FaaS) settings. Several optimization strategies may be used to raise the efficacy of FaaS platforms:

Function Sizing: Performance and cost may be greatly impacted by optimizing memory use and function size. Optimizing routines according to their memory and CPU demands guarantees effective resource management and minimizes superfluous overhead.

Concurrency Management: Managing scaling rules and concurrency limitations effectively is crucial for dealing with fluctuating workloads. Comprehending the FaaS platform's concurrency mechanism and setting suitable limitations guarantees efficient resource usage without excessive provisioning.

Cold Start Mitigation: Reducing cold start latency is essential to enhancing the responsiveness of applications. Techniques like optimizing container starting speeds, using supplied concurrency, and pre-warming functions

Resource Reuse: You may increase performance and lower overhead by utilizing strategies like connection pooling, caching, and resource reuse across function calls. Reusing API clients, database connections, and other resources reduces startup time and boosts overall efficiency.

Asynchronous Processing: You may maximize resource utilization and enhance responsiveness by using asynchronous processing for background or ongoing processes. The impact on synchronous function invocations is minimized by shifting laborious or computationally demanding activities to asynchronous workflows or queues.

Cost Optimisation: Reducing operating costs may be achieved by putting cost optimization techniques like spot instances or preemptible virtual machines (VMs) to use, memory allocation adjustments, and function execution time optimization into practice.

Scalability Metrics

In Function as a Service (FaaS) environments, scalability is essential for effectively managing fluctuating load and guaranteeing best practices for resource use. Scalability in FaaS platforms may be assessed using a variety of criteria.

Concurrency

The amount of method instances that may respond to incoming requests or events simultaneously is referred to as concurrency.

Formula

Concurrency = Requests per Second / Execution Time per Function Instance

Flow Rate

The pace when a FaaS platform can handle new inquiries or events is measured by its throughput.

Formula

Throughput = Requests per Second

Scaling Efficiency

The accuracy with which a FaaS platform adjusts resources up or down in response to workload variations is measured by its scaling efficiency.

Formula

Scaling Efficiency = (Change in Throughput) / (Change in Resources)

Resource Utilization

In a FaaS system, resource utilisation measures how well resources are allocated and used.

Formula

Resource Utilization = (Actual Resources Used) / (Allocated Resources)

7. FUTURE SCOPE

Function as a Service (FaaS) is expected to make significant strides in the future and present chances for more innovation:

i. **Increased Language Support:** In order to enable developers to use their favourite language for serverless development, FaaS platforms are probably going to increase language support to support a wider variety of programming languages.
ii. **Higher Performance**: Runtime environments, infrastructure optimisations, and containerisation technology advancements will all contribute to better resource usage, lower cold start delay, and higher performance on FaaS platforms.
iii. **Growth of the Serverless Ecosystem:** New tools, frameworks, and services that make serverless development easier, increase developer productivity, and make it easier to integrate seamlessly with current workflows will all contribute to the serverless ecosystem's continued expansion.
iv. **Integration of AI and ML:** By integrating AI and ML capabilities into FaaS platforms, developers will be able to create and implement intelligent serverless applications for tasks like image recognition, natural language processing, and predictive analytics.
v. **Event-Driven Architectures:** Using the capabilities of FaaS platforms for event-driven execution, the popularity of event-driven architectures will increase due to the growing need for instantaneous processing of data, dependent on events automation, and reactive application design.

All things considered, the future of FaaS is defined by ongoing innovation, growing capacities, and wider acceptance across diverse sectors and use cases, propelling the development of serverless computing as a paradigm-shifting cloud computing technology.

8. CONCLUSION

To sum up, Function as a Service (FaaS) offers developers a serverless approach for creating and deploying applications with more flexibility, scalability, and economy. This is a big leap in cloud computing.

We have examined the fundamental ideas of FaaS, its function in serverless computing, important jargon, and the several FaaS environments that are on the market during this investigation.

Developers may concentrate on developing code for specific functions by using FaaS platforms like AWS Lambda, Azure Functions, Google Cloud Functions, and others, which abstract away the complexity of infrastructure management. FaaS makes it possible to create extremely scalable and responsive systems that can adjust to shifting workloads and demands by utilising stateless execution and programming driven by events. Serve as a Service transforms the way cloud-based applications are created, implemented, and maintained, providing unmatched efficiency, scalability, and flexibility for contemporary software development. FaaS will continue to be at the forefront of cloud innovation, enabling developers to create the next wave of scalable and responsive apps as businesses and developers adopt serverless computing.

REFERENCES

Alam, F., Toosi, A. N., Cheema, M. A., Cicconetti, C., Serrano, P., Iosup, A., Tari, Z., & Sarvi, M. (2023). Serverless Vehicular Edge Computing for the Internet of Vehicles. *IEEE Internet Computing*, *27*(04), 40–51. doi:10.1109/MIC.2023.3271641

Cinque, M. (2023). Real-Time FaaS: Serverless computing for Industry 4.0. *Service Oriented Computing and Applications*, *17*(2), 73–75. doi:10.1007/s11761-023-00360-0

Dantas, J., Khazaei, H., & Litoiu, M. (2022). Application Deployment Strategies for Reducing the Cold Start Delay of AWS Lambda. *IEEE 15th International Conference on Cloud Computing (CLOUD)*, 1-10. 10.1109/CLOUD55607.2022.00016

Lynn, T., Rosati, P., Lejeune, A., & Emeakaroha, V. (2017). A Preliminary Review of Enterprise Serverless Cloud Computing (Function-as-a-Service) Platforms. *2017 IEEE International Conference on Cloud Computing Technology and Science (CloudCom)*, 162-169. 10.1109/CloudCom.2017.15

Szalay, M., Matray, P., & Toka, L. (2023). Real-Time FaaS: Towards a Latency Bounded Serverless Cloud. *IEEE Transactions on Cloud Computing*, *11*(02), 1636–1650. doi:10.1109/TCC.2022.3151469

Yu, H., Zhang, H., Shen, J., Geng, Y., Wang, J., Miao, C., & Xu, M. (2023). Serpens: A High Performance FaaS Platform for Network Functions. *IEEE Transactions on Parallel and Distributed Systems*, *34*(08), 2448–2463. doi:10.1109/TPDS.2023.3263272

Chapter 10
Review of Grid–Cloud Distributed Environments:
Fusion Fault Tolerance Replication Model and Fragmentation

Dharmesh Dhabliya

https://orcid.org/0000-0002-6340-2993

Vishwakarma Institute of Information Technology, India

Ananta Ojha

Jain University, India

Amandeep Gill

Vivekananda Global University, India

Asha Uchil

ATLAS SkillTech University, India

Anishkumar Dhablia

Altimetrik India Pvt. Ltd., India

Jambi Ratna Raja Kumar

https://orcid.org/0000-0002-9870-7076

Genba Sopanrao Moze College of Engineering, India

Ankur Gupta

https://orcid.org/0000-0002-4651-5830

Vaish College of Engineering, India

Sabyasachi Pramanik

https://orcid.org/0000-0002-9431-8751

Haldia Institute of Technology, India

ABSTRACT

Users who may be geographically distant from organizations must be provided with up-to-date info. Replication is one approach to make such data accessible. The process of duplicating and maintaining database items across many databases is known as distributed database replication. Distributed databases safeguard application availability while providing quick local access to shared data. Distributed databases are often divided up into pieces or replica divisions. In distributed databases, fragmentation is advantageous for utilization, effectiveness, parallelism, and security. Locality of reference is strong if data items are found in the location where they are utilized the most. Users may still query or edit the remaining pieces even if one is unavailable. It's critical to manage fragmented data replication availability even in the event of a failure. Failure scenarios include a server that responds improperly or

DOI: 10.4018/979-8-3693-1682-5.ch010

returns an inaccurate value. Enabling fault tolerance and data management systems like SAS, Oracle, and NetApp is the only way to fix these errors. This study reviews the research on data replication and fragmentation techniques used in cloud environments. It is easy to implement, takes into consideration cloud databases, considers both fragmentation and replication strategies, and is focused on enhancing database performance. All the necessary information to implement the approach is included in the chapter.

1. INTRODUCTION

Cloud computing (Dhamodaran S, et al. 2023) and grid computing (Pandey, B. K. et al. 2023) are frequently confused and have similar conceptual foundations. Both approaches have the same objective of providing services to consumers via resource sharing across a large user base, and their principles are quite similar. Because they are both network-based and multitasking (Talukdar, V. et al. 2023), users in various places may access one or more program instances to do various tasks. Grid computing uses virtualized computer resources to store massive volumes of data, while cloud computing uses an internet service to provide an application with indirect, rather than direct, access to resources. While cloud computing maintains resources centrally, grid computing distributes resources across grids.

With the aid of a group of networked computers that collaborate to solve an issue, grid computing is a network-based computational paradigm that can manage massive volumes of data. In essence, it is a vast computer network that collaborates to find a solution to a common issue by dividing it into many smaller components known as grids. Because of its distributed design, tasks are presumably planned and handled without consideration for time. As shown in Figure 1, the collection of PCs performs the role of a virtual supercomputer, offering scalable and seamless access to geographically dispersed wide-area computing resources and presenting them as a single, cohesive resource for carrying out massive tasks like data processing.

Figure 1. Grid computing

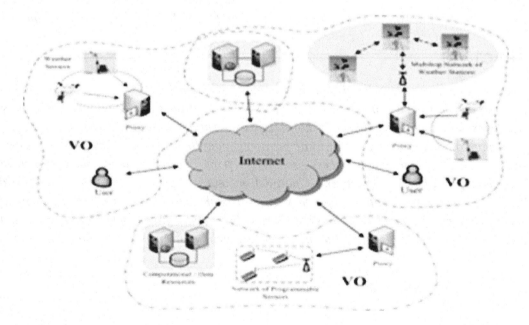

Cloud computing is a kind of internet-based computing where an application shares resources to build a big resource pool instead of directly accessing resources. It is a contemporary computing paradigm designed with the purpose of remotely providing quantifiable and scalable IT resources. It is based on network technology. It eliminates the need for large investments in local infrastructure by providing on-demand access to a shared pool of dynamically configured computer resources and higher-level services. The widely dispersed computer resources are controlled centrally. Users do not need to know the precise location of their data in order to use software and program from anywhere. Which translates to "pay only for what you require." as seen in Figure 2.

By distributing resources across several servers in clusters, grid and cloud computing are network-based computing technologies that make effective and efficient use of computer resources (Veeraiah, V. et al. 2023). This makes acquiring hardware and software for application construction easier. By itself, grid computing is a computer approach that pools resources from several fields to accomplish a common goal. In order to store enormous quantities of data, grid computing involves virtualizing computer resources, which is reviewed in this work. Ascending the spectrum, cloud computing involves a program that, instead of directly accessing resources and data, does so indirectly via an internet service. Data are distributed via a centralized or decentralized replication mechanism to a predefined geographically dispersed environment. Fragmentation imputes data into multiple little independent fragments. Replication maintains data transparency in distributed database systems by keeping several copies at each location, contingent on user access or work behavior. In a Grid Computing or Cloud Computing context, a system loses confidence or malfunctions when it does not perform as planned. In addition, fusion fault tolerance in distributed grid-cloud setups is reviewed in this work. The structure of this article is as follows: a review of the literature serves as the foundation for the discussions that follow in the first part. The fragmentation is reviewed in the second part. The replication is reviewed in the third part. Fault Tolerance is covered in Section 4. The study's conclusion is given in the last part.

Figure 2. Cloud computing

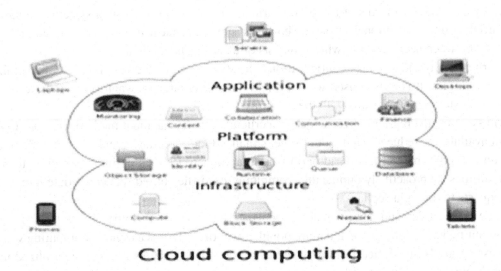

2. LITERATURE REVIEW

Data-intensive activities and data exchange are addressed by Data Grid and cloud settings. Because data-intensive activities demand enormous volumes of data and significant latency, it may be challenging to ensure data availability and speedy access. Grid computing is categorized into three forms and may be used in different ways to satisfy different application demands. Naturally, there are many grids that mix two or more of these grid types, and there are no hard and fast rules when it comes to them. The different grid types are as follows:

Computational grid: This kind of resource allocation concentrates on assigning just processing power. For instance, the majority of the apparatus consists of high-performance servers.

Scavenging grids: Usually used in conjunction with a large number of desktop computers that are scavenging for spare CPU cycles (Taviti Naidu, G. et al. 2023) and other resources. Desktop workstation owners are usually granted discretion over the times at which their resources are available for grid participation.

Data grid: A data grid is an assemblage of geographically dispersed computer resources, which might be located in different parts of the same nation or even in other nations. For instance, life science research may be carried out by two universities, each having a separate dataset. All of these locations are connected by a grid, which enables them to control communication and handle security issues like data access control.

The underlying architecture of the grid has a significant impact on replication strategy performance as well as providing a high-level overview of main grid topologies. When a single data source has to be shared across many international partnerships, hierarchical and tree models are used.

Tree topology is not without problems, though. The tree structure of the grid allows files and messages to follow precise pathways to their destination. Moreover, data transmission is not feasible between nodes that are siblings or on the same tier.

Peer-to-peer (P2P) systems, on the other hand, get over these restrictions and provide more freedom in component communication. Applications that use dispersed resources to carry out decentralized tasks set a P2P system apart. In terms of resource sharing, a P2P system and a grid system overlap. A P2P system differs from conventional resource-sharing systems in that it uses symmetric communication architecture between peers, each of which consists of a server and a client.

Furthermore, a hybrid topology configuration consists of an architecture composed of any mix of the previous topologies. It is mostly used when project-related researchers want to collaborate with other researchers by sharing their results with them readily.

In grid systems, the replication technique is a crucial data management method. In order to provide high data availability, reduced bandwidth usage, enhanced fault tolerance, and greater scalability, data replication is seen to be a crucial Grid optimization approach. Replica optimization aims to decrease file access times by proactively duplicating commonly used files based on access data and allocating access requests to the right replicas.

Because of the on-demand capacity management paradigm's benefits, both technically and financially, cloud computing has become more and more popular over time. This is a trend in computing where data and processing are being shifted from personal computers and desktops to large, centralized facilities managed by outside computing and storage companies. Because cloud computing offers a flexible and elastic service at a lower cost of infrastructure and resource management, it attracts users. Cloud computing is widely recognized as not being a novel notion, even if its definition, architecture, and models are the subject of considerable dispute within the academic community. Instead, it is the coming together of important and previously existent distributed computing concepts and technologies, including Web services, virtualization, Grid and cluster computing (K.aushik, D. et al. 2022), and Service Oriented Architecture (SOA).

These days, there are a lot of cloud service providers on the market that provide a wide variety of services that users may access via web browsers and the Internet, such Infrastructure as a Service (IaaS) (Bhattacharya, A. et al. 2021), Platform as a Service (PaaS), and Software as a Service (SaaS). Although cloud computing offers specialized cloud services that fulfill dynamic QoS (Jain, V. et al. 2023) needs and prevent Service-Level Agreement (SLA) breaches while being cost-effective, it has also considerably reduced numerous difficult tasks for clients. SLAs outline acceptable costs for SLA violations as well as QoS objectives. Availability, reaction time, security, latency, and reliability are among the frequently used QoS measures.

Availability in particular is seen to be the most important need for cloud computing. Availability is #1 among the top ten challenges associated with cloud computing, according to (Veeraiah, V. et al. 2023). Service outages not only make users' experiences worse, but they also cause large financial losses. Cloud service providers often utilize replication strategies that are seen to be successful in providing the high scalability, fault tolerance, flexibility, and availability of cloud computing in order to handle this problem and ensure SLA compliance. Replication in cloud computing may be done at different granularities based on the tier that the service is being delivered at. For instance, virtual machines are often duplicated for IaaS services, whereas service, application, or data replication is more common for SaaS services.

Data replication is one of the key strategies for enhancing data access performance and availability, which are drawbacks of cloud computing]. It has several benefits. For instance, it may cut down on bandwidth use and data access times. Additionally, it may enhance load balancing, scalability, and availability. Files are duplicated and stored close to the data requester using replication techniques. Database Management technologies (DBMS), distributed databases, cloud, peer-to-peer (p2p), and fog are among the technologies that often employ data replication. Large volumes of data are increasingly being contributed to common resources in some scientific application domains, such water and rain monitoring. Usually, these massive datasets are spread among many data centers. Data replication is a common strategy for managing large volumes of data in a distributed manner.

2.1 Disintegration

Because the distributed database is divided into split replica partitions or pieces, administrators must deal with fragmented database replication, which presents a difficult problem. The process of breaking up a database into multiple tiny, independent bits known as fragments is referred to as data fragmentation. Partial data access and a table view context are introduced when data is accessed through fragments. It is the first stage of choosing data items using a finer grained approach as opposed to a coarser one. After fragmentation, a centralized fragmentation, full replication, or partial replication approach is used to assign the data pieces to a predefined geographically dispersed environment. Replication maintains data transparency in distributed database systems by keeping several copies of the data at each location, contingent on user access or work behavior. At the foundational level of each site, it guarantees reliability, fault tolerance, and data availability.

The only objective of different data distribution strategies is to get dispersed performance overall through:

(1) Breaking up the workforce's burden into manageable chunks and making sure that data is immediately and without delay accessible to them.
(2) Subqueries are done rapidly thanks to a modular architecture.
(3) Permitting simple network expansion.
(4) Organizing the storage space that is available.
(5) Making sure that data sites are simple to maintain.

A decentralized method was chosen since the prior centralized system had several flaws. Among them are:

(1) Burden Balance and Performance: User queries are handled in a concurrent environment in a centralized system, where several users access the database at the same time, adding to the system's burden. Rapid response to database queries is commonly hindered, and it slows down the database, making it more difficult to answer to several users at once for the same data items.
(2) Complexity and Expansion: The centralized system's data is expanding at an alarming pace as a result of the big workforce. As a consequence, more storage space is needed to keep data organized, and understanding the logical structure is harder. In this situation, expanding the database further increases the risk of inadvertent data loss.
(3) Data Maintenance and Availability: Keeping massive volumes of data up to date in a centralized database affects the data's availability temporarily and interferes with user service. To remedy this disadvantage, a distributed database makes data availability and maintenance simple. In a decentralized system, any network node may access data.
(4) Fault Tolerance: Data availability is hampered by the centralized system's lack of fault tolerance. But a distributed approach makes this simpler since it provides fault tolerance through replication. By guaranteeing that the loss of any node has no impact on system performance as a whole, it assures data availability.

A heuristic technique to query fragmentation is presented to reduce the transmission costs (TC) of queries in a distributed context. Fragmentation is initially predicated on a relational model that is cost-effective, and then on the design of a DDBS. A mixed replication-based allocation scenario (MAS), a full replication-based allocation scenario (FAS), and a non-replication-based allocation scenario (NAS) are among the many replication-based allocation scenarios that have since been introduced.

A modified Bond Energy Algorithm (BEA), a hierarchical method for vertically splitting the network into fragments and assigning the pieces to specific places within the network, is offered as a solution to these problems. This method, which clusters attributes, calculates cluster allocation costs, and selects the best allocation locations, makes use of attribute affinity. In this case, every property that can be retrieved with a single query is consolidated into one piece. The study's goal was to compare and evaluate current algorithms from a design perspective in order to identify their advantages and disadvantages. This just serves to illustrate a dynamic architecture for the dissemination of data fragments in a scattered situation.

A non-redundant dynamic fragment allocation method is recommended for improved performance. It is predicated on how access patterns vary throughout locations. In this case, the quantity of data accessible on each fragment is taken into account when reallocating pieces, together with a time limit and threshold value. By modifying the read and write data volume factors, adding a threshold time volume, and implementing the Distance Constraints Algorithm, this novel method alters the reallocation approach.

Because of this, a lot of websites handle fragments and take the write data volume into account when reallocating resources. Distributed systems perform better overall as a consequence of this.

Furthermore, in order to provide effective and fault-tolerant data access in the systems, the replication technique aims to store numerous copies. While data management has been addressed in the past, only few algorithms now in use thoroughly analyze the benefits and drawbacks of different replication techniques. Replication is a common strategy used by them to increase data efficiency and availability. As the quantity of copies in the system increases, these measures become better. The most crucial point, however, that they failed to mention is that data duplication costs the provider money and energy. Implementing a data replication strategy that takes into account balancing many trade-offs is thus necessary.

Note that there has been prior research on the topic of table fragmentation for local data access. It also has some relevance to some of the distributed file system studies. The usual granularity of the data being considered (files vs. tables) and the necessity in distributed database systems for a fragmentation feature that may be used for partitioning are two important differences between distributed file systems and distributed database systems.

There is an unbreakable link between fragment allocation and fragmentation. Certain techniques just handle fragmentation, whereas others solely handle fragment allocation. Furthermore, a number of methods combine the two duties. However, fragmentation, allocation, and replication are often handled independently from replication. In contrast, some methods—like ours—adopt an integrated approach to fragmentation, allocation, and replication. While there are dynamic replication algorithms that may optimize for different metrics, we believe that reallocation and re-fragmentation should be investigated as options for replication.

2.2 Repeating

Replication solutions almost always aim to improve grid performance, decrease task response time, and lower access latency. In a similar vein, almost all replication techniques boost system performance and data availability while using less bandwidth. The idea is to store data as near to the user as feasible for fast access. Some replication techniques seek to distribute the workload evenly across all data servers. This improves system performance and offers a quicker reaction time. But when a system's replica count grows, the expense of keeping additional clones becomes an overhead for the system. In the data grid, some algorithms try to produce the fewest number of clones feasible. This guarantees the best possible use of the storage and minimal maintenance expenses for the replica. Certain solutions concentrate on both the ideal quantity of copies and their location strategically. The positioning of replicas strategically is important since it affects a few other important elements. For instance, arranging the copies in the best possible places helps to balance the workload across several servers. It is connected to maintenance costs as well. An approach that replicates a popular file blindly would produce an excessive number of duplicates, which will strain the system when replica maintenance costs rise to an unaffordable level.

The time it takes to complete a task is another important factor. By placing replicas optimally, certain replication algorithms try to shorten the time it takes to execute an operation. Replicas should be positioned closer to users in order to minimize response times and, therefore, task execution times. The throughput of the system will rise as a result. Replication hasn't been examined as a means of ensuring fault tolerance and quality control in many replication systems. Every replication strategy makes use of a subset of these parameters.

Other replication algorithms are built upon a number of replication replacement schemes that have been previously developed. The details of a few significant new and fundamental replication algorithms are as follows:

One example of an implemented technique is the SimpleOptimizer algorithm, which reads the necessary replica remotely rather than replicating anything. In terms of task execution time and network consumption, the SimpleOptimizer algorithm performs better than other algorithms, but it is also easier to construct. It also uses less storage space than other algorithms. The customer who receives the most requests for a file is considered the best client and is the one who makes a copy of themselves. Each node determines the best client for a file at a predefined period by monitoring whether the volume of requests for any of its files has beyond a threshold. Replication supports the architecture of Cascading Trees. At the top level, the data files are formed, and at the next level, a replica is made when the threshold for file accesses is exceeded. But until it gets to the best client itself, it is built along the best client's route at every step.

Another data replication mechanism is plain cashing. A local copy is saved by this algorithm whenever a client requests a file. Files are swiftly replaced if a client only has the capacity to hold one huge file at a time. An approach that combines cascading and ordinary cashing is called cashing out with cascading. The file is locally cached by the client, and popular files are consistently detected and distributed downward in the hierarchy by the server. It should be emphasized that while any node in the hierarchy might be a server, clients are always found at the leaves of the tree. Specifically, a client may act as a server to its siblings. Sibling nodes are those that share a parent.

Quick Spread: Using this technique, a duplicate of the file is kept at every node on the route to the client. Every time a client requests a file, a copy is created at each stage. A node removes the least popular file that came initially when it runs out of room to hold a new duplicate.

Comparably, files are always replicated to local storage systems using the Least Frequently Used (LFU) technique. The replica with the fewest accesses is eliminated to provide room for a new copy in the event that the local storage capacity is reached. LFU thus removes the duplicate with the lowest demand (popularity) from local storage, even if it has just been stored. In contrast, files are always replicated to the local storage system using the Least Recently Used (LRU) Strategy. The oldest replica in the local storage is removed to make room if the local storage is full. The requested site caches the necessary replicas in the LRU approach. The second oldest file is erased if the size of the oldest replica is less than the size of the new copy, and so on.

Also, the Cascading approach is expanded upon by the Proportionate Share Replica (PSR) policy. By assuming that the whole number of copies to be distributed as well as the number of sites already exists, this heuristic technique distributes replicas to the best available places. Replicas are deployed on candidate sites that are able to handle replica requests that are marginally higher than or equal to the ideal load after an optimal load distribution has been calculated. Once again, by preventing network congestion, Bandwidth Hierarchy Replication (BHR) is a cutting-edge dynamic replication technique that shortens the time it takes to access data in a data grid network. "Network-level locality," which denotes that the necessary file is situated at a site with high bandwidth to the site of task execution, is an advantage of the BHR method. The BHR approach was put to the test using the OptorSim Simulator. The findings demonstrate that when a bandwidth hierarchy develops on the internet, the BHR approach performs better in terms of data access time than alternative optimization methods. The present site-level replica optimization research is expanded to the network level by BHR.

Similarly, the multi-tier data grid design proposes two dynamic replication mechanisms: Simple Bottom-Up (SBU) and Aggregate Bottom-Up (ABU). When a client's data file surpasses a certain threshold, the SBU algorithm duplicates it. SBU's primary flaw is its disdain for the connection to historical access records. ABU is designed to aggregate historical data to the highest layer until it reaches the root in order to remedy the problem. The Fast Spread method outperformed the others, according to the data. The data access arrival rate, distribution, and replica server capacity were used to calculate the interval checking and threshold values.

The multi-objective strategy, which uses operations research approaches for replica placement, is a noteworthy methodology. This approach takes into account the data request pattern as well as the current network state while deploying a replica. In order to determine the p replica placement locations, the issue is phrased in p-median and p-center models. Reducing the maximum response time between the replica server and the user site is the aim of the p-center issue. The p-median approach, on the other hand, aims to shorten the overall response time between the replication and request sites. Additionally, replica weight is computed using the latest access history's access time in the future window using the Weight-based Dynamic Replica Replacement Strategy. Next, it calculates the access cost, which takes into account the current bandwidth of the network and the number of replicas. Replicas with a high weight are useful for increasing the efficiency of data access and should be retained; replicas with a low weight should be removed since they do not contribute to this improvement. A distribution akin to a zipfile is used to describe the access history.

The Latest Access Largest Weight (LALW) mechanism is a system for dynamic data replication on its part. LALW determines the quantity of copies and grid locations needed for duplication of a popular file. By giving each historical data access record a unique weight, the significance of each record is distinguished. A record of data access that is more recent has greater weight. This suggests that the document is more relevant to the state of data access as it is right now.

The agent-based replica placement method is an additional replica algorithm. The potential location for replica placement is identified using this suggested approach. For every site where master copies of the shared data files are kept, an agent will be installed. Selecting a prospective location for replica placement that minimizes application response times, network traffic, and access charges are the main objective of an agent. Additionally, an agent prioritizes grid resources according to resource configuration and network bandwidth, demands that the replica be created at their sites, and then generates the duplicate at appropriate resource locations.

The Adaptive Popularity Based Replica Placement (APBRP) is equally important. Placing replicas near to clients reduces data access time while maximizing the usage of network and storage resources. The approach is a hierarchical data grid dynamic replica placement algorithm driven by "file popularity." The threshold value selected with respect to file popularity determines how successful APBRP is. APBRP uses data request arrival rates to dynamically establish this threshold.

Additionally, an efficient replication approach that takes site dynamics into account is another successful replica algorithm. This technique has the capacity to decrease bandwidth use, enhance response time, and boost file availability for dynamic data grids. Replica placement and file requests are used to eventually arrive at a global grid load balancing solution. Because most grids utilize a "load" approach instead of a "update" strategy, which results in relatively few dynamic changes, this strategy will emphasize read-only access. Three stages are provided by this method and they are as follows:

(1) Based on the quantity of copies and requests for each file, the best candidate files were chosen for replication.

(2) Selecting the optimal locations for file placement from those selected in the preceding stage; these locations are chosen based on the quantity of requests and the usefulness of each site with respect to the grid.

(3) Selecting the most useful replica while taking each site's bandwidth and usefulness into account.

Replication algorithms would also benefit from the inclusion of the Value-Based Replication Strategy (VBRS). The VBRS was developed to enhance system performance by decreasing network latency. After a threshold was established in VBRS to decide whether or not to copy the requested file, the issue of replica replacement was resolved. Two steps make up VBRS. Calculating the threshold is the first step in deciding whether to copy the requested file to the local storage location. When the requested file has to be duplicated but there is not enough space at the local storage location, the replacement mechanism will then be triggered in the second step. The value of the replica—which is based on the frequency and duration of file access—is taken into account when developing the replica replacement policy. The studies' findings demonstrate how well the VBRS algorithm works to lower network latency.

Another useful technique is the Enhance Fast Spread (EPS). The enhanced Fast Spread for data grid replication approach is known as the EPS. The goal of this suggested technique is to reduce overall bandwidth use and reaction time. It takes into account a variety of variables, such as the volume and frequency of requests, the replica's size, and the duration since the previous request for the replica. The EFS method replaces less important copies with more important replicas, keeping only the important replicas. This is achieved by utilizing a dynamic threshold to decide at each node along the replica's journey to the requester whether or not to store the requested replica.

Another enhanced fast spread technique used in multi-tier data grid systems is predictive hierarchical fast spread (PHFS). The PHFS makes an effort to predict future requirements and pre-replicate in a minimal hierarchical fashion in order to enhance performance that takes spatial locality into account and boost access locality. In order to get more access locales, this approach replicates data objects hierarchically in multiple levels of the multi-tier data grid, hence optimizing the usage of storage resources. This method is intended for data grids with a lot of reading. To dynamically adjust the replication configuration to the available situation, the PHFS technique makes use of a priority mechanism and a replication configuration modification component. Additionally, it makes the high likelihood assumption that users operating in the same environment would request certain files.

In a similar vein, clones are positioned appropriately via the hierarchical replication method Dynamic Hierarchical Replication (DHR). The top site so has the most access to that copy. This method chooses the optimal replica when numerous locations host replicas in order to minimize access delay. Based on the quantity of replica requests in the queue and the data transfer time, the DHR algorithm's replica selection approach selects the optimal replica site for users who are now executing tasks. Rather of spreading out file storage over many places, it keeps the duplicate in the most visited area.

The Enhanced the Most Recent Access Largest Weight (MLALW) approach, a dynamic data replication strategy, is among the finest replication algorithms available. The Latest Access Largest Weight approach has been enhanced with this version.

When deleting files, MLALW considers three crucial factors:

(1)   The least utilized replicas

Two Replicas that is no longer in use

(3)   The size of the replica

Every replica is kept by MLALW in a suitable location in the area where it will be most accessible in the future. According to the trial findings, the MLALW method works better than the other algorithms and avoids making duplicates unnecessarily, which leads to effective storage utilization [46].

2.3 Belief Tolerance

The term "cloud computing" refers to the idea of virtualization being made available through the Internet for computer resources including storage, operating systems, and other things. While pay-per-use on-demand services, cheap pricing, and assured quality of service are some of the benefits of cloud computing, consumers' top worry in a cloud computing environment is dependability. "Reliability" describes a task's ability to be finished without fail within a certain amount of time. In a context of cloud computing or grid computing, a system fails or loses confidence when it does not perform as planned. Fault tolerance is the ability to overcome the effects of system faults and finish a job successfully when a fault occurs. A failure occurs when hardware or software cannot perform its intended function.

There are many different kinds of errors that may happen]:

Network Faults: A network may experience packet loss, network segmentation, or connection failure.

Physical Failures: These kinds of errors may happen to memory, CPUs, or storage devices, among other pieces of hardware.

Processor errors: The operating system's activities may lead to certain kinds of errors in the processor.

Process faults: These kinds of errors might be brought on by a lack of resources, issues with software, etc.

Faults related to Service Expiry: These errors arise when a resource's service timeout period ends while the application is in use.

In cloud computing, there are three different techniques to fault tolerance:

(1) Proactive Fault Tolerance Method: This approach replaces tainted components proactively and finds issues before they arise. It involves predicting faults and preventing recovery from mistakes.

The Proactive Fault Tolerance approach incorporates the following tactics:

1. Software rejuvenation: under this process, the system is launched in an entirely new state each time it is restarted after a certain amount of time.

Two. Self-Healing: This technology takes over an application on its own when a failure happens in an instance of a certain program that is running across several virtual machines.

ivy.Preemptive Migration: In this approach, a virtual machine's resources are moved to another virtual machine if it gets overcrowded after being examined and assessed many times.

The second technique is called the "Reactive Fault Tolerance Method," which is used to reduce or completely eradicate system faults. The following strategies are included in this method:

1.   Checkpointing: A task is resumed from the most recent checkpoint rather than from the beginning if it fails. Checkpoints are stored in the resource cache. This method is used in large-scale settings.

2.   Task Resubmission: Using this technique, failed tasks are sent back to the same computer or another one for further execution.

ivy.S-Guard: This HADOOP and Amazon EC2 technique makes sure that the job is rolled back in case of failure.

3.   Job migration is the process of moving a task from one malfunctioning machine to another that is capable of completing the assignment. Some algorithms are capable of fixing bugs and moving batches of applications across many data centers in a cloud. HAProxy is used to achieve this operation. HAProxy is used to achieve this operation.

   v.   User-defined exception handling: - With this method, the user designates the precise course of action to be followed in workflows in case of a task failure.

(3) Adaptive Fault Tolerance Method: -All actions in this method are taken automatically based on the status of the system at any given time. It guarantees the dependability of critical modules and keeps an eye on the dependability of virtual computers process by process.

By combining proactive and reactive fault tolerance techniques, one may use the adaptive fault tolerance approach to get rid of faults. Checkpointing, replication, and fragmentation are a few tactics. The process of "fragmenting" a single file into many files ensures that no data is lost when merging the files and creates the original file. By using this technique, applications obtain less irrelevant data.

The Assure technique, which stands for Automatic Software Self-healing through Rescue Points, is an additional approach to tolerance. For rescue points that handle the predicted failures of the coder, it works well. When a program fails at a certain moment, ASSURE encourages the program to recover through virtualization and resumes execution at the closest rescue point.

Apart from the aforementioned, HAProxy is quite efficient. The acronym for High Availability Proxy is HAProxy. This tool distributes the load across many computers to enhance a server cluster's consistency and performance. It is an open-source program designed to provide websites load-balancing options. It uses memory and CPU resources brilliantly. It is also well known for being dependable and stable. This approach is used by websites like Stack Overflow, GitHub, Twitter, and others to reduce heavy traffic.

An important development in this regard is SHelp, a runtime configuration that utilizes error virtualization and rescue points to assist virtual machines. It reduces repetition and bounces back fast from mistakes that are made again due to similar flaws. Server applications may quickly recover from these issues thanks to SHelp.

AmazonEC2, also known as Amazon Elastic Compute Cloud, is a very effective platform. One popular online service that offers cloud storage according to customer needs is AmazonEC2. Time management is facilitated by this, and developers are provided with tools to construct resilient program.

In a similar vein, Hadoop has seen tremendous growth recently. Many services related to cloud computing are offered by Hadoop. It is an open source project from the Apache Software Foundation that allows large datasets to be processed in a distributed manner across many workstations in a cluster. It provides public and private cloud services in the forms of IaaS, PaaS, and SaaS.

A multitude of models derived from the aforementioned technologies are employed:

(Pramanik, S. 2022) developed the Low Latency Fault Tolerance (LLFT) paradigm, which is based on replication and is used to provide fault tolerance for distributed applications deployed in cloud computing environments. This paradigm uses several replication procedures to copy programs and shield them from different types of errors. The issues and difficulties pertaining to the dependability, accessibility, and security of cloud computing (RAS) are the main topic of (Pramanik, S. 2023). It looks at intrusion detection techniques and concentrates on how to employ virtualization technology to improve RAS. (Khanh, P. T. et al. 2023) proposed a concept to improve the reliability of grid computing. It is based on the idea that resources and processing power required to maintain a dependable cloud infrastructure can only be obtained from trustworthy suppliers. Furthermore, it has focused on several dependability attributes to improve the integration of various constraints. (Ngọc, T. H. et al. 2023) shows a significant improvement in the reliability and availability of cloud computing systems by presenting a fault tolerance management (FTM) strategy based on virtualization technologies.

A noteworthy addition comes from (Bansal, R. et al. 2021), who put out a Dynamic Adaptive Fault Tolerance (DAFT) paradigm that is both semantically and ethically compatible with cloud fault tolerance. Replication and checkpointing are used for fault tolerance in order to improve this architecture's serviceability. In order to foresee the failure task in scientific workflow applications, (Khanh, P. T. et al. 2024) proposed a paradigm for proactive fault tolerance-based intelligent task failure detection. Additionally, (Ahamad, S. et al. 2024) put out the idea of an agent-based Fault Tolerance and Recovery System (FRAS). The recovery agent employs the rollback mechanism in the event of a failure. This method suggests an agent recovery mechanism to maintain the steady state of a system.

Additionally, (Veeraiah, V. et al. 2024) presented the idea of migration-based virtual data centers (VDCs). Certain resources are transferred to another virtual machine in case of a server failure or one virtual machine gets overcrowded. (Ashisha G. R., et al. 2023) put out a cloud fault tolerance (FTMC) idea. In this paradigm, computer nodes are chosen on the basis of their dependability, which is tracked. The node that is generating erroneous results on a regular basis is eliminated. (Andrushia, A. D. et al. 2023) introduced a fault tolerance model that relies on decisions. According to this paradigm, the precision and reaction time of a node define its dependability. This is a method of adaptation. Backward recovery is tried in the event that a node malfunctions, and nodes are added or deleted according on how reliable they are.

Once more, (Jayasingh, R. et al. 2022) suggested a number of fault tolerance and monitoring techniques to raise the dependability of the cloud computing ecosystem. This article addresses future research directions in cloud fault tolerance in addition to offering information about the different techniques and methodology used for fault tolerance. For cloud-based software rejuvenation, (VidyaChellam, V. et al. 2023) proposed a software reliability model based on dynamic fault trees. This model draws attention to the issue of software ageing, in which fault accumulation, resource depletion, and system fragmentation may continuously impair system performance proposed a method for fault tolerance in cloud computing. The author of this model explains the way in which faults lead to major problems. This model makes use of a variety of fault tolerance techniques to forecast these faults and take appropriate action either before or after a failure occurs. By (Praveenkumar, S. et al. 2023), the FT-Cloud idea was first presented. It's a part that's decided by how well cloud application developers are rated. An algorithm in this module enables direct fault tolerance by default. An adaptive fault tolerance technique (AFTRC) was proposed in real-time cloud computing by (Veeraiah, V. et al. 2023). The foundation of this concept is cloud-based real-time computing. The benefit of forwarding recovery is offered. There is a significant degree of fault tolerance in this paradigm. Additionally, this paradigm stresses checkpointing as a means of backward rehabilitation.

In conclusion, the literature researches on fault tolerance in cloud computing revealed a number of problems, the most significant of which are as follows:

(1) Because the processing is done by distant equipment, there is a significant chance of mistakes.
(2) The development of effective fault location techniques is required.
(3) Clients get limited data because of the system's high density.
(4) It is necessary to build more real-time fault prediction technology.
(5) It is challenging to understand how the system status is changing because of how dynamic the cloud environment is.
(6) Although the customer's organization is unaffected by data centre problems, fault tolerance measures nevertheless need to be put in place.

3. CONCLUSION

The article begins with a quick summary of cloud computing and grid computing settings before delving more into the different fault tolerance replication methods and fragmentation strategies used in distributed database systems. This study discusses many strategies for increasing the efficiency of distributed database system performance, reducing transfer/communication costs, and shortening access/response times. These techniques include fusion fault tolerance replication models and fragmentation techniques. It is feasible to draw the conclusion that fusion fault models and fragmentation tactics are significant techniques that may be used to enhance distributed database systems and data validity based on the researchers' results. In order to maximize the resources, it is also essential to keep up a sufficient data fragmentation and fusion fault structure. It is reasonable to say that the best way to optimize the performance of the distributed database system is to use a fusion and fragmentation fault structure that is both dependable and efficient. For fault tolerance, recovery, and identification, we must use certain algorithms. Nonetheless, there is currently a dearth of research on data fragmentation and fusion fault solutions in distributed database systems. In order to increase application efficiency, more data fragmentation and fusion fault mechanisms should be researched and used in distributed database systems in the future.

REFERENCES

Ahamad, S., Janani, S., Talukdar, V., Sharma, T., Sahu, A., Pramanik, S., & Gupta, A. (2024). *Apollo Hospital's Proposed Use of Big Data Healthcare Analytics, Big Data Analytics Techniques for Market Intelligence*. IGI Global.

Andrushia, A. D., Neebha, T. M., Patricia, A. T., Sagayam, K. M., & Pramanik, S. (2023). Capsule Network based Disease Classification for VitisVinifera Leaves. *Neural Computing & Applications*. doi:10.1007/s00521-023-09058-y

Ashisha, G. R., Anitha Mary, X., George, T., & Martin Sagayam, K. (2023). Unai Fernandez-GamizHatıraGünerhan, Uddin, M. N. and Pramanik, S. (2023). Analysis of Diabetes disease using Machine Learning Techniques: A Review. *Journal of Information Technology Management*.

Bansal, R., Obaid, A. J., Gupta, A., Singh, R., & Pramanik, S. (2021). Impact of Big Data on Digital Transformation in 5G Era. *2nd International Conference on Physics and Applied Sciences (ICPAS 2021)*. IOP Science. , 2021.10.1088/1742-6596/1963/1/012170

Bhattacharya, A., Ghosal, A., Obaid, A. J., Krit, S., Shukla, V. K., Mandal, K., & Pramanik, S. (2021). Unsupervised Summarization Approach with Computational Statistics of Microblog Data. In D. Samanta, R. R. Althar, S. Pramanik, & S. Dutta (Eds.), *Methodologies and Applications of Computational Statistics for Machine Learning* (pp. 23–37). IGI Global. doi:10.4018/978-1-7998-7701-1.ch002

Dhamodaran, S., Ahamad, S., Ramesh, J. V. N., Sathappan, S., Namdev, A., Kanse, R. R., & Pramanik, S. (2023). *Fire Detection System Utilizing an Aggregate Technique in UAV and Cloud Computing, Thrust Technologies' Effect on Image Processing*. IGI Global.

Jain, V., Rastogi, M., Ramesh, J. V. N., Chauhan, A., Agarwal, P., Pramanik, S., & Gupta, A. (2023). FinTech and Artificial Intelligence in Relationship Banking and Computer Technology. In K. Saini, A. Mummoorthy, R. Chandrika, N. S. Gowri Ganesh, & I. G. I. Global (Eds.), *AI, IoT, and Blockchain Breakthroughs in E-Governance*. doi:10.4018/978-1-6684-7697-0.ch011

Jayasingh, R. (2022). Speckle noise removal by SORAMA segmentation in Digital Image Processing to facilitate precise robotic surgery. *International Journal of Reliable and Quality E-Healthcare*, *11*(1), 1–19. doi:10.4018/IJRQEH.295083

K.aushik, D., Garg, M., Annu, Gupta, A. and Pramanik, S. (2022). Application of Machine Learning and Deep Learning in Cyber security: An Innovative Approach. In M. Ghonge, S. Pramanik, R. Mangrulkar and D. N. Le, (eds.). *Cybersecurity and Digital Forensics: Challenges and Future Trends*. Wiley. doi:10.1002/9781119795667.ch12

Khanh, P. T., Ngọc, T. H., & Pramanik, S. (2023). Future of Smart Agriculture Techniques and Applications. In A. Khang & I. G. I. Global (Eds.), *Advanced Technologies and AI-Equipped IoT Applications in High Tech Agriculture*. doi:10.4018/978-1-6684-9231-4.ch021

Khanh, P. T., Ngoc, T. T. H., & Pramanik, S. (2024). *AI-Decision Support System: Engineering, Geology, Climate, and Socioeconomic Aspects' Implications on Machine Learning, Using Traditional Design Methods to Enhance AI-Driven Decision Making*. IGI Global. doi:10.4018/979-8-3693-0639-0.ch008

Ngọc, T. H., Khanh, P. T., & Pramanik, S. (2023). Smart Agriculture using a Soil Monitoring System. In A. Khang & I. G. I. Global (Eds.), *Advanced Technologies and AI-Equipped IoT Applications in High Tech Agriculture*. doi:10.4018/978-1-6684-9231-4.ch011

Pandey, B. K., Pandey, D., Nassa, V. K., George, A. S., Pramanik, S., & Dadheech, P. (2023). Applications for the Text Extraction Method of Complex Degraded Images. In *The Impact of Thrust Technologies on Image Processing*. Nova Publishers. doi:10.52305/ATJL4552

Pramanik, S. (2022). Carpooling Solutions using Machine Learning Tools. In *Handbook of Research on Evolving Designs and Innovation in ICT and Intelligent Systems for Real-World Applications, K. K. Sarma, N. Saikia and M. Sharma*. IGI Global. doi:10.4018/978-1-7998-9795-8.ch002

Pramanik, S. (2023). Intelligent Farming Utilizing a Soil Tracking Device. In A. K. Sharma, N. Chanderwal, R. Khan, & I. G. I. Global (Eds.), *Convergence of Cloud Computing, AI and Agricultural Science*. doi:10.4018/979-8-3693-0200-2.ch009

Praveenkumar, S., Veeraiah, V., Pramanik, S., Basha, S. M., Lira Neto, A. V., De Albuquerque, V. H. C., & Gupta, A. (2023). *Prediction of Patients' Incurable Diseases Utilizing Deep Learning Approaches, ICICC 2023*. Springer. doi:10.1007/978-981-99-3315-0_4

Talukdar, V., Kurniullah, A. Z., Keshwani, P., Khan, H., Pramanik, S., Gupta, A., & Pandey, D. (2023). *Load Balancing Techniques in Cloud Computing, Emerging Trends in Cloud Computing Analytics, Scalability, and Service Models*. IGI Global.

Taviti Naidu, G., & Ganesh, K. V. B. (2023). Technological Innovation Driven by Big Data. Advanced Bioinspiration Methods for Healthcare Standards, Policies, and Reform. IGI Global. doi:10.4018/978-1-6684-5656-9

Veeraiah, V., Shiju, D. J., Ramesh, J. V. N., Ganesh, K. R., Pramanik, S., Pandey, D., & Gupta, A. (2023). *Healthcare Cloud Services in Image Processing, Thrust Technologies' Effect on Image Processing*. IGI Global.

Veeraiah, V., Talukdar, V., Manikandan, K., Talukdar, S. B., Solavande, V. D., Pramanik, S., & Gupta, A. (2023). Machine Learning Frameworks in Carpooling. Handbook of Research on AI and Machine Learning Applications in Customer Support and Analytics. IGI Global.

Veeraiah, V., Thejaswini, K. O., Dilip, R., Jain, S. K., Sahu, A., Pramanik, S., & Gupta, A. (2024). *The Suggested Use of Big Data in Medical Analytics by Fortis Healthcare Hospital, Adoption and Use of Technology Tools and Services by Economically Disadvantaged Communities: Implications for Growth and Sustainability*. IGI Global.

Vidya Chellam, V., Veeraiah, V., Khanna, A., Sheikh, T. H., Pramanik, S., & Dhabliya, D. (2023). A Machine Vision-based Approach for Tuberculosis Identification in Chest X-Rays Images of Patients. *ICICC 2023*, Springer. doi:10.1007/978-981-99-3315-0_3

Chapter 11
Unraveling the Complex Challenges and Innovative Solutions in Microservice Architecture:
Exploring Deep Microservice Architecture Hurdles

Kaushikkumar Patel
https://orcid.org/0009-0005-9197-2765
TransUnion LLC, USA

ABSTRACT

This chapter delves into the challenges of microservice architecture within serverless computing, outlining strategic remedies. It underscores operational hurdles like sophisticated orchestration and service interactions, along with security concerns due to the system's decentralized fabric. The discourse extends to performance bottlenecks, focusing on resource management in serverless frameworks. Proposed solutions include advanced system monitoring, state-of-the-art security safeguards, and innovative optimization strategies. The chapter concludes with prospective research directions, emphasizing advanced service meshes and security enhancements, offering practitioners a pragmatic blueprint for microservice implementation in serverless infrastructures. This analysis is crucial for professionals navigating the intricacies of microservice deployment.

DOI: 10.4018/979-8-3693-1682-5.ch011

1. INTRODUCTION

In the realm of software architecture, microservices have emerged as a paradigm shift, advocating for splitting applications into smaller, interconnected services instead of building a single, monolithic structure. This approach, while offering numerous benefits such as improved scalability, enhanced resilience, and faster time-to-market, also introduces a unique set of challenges that stem from its distributed nature.

The advent of microservices is rooted in the limitations of traditional monolithic architectures, where applications are built as a single unit of software. These monoliths, while straightforward to develop, test, and deploy initially, eventually lead to numerous issues as applications grow and evolve. Developers face significant hurdles in maintaining and updating a large, intertwined codebase, which often results in slower updates and a higher risk of system-wide failures stemming from minor code alterations. Moreover, scaling specific functionalities of an application isn't feasible with monoliths, as it requires scaling the entire application, leading to inefficient resource utilization.

Microservices emerged as a solution to these bottlenecks, promising more agility and scalability for modern applications. By breaking down an application into smaller services that operate independently, developers can update, deploy, and scale each service as needed without affecting the operation of others. This architectural style aligns well with contemporary business needs, especially with the rise of cloud computing, which provides the necessary infrastructure for hosting distributed applications.

However, the transition to microservices is not without its challenges. One of the primary issues is the complexity involved in creating and maintaining a distributed system. Each service, though independently operational, must effectively communicate with others, necessitating careful network planning, data consistency, and fault tolerance strategies. Security is another critical concern, as the increased inter-service communication creates numerous attack vectors. Additionally, the operational overhead of managing multiple services can be substantial, requiring robust monitoring, logging, and automation practices.

This chapter delves into the intricacies of microservice challenges, exploring the technical, operational, and organizational hurdles that companies face when adopting this architectural style. Issues related to network complexities, data management, security vulnerabilities, and the cultural shift required within organizations to support a microservices ecosystem will be dissected. Furthermore, the discussion will extend to existing solutions to these challenges, highlighting best practices and tools that aid in creating a resilient, efficient, and secure microservice architecture.

Navigating through the landscape of microservices, it becomes evident that these challenges are not deterrents but rather considerations that, when addressed effectively, can pave the way for a more agile and responsive IT infrastructure. By embracing these complexities, organizations can harness the full potential of microservices, driving innovation and growth in an ever-evolving digital marketplace.

2. LITERATURE REVIEW

Microservices architecture, a revolutionary approach in software development, has garnered substantial attention in both industrial and academic realms due to its promise of agility, scalability, and resilience. This literature review delves into the comprehensive analyses and diverse perspectives offered by numerous studies, shedding light on the evolution, benefits, challenges, and practical implications of adopting microservices. By dissecting various facets of this architectural style, we aim to present a balanced view that encapsulates the collective wisdom and ongoing debates within this domain.

Evolution and Principles of Microservices:

    i.   The Shift from Monolithic to Microservices: The journey from traditional monolithic architectures to microservices marks a significant shift in software design philosophy (Götz, B., 2018). The limitations of monolithic structures, particularly in scaling and continuous deployment, highlighted the need for a more flexible architecture, leading to the conceptualization of microservices (Assunção, W. K., 2020).

    ii.   Defining Characteristics of Microservices: Microservices are characterized by certain foundational principles, including single responsibility, decentralized governance, and loose coupling, which collectively contribute to the architectural style's agility, resilience, and maintainability (Velepucha, V., 2023). These principles guide the decomposition of applications into manageable services that can be developed, deployed, and scaled independently (Baškarada, S., 2018).

Microservices and Cloud Computing:

    i.   Symbiosis between Microservices and the Cloud: Microservices and cloud computing have evolved in a complementary manner, with cloud platforms providing the scalable, on-demand infrastructure that microservices require (Premarathna, D., 2021). The elasticity and resource management capabilities of cloud environments are particularly conducive to the dynamic scaling requirements of microservices (Villamizar, M., 2015).

    ii.   Containerization and Orchestration: The role of containerization technologies, like Docker, and orchestration tools, such as Kubernetes, has been pivotal in the microservices revolution. These technologies simplify the deployment, scaling, and management of microservice components, addressing some of the complexity associated with operating distributed systems ((Viggiato, M., 2018).

Challenges in Microservices Architecture:

    i.   Data Management and Consistency: One of the primary challenges in a microservices environment is managing data consistency across independently operating services. This issue stems from the distributed nature of microservices and necessitates sophisticated strategies for transaction management and data replication (Kalske, M., 2018).

    ii.   Network Complexity and Service Communication: Microservices architectures introduce complexity in network communication and integration. The increased inter-service communication can lead to network latency, requiring efficient communication protocols and robust API gateways ((Söylemez, M., 2022). Additionally, the architecture must be designed with fault tolerance in mind to prevent service failures (Billawa, P., 2022).

Security Concerns in Microservices:

    i.   Securing Inter-Service Communication: The distributed nature of microservices introduces security challenges, particularly concerning secure communication between services. Implementing robust authentication and authorization mechanisms is paramount to protect sensitive data and prevent unauthorized access (Yarygina, T., 2018).

    ii.   Deployment and Access Control: Each microservice's deployment and access controls must be meticulously configured to safeguard against security breaches. This task is complicated by the need to maintain security configurations across numerous services, especially in dynamic scaling environments (Krylovskiy, A., 2015).

Testing and Monitoring Microservices:

i.   Adaptation of Testing Strategies: Microservices necessitate a shift from traditional testing strategies, demanding new approaches that accommodate the architecture's distributed and independent characteristics. This includes the adoption of contract testing, end-to-end testing, and other methodologies that ensure comprehensive coverage (Jamshidi, P., 2018).

ii. Comprehensive Monitoring Approaches: Effective monitoring in a microservices environment extends beyond simple uptime checks. It involves collecting detailed performance data, tracing requests across services, and setting up sophisticated alerting mechanisms to maintain system health and performance (Waseem, M., 2017).

Organizational and Cultural Shift:

i.   Restructuring Development Teams: The adoption of microservices often requires a reorganization of development teams and processes. The architecture's emphasis on small, autonomous services aligns with a move towards smaller, cross-functional teams that can operate with a high degree of independence (Di Francesco, P., 2018).

ii. Embracing DevOps and Agile Methodologies: Microservices have been a driving force behind the widespread adoption of DevOps and agile methodologies. These practices facilitate continuous integration and deployment, which are integral to the microservices ethos of rapid, iterative releases (Cerny, T., 2018).

Performance Engineering in Microservices:

i.   Revisiting Performance Optimization Strategies: Microservices architectures compel a rethinking of performance optimization strategies. Traditional performance engineering practices need to be adapted to address the nuances of microservices, such as network latency, service discovery, and load balancing (Zhang, H., 2019).

ii. Dynamic Performance Management: The ephemeral nature of microservices, especially in cloud environments, necessitates dynamic performance management strategies that can accommodate auto-scaling and rapid deployment cycles. This dynamic approach helps in maintaining optimal performance and resource utilization (Aksakalli, I. K., 2021).

Theoretical and Practical Divergences:

Gap between Theory and Practice: While theoretical models of microservices offer a structured view of the architecture, practical implementations often necessitate deviations from these ideals. Real-world constraints, operational demands, and legacy systems often lead to compromises in the architectural design (Bushong, V., 2021).

Pragmatism in Microservices Adoption: The practical adoption of microservices requires a pragmatic approach that balances ideal architectural principles with operational realities. This balance ensures that the architecture serves the business needs effectively while maintaining technical soundness (Wang, Y., 2021).

the literature on microservices architecture presents a domain rich in complexity and ongoing innovation. From its evolutionary roots to its current applications, microservices continue to shape the landscape of modern software development. The body of literature not only highlights the transformative potential of microservices but also cautions adopters about the significant challenges inherent in this architectural style. As microservices continue to evolve, so will the discussions and studies surrounding them, perpetually driving this field toward new advancements and solutions.

3. OPERATIONAL COMPLEXITIES IN MICROSERVICE ARCHITECTURE

Microservices architecture, while beneficial for agile and scalable systems, introduces several operational complexities. These challenges stem from the architecture's inherent characteristics - distributed deployment, dynamic scaling, and the need for robustness and resilience. Addressing these operational challenges requires innovative solutions, advanced tooling, and a paradigm shift in operational methodologies.

a. **Deployment Challenges:** The deployment in a microservices environment is intricate due to the need to handle multiple, loosely coupled services that evolve independently. These services, each with its deployment lifecycle, necessitate a robust automation strategy to ensure consistency, minimize downtime, and maintain inter-service compatibility. The complexity escalates when considering zero-downtime deployments, blue/green deployments, or canary releases, which are essential strategies for ensuring the system's stability during updates and rollbacks (Assunção, W. K., 2020), (Liu, G., 2020). Furthermore, the system must maintain high cohesion within services and low coupling between them, preserving the autonomy of individual services while ensuring seamless interaction (Wang, Y., 2021).

b. **Configuration Management:** Configuration management in microservices is a formidable task. The decentralized nature of microservices means that each service might have its own configuration, potentially leading to hundreds of configuration files that need to be managed and maintained. This decentralized approach complicates tasks like updating configurations, propagating changes, and maintaining security and compliance standards. Centralized configuration servers, dynamic configuration updates, and encryption of sensitive data are practices that tackle these challenges, ensuring configurations are consistent, secure, and adaptable to changes in the system's environment (Premarathna, D., 2021), (Krylovskiy, A., 2015), (Zhang, H., 2019).

c. **Service Discovery and Load Balancing:** Microservices operate in a dynamic environment, necessitating efficient service discovery and load balancing mechanisms. Service discovery must be intelligent and real-time, capable of automatically registering and deregistering service instances. This dynamic nature eliminates the feasibility of manual configuration, demanding automated, self-healing mechanisms embedded in the system ((Viggiato, M., 2018), (Billawa, P., 2022). Load balancing strategies, too, must be dynamic, recognizing the availability and demand of services to distribute requests efficiently. They should also be cognizant of the system's health, redirecting traffic away from failing instances and ensuring reliability and optimal resource utilization (Bushong, V., 2021).

d. **Monitoring and Logging:** Effective monitoring and logging are paramount in a distributed system like microservices. The need to monitor health metrics, performance data, and business transactions across different services requires a holistic approach that aggregates data into a centralized, coherent view. This approach helps in quick anomaly detection, efficient root cause analysis, and informed decision-making processes (Kalske, M., 2018), (Waseem, M., 2017). Logging, on the other hand, becomes complex due to the sheer volume of logs generated by services. Centralized logging solutions that aggregate and index logs are crucial for providing insights and simplifying the debugging process in such distributed environments (Aksakalli, I. K., 2021).

e. **Network Complexity:** The inter-service communication in microservices introduces network complexity, making the system susceptible to issues like network latency, partitioning, and security concerns. Efficient, lightweight communication protocols are needed to facilitate quick, reliable inter-service exchanges. Sophisticated API gateways help manage traffic flow, enforce policies, and aggregate data, ensuring smooth and secure data exchange. Strategies to ensure network resilience, like implementing timeouts, retries, and circuit breakers, are also crucial to maintaining system availability and performance ((Söylemez, M., 2022), (Jamshidi, P., 2018).

f. **Security Management:** Each microservice exposes a potential attack surface, making security a top-tier concern. Implementing security at the perimeter level is insufficient; instead, end-to-end security measures incorporating authentication, authorization, secure communication, and threat detection are imperative. Consistent security policies, API security, secret management, and regular vulnerability assessments are part of a comprehensive security strategy. The complexity arises in uniformly enforcing these measures across all services while accommodating the unique requirements of each service (Yarygina, T., 2018), (Smid, A., 2019), (Ghofrani, J., 2018).

g. **Data Management:** Data management poses unique challenges in microservices due to the distribution of services. Ensuring data consistency across microservices, managing transactions that span multiple services, and implementing effective data sharing and replication strategies are complex but essential. Techniques like Saga patterns help manage distributed transactions, while event sourcing and CQRS address data consistency and query optimization. However, these solutions also bring additional complexity and require careful consideration and expertise to implement effectively (Baškarada, S., 2018), (Villamizar, M., 2015), (Alshuqayran, N., 2016).

h. **Resilience and Fault Tolerance:** Microservices must be resilient, with the capability to recover quickly from failures. Designing systems for failure, implementing strategies like circuit breakers, and designing for graceful degradation are essential in building robust systems. Redundancy, fallback methods, and isolation techniques prevent failures from cascading through the system, ensuring high availability and reliability. Testing practices like chaos engineering can further ensure system robustness by proactively identifying weaknesses before they cause system-wide outages (Velepucha, V., 2023), (Di Francesco, P., 2018), (Heinrich, R., 2017).

i. **Scaling Challenges:** While microservices are designed for scalability, this characteristic introduces challenges. Effective scaling strategies must account for when to scale, how much to scale, and how to balance the load between instances. Auto-scaling, based on real-time performance metrics, ensures the system can handle increased load without manual intervention. However, this requires sophisticated monitoring and decision-making mechanisms. Additionally, understanding the interdependencies between services is crucial to avoid performance bottlenecks and ensure resource efficiency (Götz, B., 2018), (Cerny, T., 2018).

Managing the operational complexities of microservices architecture is a multifaceted endeavor that requires strategic planning, advanced tooling, and continuous monitoring. These complexities, while challenging, are surmountable with the right approaches and technologies, paving the way for efficient, agile, and reliable microservice ecosystems.

4. SECURITY AND COMPLIANCE CHALLENGES

Navigating the security landscape within microservice architectures demands a profound understanding of the unique challenges posed by the distributed nature of microservices. These systems, characterized by their agility and scalability, also introduce complexities in maintaining security and regulatory

Table 1. Operational complexities in microservice architecture

Challenge	Description
Deployment Challenges	Involves handling multiple services' independent evolution, requiring robust automation strategies for consistency and stability during updates.
Configuration Management	Decentralized configurations across services necessitate centralized management solutions for consistency and security.
Service Discovery and Load Balancing	Requires real-time, intelligent mechanisms for automatic service registration and efficient request distribution.
Monitoring and Logging	Essential for maintaining system health, requiring centralized solutions for effective anomaly detection and debugging.
Network Complexity	Inter-service communication introduces issues like latency and security, demanding efficient protocols and resilience strategies.
Security Management	Requires end-to-end measures, including authentication, authorization, and consistent policy enforcement across services.
Data Management	Challenges in ensuring consistency, managing distributed transactions, and effective data-sharing strategies.
Resilience and Fault Tolerance	Designing for quick recovery, isolation, and robustness to prevent system-wide outages.
Scaling Challenges	Demands effective strategies for auto-scaling and understanding service interdependencies to prevent bottlenecks.

compliance. This section explores these intricacies, highlighting the paramount importance of advanced, integrated security measures in sustaining the integrity, confidentiality, and availability of resources in microservice ecosystems.

a. **Data Security and Privacy:** Microservices operate on the principle of decentralized data management, which, while enhancing agility, also complicates data security protocols. The segmentation of services necessitates a framework where each service upholds data integrity and confidentiality, enforcing policies like data encryption at rest and in transit, and regular security assessments (Assunção, W. K., 2020). The challenge escalates with international data privacy regulations like GDPR and HIPAA, which impose stringent rules on data processing and cross-border data transfers. Organizations must incorporate data protection measures at the architectural level, ensuring that personal data undergoes anonymization and pseudonymization. Additionally, they must manage consent comprehensively and provide transparent data processing notifications to maintain compliance (Yarygina, T., 2018).

b. **Authentication and Authorization:** In a microservice environment, ensuring a unified and secure identity verification process is complex due to the disparate nature of services. While monolithic applications can rely on session-based authentication, microservices prefer stateless authentication mechanisms, such as JWT or OAuth, to reduce dependencies ((Viggiato, M., 2018). These tokens carry the risk of theft or interception, necessitating robust token management systems. Furthermore, fine-grained access control requires dynamic authorization mechanisms that consider context, roles, and attributes, challenging to implement consistently across services (Waseem, M., 2017).

c. **Network Security:** Inter-service communication, a hallmark of microservices, is a potential entry point for unauthorized access. Ensuring network security requires SSL/TLS encryption for data in transit, API security measures, and strict firewall rules (Kalske, M., 2018). The internal network, often overlooked, must also be fortified against lateral movements in case of a breach. Implementing mutual SSL or mTLS provides an additional layer of security by ensuring two-way authentication between services. However, managing SSL certificates and implementing network segmentation in a dynamic microservice ecosystem remains challenging (Di Francesco, P., 2018).

d. **Compliance and Regulatory Challenges:** Compliance in microservice architectures is a moving target due to the continuous deployment of services and evolving regulatory standards. Each microservice might fall under different compliance categories, making it imperative to have a thorough understanding of applicable laws for data protection, financial transactions, and industry-specific regulations (Premarathna, D., 2021). Automated compliance checks, policy-as-code, and real-time compliance monitoring become essential in such a dispersed environment. Additionally, preparing for compliance audits requires comprehensive logging, transparent processes, and evidence of security measures, which are resource-intensive (Bushong, V., 2021).

e. **Security Testing and Patch Management:** The autonomous nature of microservices intensifies the need for continuous security assessments. Traditional security testing methods are inadequate, prompting the integration of security into DevOps, termed DevSecOps. This approach emphasizes automated security checks, code reviews, dependency checks, and penetration testing at every stage of the CI/CD pipeline (Jamshidi, P., 2018). Simultaneously, vulnerability management and timely patching of services are complicated by the need to maintain system stability. Coordinating patch schedules, ensuring backward compatibility, and validating patches before deployment requires a systematic, automated approach to prevent service disruptions (Wang, Y., 2021).

f. **Configuration Management and Secret Handling:** The distributed configuration in microservices heightens the risk of exposure of sensitive data. Best practices discourage embedding secrets in code or configuration files, advocating for centralized secret management services (Zhang, H., 2019). These specialized services provide secure storage, tightly controlled access, and regular rotation of secrets, reducing the risk of compromise. However, implementing these practices requires careful planning, as real-time updates of secrets can cause service disruptions. Additionally, auditing access to secrets and integrating with identity providers adds to the operational overhead (Alshuqayran, N., 2016).

Securing microservice architectures is an intricate task, demanding a holistic approach that encompasses various aspects of information security. From ensuring data privacy to managing network security and maintaining compliance, each facet requires dedicated strategies tailored to the microservices paradigm. As organizations continue to embrace microservices, the importance of comprehensive security measures, continuous monitoring, and adaptive security policies cannot be overstated. The resilience of a microservice-based application hinges on the robustness of its security infrastructure, affirming the need for ongoing research and development in this critical domain.

5. PERFORMANCE AND OPTIMIZATION IN A SERVERLESS ENVIRONMENT

Serverless computing, a groundbreaking innovation in cloud computing, has significantly altered the landscape of application development and deployment. By offloading the operational overhead to cloud providers, organizations can concentrate on delivering value through business logic and user experience. However, this shift necessitates a deep understanding of unique performance hurdles and optimization

Table 2. Overview of security and compliance challenges

Challenge Category	Description
Data Security and Privacy	Ensuring data integrity and confidentiality, compliance with data protection regulations, implementing encryption, and managing consent.
Authentication and Authorization	Implementing secure and consistent identity verification processes, managing authentication tokens, and enforcing fine-grained access control.
Network Security	Securing inter-service communications, fortifying internal networks, and managing SSL certificates for encrypted connections.
Compliance and Regulatory Challenges	Navigating varying compliance requirements, automating compliance checks, and preparing comprehensive audit logs and documentation.
Security Testing and Patch Management	Integrating continuous security assessments in DevOps, coordinating vulnerability management, and systematic patch deployment.
Configuration Management and Secret Handling	Protecting sensitive configuration data, centralizing secret management, and auditing access while ensuring system stability.
Data Security and Privacy	Ensuring data integrity and confidentiality, compliance with data protection regulations, implementing encryption, and managing consent.

tactics essential for efficient, cost-effective, and robust applications. This discussion explores the depth of performance issues, optimization methodologies, and industry best practices in the serverless realm, drawing on a wealth of scholarly research and real-world experiences.

a. **Understanding Performance Implications:** Serverless architectures, characterized by their micro-level functional components, offer remarkable scalability but also introduce distinct challenges. One of the primary concerns is the cold start phenomenon, where latency is introduced during the initiation of a new function instance, significantly impacting performance-sensitive applications (Waseem, M., 2017). The issue compounds the varying languages and resource configurations, often leading to inconsistent performance (Aksakalli, I. K., 2021). Additionally, the stateless nature of functions complicates consistent resource allocation, as both over-provisioning and under-provisioning have adverse effects on performance, user experience, and costs ((Viggiato, M., 2018), (Heinrich, R., 2017). Researchers also highlight network latency in communication between functions and with other services, emphasizing the need for efficient networking solutions within the serverless infrastructure (Söylemez, M., 2022).

b. **Monitoring and Observability:** The ephemeral and distributed nature of serverless functions necessitates advanced monitoring and observability tools. Traditional methods are insufficient, lacking the granularity to provide insights into short-lived function executions (Assunção, W. K., 2020). Scholars advocate for specialized tools capable of detailed tracing, sophisticated log analytics, and real-time performance monitoring to identify bottlenecks and inefficiencies effectively (Zhang, H., 2019). These solutions must cater to the serverless model's dynamic, event-driven architecture, providing visibility into function interactions, execution paths, and external dependencies (Smid, A., 2019).

c. **Optimization Strategies:** Tackling performance inefficiencies requires a comprehensive strategy encompassing several aspects. Code optimization, such as refining the code for quicker execution or reducing the package size, can significantly reduce latency (Kalske, M., 2018). Pre-warming strategies, where functions are initialized in advance to avoid cold starts, are crucial for performance-sensitive applications (Liu, G., 2020). Resource allocation also requires meticulous management, adjusting configurations to match the function's demand accurately (Krylovskiy, A., 2015). Deployment strategies, too, play a role, with options like dedicated instances for critical functions or geographic distribution to reduce latency (Wang, Y., 2021). Researchers are exploring adaptive optimization techniques, adjusting resources in real-time based on traffic patterns and user demand (Götz, B., 2018).

d.   **Cost-Performance Trade-offs:** The serverless cost model, while potentially more cost-efficient, requires balancing performance with expenses. High-throughput applications, if not optimized, can incur substantial costs (Yarygina, T., 2018). This balance involves strategic resource allocation, where functions receive resources corresponding to their requirements, preventing over-provisioning (Cerny, T., 2018). Innovative approaches like function batching, where multiple requests are processed simultaneously, or request multiplexing, where single function instances handle multiple requests, optimize resource usage (Villamizar, M., 2015). Cost monitoring and governance strategies are also vital to prevent budget overruns while maintaining optimal performance (Jamshidi, P., 2018).

e.   **The Role of Machine Learning and Automation:** Emerging technologies, particularly machine learning and automation, are paving the way for sophisticated performance optimization in serverless environments. Predictive scaling utilizes machine learning algorithms to anticipate traffic trends and adjust resources, ensuring optimal performance and cost-efficiency (Baškarada, S., 2018). Automated performance testing tools are gaining traction, capable of simulating diverse workloads and stress conditions to identify bottlenecks preemptively and potential performance downgrades (Di Francesco, P., 2018). These systems, through continuous learning and adaptation, contribute to more resilient, efficient, and performant serverless applications (Billawa, P., 2022).

Optimizing performance in serverless environments is an intricate endeavor demanding ongoing attention and innovative approaches. The transient nature of serverless computing calls for specialized strategies and tools to monitor, comprehend, and enhance application performance effectively. A comprehensive approach, encompassing meticulous code optimization, strategic resource management, cost-control measures, and the integration of advanced technologies like machine learning, is imperative for organizations aiming to exploit serverless computing fully. Insights from academic studies and practical implementations underscore the necessity for perpetual learning and adaptation in this fast-paced, ever-evolving field.

6. CHALLENGES AND SOLUTIONS

Embracing microservice architecture is a paradigm shift that promises scalability, resilience, and agility in application development. However, it inherently introduces multifaceted challenges, primarily due to its distributed nature and the granularity of services. This complexity demands innovative solutions that encompass advanced technological tools, refined best practices, and comprehensive strategic approaches. Addressing these challenges head-on is crucial for harnessing the full potential of microservices and achieving optimized, seamless functionality within these architectures.

Table 3. Key strategies for enhancing performance in serverless environments

Performance Optimization	Description
Understanding Performance Implications	Addresses the unique performance challenges in serverless computing, including cold starts, resource allocation inconsistencies, and network latency.
Monitoring and Observability	Emphasizes the need for advanced tools to gain insights into function executions, dependencies, and interactions within the serverless architecture.
Optimization Strategies	Encompasses code refinement, pre-warming functions, precise resource allocation, and adaptive techniques for real-time performance enhancement.
Cost-Performance Trade-offs	Involves strategic resource management to balance operational costs with performance efficiency, employing innovative approaches for optimal resource utilization.
Role of Machine Learning and Automation	Highlights the integration of predictive analytics, automated testing, and continuous adaptation methods to foresee demands, identify potential issues, and ensure resilient application performance.

Network Complexity and Communication Overhead:

i. Challenge: The intricate network of microservices necessitates a substantial amount of inter-service communication, potentially leading to network congestion, increased latency, and data transmission inefficiencies. This complexity is compounded by the need for synchronous and asynchronous communication strategies, error handling, and the implementation of robust communication protocols.

ii. Solution: Solutions include the adoption of efficient communication protocols like gRPC, which is specifically designed for low-latency, high-performance applications. Furthermore, introducing a service mesh technology such as Istio or Linkerd can abstract the complexity of inter-service communication, providing features like traffic management, security, and observability. These technologies ensure a robust communication infrastructure capable of intelligent routing, load balancing, and network fault recovery.

Data Management and Consistency:

i. Challenge: Each microservice manages its own data, leading to distributed data stores that pose challenges for data consistency, transaction management, and performance optimization during data retrieval. Ensuring that all services have a consistent view of data and managing transactions that span multiple services becomes complex and critical.

ii. Solution: Strategies such as the Saga pattern can manage distributed transactions by sequencing related local transactions. Event Sourcing and CQRS (Command Query Responsibility Segregation) patterns can also be instrumental, where Event Sourcing asynchronously captures changes to the application state as events, and CQRS separates read and update operations for data. These approaches help in achieving eventual consistency, optimizing data retrieval, and maintaining data integrity across microservices.

Security Concerns:

i. Challenge: Microservices architecture opens up multiple points of entry, increasing the attack surface. The security strategy must encompass authentication, authorization, secure communication, and data security. Implementing these at each service level without a standardized approach can lead to vulnerabilities and inconsistencies.

ii. Solution: Implementing API gateways to centralize and enforce security policies can mitigate inconsistent security practices. The adoption of a zero-trust security model, where no communication is trusted by default, regardless of whether it originates from inside or outside the network, is also beneficial. Solutions like OAuth for token-based authentication, and automatic encryption of data-in-transit using service meshes, enhance security robustness.

Service Discovery and Load Balancing:

    i.   Challenge: Dynamic service discovery and efficient load balancing are paramount in a microservices environment, where services are ephemeral and can scale horizontally on demand. Manually managing service registries and network traffic distribution is impractical and error-prone.

    ii.   Solution: Automated service discovery tools like Eureka, Consul, or Zookeeper can dynamically manage service registries, ensuring services can seamlessly discover and communicate with each other. Implementing intelligent load balancers or adopting service mesh technology helps in dynamic traffic management, ensuring requests are efficiently distributed across services, even during spikes in demand.

Error Detection and Fault Tolerance:

    i.   Challenge: The distributed nature of microservices makes system failures more complex to predict and manage. Ensuring system resilience requires strategies to quickly detect failures, prevent cascading failures, and recover without human intervention.

    ii.   Solution: Implementing resilience patterns like circuit breakers, retries, fallbacks, and bulkheads can prevent system-wide outages by isolating failures and providing controlled degradation. Comprehensive logging, monitoring, and alerting systems like Prometheus and Grafana enable real-time insight into system health, facilitating quick error detection and resolution.

Deployment and Scalability:

    i.   Challenge: The need for frequent, independent deployments and dynamic scaling in microservices introduces complexities in deployment orchestration, resource management, and configuration. Achieving zero-downtime deployments and managing service-to-service dependencies require sophisticated strategies.

    ii.   Solution: Containerization technologies like Docker encapsulate services into consistent, deployable units, while Kubernetes orchestrates these containers, handling deployment, scaling, and self-healing. Advanced CI/CD pipelines automate these processes, ensuring rapid, consistent, and reliable deployments. Blue/green or canary deployment strategies can further enhance zero-downtime deployments.

Testing Complexities:

    i.   Challenge: Microservices require a shift from traditional testing strategies due to their distributed nature. Ensuring quality demands testing each service in isolation and in conjunction with others, simulating real-world conditions and accounting for unpredictable network factors.

    ii.   Solution: A multi-level testing strategy is essential, including unit testing, integration testing, contract testing, and end-to-end testing. Service virtualization can simulate components to ensure more realistic and comprehensive testing. Chaos engineering, where the system is intentionally stressed in production to uncover weaknesses, also contributes to a robust testing strategy.

Performance Monitoring:

Challenge: In a microservices architecture, understanding the intricate performance metrics of each service and the system as a whole is crucial. This includes monitoring the runtime behavior of services, analyzing response times, and ensuring system health. The distributed nature of the architecture makes pinpointing bottlenecks and performance issues challenging.

Solution: Specialized application performance monitoring (APM) tools that provide deep insights into service performance are essential. Implementing distributed tracing with tools like Jaeger or Zipkin can track a request's journey through various services, helping identify performance bottlenecks and optimization opportunities. These tools, combined with real-time monitoring and alerting systems, ensure performance issues are quickly identified and addressed.

Microservices architecture, while offering significant benefits, brings to the forefront a host of challenges that span various operational, security, and performance aspects. These challenges demand innovative, sophisticated solutions that leverage the latest in technology and strategic thinking. By understanding and addressing these challenges with appropriate solutions, organizations can build robust, efficient, and secure microservice ecosystems. Success in the microservices realm hinges on a continuous adaptation strategy, embracing modern tools and methodologies, and a proactive approach to emerging challenges and solutions.

Table 4. Challenges and solutions in microservice architecture

Challenges	High-Level Solutions
Network Complexity and Communication Overhead	Adoption of efficient communication protocols (e.g., gRPC), and utilization of service mesh technologies (e.g., Istio, Linkerd) for enhanced communication management.
Data Management and Consistency	Implementation of patterns such as Saga, Event Sourcing, and CQRS for consistent data management and integrity across services.
Security Concerns	Centralized security policies through API gateways, adoption of zero-trust security models, and utilization of protocols like OAuth for robust authentication.
Service Discovery and Load Balancing	Automated service discovery tools (e.g., Eureka, Consul), intelligent load balancing, and service mesh for dynamic traffic management.
Error Detection and Fault Tolerance	Resilience patterns (e.g., circuit breakers, retries), and comprehensive monitoring systems (e.g., Prometheus, Grafana) for real-time insights and error resolution.
Deployment and Scalability	Containerization (e.g., Docker), orchestration tools (e.g., Kubernetes), advanced CI/CD pipelines, and deployment strategies (e.g., blue/green, canary).
Testing Complexities	Multi-level testing strategies, service virtualization, and chaos engineering for thorough system evaluation.
Performance Monitoring	Application performance monitoring (APM) tools, distributed tracing (e.g., Jaeger, Zipkin), real-time monitoring, and alerting systems for performance optimization.

7. FUTURE RESEARCH DIRECTIONS

Microservice architecture is continuously evolving, with new challenges and innovations surfacing regularly. While current solutions address numerous issues in microservice environments, there is a perpetual need for more advanced research to keep up with the escalating complexity and demands of modern applications. This section delves into the prospective areas where future research could significantly impact the development, deployment, and management of microservices, pushing the boundaries of current technological practices.

a. Advanced Security Mechanisms for Microservices: The decentralized nature of microservices necessitates robust security protocols that extend beyond traditional measures. Future research could focus on developing advanced security mechanisms tailored to microservices' unique characteristics, such as enhanced encryption methods for inter-service communication and sophisticated identity propagation techniques within microservice chains (Velepucha, V., 2023),((Viggiato, M., 2018),(Krylovskiy, A., 2015).

b. Intelligent Microservice Orchestration: As applications grow, so does the complexity of orchestrating numerous microservices. Research into intelligent orchestration could explore the use of AI and machine learning to automate service coordination, optimize resource allocation, and enhance scalability and fault recovery processes in real-time, adapting to current system demands and predictive analytics (Assunção, W. K., 2020),(Waseem, M., 2017),(Zhang, H., 2019).

c. Unified Framework for Microservice Governance: With the proliferation of microservices in large-scale applications, there's a need for comprehensive governance frameworks. Research in this area could aim to establish unified standards and practices for developing, deploying, and monitoring microservices, incorporating aspects like security policies, data governance, and compliance standards, ensuring consistency across various domains and industries (Kalske, M., 2018),(Smid, A., 2019),(Wang, Y., 2021).

d. In-depth Analysis of Serverless Microservices: The intersection of serverless computing and microservices offers intriguing possibilities, particularly concerning scalability and cost-efficiency. However, this area remains underexplored. Future studies could delve into the nuances of serverless microservices, investigating optimal patterns for state management, resource provisioning, and cold start mitigation, among other pertinent topics (Premarathna, D., 2021),(Yarygina, T., 2018),(Aksakalli, I. K., 2021).

e. Enhanced Observability and Monitoring Tools: Observability is crucial in microservice architectures for diagnosing issues and ensuring system reliability. There's a gap for research into more advanced monitoring solutions that provide deeper insights into system performance, leveraging data analytics and machine learning for predictive maintenance, anomaly detection, and automated root cause analysis (Götz, B., 2018),(Jamshidi, P., 2018),(Ghofrani, J., 2018).

f. Microservices in Edge Computing: The advent of edge computing presents a novel frontier for microservices, especially for IoT and real-time applications. Research could focus on optimizing microservice deployment in edge environments, addressing challenges related to limited resources, connectivity issues, and data processing at the edge, potentially revolutionizing latency-sensitive applications (Baškarada, S., 2018),(Billawa, P., 2022),(Di Francesco, P., 2018).

g. Sustainability and Eco-Efficiency in Microservice Architectures: As global digitalization continues; the environmental impact of IT infrastructures is gaining attention. Future research could investigate eco-efficient microservice architectures, exploring energy-efficient coding practices, resource optimization algorithms, and sustainable scalability strategies, contributing to greener IT solutions (Villamizar, M., 2015),(Liu, G., 2020),(Alshuqayran, N., 2016).

Microservice architecture holds vast potential for innovation and enhancement. The outlined directions for future research signify areas ripe for exploration, promising advancements that could redefine the standards for microservice-based applications. By addressing these focal points, the academic and industrial communities can collaborate to forge new pathways in microservice technologies, contributing to more resilient, efficient, and secure digital solutions for the future. The continuous evolution of technology landscapes necessitates an unwavering commitment to research and development, ensuring that microservice architectures can meet the ever-changing demands of tomorrow's digital world.

Table 5. Future research directions

Research Direction	Description
Advanced Security Mechanisms	Developing enhanced security protocols specific to microservices, including sophisticated encryption and identity propagation techniques.
Intelligent Microservice Orchestration	Utilizing AI and machine learning for automated service coordination, resource optimization, and dynamic scalability and recovery processes.
Unified Microservice Governance Framework	Establishing comprehensive standards and practices for consistent development, deployment, and monitoring of microservices across various sectors.
In-depth Analysis of Serverless Microservices	Exploring the specifics of serverless computing within microservices, focusing on scalability, cost-efficiency, and state management patterns.
Enhanced Observability and Monitoring Tools	Advancing monitoring solutions that offer deeper system insights, using data analytics and AI for predictive maintenance and automated diagnostics.
Microservices in Edge Computing	Optimizing microservice deployment in edge environments, addressing resource constraints, connectivity, and localized data processing challenges.
Sustainability and Eco-Efficiency	Investigating practices for eco-efficient microservice architectures, including energy-saving coding, resource optimization, and sustainable scalability strategies.

8. CONCLUSION

The journey through the multifaceted landscape of microservice architecture reveals both its compelling advantages and the intricate challenges it brings. This architectural style, celebrated for its scalability and robustness, particularly in cloud-native environments, has revolutionized application development and deployment, enabling unparalleled agility and continuous delivery. However, as dissected in the preceding discussions, adopting microservices is not without its hurdles.

Operational complexities often surface, demanding sophisticated strategies for service discovery, load balancing, and failure recovery. These intricacies are further compounded by the need for intricate communication patterns and advanced monitoring and logging mechanisms to maintain system health and performance. Security and compliance present another formidable frontier. The distributed nature of microservices necessitates a fortified defense for inter-service interactions, rigorous data protection protocols, and adherence to a myriad of regulatory standards. The granularity of microservices amplifies the security perimeter, calling for innovative solutions to safeguard each autonomous unit without compromising functionality.

Performance optimization in a serverless environment remains a focal concern. The ephemeral nature of serverless computing imposes unique constraints on resource allocation, latency, and cold starts, pressing for continual refinements in performance tuning, efficient code practices, and judicious resource management. Amid these challenges, the discourse has unveiled a spectrum of solutions, from leveraging dedicated microservice platforms and employing automated testing to embracing advanced observability tools. These strategies, while diverse, converge on the necessity of a holistic approach that intertwines technological prowess with strategic foresight.

The future holds many opportunities for groundbreaking research and innovation. The quest for enhanced security mechanisms, intelligent orchestration, and eco-efficiency underscores the dynamic evolution of this domain. As organizations venture deeper into the realms of AI, edge computing, and sustainable IT, microservices will undoubtedly play a pivotal role in shaping the digital future. In conclusion, while the road to mastering microservice architecture is fraught with challenges, the rewards of resilience, scalability, and agility is compelling. By harnessing the insights, strategies, and future directions outlined in this discourse, practitioners and researchers alike are well-equipped to navigate this evolving terrain, steering toward a future where microservice architecture reaches its full potential in driving business innovation and technological advancement.

REFERENCES

Aksakalli, I. K., Çelik, T., Can, A. B., & Tekinerdoğan, B. (2021). Deployment and communication patterns in microservice architectures: A systematic literature review. *Journal of Systems and Software*, *180*, 111014. https://www.sciencedirect.com/science/article/abs/pii/S0164121221001114. doi:10.1016/j.jss.2021.111014

Alshuqayran, N., Ali, N., & Evans, R. (2016, November). A systematic mapping study in microservice architecture. In *2016 IEEE 9th International Conference on Service-Oriented Computing and Applications (SOCA)* (pp. 44-51). IEEE. https://ieeexplore.ieee.org/abstract/document/7796008/

Assunção, W. K., Krüger, J., & Mendonça, W. D. (2020, October). Variability management meets microservices: six challenges of re-engineering microservice-based webshops. In *Proceedings of the 24th ACM Conference on Systems and Software Product Line* (pp. 1–6). ACM. https://dl.acm.org/doi/abs/10.1145/3382025.3414942 doi:10.1145/3382025.3414942

Baškarada, S., Nguyen, V., & Koronios, A. (2018). Architecting microservices: Practical opportunities and challenges. *Journal of Computer Information Systems*. https://www.tandfonline.com/doi/shareview/10.1080/08874417.2018.1520056

Billawa, P., Bambhore Tukaram, A., Díaz Ferreyra, N. E., Steghöfer, J. P., Scandariato, R., & Simhandl, G. (2022, August). SoK: Security of Microservice Applications: A Practitioners' Perspective on Challenges and Best Practices. In *Proceedings of the 17th International Conference on Availability* (pp. 1–10). Reliability and Security. https://dl.acm.org/doi/abs/10.1145/3538969.3538986 doi:10.1145/3538969.3538986

Bushong, V., Abdelfattah, A. S., Maruf, A. A., Das, D., Lehman, A., Jaroszewski, E., Coffey, M., Cerny, T., Frajtak, K., Tisnovsky, P., & Bures, M. (2021). On microservice analysis and architecture evolution: A systematic mapping study. *Applied Sciences (Basel, Switzerland)*, *11*(17), 7856. https://www.mdpi.com/2076-3417/11/17/7856. doi:10.3390/app11177856

Cerny, T., Donahoo, M. J., & Trnka, M. (2018). Contextual understanding of microservice architecture: Current and future directions. *Applied Computing Review*, *17*(4), 29–45. https://dl.acm.org/doi/abs/10.1145/3183628.3183631. doi:10.1145/3183628.3183631

Di Francesco, P., Lago, P., & Malavolta, I. (2018, April). Migrating towards microservice architectures: an industrial survey. In *2018 IEEE international conference on software architecture (ICSA)* (pp. 29-2909). IEEE. https://ieeexplore.ieee.org/abstract/document/8417114

Ghofrani, J., & Lübke, D. (2018). Challenges of Microservices Architecture: A Survey on the State of the Practice. *ZEUS*, 1-8. https://www.researchgate.net/profile/Christoph-Hochreiner/publication/324517504_Proceedings_of_the_10th_ZEUS_Workshop/links/5ad1c5e9458515c60f5054d3/Proceedings-of-the-10th-ZEUS-Workshop.pdf#page=8

Götz, B., Schel, D., Bauer, D., Henkel, C., Einberger, P., & Bauernhansl, T. (2018). Challenges of production microservices. *Procedia CIRP, 67*, 167–172. https://www.sciencedirect.com/science/article/pii/S2212827117311381. doi:10.1016/j.procir.2017.12.194

Heinrich, R., Van Hoorn, A., Knoche, H., Li, F., Lwakatare, L. E., Pahl, C., & Wettinger, J. (2017, April). Performance engineering for microservices: research challenges and directions. In *Proceedings of the 8th ACM/SPEC on international conference on performance engineering companion* (pp. 223-226). ACM. https://dl.acm.org/doi/abs/10.1145/3053600.3053653

Jamshidi, P., Pahl, C., Mendonça, N. C., Lewis, J., & Tilkov, S. (2018). Microservices: The journey so far and challenges ahead. *IEEE Software, 35*(3), 24–35. https://ieeexplore.ieee.org/abstract/document/8354433. doi:10.1109/MS.2018.2141039

Kalske, M., Mäkitalo, N., & Mikkonen, T. (2018). Challenges when moving from monolith to microservice architecture. In *Current Trends in Web Engineering: ICWE 2017 International Workshops, Liquid Multi-Device Software and EnWoT, practi-O-web, NLPIT, SoWeMine,* (pp. 32-47). Springer International Publishing. https://link.springer.com/chapter/10.1007/978-3-319-74433-9_3

Krylovskiy, A., Jahn, M., & Patti, E. (2015, August). Designing a smart city internet of things platform with microservice architecture. In *2015 3rd international conference on future internet of things and cloud* (pp. 25-30). IEEE. https://ieeexplore.ieee.org/abstract/document/7300793

Liu, G., Huang, B., Liang, Z., Qin, M., Zhou, H., & Li, Z. (2020, December). Microservices: architecture, container, and challenges. In *2020 IEEE 20th international conference on software quality, reliability and security companion (QRS-C)* (pp. 629-635). IEEE. https://ieeexplore.ieee.org/abstract/document/9282637

Premarathna, D., & Pathirana, A. (2021, September). Theoretical framework to address the challenges in Microservice Architecture. In *2021 International Research Conference on Smart Computing and Systems Engineering (SCSE)* (Vol. 4, pp. 195-202). IEEE. https://ieeexplore.ieee.org/abstract/document/9568346/

Smid, A., Wang, R., & Cerny, T. (2019, September). Case study on data communication in microservice architecture. In *Proceedings of the Conference on Research in Adaptive and Convergent Systems* (pp. 261-267). ACM. https://dl.acm.org/doi/abs/10.1145/3338840.3355659

Söylemez, M., Tekinerdogan, B., & Kolukısa Tarhan, A. (2022). Challenges and solution directions of microservice architectures: A systematic literature review. *Applied Sciences (Basel, Switzerland), 12*(11), 5507. https://www.mdpi.com/2076-3417/12/11/5507. doi:10.3390/app12115507

Velepucha, V., & Flores, P. (2023). *A survey on microservices architecture: Principles, patterns and migration challenges*. IEEE Access. https://ieeexplore.ieee.org/abstract/document/10220070

Viggiato, M., Terra, R., Rocha, H., Valente, M. T., & Figueiredo, E. (2018). *Microservices in practice: A survey study*. arXiv preprint arXiv:1808.04836. https://arxiv.org/abs/1808.04836

Villamizar, M., Garcés, O., Castro, H., Verano, M., Salamanca, L., Casallas, R., & Gil, S. (2015, September). Evaluating the monolithic and the microservice architecture pattern to deploy web applications in the cloud. In *2015 10th Computing Colombian Conference (10CCC)* (pp. 583-590). IEEE. https://ieeexplore.ieee.org/abstract/document/7333476

Wang, Y., Kadiyala, H., & Rubin, J. (2021). Promises and challenges of microservices: An exploratory study. *Empirical Software Engineering*, 26(4), 63. https://link.springer.com/article/10.1007/s10664-020-09910-y. doi:10.1007/s10664-020-09910-y PMID:34149303

Waseem, M., & Liang, P. (2017, December). Microservices architecture in DevOps. In *2017 24th Asia-Pacific Software Engineering Conference Workshops (APSECW)* (pp. 13-14). IEEE. https://ieeexplore.ieee.org/abstract/document/8312518

Yarygina, T., & Bagge, A. H. (2018, March). Overcoming security challenges in microservice architectures. In *2018 IEEE Symposium on Service-Oriented System Engineering (SOSE)* (pp. 11-20). IEEE. https://ieeexplore.ieee.org/abstract/document/8359144

Zhang, H., Li, S., Jia, Z., Zhong, C., & Zhang, C. (2019, March). Microservice architecture in reality: An industrial inquiry. In *2019 IEEE international conference on software architecture (ICSA)* (pp. 51-60). IEEE. https://ieeexplore.ieee.org/abstract/document/8703917

Chapter 12
NodeJS and Postman for Serverless Computing

Rajesh Kannan Kannan

Chaitanya Bharathi Institute of Technology (Autonomous), India

Meena Abarna K. T.

Annamalai University, India

S. Vairachilai

VIT Bhopal University, India

R. Vijayalakshmi

Mahatma Gandhi Institute of Technology (Autonomous), India

ABSTRACT

Node.js is a robust, open-source cross platform server-side JavaScript runtime environment. Node.js, which Ryan Dahl created in 2009, is incredibly popular because it makes it easier to create network applications that are both scalable and high-performing. Its event-driven architecture, which permits asynchronous I/O operations and makes it ideal for managing concurrent connections and delivering quick, real-time applications, is one of its main advantages. With Node.js, coders can leverage JavaScript for both the client and server- side scripting, promoting code reuse and resulting in a smoother development process.

1. INTRODUCTION

Node.js is a robust, open-source cross platform server-side JavaScript runtime environment. Node.js, which Ryan Dahl created in 2009, is incredibly popular because it makes it easier to create network applications that are both scalable and high-performing. Its event-driven architecture, which permits asynchronous I/O operations and makes it ideal for managing concurrent connections and delivering quick, real-time applications, is one of its main advantages. With Node.js, coders can leverage JavaScript for both the client and server-side scripting, promoting code reuse and resulting in a smoother development process.

DOI: 10.4018/979-8-3693-1682-5.ch012

2. WHY NODEJS?

In the early days of web application development, HTML, CSS, and JavaScript were fundamental, but the landscape and practices were quite different compared to the sophisticated tools and frameworks available today.

HyperText Markup Language (HTML): HTML was primarily used for structuring the content of web pages.

Cascading Style Sheets (CSS): CSS is a key tool in web development that empowers developers to manage the visual aspects of a website, create responsive layouts, and enhance the overall user experience.

JavaScript (JS): In order to improve the user experience, JavaScript is frequently used for client-side validation, which verifies user input in the web browser before sending data to the server. This makes online forms more generally usable by cutting down on pointless server queries and giving users quick feedback. Every modern web browser contains a JavaScript engine, which is responsible for interpreting and executing JavaScript code on web pages. JavaScript engines are an integral part of browsers and play a vital role in enabling dynamic and interactive functionality on the web. Different browsers may use different JavaScript engines, and these engines are responsible for processing and executing JavaScript code in accordance with the ECMAScript specification, which is the standard that defines the scripting language features that JavaScript engines must support (Chhetri, N et al., 2016).

Here are some examples of popular browsers and their associated JavaScript engines:

1. Google Chrome: V8
2. Mozilla Firefox: Spider Monkey
3. Apple Safari: JavaScriptCore
4. Microsoft Edge: V8 (since the move to the Chromium project in 2020)
5. Opera: V8 (since the move to the Chromium project)

In the realm of client-side browsers, the execution of JavaScript code is fundamental to the dynamic and interactive nature of web applications. A JavaScript engine embedded within the browser interprets and executes the code, enabling the seamless interaction between users and web content. However, the versatility of JavaScript extends beyond the client-side environment. Node.js, a server-side runtime environment, provides a complementary platform for executing JavaScript code on servers. By leveraging Node.js, developers can extend the capabilities of JavaScript beyond the confines of the browser, allowing for server-side scripting and enhancing the overall efficiency and scalability of web applications. This dual capability, with client-side browsers handling user interactions and Node.js managing server-side operations, contributes to the cohesive and powerful ecosystem that defines modern web development.

Node.js is neither a programming language nor a framework or library. It functions as a runtime environment on the backend, facilitating the execution of JavaScript code.

3. NODEJS INSTALLATION.

Node.js installation is a straightforward process, ensuring developers can quickly set up the runtime environment on their machines for efficient server-side JavaScript execution.

Figure 1. NodeJS official site
(Source: https://nodejs.org/en)

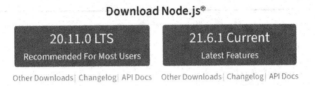

To initiate the installation, users can visit the official Node.js website, where they can find downloadable installers for various operating systems, including Windows, Linux and macOS. The installation package typically includes both Node.js and Node Package Manager, a powerful utility tool for handling dependencies and packages in Node.js projects.

The current version of Node.js is 21.6.1, while the Long-Term Support (LTS) variation is 20.11.0. It is advisable for users to opt for the LTS version, as it ensures stability and long-term support, making it the recommended choice for development endeavours. Once the MSI installer is downloaded, the installation process involves running the executable file and following the guided steps provided by the MSI installer. Node.js. After completing the installation of Node.js, users can verify the installation in the terminal by executing the command "node --version."

4. NODE PACKAGE MANAGER (NPM)

Node Package Manager (npm) stands as a fundamental tool within the Node.js ecosystem, playing a crucial role in managing JavaScript packages and dependencies. In the Java ecosystem, Maven serves a similar purpose as a build automation and project management tool. The Maven Central Repository acts as a central hub for Java libraries and artifacts. While both npm and Maven repositories facilitate the sharing and management of dependencies. With npm, developers can effortlessly install, share, and manage packages, fostering a streamlined development process.

The npm registry serves as a centralized hub for a vast array of libraries and tools, enabling developers to leverage an extensive ecosystem of open-source software. Its straightforward command-line interface and integration with Node.js projects contribute to its widespread adoption, empowering developers to efficiently handle dependencies and enhance collaboration within the JavaScript community. Currently NPM stands out as the primary repository for modules or packages, boasting over 3,000,000 packages.

Figure 2. Number of modules contributed for various repositories

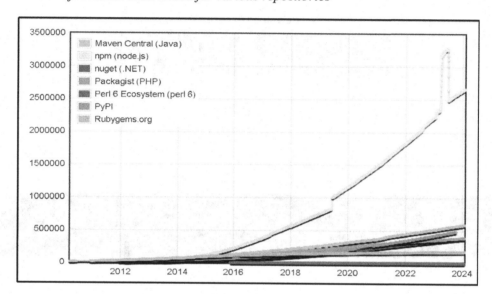

This surpasses other repositories, as indicated in Fig 2 from the source http://www.modulecounts.com/. This observation emphasizes that npm is not only the largest but also the most rapidly expanding repository.

In NPM central Repository, a module refers to an independent and reusable code unit or functionality that can be easily integrated into a Node.js project. These modules are typically JavaScript files or directories with a specific structure, encapsulating specific features, utilities, or libraries. The npm registry serves as a centralized repository where developers can publish and share their modules, making them accessible to others. Modules facilitate code organization, promote code reuse, and contribute to a modular and maintainable architecture in Node.js projects. By leveraging npm modules, developers can enhance productivity, reduce redundancy, and seamlessly incorporate pre-built functionalities into their applications, fostering a collaborative and efficient development ecosystem. Node.js modules fall into three distinct categories (Landup, D., & Sanatan, M et al., 2020).

1. Core/ Built-in Modules
2. External-Source/Third-party Modules
3. Local Modules

4.1 Core/Built-in Modules

The Node.js installation includes built-in modules known as core modules. Examples include modules like http (Both client and server), fs (file system), path (path utility), and util (utilities). You can use core modules by requiring them in your Node.js script.

Example:

const fs =require ('fs ')

4.2 External Source/Third-party Modules

Third-party modules are created by external sources (developers) and are not part of the core Node.js distribution. Typically hosted on the central repository of npm, these modules can be installed using npm and then utilized in your Node.js projects.

Example:
(installing a single module using npm):

```
> npm install express
```

(installing a multiple module using npm):

```
> npm install express mongoose mongodb
```

4.3 Local Modules

Local modules are modules that you create in your project. You can create separate files for different functionalities and then use these files as modules in other parts of your project. To use local modules, you use the require function and provide the relative path to the module file.

Example (creating a local module in a file named mathcal.js and app.js):

app.js	mathcal.js

var cal = require('./mathcal ');
var p = 100;
var q = 50;
console.log(" Add: " + cal.add(p,q));
console.log(" Sub: " + cal.sub(p,q));
console.log(" Mul: " + cal.mul(p,q));
console.log(" Div: " + cal.div(p,q));
	const arithmeticOperations = {
	add: (p, q) => p + q,
	sub: (p, q) => p - q,
	mul: (p, q) => p * q,
	div: (p, q) => p / q,
	};
	module.exports = arithmeticOperations;

5. NODE.JS MODULES MANAGEMENT

The `package.json` file in a Node.js project serves as a crucial configuration file, encapsulating essential information about the project and its dependencies. It is a JSON (JavaScript Object Notation) file that typically includes metadata such as the project name, version, description, entry point file, and scripts for various tasks. Additionally, `package.json` lists the project's dependencies, specifying the external modules or packages required for the application to run. This file plays a pivotal role in facilitating project management, enabling easy sharing of code, and ensuring that others can replicate the development environment effortlessly. Developers often interact with `package.json` to install project dependencies, run scripts, and manage project settings, making it a central component in Node.js projects.

NPM installs dependencies required only during the development phase of a project but are not required for the actual execution of the application (*devDependencies*) listed in the package.json file. The **'npm install'** command automatically adds all dependencies, including devDependencies, during installation. To add particular devDependencies to your project, you can use the command *'npm install --save-dev'*. Figure 3 displays the package.json file with relevant details included in the comments section (Gackenheimer, C., & Gackenheimer, C., 2013).

Figure 3. Node.js modules management with package.json

```
{
    "name"          : "demo",
    "version"       : "1.0.0",
    "description"   : "",
    "main"          : "app.js",
    "scripts"       : {        "start": "nodemon app.js"      }, //Script to run the the app.js File
    "author"        : "",
    "license"       : "ISC",
    "dependencies"  : {                                        //5 Dependecies are Installed
                       "body-parser": "^1.20.0",              //"^" Symbol represents the recent version is installed.
                       "cors": "^2.8.5",                      //"2.8.5 represents the version number.
                       "express": "^4.18.1",
                       "mongodb": "^4.9.0",
                       "mongoose": "^6.5.2"
                      },
    "devDependencies": {                                      //Only One dependencies is installed
                       "nodemon": "^2.0.19"
                      }
}
```

6. DEVELOPMENT OF NODE.JS SERVERS

Node.js server development involves creating robust, scalable, and efficient servers using the Node.js runtime environment. The Node.js runtime built on the V8 JavaScript engine, making it well-suited for server-side development. Start by initializing a Node.js project using the *npm init* command. This command guides you through creating a *package.json* file that holds project metadata and dependencies. Use Node.js's core http module to create a basic HTTP server (Brown et al., 2019).

```
index.js
// Import the 'http' module to set up an HTTP server.
```

```
const http = require('http');
// Create a new HTTP server using the 'createServer' method.
const server = http.createServer((req, res) => {
res.writeHead(200, { 'Content-Type': 'text/plain' });
res.end('Hi! Welcome to Nodejs!');
});
// Specify the port on which the server will receive inbound requests
const PORT = 4000;
// Start the server to listen on the specified port.
server.listen(PORT, () => {
console.log(`Server is operational at http://localhost:${PORT}/`);
});
```

The code provided in *"index.js"* exemplifies the fundamental structure of a basic HTTP server implemented in Node.js. It commences by importing the *'http'* module, a core component in Node.js that facilitates the creation of web servers. The *'createServer'* method is then employed to instantiate an HTTP server, defining a callback function responsible for handling incoming requests and formulating responses. In this scenario, the server responds with a '200 OK' status code and a plain text message, namely 'Hello, Nodejs!'. Configured to listen on port 4000, the server, upon initiation, logs a message to the console confirming its operational status and providing the URL (http://localhost:4000/) for access as shown in fig 4. This concise implementation serves as a foundational introduction to building web servers in Node.js, highlighting its simplicity and flexibility in handling HTTP requests.

Figure 4. Accessing the server running on localhost at Port 3000

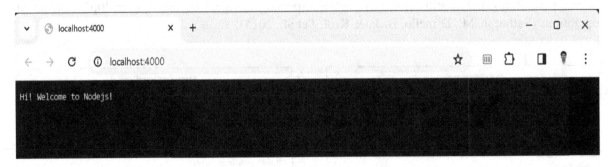

7. FILE SYSTEM IN NODEJS

Node.js provides a robust file system *(fs)* module that allows developers to interact with the file system on their server. The fs module includes various methods for performing file-related operations, such as reading, writing, updating, and deleting files. One of the fundamental functions is `fs.readFile`, which enables asynchronous file reading. This function takes a file path and a callback function, executing the callback with the file content once the reading operation is complete. Similarly, `fs.writeFile` allows for asynchronous file writing, while `fs.appendFile` adds content to an existing file. The fs module also supports synchronous alternatives for these operations, providing flexibility for different programming preferences. Additionally, features like `fs.readdir` assist in reading the contents of directories, and `fs.unlink` facilitates the removal of files.

Furthermore, the fs module in Node.js supports more advanced operations, such as working with streams for reading and writing large files efficiently. The ability to manipulate the file system seamlessly within the server environment makes the fs module a crucial component for various applications, including web servers, file management systems, and data processing tasks. By leveraging the fs module, developers can create powerful and efficient file-handling functionality within their Node.js applications.

The Node.js File System (fs) module offers both synchronous and asynchronous operations, catering to different programming needs. Synchronous operations, such as `fs.readFileSync` and `fs.writeFileSync`, execute in a blocking manner, meaning the program halts until the operation is completed. While this simplicity might be suitable for certain scenarios, it can potentially lead to performance bottlenecks in applications with numerous simultaneous tasks. On the other hand, asynchronous operations, exemplified by `fs.readFile` and `fs.writeFile`, operate non-blocking, allowing the program to continue executing other tasks while waiting for the file operation to conclude. Asynchronous operations are particularly advantageous in scenarios where responsiveness and scalability are paramount, enabling the system to handle multiple operations concurrently without significant delays. The choice between synchronous and asynchronous file system operations in Node.js depends on the specific requirements of the application, balancing simplicity with the need for efficient and responsive performance (Ihrig, C. J et al .2014).

The code in *'SynchronousRead.js'* reads the contents of a file *('input.txt')* synchronously using the `readFileSync` method, implying that the program execution halts until the entire file is read. While synchronous operations are straightforward, they can potentially introduce delays in the overall program execution, especially in scenarios where multiple operations need to be performed concurrently.

The code in *'AynchronousRead.js'* demonstrates the asynchronous file reading approach in Node.js, where the program does not pause during the file read operation. Instead, it continues with other tasks, allowing for more efficient utilization of resources, especially in scenarios involving multiple concurrent operations (Satheesh, M., D'mello, B. J., & Krol, J et al., 2015).

SynchronousRead.js

var fs = require(' fs ');
console.log("Start Synchronous read method:");
var FileInfo = fs.readFileSync('input.txt');
console.log("Data in the file is - " + FileInfo.toString());
console.log("End Synchronous read method.");

Result: **> node SynchronousRead.js** Start Synchronous read method: Data in the file is - Welcome to NodeJS End Synchronous read method.

AsynchronousRead.js

var fs = require(' fs ');
console.log("Start Asynchronous read method:");
fs.readFile('input.txt', function (err, FileInfo) {
if(err)
{
return console.error(err);
}
console.log("Data in the file is - " + FileInfo.toString());
});
console.log("I am outside the function");

Result: **> node AsynchronousRead.js** Start Asynchronous read method: I am outside the function Data in the file is - Welcome to NodeJS

POSTMAN FOR SERVERLESS COMPUTING

Postman is a powerful and widely-used collaboration platform for API development that simplifies the process of designing, testing, and documenting APIs. This tool provides a user-friendly interface to construct and send HTTP requests, facilitating comprehensive testing of API endpoints. Postman offers a wide range of request types, including GET, POST, PUT, and DELETE, and users may customise headers, arguments, and authentication methods. Beyond testing, Postman offers robust features for API documentation, enabling developers to create and share detailed API documentation with team members or external stakeholders. Its versatility, ease of use, and collaborative functionalities make Postman an indispensable tool for developers, QA engineers, and other professionals involved in the API development lifecycle (Westerveld et al., 2021).

Figure 5. Utilizing Postman to Access the GET API on Port 4000

Postman offers flexibility in its usage by providing two primary options for access. Users can either download and install the Postman application on their local machines, providing a dedicated environment for API development and testing, or they can opt for the web version by creating an account on the Postman platform. The downloadable version allows for offline access and enhanced performance, ensuring a seamless experience for developers working on API projects. On the other hand, the web version, accessible through a web browser, provides a convenient option for collaborative work and easy accessibility from any location. By accommodating both local installations and a web-based interface, Postman caters to the diverse preferences and needs of developers and teams engaged in API development and testing processes.

REFERENCES

Brown, E. (2019). *Web development with node and express: leveraging the JavaScript stack*. O'Reilly Media.

Chhetri, N. (2016). *A comparative analysis of node. js*. Server-Side Javascript.

Gackenheimer, C., & Gackenheimer, C. (2013). Understanding Node. js. *Node. js Recipes*, 1-26.

Ihrig, C. J. (2014). *Pro node. js for developers*. Apress.

Landup, D., & Sanatan, M. (2020). *How to code in Node. JS*. DigitalOcean.

Satheesh, M., D'mello, B. J., & Krol, J. (2015). *Web development with MongoDB and NodeJs*. Packt Publishing Ltd.

Subramanian, V. (2017). *Pro MERN Stack* (Vol. 13). Apress. doi:10.1007/978-1-4842-2653-7

Westerveld, D. (2021). *API Testing and Development with Postman: A practical guide to creating, testing, and managing APIs for automated software testing*. NodeJS. https://nodejs.org/en https://www.npmjs.com/

Chapter 13
Serverless Computing:
A Security Viewpoint

Padmavathi Vurubindi

https://orcid.org/0000-0002-5524-5983

Chaitanya Bharathi Institute of Technology, Hyderabad, India

Sujatha Canavoy Narahari

Sreenidhi Institute of Science and Technology, India

ABSTRACT

Recently, serverless computing has become a newfound computing platform for the cloud-based deployment of applications and it took over all other contemporary computing platforms. It has two significant advantages over its contemporary computing platforms. First off, it enables software developers to delegate to cloud service providers all infrastructure maintenance and operational chores, allowing them to concentrate solely on the business logic of their applications. The second is that it has a strict pay-per-use business model, where customers are only charged for the resources, they utilize. Despite its advantages, researchers have been deeply examining the actual security guarantees offered by the current defences employed to safeguard container-based infrastructures over the past few years. This led to the discovery of significant flaws in the security controls employed for network security and process isolation. In this chapter, the authors highlight the security attacks/issues with the investigated serverless architecture platforms and suggest potential countermeasures.

1. INTRODUCTION

Serverless computing has transformed cloud application development by removing the burden of managing servers and infrastructure, allowing developers to focus only on writing code and business logic. In this, the application logic is broken down into a collection of small, transient, and stateless functions, each of which executes in a different execution environment such as a container and interacts with other functions and various cloud services such as storage services to complete its tasks. Developers use this strategy to deploy their application code to containers controlled by a cloud service provider. The cloud

DOI: 10.4018/979-8-3693-1682-5.ch013

provider handles infrastructure provisioning and scaling, as well as normal maintenance duties including security management, operating system updates, capacity planning, and system monitoring. This method simplifies development, increases productivity, and lowers the difficulties of server management.

The pay-as-you-go pricing model of serverless computing differs significantly from traditional server-based approaches. Users are invoiced based on actual computation and resource consumption, which eliminates the need to reserve and pay for predetermined quantities of bandwidth or server resources. The ability to auto-scale ensures efficient resource allocation, making it a cost-effective alternative. This is in contrast to the old strategy, in which over-purchasing of server capacity to address projected traffic spikes is widespread, resulting in unnecessary expense. Figure 1 illustrates various components of serverless architecture.

While the phrase "serverless" may appear to be deceptive, it truly describes the development experience. Backend services are still provided by physical servers, but developers are protected from server-related problems. This frees them from the constraints of servers, allowing for a more efficient and simplified development process. Serverless computing represents a paradigm shift in application development, providing modern development needs with simplicity, scalability, and cost-efficiency.

The breakdown of application logic into a constellation of tiny, stateless functions is at the foundation of serverless computing. These functions run in discrete execution environments, frequently in the form of containers, and communicate smoothly with other functions and cloud services. This architectural paradigm enables developers to more effectively exploit cloud capabilities than ever before.

1.1 Security in Serverless Computing

Serverless computing is an increasingly popular approach for building and deploying applications due to its ability to abstract away infrastructure management and its promise of enhanced security. However, as the examination of serverless platform security defenses reveals, there are still notable concerns that demand a closer look.

Concerns like this include network security. Functions communicate via networks and APIs in serverless systems. Data integrity and secrecy must be guaranteed when using these channels. Even though encryption is frequently provided by serverless platforms for both data in transit and data at rest, developers must take care while setting up and executing safe network profiles. Inadequate network configuration may leave confidential information vulnerable to intrusions.

Another subject that is under investigation is process isolation. In order to stop attackers from moving laterally within the system, serverless systems try to separate different functions from one another. To find and fix any possible flaws, it is crucial to test and evaluate this isolation's efficacy on a regular basis.

In fact, serverless computing's security posture is strengthened by its layers of protection, which include automatic scaling and reduced attack surfaces. Still, the shared responsibility paradigm is critical. Developers and companies must take proactive steps to secure their serverless apps by using continuous monitoring, frequent code audits, and least privilege access, among other measures.

In closing, serverless computing offers a desirable security architecture, but there are drawbacks as well. To ensure that serverless applications remain resilient and robust in the face of constantly changing security threats, effective security assurance requires a comprehensive solution that addresses network security, process isolation, and a shared responsibility paradigm.

Figure 1. Serverless architecture

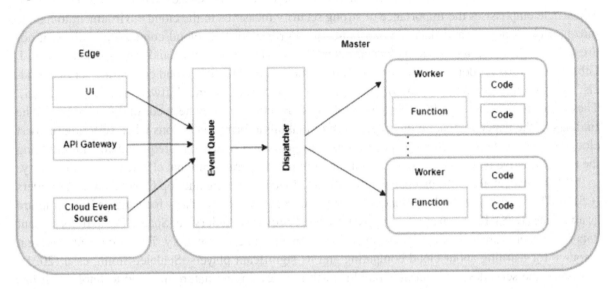

2. LITERATURE REVIEW

This section outlines views on various papers referred in the course of research. These papers provide valuable insights into "Serverless Computing", and their findings have played a significant role in shaping the context and understanding of this field.

Won Kim (2009) gives an informative review of cloud computing by emphasising its numerous service offerings and benefits such as cost savings and scalability. The study also looks into important adoption factors including security and compliance, while forecasting the expansion of cloud services, integration solutions, and hybrid cloud adoption. Kim also identifies technical difficulties that merit attention in the emerging cloud computing landscape, such as software platforms, collaboration tools, data integration, multimedia transmission, and service administration. The research that Dilon, T, et.al. (2010) delves further into cloud computing, examining its features, service models, deployment patterns, and interactions with other computing paradigms such as SOC, Grid Computing, and HPC. It focuses on the critical topic of cloud computing interoperability, covering solutions such as intermediary layers, standardisation, and open APIs for smooth integration among cloud providers and with on-premise systems.

Alouffi, B. et.al (2021) presented a Systematic Literature Review (SLR) on cloud computing security. It highlights major findings and issues of cloud security. Data tampering and leaking have been identified as dangers, with consumer trustworthiness highlighted as a challenge. The text also discusses data outsourcing concerns and issues that cloud service companies confront. It also considers blockchain as a viable method to improve security and emphasises the general significance of effective security measures in cloud computing. J. Keung, et.al (2012) study provides a comprehensive analysis of cloud deployment models, emphasising their different benefits and trade-offs. This analysis provides readers with a thorough overview of cloud deployment alternatives, allowing them to make informed selections based on their individual needs and goals.

L. Savu (2011) analyses the history, characteristics, delivery strategies, security risks, commercial products, and research problems of cloud computing. Cloud computing is portrayed as a game-changing

IT model that allows for greater flexibility in resource allocation and service delivery over the Internet. The article emphasises the importance of strong security measures in the cloud environment to handle threats such as attacks and data security concerns. Furthermore, as cloud computing evolves, it addresses emergent research concerns such as automated service provisioning and energy management. J. Gibson, et.al (2012) addressed the benefits and limitations of three key cloud computing service models: Infrastructure as a Service (IaaS), Platform as a Service (PaaS), and Software as a Service (SaaS). These models provide variable levels of control and abstraction to meet the needs of different users. The findings of the paper emphasise the importance of making informed decisions when selecting the best cloud service model to align with specific business goals and operational requirements, highlighting the transformative potential of cloud computing in improving organisational efficiency and flexibility.

M. Saraswat, et.al (2020) extensively investigate cloud computing and top Cloud Service Providers (CSPs). They emphasise the importance of cloud technology in modern IT by focusing on Infrastructure as a Service (IaaS), Platform as a Service (PaaS), and Software as a Service (SaaS). The authors present data on market share and growth rates for major companies in each category. This document is a great resource for learning about cloud computing and its significant players. Schleier-Smith, et al (2021). illustrated the serverless computing's rapid growth and developing nature in cloud technology. It has proven to be a profitable industry, with simpler system management and significant annual growth approaching 50%. According to the report, serverless computing will enter a new phase fueled by easier cloud programming, similar to how ride-sharing simplifies transportation. In the future decade, this evolution is predicted to bring about greater abstractions, cost competitiveness, machine learning integration, and diversified hardware, making serverless computing the dominating paradigm in the Cloud Era.

T. Lynn, et.al (2017) examined seven enterprise serverless computing technologies, with AWS Lambda standing out as a focus point for academic research due to its prominence. It emphasises the cost-efficiency and scalability benefits of serverless computing while highlighting issues in areas such as cost modelling and security. The paper's limited investigation of alternative platforms highlights the need for additional research in this expanding topic, making it a useful resource for understanding the serverless computing ecosystem. S. Eismamm, et. al (2021) have analysed 89 serverless applications from diverse sources, and it was discovered that serverless computing had multiple advantages, such as faster development, less operating work, and scalability. Contrary to popular opinion, serverless apps are employed for both core functionality and scientific workloads in addition to utility functions. Languages like Python and JavaScript are commonly used to develop serverless applications, which significantly rely on Backend-as-a-Service (BaaS) solutions for storage, databases, and communications. Serverless functions are more like microservices or API endpoints in terms of granularity. The study's findings dispel myths about serverless computing's limits by highlighting the variety of uses and potential benefits of this technology.

H. Lee, et.al (2018) provided a detailed examination of production serverless computing infrastructures. Their research is centred on four main serverless platforms: Amazon Lambda, Microsoft Azure Functions, Google Cloud Functions, and IBM Cloud Functions (Apache OpenWhisk). The authors evaluate these systems' performance in terms of CPU capability, network bandwidth, and file I/O throughput, particularly when dealing with concurrent function invocations. Their findings underscore serverless computing's capabilities in terms of flexibility, cost-effectiveness, and quick resource provisioning, making it a tempting solution for distributed data processing and dynamic workloads. Hassan, H.B., et.al (2021) undertook a thorough study on serverless computing, addressing the field's lack of in-depth expertise. The survey covers serverless principles, platforms, advantages, disadvantages, and use cases. Its contributions include summarising previous research, comparing serverless systems, and offering insights into the complexities of serverless. This work is a great resource for both newbies and specialists in serverless computing, since it reduces complexity and guides future research in this novel cloud computing paradigm.

M. Sewak and S. Singh (2018) talked about the importance of serverless computing and Function as a Service (FaaS) in current technologies. The article will most likely investigate how certain architectural styles provide benefits such as cost reductions, quick development, and event-driven processing. It may also discuss real-world serverless and FaaS applications and use cases.

D. Taibi, et.al (2021) defined serverless computing as an application development paradigm that abstracts infrastructure administration and concentrates on event-driven, cloud-based systems. Backend as a Service (BaaS) and Functions as a Service (FaaS) are choices provided by major cloud providers. Serverless operations, like microservices, operate at a finer granularity. They have advantages such as NoOps, quick deployment, and cost savings, but they also have drawbacks such as testing difficulties and vendor lock-in. The serverless world is evolving, with issues such as optimising architectural patterns and dealing with long-term system evolution. Serverless computing, developed by Amazon Lambda in 2014, provides a framework for executing code without maintaining infrastructure, according to H. Lee, et. al (2018). It has grown to be capable of supporting thousands of concurrent invocations, making it suited for distributed data processing and event-driven microservices. This research compares the performance of serverless setups from Amazon, Google, Microsoft, and IBM in terms of throughput, CPU, disc, and network. The results show that serverless computing is appropriate for some workloads, such as concurrent processes, but it is less expensive for infrequent workloads. Language support and capabilities varies amongst serverless systems, with Amazon Lambda offering high throughput and dynamic scalability.

I. Odun-Ayo, et.al (2018) investigated the history and importance of cloud computing, emphasising its role in altering IT practises. It introduces major players in cloud computing, defines its features, analyses several deployment techniques (private, public, community, hybrid), and goes into the primary service types (SaaS, PaaS, IaaS). It also discusses developing "as-a-Service" models and security concerns as well as industry developments. The paper emphasises the importance of more research in cloud architecture. This systematic mapping research investigates the interface of Machine Learning Operations (MLOps) and serverless computing, demonstrating how their connection is growing by A. Barrak, et. al (2022). The analysis, which is based on 53 relevant academic publications, emphasises the growing use of serverless computing, specifically AWS Lambda, for machine learning workloads. It focuses on the use of serverless architecture at various stages of the machine learning pipeline, with major problems such as cost optimisation and resource scalability. The study uncovers new publishing patterns, priority areas within applied machine learning on serverless platforms, and prospective difficulties and possibilities in this creative field, benefiting both researchers and practitioners.

The paper entitled "SelectiveCrypt: Efficient and Secure Serverless Computing for IoT," B. Kim et al. B. Kim, et. al (2021) presents SelectiveCrypt, an encryption technique designed for IoT services on serverless platforms. SelectiveCrypt uses a compiler and runtime framework for automated selection and code modification to dynamically pick encryption techniques depending on data consumption patterns. In real-world IoT scenarios, such as face recognition and gas leak monitoring, SelectiveCrypt reduces reaction times by 1.59 times and communication overhead by 9.61 times when compared to complete homomorphic encryption. This advancement improves data privacy in IoT applications while improving serverless computing efficiency. G. Somma, et.al (2020) described an effective container-based cloud computing provisioning method for dealing with resource allocation issues in dynamic cloud applications.

It emphasises the advantages of containers for quick resource scaling and offers an auto-scaling system based on Q-Learning to optimise resource allocation. Experiments in Docker and Kubernetes settings reveal that the approach saves money, has more predictable service times, and has lower blocking rates than conventional provisioning and Kubernetes' Horizontal Pod Autoscaler. Overall, the suggested approach provides an efficient method for managing resources under varying cloud workloads.

A device-driven on-demand deployment approach for serverless computing tasks in IoT edge contexts is presented by T. Quang, et.al (2020). Unlike the typical user-driven push-model method, this strategy enables IoT devices to request and indicate where serverless operations should be executed, resulting in improved responsiveness. The system consists of IoT devices, edge devices, and cloud resources that use cloud services such as AWS Greengrass.If the required function is not accessible on the edge, the deployment procedure involves interacting with the cloud for deployment. AWS Greengrass greatly contributes to deployment delay. Function invocation, whether on the edge or in the cloud, adds just a little amount of delay. Integrating Azure IoT Edge and optimising deployment methodologies are among the next steps. L. Schuler, et. al (2021) investigated the influence of serverless computing on resource management. Within the Knative framework, they develop a request-based auto-scaling strategy and examine the use of reinforcement learning to optimise auto-scaling for serverless settings. Their studies show significant performance improvements over default setups.

S. Werner, et.al (2018) investigated serverless computing (FaaS) as a big data processing alternative, with an emphasis on matrix multiplication. It establishes the criteria for creating serverless large data applications, creates a prototype, and runs tests. Serverless alternatives can cut costs while retaining performance and scalability, perhaps beating cluster-based frameworks, according to the findings. The research emphasises the significance of parameter tweaking, such as split size, in optimising the trade-off between work runtime and cost. Finally, serverless architecture holds the promise of cost-effective and efficient large data processing. The junction of IoT applications, age of information (AoI) as a timeliness metric, and serverless computing (FaaS) is the focus of this article authores by S.Wakisaka, et. al. (2021) It emphasises how information updates from IoT devices affect the freshness of serverless services, an element that has received less attention in previous studies. This is expressed in the study as an integer linear programme (ILP) with the goal of minimising the AoS of serverless functions. To overcome this issue, it proposes both offline and online algorithms. The simulation findings show that these methods are successful at providing serverless functions with timely information updates, hence improving AoS performance over a wide range of parameter settings.

D. Chahal, et. al (2020) discussed the deployment of large machine learning and deep learning models on serverless computing platforms, with a focus on AWS Lambda. The study emphasises the benefits of serverless computing for the cost-effective and efficient deployment of complicated applications with deep learning models. It solves issues like as cold starts, memory allocation, and Elastic File System (EFS) interaction with Lambda. The study demonstrates how serverless architecture improves performance and cost competitiveness for large model installations. J. L. Vazquez-Poletti, et.al (2021) delved into serverless computing for scientific data processing, concentrating on AWS Lambda's use in analysing data from the MARSIS instrument on the Mars Express orbiter. It compares Lambda's event-driven, serverless paradigm against a typical server-based solution utilising AWS EC2. The programme analyses ionospheric events and analyses data to identify Martian magnetic fields, emphasising the need of rapid data processing throughout the prolonged Mars Express mission. The paper covers Lambda's architecture, container warming times, and cost factors, finding that while EC2 is marginally less expensive, Lambda provides quicker execution speeds and lower delays for low-latency data processing.

Yelam. A, (2021) explored the possibility of leveraging serverless cloud services such as AWS lambdas to create secret communication channels. The paper focuses on the difficulties posed by these transient, lightweight functionalities, highlighting the necessity of quick co-residence identification in order to enable hidden channels. The researchers create a scalable and dependable memory bus hardware-based co-residence detection method that allows for the quick and dynamic finding of co-resident lambdas. The research validates that it is possible to set up secret communication channels using lambdas. It can generate hundreds of these channels for each 1000 lambdas that are deployed, and it can send data at a speed of 200 bits per second. Wang L, et. al (2018) provided a thorough examination of these platforms, illuminating their structures, functionality, and effectiveness in resource management. The detection of resource accounting issues, the scalability and cold start delay of various platforms, and the security implications of resource isolation techniques are some of the noteworthy discoveries. Both platform developers and consumers may benefit from the research's useful picture of the resource management and performance of serverless platforms.

Kelly D, (2021) examined the growing risk of Denial of Wallet (DoW) attacks in serverless computing, emphasising the possible harm to finances that these attacks may inflict. DoW attacks use a serverless platform to repeatedly invoke functions in an attempt to deplete the financial resources of its victims. The impact of DoW assaults is illustrated through simulations in the paper, which highlights how dispersed efforts are necessary for DoW to be effective and how this sets it apart from more conventional Denial of Service operations. The study highlights the significance of creating mitigation techniques for serverless systems and offers a springboard for more research into this new cybersecurity issue. Liu G, et.al (2022) provided a thorough analysis of the typosquatting attack vulnerability of container registries, where malicious pictures are posted under names that resemble innocuous ones, potentially causing users to inadvertently download destructive stuff. The research includes cross-platform assaults including both public and private registries. In order to protect against typosquatting from both registry and user viewpoints, the authors underline the significant security vulnerabilities that this presents to the container ecosystem and provide a solution termed 'Crystal'. In order to safeguard consumers and organisations, the research highlights how critical it is to address this emerging issue in container technology.

An overview of serverless computing, its benefits, and security issues is given Marin, et.al. (2022) With serverless computing, cloud providers handle infrastructure administration while developers concentrate only on the logic of their applications. Because the functions in this paradigm are tiny, stateless, and have a limited lifespan, they provide fine-grained security by making it difficult for attackers to launch persistent assaults. Developers and cloud providers share security obligations; the latter is in charge of protecting the underlying infrastructure. Potential security vulnerabilities including wider attack surfaces, evading authentication, misconfigured privileges, and assaults at the infrastructure level are also highlighted in the study. We talk about countermeasures and the need for further serverless security research.

3. BENEFITS OF SERVERLESS COMPUTING

In this section, we will explore several benefits of serverless computing, each of which has a significant impact on the way that contemporary applications are developed and deployed. Serverless computing offers a multitude of benefits that companies and developers find more enticing, from its affordability and seamless scalability to its streamlined management and decreased latency. Let's delve more into these advantages.

1.   Cost-Effective and Usage-Based Billing:

Serverless computing offers a cost-effective solution since applications are priced based on actual usage, which is known as usage-based billing. This indicates that consumers are only billed for the computing resources used when performing functions or using services. Businesses may properly optimise their use of cloud resources since there are no fees for downtime.

2.   Seamless Scalability and Autoscaling:

The serverless architecture's ability to scale automatically is one of its most notable features. By dynamically assigning resources in response to rising demand, serverless apps can handle a variety of workloads. This feature makes it an appealing choice for applications with unpredictable usage patterns because it automatically assures optimal performance during traffic spikes.

3.   Simplified Management and No Operations (NoOps):

Serverless computing streamlines the development process by relieving developers of the need to worry about server provisioning, scaling, or system orchestration. Operations teams also follow this "NoOps" philosophy. Developers can concentrate on development by delegating infrastructure management responsibilities to the cloud provider, such as database maintenance, which reduces resource ownership.

4.   Independence and Simple Code Deployment:

Serverless solutions simplify code deployment by enabling programmers to upload and modify certain functions on their own. With this degree of granularity, updates and modifications may be made more quickly without requiring a whole application redeployment. In order to improve time-to-market, developers can deploy new features and patches more quickly.

5.   Elimination of Infrastructural Costs:

Serverless models reduce the requirement for enterprises to invest in and maintain real servers or pay for fixed resources. Only when code is run in response to events are costs incurred, matching cost structures to real usage patterns. Significant cost reductions may result from this, particularly for applications with fluctuating workloads.

6.   Quick Time-to-Market:

Serverless development's simplicity hastens the introduction of new features and products. Instead of becoming bogged down in infrastructure worries, developers can concentrate on writing code and coming up with new ideas. By speeding up the time it takes to market products, this agility can give organisations a competitive edge.

7.   Proximity to End Users and Reduced Latency:

Serverless apps can run on servers that are close to end users, which reduces latency. This results in faster response times and a better user experience because data and requests do not need to travel over the internet over great distances.

8.   Automatic Autoscaling:

Regardless of the load, serverless functions scale automatically. Serverless apps can effectively expand to meet demand, whether they are managing a vast stream of requests or a single client request. Applications with variable workloads benefit most from this elasticity.

9.   Redeployment independence:

Serverless architectures allow for the redeployment of specific functions without affecting the system as a whole. This granular control over updates and changes makes maintenance easier and lowers the chance of making mistakes when making changes.

4. SECURITY GUARANTEES OF SERVERLESS COMPUTING

Serverless computing comes with various intrinsic security assurances, making it an appealing option for modern application development.

1.   *Automatic Scaling for Resilience:* Serverless solutions are designed to scale resources automatically in response to incoming workload. This means that increased computer resources are supplied during periods of high demand, while resources are de-provisioned during periods of low demand. This elastic scaling ensures that the application can adapt to changing demands while remaining available. In essence, serverless architectures are more robust to resource depletion caused by abrupt traffic spikes or Distributed Denial of Service (DoS) assaults by definition. The system can adjust to increased traffic without operator intervention, increasing its resilience to availability concerns.

2.   *Function Isolation and Security:* Each serverless function is run within an isolated environment or container. This isolation guarantees that the execution of one function does not interfere with or jeopardise the security of other functions. This isolation is an important security element in a shared infrastructure paradigm, where numerous users may be performing tasks concurrently. Any vulnerabilities or breaches in the execution environment of one function are contained within that unique instance, avoiding lateral movement of threats and improving overall programme security.

3.   *Reduced Attack Surface:* Serverless functions are often small, concentrated bits of code that execute certain tasks or microservices. These functions offer fewer attack surfaces than typical monolithic programmes with large codebases due to their compact design. There are fewer possible vulnerabilities and attack vectors available for exploitation when there are fewer lines of code and dependencies. This smaller attack surface makes it more difficult for bad actors to find and exploit programme flaws.

4. ***Short-Lived Instances for Enhanced Security:*** Serverless functions are short-lived, with instances produced and then destroyed for the length of the function's execution. The ephemeral nature of a running function restricts its exposure, minimising the time available for prospective attackers to exploit flaws. Because functions are stateless and controlled automatically, there is less chance for long-term assaults or unauthorised access. The short duration of these incidents helps to the overall security posture.

5. ***Controls for Authentication and Authorization:*** Many serverless solutions have integrated authentication and authorization procedures. These technologies allow developers to manage function access by implementing API gateways, role-based access control, and fine-grained permissions. Only authorised users or systems can execute serverless operations when authentication and authorization are properly established. This level of access restriction is critical for ensuring the security and integrity of serverless applications.

6. ***Managed Infrastructure Security:*** Cloud providers are responsible for safeguarding the underlying infrastructure, which includes servers, networking, and data centres. This involves physical security, frequent upgrades, and hardware and software layer maintenance. Users can use the powerful security mechanisms developed by cloud providers to secure the infrastructure underlying their serverless apps, hence improving overall environment security.

7. ***Payment-Based DoW Mitigation:*** Serverless solutions frequently use a payment approach based on actual resource use. Users are charged based on the resources used during execution. This pricing mechanism can inhibit abusive behaviour such as DoW assaults presented by Kelly D, et.al (2022), in which attackers overwhelm the system with requests in order to exaggerate expenses. The financial consequences of resource usage provide built-in defence against such assaults, preventing hostile acts that try to financially disrupt services.

Serverless computing provides a dynamic and safe way to application deployment, with these assurances contributing to the resilience and strong security posture of the technology. Organisations may benefit from automatic scalability, isolation, and reduced attack surfaces by using serverless architectures, all while leveraging the security controls and managed infrastructure provided by cloud service providers.

5. SERVERLESS COMPUTING AS A SECURITY ENHANCER

In this section some guidelines and examples pertaining to the advantages of serverless computing from a security perspective is discussed.

5.1 Attacks against serverless and its countermeasures

In this section, we outline the primary kinds of attacks against serverless computing. We divide them into two primary groups: (i) attacks at the application level, which take advantage of flaws in the functions' code explained by Owasp (2023) (ii) attacks at the infrastructure level, which target the serverless architectures' structure and functionality.

5.1.1 Attacks at Application Level

In serverless computing, software developers are still in charge of ensuring the security of their apps, or the security in the cloud.

Therefore, if programmers write their functions' code in an insecure manner or fail to follow standard secure coding practises, their functions may contain vulnerabilities that leave them open to common application-level attacks like SQL Injection, Cross-Site Scripting (XSS), Denial of Service (DoS) explained by Owasp (2023).

5.1.1.1 Bypassing the Authentication

When serverless functions are used in isolation, they lack the context and knowledge needed to understand other features and cloud services that they are a part of. In order for serverless systems to verify if a function invocation request is valid and possesses the necessary permissions to access a function or a piece of data, a strong access control mechanism is necessary. In serverless systems, a strong access control mechanism is necessary to verify whether a function invocation request is valid and possesses the necessary authorizations to access a function or a piece of data presented by Marin, Eduard, et. al (2022).

5.1.1.2 Utilising and De-Serializing Third-Party Libraries

Many programming languages, including scripting languages like Python and NodeJS, are used to write serverless functions. These languages frequently use serialised data types like JSON. Due to the peculiarities of each of these programming languages, unanticipated conclusions about unreliable data may result. This stems from the programming language itself as well as from frameworks that are integrated into the application, usually to facilitate quicker code development. User input deserialization should be avoided until absolutely essential, as safeguarding against deserialization vulnerabilities is challenging. If this is not possible, then, software developers need to think about and include strong security services like integrity checks and authentication using digital signatures to ensure the data hasn't been altered.

Furthermore, functions frequently rely on numerous (perhaps unsafe) third-party libraries to perform a variety of crucial activities. Software developers must monitor the third-party libraries they utilise and take the appropriate steps to guarantee that each function has its own security boundary shown by Sbom (2020).

5.1.1.3 Injection Attacks

In order to take advantage of flaws in the way functions parse input data, adversaries can transmit deliberately constructed packets to those functions. Because there are numerous function entry points that an adversary can fully control, serverless functions can be subject to new sorts of injection attacks in addition to existing ones (such as those based on OS commands or SQL/NoSQL). For instance, injection attacks could be used to obtain the secrets kept in the execution environment or the source code of the routines. Inorder to resolve this issue each function should always thoroughly verify and sanitise any received input data presented by Marin, Eduard, et. al (2022).

5.1.1.4 Incorrect Privilege Setup

The process of granting privileges to serverless functions is difficult, and it frequently leads to processes receiving more privileges than necessary. Attacks that take advantage of these vulnerabilities exist for a number of reasons. Firstly, the expertise required to establish fine-grained security controls that restrict the capabilities of their functions is typically lacking in software engineers. Second, due to the pressure of meeting deadlines to deploy their apps in live environments, software developers frequently neglect to adequately evaluate the rights provided to their services. Perhaps most significantly, there are no systems in place to determine and set up the minimal set of privileges required by programmes presented by Marin, Eduard, et.al (2022) dynamically and automatically.

5.1.2 Attacks at Infrastructure-Level

5.1.2.1 Race Conditions

Any component whose functionality is dispersed across different nodes or that has multiple replicas might be a source of inconsistencies in serverless platforms. Let's take an example where software engineers choose to alter a function's code while it's being executed by several copies. When this occurs, there may be a brief period of time during which the serverless platform is inconsistent, processing some incoming requests using the older version of the function and some using the updated version explained by Wnag L et.al. (2018). Such unwanted behaviour could be exploited by adversaries to launch security attacks, with the aim of obtaining or altering data that would otherwise be inaccessible to them. Such attacks could also be conducted when many replicas of the same function are running concurrently and other factors (such memory sizes, IAM roles, or environment variables) are changed. By changing these factors during runtime, hackers may be able to create race situations that compromise the serverless platform's overall security. Although race problems can also occur in microservices architectures, the likelihood of conflicts between function versions is increased by the lower granularity provided by serverless platforms.

5.1.2.2 Billing Attacks

While serverless offers better defence against DoS/DDoS attacks, these techniques can be redesigned to create new, serverless-specific attacks by leveraging the fact that uses pay for the resources their functions use. Adversaries can now carry out Denial-of-Wallet (DoW) attacks presented by Kelly D, et.al (2022) explains flooding services with requests in an attempt to force users to pay a much higher price. While there are several existing mitigating countermeasures against DoW attacks, these attacks are difficult to safeguard against and necessitate the implementation of additional control measures. These methods include the detection of anomalous behaviour and the subsequent discrimination of which legal invocations to allow and which to drop.

5.1.2.3 Persistent Attacks

In serverless computing perspective, classic persistent attacks against servers are inapplicable. Researchers have discovered, however, that attackers may carry out a new kind of persistent attacks by inserting malicious code in the writable /tmp/disk space, which warm containers use to hold temporary data between invocations presented in Gone in 60 ms and AWS containers (2021). In terms of countermeasures, cloud providers could minimise the size of the /tmp/ folder and observe its contents after each function call in order to mitigate the exposed issue, inorder to use the warm containers which are necessary to meet application performance requirements.

5.1.2.4 Side Channel Attacks

Attackers may try to take advantage of the way serverless systems are built and set up to launch new kinds of side channel attacks. To acquire host-system state information such as performance data or power consumption or information on the execution of specific processes like running status, scheduling,) for instance, they could take advantage of flaws in the execution environments where functions are executed. By using this information, adversaries may be able to more successfully and efficiently launch attacks by using it to identify a worker node or function instance. Given that there are numerous components and cloud services that are shared by users, more complex side channels can also be created. Adversaries are particularly interested in any shared component that is subject to a state change built on the processed data, as these components have the potential to leak private information about users and functions via a side channel presented by Marin, Eduard, et. al (2022).

Finally, serverless computing offers a dynamic and scalable method to application deployment that comes with intrinsic security benefits. However, in order to maximise these benefits while also addressing the security concerns and limits, developers and organisations must follow best practises. Thorough code review, safe configuration management, and proactive threat modelling are examples of best practises. An important part of guaranteeing the security of serverless apps is the shared responsibility paradigm, in which both cloud providers and users contribute to security.

6. CONCLUSION

To sum up, serverless computing is a revolutionary change in the creation of cloud-based applications. It delivers cost-effectiveness, smooth scalability, powerful security features, and streamlines the development process. It does, however, also bring with it additional security concerns and constraints. Strong authentication and permission restrictions, function separation, robustness, and automated scalability are all made possible by serverless computing. The security of the underlying infrastructure is handled by cloud providers, while these elements help to create a secure environment. Developers, however, are accountable for application-level security, which includes safe coding techniques and proactive threat mitigation. They also need to understand the concept of shared accountability. Issues including side channel attacks, cold start delays, and poor visibility need to be taken seriously.In order to optimise serverless computing's security and realise its full potential, developers and organisations have to use best practises such as rigorous code reviews, safe configuration management, and ongoing security monitoring. To guarantee the security and integrity of serverless apps, consumers and cloud providers must work together. With its flexibility, scalability, and strong security, serverless technology offers an intriguing opportunity in the ever-changing field of cloud computing. Developers and organisations may confidently tackle the challenges of serverless computing while fully using its benefits by comprehending and proactively managing its security implications.

REFERENCES

Alouffi, B., Hasnain, M., Alharbi, A., Alosaimi, W., Alyami, H., & Ayaz, M. (2021). A Systematic Literature Review on Cloud Computing Security: Threats and Mitigation Strategies. *IEEE Access*. IEEE.

Barrak, A., Petrillo, F., & Jaafar, F. (2022). Serverless on Machine Learning: A Systematic Mapping Study. *IEEE Access : Practical Innovations, Open Solutions*, *10*, 99337–99352. doi:10.1109/ACCESS.2022.3206366

Chahal, D., Ojha, R., Ramesh, M., & Singhal, R. (2020). Migrating Large Deep Learning Models to Serverless Architecture, *2020 IEEE International Symposium on Software Reliability Engineering Workshops (ISSREW)*, Coimbra, Portugal. 10.1109/ISSREW51248.2020.00047

Dillon, T., Wu, C., & Chang, E. (2010), Cloud Computing: Issues and Challenges. *2010 24th IEEE International Conference on Advanced Information Networking and Applications*, (pp. 27-33). IEEE.

Eismann, S., Scheuner, J., van Eyk, E., Schwinger, M., Grohmann, J., Herbst, N., Abad, C. L., & Iosup, A. (2021). Serverless Applications: Why, When, and How? *IEEE Software*, *38*(1), 32–39. doi:10.1109/MS.2020.3023302

Gibson, J., Rondeau, R., Eveleigh, D., & Tan, Q. (2012). *Benefits and challenges of three cloud computing service models. 2012 Fourth International Conference on Computational Aspects of Social Networks (CASoN)*, Sao Carlos, Brazil. 10.1109/CASoN.2012.6412402

Hassan, H. B., Barakat, S. A., & Sarhan, Q. I. (2021). Q.I. Survey on serverless computing. *Journal of Cloud Computing (Heidelberg, Germany)*, *10*(1), 39. doi:10.1186/s13677-021-00253-7

Kelly, D., Glavin, F. G., & Barrett, E. (2021). Denial of wallet–Defning a looming threat to serverless computing. *Journal of Information Security and Applications*, (60), 2214–2126.

Keung, J., & Kwok, F. (2012). *Cloud Deployment Model Selection Assessment for SMEs: Renting or Buying a Cloud. IEEE Fifth International Conference on Utility and Cloud Computing*, Chicago, IL, USA. 10.1109/UCC.2012.29

Kim, B., Heo, S., Lee, J., Jeong, S., Lee, Y., & Kim, H. (2021). Compiler-Assisted Semantic-Aware Encryption for Efficient and Secure Serverless Computing. *IEEE Internet of Things Journal*, *8*(7), 5645–5656. doi:10.1109/JIOT.2020.3031550

Kim, W. (2009). Cloud Computing: Status and Prognosis. *Journal of Object Technology*, *8*(1), 65–72. doi:10.5381/jot.2009.8.1.c4

Lee, H., Satyam, K., & Fox, G. (2018). *Evaluation of Production Serverless Computing Environmentts.* 2018 IEEE 11th International Conference on Cloud Computing (CLOUD), San Francisco, CA, USA.

Lee, H., Satyam, K., & Fox, G. (2018). *Evaluation of Production Serverless Computing Environments.* 2018 IEEE 11th International Conference on Cloud Computing (CLOUD), San Francisco, CA, USA, 442-450.

Liu, G., Gao, X., Wang, H., & Sun, K. (2022) *Exploring the Unchartered Space of Container Registry Typosquatting*. In: USENIX Security Symposium (USENIX Security), USENIX Association, Boston.

Lynn, T., Rosati, P., Lejeune, A., & Emeakaroha, V. (2017). A Preliminary Review of Enterprise Serverless Cloud Computing (Function-as-a-Service*) Platforms. IEEE International Conference on Cloud Computing Technology and Science (CloudCom)*, Hong Kong, China. 10.1109/CloudCom.2017.15

Marin, Eduard and Perino, Diego and Di Pietro, Roberto (2022) Serverless computing: a security perspective. pp 1–12. Journal of Cloud Computing, SpringerOpen.

Odun-Ayo, I., Ananya, M., Agono, F., & Goddy-Worlu, R. (2018). *Cloud Computing Architecture: A Critical Analysis*. 2018 18th International Conference on Computational Science and Applications (ICCSA), Melbourne, VIC, Australia.

Quang, T., & Peng, Y. (2020). *Device-driven On-demand Deployment of Serverless Computing Functions*. 2020 IEEE International Conference on Pervasive Computing and Communications Workshops (PerCom Workshops), Austin, TX, USA.

Saraswat, M., & Tripathi, R. C. (2020). *Cloud Computing: Analysis of Top 5 CSPs in SaaS, PaaS and IaaS Platforms*. 2020 9th International Conference System Modeling and Advancement in Research Trends (SMART), Moradabad, India.

Savu, L. (2011).Cloud Computing: Deployment Models, Delivery Models, Risks and Research Challenges. *2011 International Conference on Computer and Management (CAMAN)*, Wuhan, China. 10.1109/CAMAN.2011.5778816

Schleier-Smith, J., Sreekanti, V., Khandelwal, A., Carreira, J., Yadwadkar, N. J., Popa, R. A., Gonzalez, J. E., Stoica, I., & Patterson, D. A. (2021). What serverless computing is and should become. *Communications of the ACM, 64*(5), 76–84. doi:10.1145/3406011

Schuler, L., Jamil, S., & Kühl, N. (2021). *AI-based Resource Allocation: Reinforcement Learning for Adaptive Auto-scaling in Serverless Environments*. 2021 IEEE/ACM 21st International Symposium on Cluster, Cloud and Internet Computing (CCGrid), Melbourne, Australia.

Sewak, M., & Singh, S. (2018). *Winning in the Era of Serverless Computing and Function as a Service*. 2018 3rd International Conference for Convergence in Technology (I2CT), Pune, India.

Somma, G., Ayimba, C., Casari, P., Romano, S. P., & Mancuso, V. (2020). *When Less is More: Core-Restricted Container Provisioning for Serverless Computing*. IEEE INFOCOM 2020 - IEEE Conference on Computer Communications Workshops (INFOCOM WKSHPS), Toronto, ON, Canada.

Taibi, D., Spillner, J., & Wawruch, K. (2021). Serverless Computing-Where Are We Now, and Where Are We Heading? *IEEE Software, 38*(1), 25–31. doi:10.1109/MS.2020.3028708

Vázquez-Poletti, J. L., & Llorente, I. M. (2021). Serverless Computing: From Planet Mars to the Cloud. *Computing in Science & Engineering, 20*(6), 73–79. doi:10.1109/MCSE.2018.2875315

Wakisaka, S., Chiang, Y.-H., Lin, H., & Ji, Y. (2021). *Timely Information Updates for the Internet of Things with Serverless Computing*. IEEE International Conference on Communications, Montreal, QC, Canada.

Wang, L., Li, M., Zhang, Y., Ristenpart, T., & Swift, M. (2018). Peeking behind the Curtains of Serverless Platforms. In: *USENIX Conference on Usenix Annual Technical Conference (USENIX ATC)*. USENIX Association, Boston.

Werner, S., Kuhlenkamp, J., Klems, M., Müller, J., & Tai, S. (2018). *Serverless Big Data Processing using Matrix Multiplication as Example*. 2018 IEEE International Conference on Big Data (Big Data), Seattle, WA, USA.

Yelam, A., Subbareddy, S., Ganesan, K., Savage, S., & Mirian, A. (2021). CoResident Evil: Covert Communication. In *The Cloud With Lambdas. In: The Web Conference (WWW)* (pp. 1005–1016). Association for Computing Machinery.

Chapter 14
Applications of Serverless Computing:
Systematic Overview

A. Kathirvel

iD https://orcid.org/0000-0002-5347-9110

Panimalar Engineering College, India

ABSTRACT

Applications that are serverless can be distributed (many services are connected for smooth operation), elastic (resources can be scaled up and down without limit), stateless (interactions and data aren't stored), event-driven (resources are allocated only when triggered by an event), and hostless (apps aren't hosted on a server). Serverless computing is becoming more and more popular as cloud adoption rises. In many respects, serverless computing unleashes the entire potential of cloud computing. we pay only for the resources consumed, and resources are allocated, increased, or decreased dynamically based on user requirements in real-time. It makes sure that when there are no user requests and the application is effectively dormant, resources are immediately scaled to zero. More scalability and significant cost reductions are the outcomes of this. According to research by Global industry Insights, the serverless industry is expected to reach $30 billion in market value by the end of the forecast period, growing at an above-average rate of 25% between 2021 and 2027.

1. INTRODUCTION

Serverless computing (SC) is a method of providing backend services on a need-based basis. Through serverless providers, users can create and execute applications without having to consider the underlying infrastructure. When a business uses a serverless vendor for backend services, the cost is determined by the vendor's computation; no set bandwidth or server count needs to be reserved or paid for because the service is auto-scaling. Even though it has a different name, the physical server is still used; Developers don't necessarily know this.

DOI: 10.4018/979-8-3693-1682-5.ch014

When the Web was born, anyone who wanted to build a Web application had to buy the expensive and time-consuming physical hardware needed to run a server.

In cloud computing, where one could rent a set number of servers or a set amount of server space remotely. In order to make sure that a surge in activity or traffic won't surpass their monthly allotment and disrupt their applications, developers and businesses that rent these fixed units of servers typically overbuy. It can therefore be the case that a large portion of the paid server space is wasted. To alleviate this problem, cloud manufacturers have come up with auto-scaling models. However, even with auto-scaling, unintended increases in activity, such as DDoS attacks (Bhupathi & Kathirvel, 2022; Kathirvel & Pavani, 2023; Kathirvel & Shobitha, 2023; Sudha & Kathirvel, 2022a; Sudha & Kathirvel, 2023), can impose significant costs. Developers use pre-packaged functions such as Google Cloud Functions and Microsoft Azure Functions to operate so-called serverless applications that either work Function as a service (FaaS) or computation as a service (CaaS).

1.1 Fundamentals of SC

Developers can purchase back-end services using serverless computing on a flexible "pay-as-you-go" basis, meaning they only pay for the services they need. This is like switching from your cell phone data plan that has a set monthly limit to a plan that only charges for the actual amount of data used.

Although these backend services are still provided by the server, the term "serverless" is a bit confusing because the provider manages all aspects of the infrastructure and server space. Developers don't have to worry about servers at all when their work is serverless.

1.2 Techniques in Serverless Computing

The two domains of application development are often separated into 1. frontend and 2. backend. The portion of the program, people can view and interact with SC, (i.e) the layout visually, is called the frontend (Kathirvel & Pavani, 2023). Portion of the program that is hidden from the user's view is called the backend, and it consists of the database and server that store user information and business logic as shown in the Figure 1.

Figure 1. Front end and back end server request

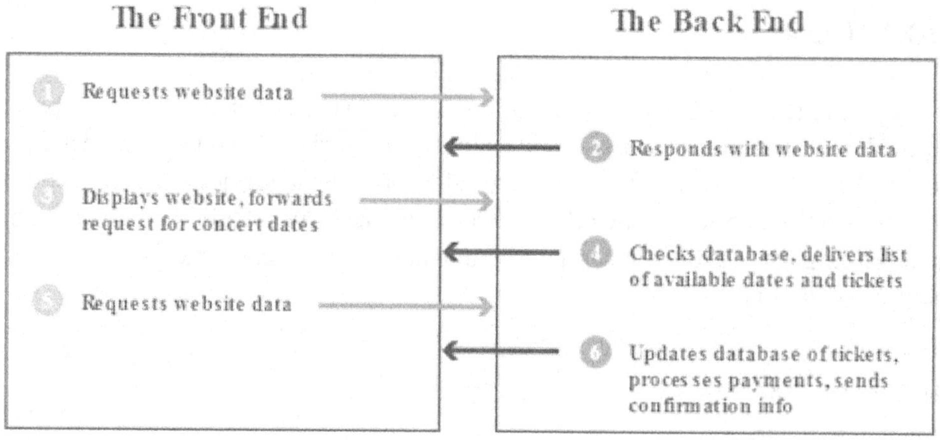

The Front End

The Back End

1. Requests website data
2. Responds with website data
3. Displays website, forwards request for concert dates
4. Checks database, delivers list of available dates and tickets
5. Requests website data
6. Updates database of tickets, processes payments, sends confirmation info

Consider, for illustration, a website that offers concert tickets. The browser sends a request to the back-end server, which returns website information in response when the user types the website address in the browser window. The user then sees the website and the user interface, which may include form fields that the user can fill in as well as text and graphic content. After that, the user can use one of the frontend form fields to look up their preferred musical act. The user will send another request to the backend when they click "submit." The background function queries its database to see if the performer with that name is present and if, what their upcoming performance date and quantity of ticket is available.

In addition to providing database and storage capabilities, the majority of serverless providers also offer FaaS platforms, such as Cloudflare Workers. A developer can run brief code segments on the network server edge with Function as a Service. By creating a sectional architecture using FaaS, developers may create a more scalable codebase without having to invest resources in maintaining the underlying backend.

1.2.1 FaaS

Function-as-a-Service is a serverless approach for running modular programs at the boundary. With FaaS, developers can quickly build and modify code that will be performed when a certain event occurs, such the user clicks on an element in the web application. This mechanism is a low-cost approach to implementing microservices and facilitates code scalability.

1.2.2 Microservices

Using microservice architecture in a web application would be like creating a work of visual art out of a mosaic tile collection as shown in the Figure 2. An artist can easily add, change and fix one record at a time. It is like to painting the entire composition on a single canvas if architecture were monolithic.

Figure 2. Microservice architecture

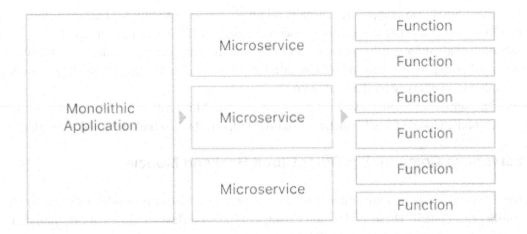

Microservices architecture is the process of building an application from a collection of modular parts. Developers find it attractive when an application is divided into microservices because it allows them to easily generate and alter small code parts that can be integrated into their codebases (Leitner et al., 2019). As opposed to this, uniform architecture integrates totally of the code into a single, massive system. Uniform minor application modifications in large monolithic systems necessitate a laborious deploy procedure. This deployment difficulty is removed with FaaS.

Web developers can concentrate on creating application code by using serverless code, such as FaaS, which handles server allocation and backend services.

Figure 3. Cost benefits of serverless computing

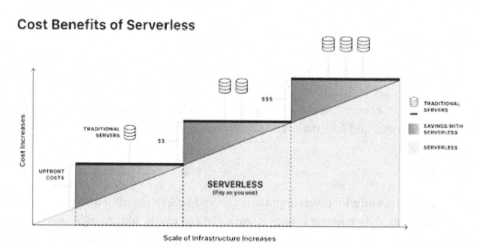

1.3 Advantages of Serverless Computing

Reduced costs: Serverless computing is usually relatively cheap, as traditional back-end cloud providers (server allocation) often charge users for unused CPU time or free space (see Figure 3).

Scalability made simple: When utilizing serverless architecture, developers don't need to worry about regulations when expanding their code (Gobinath et al., 2024; Kathirvel et al., 2023). A serverless service provider takes care of every on-demand scale.

Serverless services provided by cloud providers include Microsoft Azure Functions, Amazon Web Services Lambda, Google Cloud Functions, and IBM OpenWhisk, which are good examples.

1.4 Serverless Compared to Other Cloud Backend Models

Two terms that are frequently used interchangeably with SC are Platform-as-a-Service (PaaS) and Back-end-as-a-Service (BaaS). These models don't always fit the serverless requirements, despite their shared commonalities (Kathirvel & Shobitha, 2023).

With the help of the BaaS service model, front-end developers may focus on writing front-end code while the cloud service provider takes care of backend tasks like data storage. BaaS applications, on the other hand, might not meet either of these requirements, whereas serverless applications function on the edge and are event-driven.

The platform-as-a-service (PaaS) concept allows architects to construct and launch applications by basically renting middleware and operating systems from a cloud provider, among other essential tools. However, scaling PaaS applications is more challenging than scaling serverless apps. Furthermore, PaaS often function off-the-edge and have a noticeable initialization period that is missing from server-based applications (Kathirvel & Pavani, 2023).

Cloud suppliers that host infrastructure on behalf of their clients are collectively referred to as infra-structure-as-a-service (IaaS) providers (Sudha & Kathirvel, 2022b). Although serverless functionality may be offered by IaaS providers, the phrases are not interchangeable.

1.5 What is Next for Serverless?

As serverless providers find ways to get around some of the problems with serverless computing, the technology continues to advance. Cold beginnings are one of these disadvantages.

The provider typically deactivates a serverless service that hasn't been used for a while in order to save energy and avoid over-provisioning. When a user launches an application that calls it later, the serverless provider will have to start it up again and host that function. Term "cold start" refers to the substantial lag that this initial period contributes (Bhupathi & Kathirvel, 2022).

Once the function is operational, following requests will be delivered significantly more quickly (warm begins); but, if the function is not used again for some time, it will eventually go for dormant.

In order to solve this issue, Cloudflare Workers has spun up serverless tasks ahead of time, during the TLS handshake. The outcome is a FaaS platform with no cold starts since Workers functions spin up at the edge in much less time—even less time than it takes to finish the handshake. Check out our Developer guide to learn how to use Cloudflare Workers.

We should anticipate a greater use of serverless architecture when the disadvantages of doing so are resolved and edge computing gains traction.

Simplified backend code: With FaaS, programmers can create basic applications that each perform a specific function, such initiating a request to an API, independently.

Faster turnaround: Serverless architecture has an opportunity to significantly shorten the time to market. to release corrections for bugs and fresh functionality, developers don't need to go through a laborious deploy procedure; instead, they may add and edit code as needed.

2. SERVERLESS MODEL WORKS

The programmer creates an application with a function that controls the program's reaction to a specific user activity (Sudha & Kathirvel, 2023). Pre-packaged FaaS products are typically offered by cloud providers to ease developers' coding and incorporate pre-built backend components.

The method and time at which the function will be activated are defined in an event. For instance, the program might wish to retrieve and send specific data when the user makes an HTTP request. An event is the term for this "if-then" sequence.

A user action triggers the event after the program is deployed and available to the user.

After receiving the event from the application, the cloud provider dynamically allots the resources required to react to the action in accordance with the predetermined function.

The client receives the information or any additional outcome that the function's parameters specifies. Crucially, no resources will be allotted and no data will be kept in an intermediate stage if there is no user request (Sudha & Kathirvel, 2022a). This minimizes storage costs and guarantees that the user receives just the most recent and updated data, making your apps real-time (Sudha & Kathirvel, 2022b).

2.1 Key Components of Architecture

FaaS, the core element of serverless technology, is responsible for executing the computation that determines how services are allocated in a given scenario. Whichever is the kind of cloud infrastructure that is being utilized, you can select from purpose-built FaaS offerings like AWS Lambda for Amazon Web Services (AWS), Microsoft Azure Functions for Azure, Google Cloud Functions for the Google Cloud Platform (GCP), and IBM Cloud Functions for private or hybrid environments. These steps will read the backbone database, retrieve the reply, and deliver it when the user starts an event.

A significant component of serverless functioning is the client interface. Serverless architecture cannot be forced into any application. Short bursts of queries, stateless interactions, and adaptable integrations must all be supported by the interface. Additionally, the interface needs to be built to work with both very high and low volume data transmissions as shown in the Figure 4.

A stateless interaction will begin on the web server, following the user's inception and ending before the FaaS service does. The backend database, which houses the data that is sent to users, is separate from the web server. Let's say you are a provider of internet video content. The internet server is therefore at which customer inquiries, applications, FaaS answers, and additional data are hosted until they are stopped due to serverless computing is transient. Conversely, video material will be retained in the backend storage, ready to be retrieved in response to user queries.

One of the main reasons serverless operations need security is:

Thousands of queries are handled concurrently by the application. Before responding to a request, it must first undergo authentication.

Its stateless architecture prevents the storage of previous interaction histories. Future interactions cannot be validated by the application based on past ones.

The serverless paradigm complicates matters of openness and oversight. Security intelligence must be gathered from the millions of occurrences that are daily logged.

There are several services and providers engaged since serverless architecture is spread. The entire terrain needs to be safeguarded.

The data that has to be shared with the user is kept in the backend database. Static content repositories, SQL databases, media storage, and live broadcasting modes are a few examples of this. Designers usually employ Backend as a service (BaaS) services to further minimize managerial and upkeep work. Most cloud providers also have BaaS alternatives that integrate with their FaaS packages.

FaaS and the client interface, or components 1 and 2, are connected by the API gateway. The FaaS service uses an action that the user takes to initiate an event, which is relayed via the API portal. The client interface's functionality can be increased by connecting it through the intermediary to a variety of FaaS services.

Figure 4. Key components

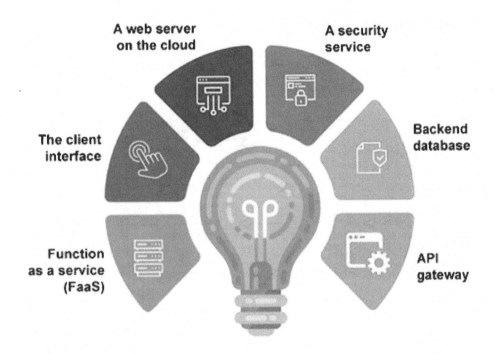

KEY COMPONENTS OF SERVERLESS ARCHITECTURE

3. SERVERLESS COMPUTING

3.1 Overview of Architecture

Typically, hosting a software program online entails overseeing a server architecture. This usually refers to a physical or virtual server that requires management in addition to the OS and additional internet hosting functions required for the app to run correctly as shown in the Figure 5. While using a server that's virtual from an internet-based service like Amazon eliminates real problems with hardware or Microsoft, some level of operating system and web server software maintenance is still necessary.

"Serverless technology computing" is an execution model for cloud-based services that enables the cloud service to operate servers on behalf of the customers it serves by providing resources such as machines as needed. Because cloud service providers still utilize server to run client code, the term "serverless" is deceptive. For architects of serverless applications, however, challenges related to capacity planning, virtualization or physically server installation and management, resilience to faults, and scalability do not arise. Serverless computing uses short bursts of computing, storing the result, rather than storing assets within volatile memory. An application does not have any computer resources assigned to it when it is not in use. The real amount of resources used by an application determines pricing (Kounev, et al., 2023). Code deployment into production can be made easier with serverless computing. Code distributed in conventional ways, like microservices or monoliths, can be combined with serverless code. As an alternative, programs can be developed to run entirely without provided servers (Aske & Zhao, 2018). This is not to be confused with networking or computer methods like peer-to-peer (P2P) that operate without a physical server.

Figure 5. Working of serverless computing

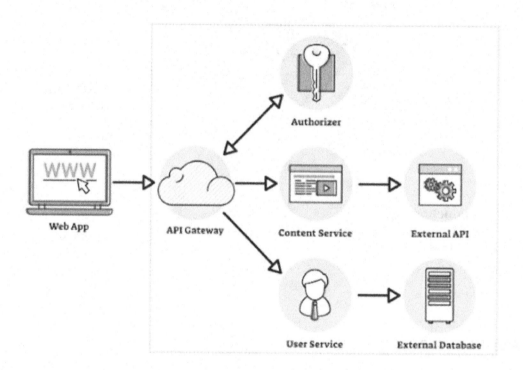

4. EXAMPLE OF SERVERLESS COMPUTING

Global leaders in business have been using serverless computing to provide their clients with high-availability, high-performance online services. Among the noteworthy instances are:

4.1 Major League Baseball Advanced Media (MLBAM)

The Major League Baseball Association is one of the larger and most established athletic associations in the USA. The company runs a program called Statcast that gives customers access to precise and up-to-date sports analytics. You may perform intricate searches on the Statcast website using information such as pitch velocity, pitch type, season type, and individual player names. It can provide accurate data and help users make decisions about baseball games by utilizing serverless computing.

4.2 Autodesk

For the bandwidth-intensive and mission-critical construction, architecture, and engineering sectors, Autodesk provides robust software. It released a new tool named Tailor that could swiftly generate unique Autodesk accounts for businesses with all the required setups. With just two FTES handling the solution, Autodesk was able to launch Tailor in just two weeks by utilizing a serverless architecture.

4.3 Netflix

Netflix, one of the biggest over-the-top (OTT) video companies in the world, has long supported serverless computing. Since 2017 and before, it has been utilizing serverless to create a platform that can manage thousands of modifications every day. The only thing that Netflix developers have to do is define the adapter code, which controls how the platform reacts to user requests and system requirements. At the core of Netflix's exclusive Dynamic Scripting Platform is serverless architecture, which manages platform modifications, provisioning, and end-user delivery.

5. RAPID TECHNOLOGICAL ADVANCEMENT AND INDUSTRY

IR 5.0 is characterized by cutting-edge technologies such as quantum computing, advanced artificial intelligence, and nanotechnology. The rapid pace of innovation can be challenging for industries and governments to keep up with. With this dimension we can further explore the multifaceted challenges posed by rapid technological advancement and their implications in the context of IR 5.0. The technological advancement can be divided into two main dimensions:

5.1. Disruption and Adaptation

Rapid technological advancement drives disruptive changes in industries. Traditional business models and operations are upended as emerging technologies offer new opportunities and efficiencies. This challenges industries to constantly adapt to remain competitive. Failure to do so can result in obsolescence, as witnessed in sectors that couldn't keep pace with digitization. Apart of that deciding where to allocate resources for technological innovation is a complex task. Industries must identify which technologies are most relevant to their operations and invest strategically. Poor resource allocation may lead to missed opportunities or wasted investments. Besides that, the rapid technological advancement can exacerbate economic inequality. While some sectors flourish, others decline, leading to job displacement and wage disparities. Addressing these social and economic disparities becomes an imperative for industries to ensure inclusive growth and societal cohesion (Sudha & Kathirvel, 2022a).

5.2. Regulatory and Ethical Hurdles

Rapid technological change often outpaces the development of regulatory and ethical frameworks. This regulatory lag poses legal and ethical challenges for industries. They must navigate issues such as data privacy, intellectual property rights, safety, and ethical technology use. The absence of clear guidelines can lead to misuse, privacy breaches, or ethical dilemmas. In other words, this has also created a demand for skilled professionals in emerging technologies frequently outstrips supply. Industries struggle to attract, retain, and upskill a workforce capable of harnessing these technologies. The scarcity of talent in fields like AI, quantum computing, and cybersecurity can hinder innovation and competitiveness.

6. RAPID TECHNOLOGICAL ADVANCEMENT AND GOVERNMENT

6.1. Regulation and Legislation

Governments must develop and adapt regulatory frameworks to address the rapid advancement of technology. This includes rules regarding data privacy, intellectual property rights, and the ethical use of technologies. Striking the right balance between enabling innovation and protecting public interests is a challenge. This gap raises legal and ethical challenges. Government and industry must navigate issues like data privacy, intellectual property, safety, and ethical use of technologies. The absence of clear guidelines can lead to misuse, privacy breaches, or even ethical dilemmas. The global nature of IR 5.0 necessitates international collaboration. Governments must work together to address cross-border issues, such as data flows and technology standards, while safeguarding their national interests and security. Nevertheless, as technological advancements increase the vulnerability of digital infrastructure, governments must focus on enhancing cybersecurity measures. Cyberattacks can have national security implications. Collaborating with industries to safeguard critical infrastructure is crucial.

6.2. Workforce Development

Government plays a role in promoting workforce development and reskilling initiatives. Ensuring that the labour force is equipped with the skills required in the rapidly evolving job market is essential for societal stability and economic growth. IR 5.0 brings with it a demand for new and advanced skills, such as data analytics, AI, quantum computing, and cybersecurity. The existing workforce may not possess these skills, leading to a significant skill mismatch. Governance needs to facilitate the rapid acquisition of these skills through education and training programs. Automation and AI can displace traditional jobs. Governance has the responsibility to manage the societal impact of job loss. This may involve designing policies for reskilling and upskilling the workforce to transition into new, tech-related roles. Ensuring that all segments of the population, including disadvantaged groups, have access to the opportunities created by IR 5.0 is a governance challenge. This requires addressing the digital divide, making education and training accessible to everyone, and creating policies that promote inclusivity. Governance needs to adapt labour market policies to align with the changing nature of work. Policies related to contract work, benefits, and worker protections may need to be reevaluated and updated to suit the needs of a more technology-driven workforce. Encouraging and facilitating public-private partnerships can be essential in addressing workforce development challenges. This collaboration can help in the creation of specialized training programs and research initiatives that bridge the gap between the workforce and industry requirements.

In the transition to Industrial Revolution 5.0 (IR 5.0), we confront an array of intricate technological challenges that will shape the course of our future. The rapid pace of technological obsolescence necessitates constant adaptation and upskilling for individuals and organizations, with the risk of lagging behind ever-present. Bridging the digital skills gap and ensuring that all members of society can harness the potential of advanced technologies is not only a challenge but also a moral imperative. Moreover, the ethical and regulatory complexities of IR 5.0 are paramount. As we grapple with the ethical dilemmas posed by artificial intelligence, data privacy, and the responsible use of technology, the development of robust frameworks and regulations becomes crucial. Simultaneously, the expanding threat landscape of cybersecurity looms large. Protecting our digital infrastructure and safeguarding sensitive information require continuous vigilance and innovation. Balancing the demands of a transforming workforce with evolving skills and preparing for jobs that are yet to emerge is a formidable task. The global scale of these challenges necessitates international collaboration in technology and governance. In addressing these hurdles, we must find a delicate equilibrium between technological innovation and responsible use, ensuring that the benefits of IR 5.0 are accessible and beneficial to all. Meeting these technological challenges head-on will define our ability to navigate the complexities of this new industrial era and harness its potential for the greater good of society.

7. INCORPORATING SOFT SKILLS

Incorporating soft skills in education is a crucial challenge in the context of Industrial Revolution 5.0 (IR 5.0) due to the transformation of the job market and the evolving needs of the modern workforce. IR 5.0 places a significant emphasis on holistic development, recognizing that success in the modern world goes beyond technical skills. Soft skills like communication, collaboration, adaptability, and emotional intelligence are considered essential for personal and professional success. The challenges of IR 5.0 often require cross-disciplinary solutions. Incorporating soft skills into the curriculum prepares students to work effectively in multidisciplinary teams, fostering creativity and innovative problem-solving. IR 5.0 introduces adaptive and personalized learning environments, which allow students to progress at their own pace. This personalized learning approach provides opportunities to assess and develop individual soft skills. In IR 5.0, collaboration is key, not only among students but also between educators. The educational approach is more collaborative, mirroring the soft skills being taught. Educators and students work together to create a learning ecosystem that nurtures these skills.

Soft skills encompass digital citizenship, which includes digital etiquette, online collaboration, and responsible use of technology. Students need to develop these skills to navigate the digital landscape of IR 5.0 effectively. IR 5.0 raises ethical issues related to technology and data use. Soft skills like ethical reasoning and decision-making become crucial in navigating these complex ethical considerations in education and beyond. Educators must be competent in teaching soft skills. This requires their own professional development to effectively foster these skills in students. Strategies for experiential learning, feedback, and reflection are essential components of this development. Assessing soft skills can be challenging. Educators must develop valid and reliable methods to assess communication, collaboration, adaptability, and other soft skills. Traditional assessment methods may need to evolve to capture these skills effectively. Soft skills like cross-cultural understanding, empathy, and effective communication across diverse backgrounds are increasingly important in a globalized world. Preparing students for global competence is a challenge that requires an international perspective in education.

7.1 Lifelong Learning

The challenge of lifelong learning in education is significantly impacted by Industrial Revolution 5.0 (IR 5.0) due to the changing nature of work, the rapid evolution of technology, and the need for individuals to continuously adapt and acquire new skills throughout their lives. In IR 5.0, technological advancements are occurring at an unprecedented rate. This requires individuals to continuously update their skills and knowledge to remain relevant in the job market. Lifelong learning becomes imperative for staying employable. IR 5.0 emphasizes skill-based education over traditional degree-based education. Lifelong learners need access to target. The use of technology in education facilitates personalized learning paths, enabling individuals to learn at their own pace and tailor their educational journeys to their specific needs and career goals. ed, just-in-time learning opportunities to acquire specific skills required for their chosen careers.

Lifelong learning often involves online education platforms. Individuals must be digitally literate to navigate these platforms effectively. This presents challenges for those who are less familiar with technology. Lifelong learning resources, including online courses and educational materials, need to be accessible to a diverse population, regardless of socio-economic background. Overcoming barriers to access and affordability is a challenge in promoting lifelong learning. As the nature of work evolves, traditional degrees may become less important. Individuals need a system of flexible credentials and certifications that reflect their ongoing skill development. Education institutions must adapt to provide these. Lifelong learning often involves the integration of knowledge and skills from multiple disciplines. Education systems need to promote interdisciplinary learning to enable individuals to solve complex, multifaceted problems. Assessing the effectiveness of lifelong learning is challenging. Traditional metrics like degrees may not reflect the breadth and depth of skills and knowledge acquired through lifelong learning. Developing new assessment methods is essential.

In conclusion, Industrial Revolution 5.0 (IR 5.0) has ushered in a transformative era for education, replete with intricate challenges. The rapid evolution of technology requires constant adaptation of curricula and teaching methods, underscoring the importance of lifelong learning for educators and students alike. Bridging the digital divide and ensuring equitable access to advanced technologies remains a pressing concern. Moreover, the paradigm shifts toward soft skills, ethical technology use, and interdisciplinary learning necessitates a profound overhaul of educational models. Assessment methods must evolve to accurately measure the dynamic skills demanded in this new era. The development of global perspectives and international collaboration is pivotal in an interconnected world. As we navigate these challenges, we must invest in resources, professional development, and educational policies that enable a seamless transition into IR 5.0. Educators play a central role in cultivating adaptive, ethically aware, and digitally proficient learners who possess not only technical skills but also the soft skills and ethical grounding to thrive in this rapidly changing landscape. By addressing these challenges, education can remain a vital force in individual empowerment and societal progress amidst the dawn of IR 5.0.

8. CONCLUSION

A new cloud computing paradigm called serverless computing is being used to create a variety of software applications. It releases developers from laborious and prone to error infrastructure administration, allowing them to concentrate on the application logic at the granularity of function. Its distinct feature, however, presents fresh difficulties for the creation and implementation of serverless-based systems. There have been significant scientific efforts made to address these issues. An extensive survey of the literature is presented in this article to describe the current state of serverless computing research. Additionally, it determines research priorities, trends, and widely-used serverless computing platforms.

REFERENCES

Aske, A., & Zhao, X. (2018). Supporting Multi-Provider Serverless Computing on the Edge. In *Proceedings of the 47th International Conference on Parallel Processing Companion*. Association for Computing Machinery. 10.1145/3229710.3229742

Bhupathi, J. & Kathirvel, A. (2022). MMF Clustering: A On-demand One-hop Cluster Management in MANET Services Executing Perspective. *International Journal of Novel Research and Development, 8*(4), 127-132.

Gobinath, V., Ayyaswamy, K., & Kathirvel, N. (2024). Information Communication Technology and Intelligent Manufacturing Industries Perspective: An Insight. *Asian Science Bulletin*, *2*(1), 36–45. doi:10.3923/asb.2024.36.45

Kathirvel, A, Blesso, D., Preetham, S., Hinn, J. T O, Kennedy, R. C, & Immanuel, A. (2023). *Systematic Number Plate detection using improved YOLOv5 detector*. Institute of Electrical and Electronics Engineers Inc. . doi:10.1109/ViTECoN58111.2023.10157727

Kathirvel, A. & Pavani, A. (2023). *Machine Learning and Deep Learning Algorithms for Network Data Analytics Function in 5G Cellular Networks*. Institute of Electrical and Electronics Engineers Inc. . doi:10.1109/ICICT57646.2023.10134247

Kathirvel, A. & Shobitha, M. (2023). *Digital Assets Fair Estimation Using Artificial Intelligence*. Institute of Electrical and Electronics Engineers Inc. . doi:10.1109/ViTECoN58111.2023.10157310

Kounev, S., Herbst, N., Abad, C., Iosup, A., Foster, I., Shenoy, P., Rana, O., & Chien, A. (2023). Serverless Computing: What It Is, and What It Is Not? *Communications of the ACM*.

Leitner, P., Wittern, E., Spillner, J., & Hummer, W. (2019). A mixed-method empirical study of Function-as-a-Service software development in industrial practice. *Journal of Systems and Software*, *149*, 340–359. doi:10.1016/j.jss.2018.12.013

Sudha, D., & Kathirvel, A. (2022a). The effect of ETUS in various generic attacks in mobile ad hoc networks to improve the performance of Aodv protocol. *International Journal of Humanities, Law, and Social Sciences, 9*(1), 467-476.

Sudha, D., & Kathirvel, A. (2022b). An Intrusion Detection System to Detect and Mitigating Attacks Using Hidden Markov Model (HMM) Energy Monitoring Technique. *Stochastic Modeling an Applications, 26*(3), 467-476.

Sudha, D., & Kathirvel, A. (2023). The performance enhancement of Aodv protocol using GETUS. *International Journal of Early Childhood Special Education, 15*(2), 115-125. DOI: doi:10.48047/INTJECSE/V15I2.11

Chapter 15
Development Environment, Tools, and SDKs for Serverless Computing

Ashwin Raiyani

https://orcid.org/0000-0001-5085-5822

Nirma University, India

Sheetal Pandya

Indus University, India

ABSTRACT

Serverless applications require a good development environment and the right tools. This chapter guides serverless computing application developers through installing and utilising essential components and technologies. VSCode is a robust code editor and debugger. Easy installation provides developers with a diverse code editing and debugging platform. AWSToolkit for VS Code simplifies serverless application development, testing, and release on Amazon web services (AWS). Fast setup with step-by-step instruction makes AWS serverless development easy for developers. Node.js is needed for serverless apps. Developers require Node.js for local and cloud serverless operations. This chapter briefly describes installation. Postman is essential for serverless API testing. Postman installation and use for serverless API testing and troubleshooting are covered in this chapter. Developers seeking efficiency will benefit. These concepts let developers build a strong development environment, integrate AWS resources, and leverage SDKs to build serverless apps.

1. OVERVIEW ON SERVERLESS COMPUTING

Serverless computing has evolved as a new solution within the field of cloud computing, drastically altering how applications are hosted, created, and managed. At its very foundation, serverless computing enables developers to launch apps without the need to setup or manage server infrastructure manually. Instead of dealing with server deployment, setup, and maintenance, developers focus only on develop-

DOI: 10.4018/979-8-3693-1682-5.ch015

ing code in the form of functions, which are performed in response to various events or triggers. These events might vary from HTTP requests to changes in data within a database or messages coming in a queue. This event-driven architecture separates serverless computing from traditional hosting techniques, where developers often engage directly with servers or virtual machines, managing their configurations and scalability.

The transition to serverless computing signals a change from the old server-centric architecture, where developers are saddled with the intricacies of infrastructure administration. In conventional hosting set-ups, developers must provision servers or virtual machines, install and configure software dependencies, and manage scale and availability. This technique frequently involves considerable upfront investment in infrastructure and continuing maintenance efforts to maintain optimal performance and availability. In contrast, serverless computing abstracts(Vashishth et al., 2024) away these infrastructure issues, allowing developers to focus completely on building application logic. By removing the requirement for server supply and administration, serverless computing offers considerable advantages in terms of agility, scalability, and cost-effectiveness.

The historical growth of serverless computing dates back to the early days of cloud computing, with Amazon Web Services (AWS) launching AWS Lambda in 2014 as one of the pioneering serverless platforms. AWS Lambda allows developers to upload functions and describe the events that trigger their execution, ushering in a new age of event-driven computing. This constituted a substantial divergence from typical cloud computing methods and established the framework for the mainstream acceptance of serverless computing. Since then, additional cloud providers such as Microsoft Azure with Azure Functions and Google Cloud Platform (GCP) with Google Cloud Functions have entered the serverless market, offering their own platforms and services targeted to serverless application development.

The popularity of serverless computing may be linked to various causes, including its capacity to promote developer productivity, minimize operational overhead, and improve cost efficiency. By abstracting away infrastructure administration responsibilities, serverless computing allows developers to focus more on creating code and less on maintaining servers, leading to higher productivity and a faster time-to-market for apps. Additionally, the pay-per-use payment approach of serverless computing assures that customers only pay for the resources utilized by their functions, delivering cost savings compared to traditional hosting models where resources must be supplied ahead. Furthermore, the automated scaling features inherent in serverless systems enable applications to handle variable workloads easily, ensuring maximum performance and scalability without any intervention.

In essence, serverless computing represents a paradigm shift in cloud computing, providing a more efficient, flexible, and cost-effective alternative to hosting and delivering applications. Its history, from the early days of cloud computing to its broad acceptance, now illustrates the rising desire for simpler, scalable, and developer-friendly cloud solutions. As serverless computing continues to advance, it is positioned to play an increasingly critical role in influencing the future of application development and cloud computing architecture.

Importantly, this chapter effectively outlines crucial facets of serverless application development, encompassing development tools, runtime environments, and essential considerations. These tools serve as the cornerstone of serverless development. It is important to note that this chapter does not delve into other aspects of serverless computing such as security, deployment, monitoring, and collaboration, except to a certain extent necessary for understanding serverless application development.

1.1. Development Environments for Serverless Computing

In this literature review, we delve into the vast array of research and scholarly works surrounding the development environment, tools, and software development kits (SDKs) essential for serverless application development. Through an in-depth analysis of existing literature, we aim to provide insights into the current state-of-the-art practices and emerging trends in the field of serverless computing.

The choice of a development environment plays a pivotal role in the success of serverless application development. Visual Studio Code (VSCode), a lightweight and extensible IDE developed by Microsoft, has gained widespread popularity among developers due to its robust features and seamless integration with cloud platforms. Real-time case studies have demonstrated how integrating VSCode with cloud-specific toolkits, such as the AWS Toolkit, enhances the development workflow by providing developers with a unified environment for writing, testing, and deploying serverless functions. Additionally, research has explored the use of alternative development environments, such as JetBrains' IntelliJ IDEA and Eclipse IDE, in the context of serverless application development, highlighting the importance of flexibility and interoperability in modern development workflows.

1.2. Software Development Kits (SDKs) for Serverless Computing

SDKs serve as the bridge between developers and cloud services, providing the necessary abstractions and APIs to interact with cloud resources programmatically. In the realm of serverless computing, SDKs play a crucial role in enabling developers to leverage the full potential of cloud platforms such as Amazon Web Services (AWS), Microsoft Azure, and Google Cloud Platform (GCP). The AWS SDK for JavaScript, commonly known as the AWS SDK for Node.js, is a prominent example of an SDK tailored for serverless application development on AWS Lambda. Real-world case studies have highlighted how the AWS SDK simplifies tasks such as authentication, data storage, and messaging, enabling developers to focus on implementing business logic rather than dealing with low-level infrastructure concerns. Similarly, research has explored the use of SDKs for other cloud providers, such as the Azure Functions Core Tools for Microsoft Azure and the Google Cloud Functions Framework for Google Cloud Platform, emphasizing the importance of platform-specific SDKs in enabling seamless integration with cloud services.

1.3. Programming Languages and Runtimes for Serverless Computing

The choice of programming language and runtime environment significantly influences the performance, scalability, and maintainability of serverless applications. Languages like JavaScript, Python, and Go have gained traction in the serverless community due to their lightweight runtime environments and support for asynchronous, event-driven programming models. Node.js, in particular, has emerged as a popular choice for serverless application development, thanks to its non-blocking I/O model and extensive ecosystem of libraries and frameworks. Real-time case studies have demonstrated how leveraging Node.js enables developers to build responsive and scalable serverless applications capable of handling unpredictable workloads. Moreover, research has explored the performance implications of different programming languages and runtimes in the context of serverless computing, highlighting the trade-offs between developer productivity, execution speed, and resource utilization.

2. CONFIGURING DEVELOPMENT ENVIRONMENT AND ESSENTIAL TOOLS

To develop serverless applications efficiently, it is required to have a properly configured application development environment and the right set of tools. This chapter provides detailed instructions and guidelines for developers, walking them through important steps such as installing key components and using essential tools for serverless computing application development.

VSCode is a versatile integrated development environment (IDE) that provides an optimal code editing and debugging platform. The installation process is simple, providing developers with a flexible code editing and debugging platform.

The AWSToolkit for VS Code provides developers a convenient solution for constructing, evaluating, and releasing serverless applications on Amazon Web Services (AWS) with minimal hassle and maximum efficiency. You'll get a step-by-step guide that's easy to follow and will have you up and running in no time, making it easier for developers to utilize its features in AWS serverless development.

Node.js is an essential runtime for developing serverless applications. This chapter offers a concise guide on installing Node.js, ensuring that developers have the required runtime to run serverless functions locally and in cloud environments.

Postman is an incredibly useful tool for testing APIs, making it an essential part of serverless development. This chapter provides a step-by-step guide for installing Postman and utilizing its features to test and debug serverless APIs effectively. It offers valuable insights for developers looking to enhance their efficiency.

By adhering to these guidelines, developers can create a strong development environment, seamlessly integrate AWS tools, and make the most of essential SDKs, setting the stage for successful serverless application development.

2.1. VSCode: Integrated Development Environment (IDE) Tool

VSCode (Chowhan, 2018) is a powerful code editor that has been developed by Microsoft. It is an open-source and cost-free platform that can be used on all major platforms such as Windows, macOS, and Linux. This tool provides a wide range of development processes which includes debugging, task execution, and version control. VSCode is an ideal choice for daily utilization as it exhibits exceptional speed and efficiency. It supports a variety of programming languages and offers features such as automatic indentation, syntax highlighting, code snippets, and matching of brackets.

In addition, it features a user-friendly keyboard shortcut interface that can be easily personalized with user-defined configurations. The community also contributes to the keyboard shortcut mappings, which greatly facilitates the navigation of source code. VSCode also possesses inherent functionality for code completion, IntelliSense, and user interface navigation, offering comprehensive semantic code comprehension and code refactoring capabilities.

Debugging (Chowhan, 2018) is one of the most important features of a code editor, and VSCode provides not just debugging capabilities but also simplifies the process of debugging your programs. The software features an interactive debugger that enables the examination of variables, navigating through source code, examining call stacks, and issuing console commands. VSCode seamlessly incorporates scripting and build tools, streamlining routine processes and enhancing efficiency in daily workflows.

Figure 1. VSCode IDE and download VS code

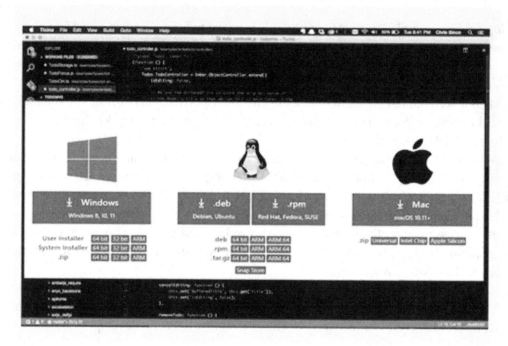

2.1.1. Why VSCode?

VS Code is a Microsoft-developed integrated programming environment with advanced features that cater to various developers' needs, enhancing the development process.

1. **Versatile Language Support:** VS Code offers exceptional adaptability for multiple programming languages, allowing developers to seamlessly transition between different codebases without compromising functionality.
2. **Intelligent Code Editing:** VS Code utilizes IntelliSense features to enhance developers' code completion, providing real-time suggestions for functions and variables, thereby reducing errors and expediting the development process.
3. **Integrated Version Control:** VS Code's integrated feature with Git allows developers to manage version history within the editor, simplifying collaborative workflows and enhancing code review efficiency.
4. **Robust Debugging Capabilities:** VS Code offers a robust debugging interface compatible with multiple programming languages, allowing developers to easily establish breakpoints, examine variables, and navigate their code.
5. **Enhanced flexibility via extensions:** The VSCode Marketplace provides a variety of extensions to meet specific development needs, allowing users to customize and enhance their coding environment.
6. **Integrated Terminal:** The integrated terminal feature is a powerful tool that enables developers to use the command line within the editor itself. This feature simplifies the development process by eliminating the need to switch back and forth between the terminal and the editor. Moreover, it

enhances frequent command-line interactions by providing a more intuitive and efficient way to execute commands, making it easier to manage and navigate your project.

7. **Powerful Theming and Customization:** VS Code offers a customizable interface, allowing developers to personalize their coding environment with themes and customization options, enhancing the user experience and convenience.

8. **Live Share Collaboration:** VS Code's Live Share feature enables real-time developer communication, streamlining collaborative development sessions on a shared codebase without complicated setup processes.

VSCode is a top-tier integrated development environment in the software development industry, known for its adaptability, intelligence, and collaborative functionalities.

2.1.2. VSCode: Hardware Requirement

VS code doesn't have stringent hardware requirements. However, the performance of the editor can vary based on your project size and complexity. As a general guideline:

Processor. A multi-core processor is recommended for improved performance.
RAM. A minimum of 4 GB RAM is recommended, but for larger projects, 8 GB or more is preferable.
Storage. At least 200 MB of available hard disk space.

2.1.3. Platform Compatibility

VSCode is a cross-platform code editor, and it can be set up on the following platforms:

*   **Windows**: Windows 7 (64-bit) and newer versions are supported. Ensure .NET Framework 4.5.2 is installed if using Windows 7.
*   **Linux**: Compatible with various distributions, including Ubuntu, Debian, Fedora, and more.
*   **macOS**: Compatible with macOS 10.9 (Mavericks) and later.

2.2. Configuration of Visual Studio Code in Various OS Platform

2.2.1. Installing VSCode on Windows

VSCode is a widely used (Microsoft, 2021), open-source code editor developed by Microsoft. It provides a lightweight and extensible platform for various programming languages. To set it up:

*   Go (Del Sole, 2021)to the official VSCode website: https://code.visualstudio.com/.
*   Download the latest version of VSCode that is compatible with your operating system (Windows, Linux, or macOS).
*   Run the downloaded installer and carefully follow the on-screen instructions to complete the installation process.
*   By default, VSCode is installed to the C:\Program Files\MicrosoftVS Code directory on a 64-bit machine.

Figure 2. Download installer for Windows

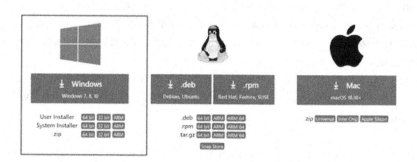

If you are using Windows 7 and want to use VSCode without any issues, you need to have .NET Framework 4.5.2 or a newer version installed on your computer. .NET Framework is a software framework developed by Microsoft that supports building and running applications on Windows. VSCode is built on top of .NET Framework, which is why it is essential to have it installed.

You can download .NET Framework 4.5.2 and it needs to be install it properly to ensure that VSCode runs smoothly. You can follow the instructions provided during the installation process to complete the installation successfully.

By installing .NET Framework 4.5.2 or a newer version, you can enjoy all the features of VSCode without any issues on your Windows 7 computer.

2.2.2. Installing VSCode on Ubuntu

Installation of VSCode on your Ubuntu machine (Microsoft, 2021), follow these detailed steps:

Step 1: Open the terminal on your Ubuntu machine

Step 2: To get started with VSCode, head over to their official website and download the package you need. Once you've found the package you're after, just copy its URL and use the wget command in your terminal to download it. You can use the following command:

```
wget https://code.visualstudio.com/sha/download?build=stable&os=linux-deb-x64
-O vscode.deb
```

This will download the package and save it in the current directory with the name "vscode.deb".

Step 3: Once you have downloaded the package, you can use the dpkg package manager to install it. Use the following command to install the downloaded package:

```
sudo dpkg -i vscode.deb
```

This will start the installation process. Follow the on-screen instructions to complete the installation.

Step 4: If there are any unmet dependencies, the installation process might be interrupted. In such cases, use the following command to fix and install the dependencies:

```
sudo apt-get install -f
```

This command will download and install any missing dependencies.

Step 5: After the installation process is finished, you can easily launch VSCode by searching for it in the applications menu or simply by entering "code" in the terminal. This will launch VSCode on your Ubuntu machine.

Step 6: In order to execute VSCode from the terminal without explicitly giving the complete file path, you may include it in the PATH environment variable of your operating system. Open your shell configuration file (e.g., ~/.bashrc or ~/.zshrc) and add the following line:

```
export PATH=$PATH:/usr/share/code/bin
```

Save the file, and then run:

```
source ~/.bashrc # or source ~/.zshrc
```

Step 7: VSCode receives regular updates. You can update it manually by repeating the download and installation process with the latest package. To do this, use the following commands:

```
wget https://code.visualstudio.com/sha/download?build=stable&os=linux-deb-x64
-O vscode.deb
sudo dpkg -i vscode.deb
sudo apt-get install -f
```

These commands will download the latest package, install it and fix any dependencies. You can now use it as your integrated development environment for various programming languages and frameworks.

2.2.3. Installing VSCode on MacOS

1. Visit the official VSCode (VScode Mac, 2022) website: https://code.visualstudio.com/
2. Then, choose Apple Silicon from the options available beneath the Mac icon in order to obtain the package installer for VS Code for Mac. The installer will be provided in a ZIP file format (refer figure 3)
3. To confirm that the VS Code's package installer you downloaded is correct, you need to open your terminal and enter the 'ls' command. This command will display a list of all the files and directories in your current location. Look for the package installer file in this list and ensure that it matches the name and version you downloaded. If you do not see the installer file or if it has a different name or version number, it could be corrupted or not the correct version. In that case, you should re-download the correct package installer file from a trusted source and try again.

```
ls -la ~/Downloads/VSCode-darwin-arm64.zip
```

4. To unzip the downloaded VS Code zip file, follow these steps:
   ○ Locate the VS Code zip file you downloaded and open it.
   ○ To proceed, please select the ellipsis icon in the window's upper-right quadrant.
   ○ From the drop-down menu, select "Open".

○   This will unzip the ZIP file and extract its contents to a new folder.

Once the extraction is complete, you can open the newly created folder to access the extracted files. You can then proceed to install VS Code on your system using the extracted files.

To verify that the Visual Studio Code application file has been properly downloaded, you can run the "ls" command. This command will display a list of all the contents within the VSCode application file.

To execute this command, open the terminal and type "ls -la ~/Downloads/Visual\ Studio\ Code.app". This will display all the files within the Visual Studio Code application.

To launch the installer, you'll need to run the "open" command. This command will open a new instance and initiate the installation process. To do this, type "open -n ~/Downloads/Visual\ Studio\ Code.app" into the terminal.

After the installation process is complete, you will have a new VSCode application in your Downloads folder. You can find it by navigating to the Downloads folder and looking for the newly installed Visual Studio Code application.

Figure 3. Click on Apple silicon

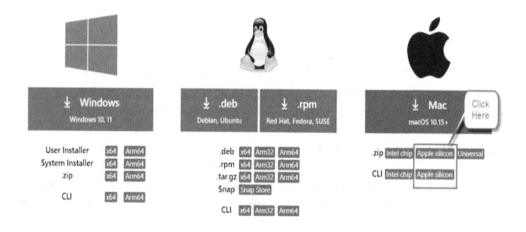

Figure 4. VS code unzip file

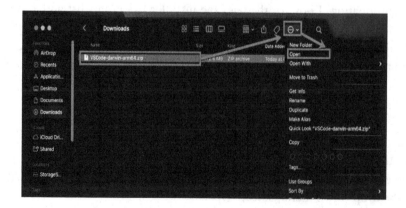

Click Open to continue installation, ignore internet warnings (refer figure 5 (a)), and open VS Code application. Get Started page appears (refer figure 5(b)) after installation.

Figure 5. (a) Warning message; (b) Viewing VS code's main window

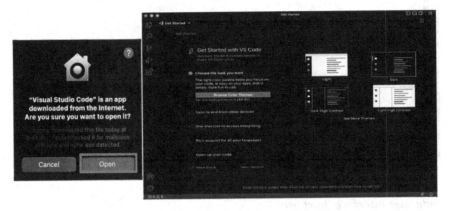

2.3. VSCode: Basic User Interface Overview

VS Code's user-friendly design optimizes editor area, enabling easy navigation and access to full folder or project content. The user interface is partitioned into seven primary sections:

1. **Activity Bar:** On the side of the window, the Activity Bar contains icons for different views such as Explorer, Source Control, Run and Debug, and Extensions. Users can quickly switch between these views to access various features. *(refer image 6)*
2. **Side Bar:** The Side Bar, located within the Activity Bar, provides quick access to key functionalities like file Explorer, Search, Git integration, and Extensions. *(refer image 6)*
3. **Editor Area:** The Editor Area is where users write and edit their code. It supports syntax highlighting, IntelliSense (code completion), and various productivity features. Users can split the editor into multiple panes for simultaneous editing. *(refer image 6)*
4. **Status Bar**: It is situated at the bottom of the window, provides you with pertinent details regarding the ongoing project, including information about the current Git branch, and other relevant contextual information. It also includes shortcuts for selecting coding languages and changing the file encoding. *(refer image 6)*
5. **Extensions**: The Extensions view (accessed through the Activity Bar) (Del Sole, 2021)allows users to manage and install extensions to customize and extend the functionality of VS Code.
6. **Command Palette**: The Command Palette (accessed with Command + Shift + P) allows users to access and execute commands quickly. It's a powerful tool for navigating VS Code's features without relying on the mouse.
7. **Integrated Terminal**: VS Code includes an integrated terminal at the bottom of the window, enabling users to run command-line tasks directly within the editor.

Figure 6. VS code user interface, part one

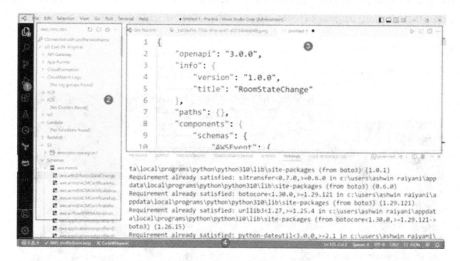

Figure 7. VS code user interface, part two

Hint: An additional sidebar, known as the Secondary Side Bar, can be used to show views that are different from those displayed in the Primary Side Bar. To display it, use the keyboard shortcut Ctrl+Alt+B.

VS Code resumes in its previous state, maintaining folder, layout, and opened files. Tabbed headers display open files at the top of the editor zone.

In the realm of serverless development, various cloud providers (like AWS, Azure, Google etc) and open-source solutions offer unique platforms and services. However, this chapter, AWS serverless development configuration is a strategic choice aimed at providing learners with a comprehensive and in-depth understanding of a leading cloud provider's offerings. AWS's dominance, extensive service ecosystem, mature tooling, security measures, industry standardization, diverse use cases, and community support collectively make it a compelling focus for developers seeking to excel in the serverless computing landscape.

Before commencing with the **AWS Toolkit for VSCode**, it is imperative to have the subsequent components installed on our local workstation.

- **AWS Account** - A valid AWS account is required to begin using it. Access the website https://console.aws.amazon.com/ in order to begin using Amazon Web Services.
- **Install VSCode** on your computer. VS Code is compatible with Windows, Linux, and Mac operating systems.
- **Install the appropriate Software Development Kit (SDK)** for coding your application. The available options are the .NET SDK, Node. JS SDK, or the Python SDK.
- The **AWS SAM CLI** is a command line tool provided by Amazon that allows for the local development and testing of serverless applications. While the installation of the toolkit on the local system is not obligatory, it is advisable to do so.

Now delves into the intricate role of VSCode in the serverless development workflow, elucidating its integration with pivotal tools and technologies such as the AWS Toolkit, Node.js, and Postman, thereby elucidating its multifaceted contributions to the realm of serverless computing.

3. AWS TOOLKIT INSTALLATION IN VSCODE

Open VSCode and click on the Extensions icon available in the left pane of the editor:

Figure 8. Extensions in VS code

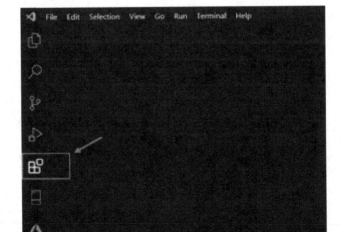

Enter "AWS Toolkit" in the search box and press Enter.

After successfully installing the toolkit on your device, a new icon will be shown on the left sidebar. It enables you to utilize all the resources accessible within your AWS subscription. Our immediate priority is to establish a connection to our AWS account using designated credentials, which will be elaborated upon in a subsequent portion of this article.

Figure 9. Install AWS toolkit in VS code

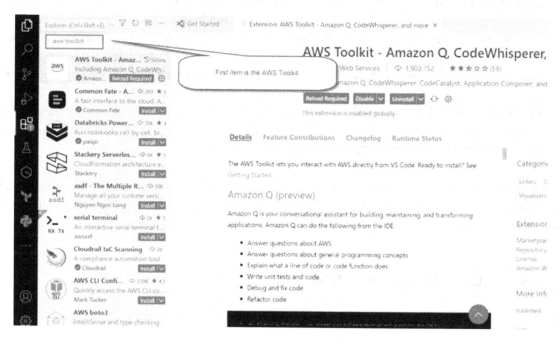

Figure 10. Connecting AWS account

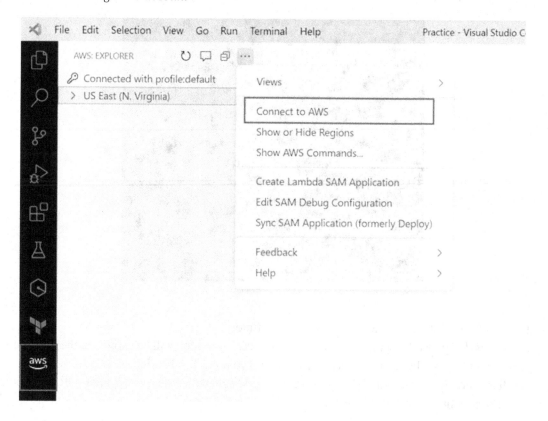

Before proceeding further, Please configure the authentication details in order to establish a connection with AWS. There are two methods:

1. **AWS supported credentials**- directly from Amazon using a shared AWS credential file or a shared AWS config file.
2. An *external authentication procedure* (which is not endorsed by Amazon) - This procedure may be employed when you possess a mechanism that produces or retrieves the authentication details that Amazon does not immediately endorse.

Figure 11. IAM: Users section

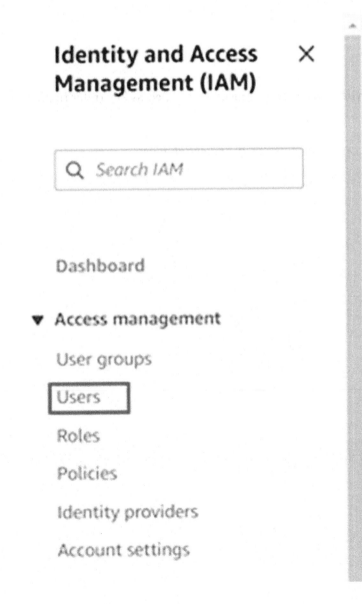

In this chapter, we shall proceed with the **AWS Supported Credentials**. Let's create the credentials for AWS Console which consists of two parts - the Access Key ID and the Access Key Secret.

Access https://console.aws.amazon.com/iam/ using admin account(if wish to create new user) or normal user. Goto IAM → Users section of console management (refer figure 11)

On the Users page, click on the username to see the details (refer figure 12)

Figure 12. Select user

Goto **Security Credentials** page and select **Create access key** (refer figure 13)

Figure 13. Create access key using security credential page

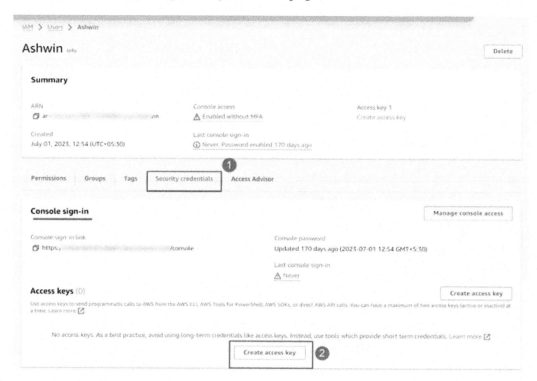

Once you click Create Access Key, new windows will be open to ask use case of creating access key. As per your application select any one option (refer figure 14) (in this case, select CLI) and click next.

Figure 14. Access key: Use case

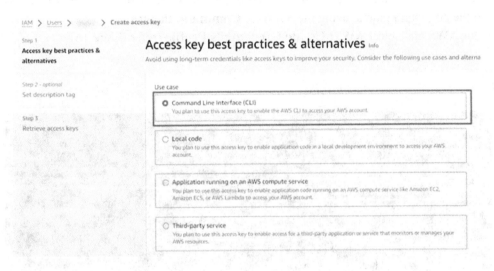

You will be able to download the CSV file that contains the credentials. Retrieve the (Del Sole, 2021) Access Key ID and the Secret Access Key and save them in a secure location. Then, proceed to click on the Close button.

Figure 15. Generate access key

3.1. Setting up the AWS Credentials in VSCode

We would now need to setup the credentials that we obtained from AWS in the toolkit in VS Code. This can be done by using the shared AWS files that is provided by AWS. When using Amazon Web Services (AWS), we often need to store the credential information that we receive. AWS provides two files, AWS config file and AWS credentials file, for this purpose. Having the config and credentials files in your ".aws" directory is essential for seamless access to your Amazon Web Services account. It's always a good idea to keep them in a safe place and ensure they are up-to-date to avoid any inconvenience. By storing the credentials in these files, we can easily access them whenever we need them.

Let us now go ahead and create the shared credential and config files in the VS Code. Inside VS Code, open the command palette using the **View -> Command Palette**.

Search for **AWS** and select **AWS: Create Credentials Profile** (refer figure 16)

Figure 16. Select AWS credentials profile

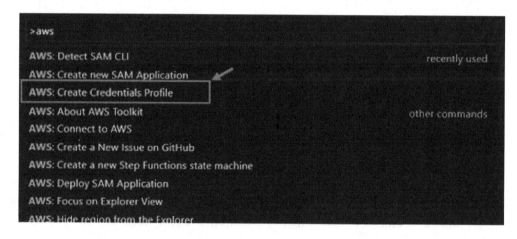

Provide a suitable profile name. Let me say it as "*default*" (refer figure 17):

Figure 17. Profile name selection

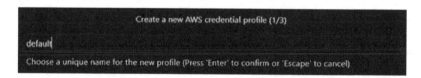

In the next step, we need to provide the **AWS Access Key** that we have created in the previous step. Paste the access key (refer figure 18) here and hit **Enter**:

Figure 18. AWS access key

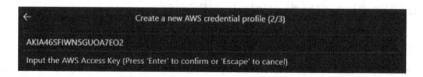

Finally, enter the **AWS Secret Key** and press **Enter** to create the **Credential profile**:

Figure 19. AWS secret key

3.2. Connect to AWS From VSCode

Now that we successfully have setup our credentials profile, we can go ahead and connect to our AWS environment. Open the command palette in VS Code as previously done. Search for **AWS** and select **AWS: Connect to AWS** (refer figure 20) from the menu:

Figure 20. Connecting to AWS through VS code

In the next step, select the profile that you have created in the previous step. Let us select the **default** (refer figure 21)profile:

Figure 21. Select the default profile

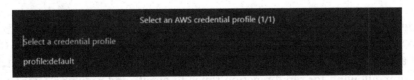

Once you select the profile, the AWS Toolkit for VSCode will connect to the AWS resources using the credentials and fetch the information within the VS Code environment as follows:

Figure 22. AWS toolkit for VSCode

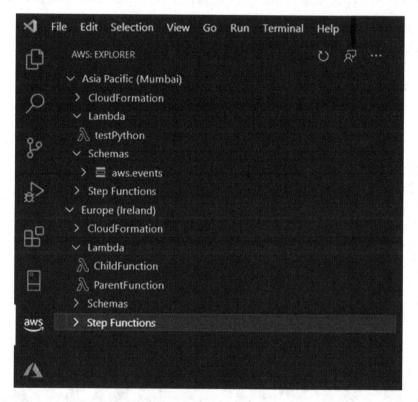

As you can see in the above figure, that we have two regions defined in our AWS account and both of them are shown in the list. Also, all the lambda functions, schemas and step functions also appear under each region separately so that we can easily organize them and code efficiently.

4. NODE.JS

Node.js is a freely available runtime environment for the JavaScript programming language that modifies JavaScript's attributes and enhances its capabilities. Consequently, JavaScript may be utilized for both frontend and backend development, allowing for the exclusive usage of JavaScript in full-stack development.

Lets understand how Node.js enhances serverless application development

Node.js offers substantial advantages to serverless architecture, increasing the efficiency and responsiveness of apps. This system's asynchronous, event-driven approach perfectly integrates with the serverless paradigm, allowing for rapid reaction times to events and reducing latency to a minimum. Node.js's lightweight design enables fast invocation and optimal resource use, essential in the serverless environment where functions dynamically scale.

Furthermore, Node.js possesses an extensive ecosystem of npm packages, enabling developers to utilize pre-built modules and expedite development cycles. The support for microservices architecture in serverless applications aligns with the modular design principles, which enhances scalability and maintainability. Node.js is a supported runtime in popular (Leipzig, 2019) serverless platforms such as AWS Lambda, Azure Functions, and Google Cloud Functions. This allows developers to enjoy cross-platform compatibility and the freedom to choose their cloud provider.

The event-driven architecture of Node.js promotes extensive information exchange and assistance, boosting the serverless programming experience. Node.js is an excellent option for serverless architecture, offering a flexible, effective, and community-backed platform for developing scalable and responsive serverless apps.

Figure 23. Node.js logo
(Image source: https://nodejs.org/en/about)

4.1. Node.js Pre-Requisite

Prior to installing Node.js, it is imperative to verify that you have acquired all the essential information and downloaded all the necessary installation files and components. Prior knowledge of JavaScript and its syntax is beneficial when learning Node.js. Furthermore, possessing a fundamental comprehension of an object-oriented programming (OOP) language will facilitate your ability to engage in server-side development.

To ensure optimal performance, it is necessary to meet the following hardware requirements:

- at least 4GB of RAM,
- an Intel Core i3TM i3 HQ processor running at CPU @2.50 GHz, and
- ROM 256 GB of storage capacity.

These specifications are critical for running demanding applications and handling complex tasks with ease. Please check your system specifications before attempting to install the software to ensure that your system meets these requirements.

In order to utilize the JavaScript-based NodeJS effectively for product development including real-time features and resource-intensive I/O activities, it is crucial to understand the process of utilizing NPM packages. This chapter provides comprehensive instructions on the optimal procedures for installing NodeJS and NPM on your machine, including thorough step-by-step guidelines.

4.2. What is NPM?

The NPM, or Node Package Manager, serves as the primary package manager for NodeJs. NPM facilitates the sharing and borrowing of packages among open-source web developers for the purpose of app development. Additionally, it functions as a command-line utility for the program, facilitating the installation of packages in the project, managing dependencies, and even overseeing version control.

4.3. Step by Step Procedure to Install Node.js and NPM on Windows

Step 1: To start with the installation process for Node.js on your Windows machine, you need to download the Windows Installer that includes the NPM package manager (Calles, 2020). You can get this installer by visiting the official website of Node.js (https://nodejs.org/en/download/). Find the download link for the Windows Installer and click on it. The download will begin automatically, and you'll be able to access the installer once the download is complete.

Figure 24. Select the version

Here selected the Node.js installer that is specifically designed to work with 64-bit operating systems
Step 2: Install Node.js and NPM
Run the downloaded installer and Follow the installation wizard (refer figure 25), accepting the default settings. Please refer the images in sequential order.
Step 3: Check Node.js and NPM Version
The installation procedure has been completed. Now, you must verify if Node.js has been successfully installed or not. To validate the installation and ascertain the proper version, use the command prompt on your personal computer and input the specified command (refer figure 26):
Step 4: To update the npm to its latest version, you can run a simple command. Execute the below command for the quick update the npm:

```
npm install npm –global
```

This will update the 'CLI' client and ensure that you have the latest version of npm installed locally.

Figure 25 Node.js installation wizards

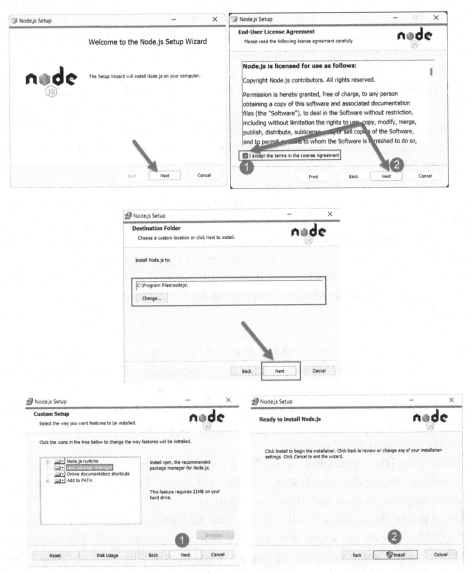

Figure 26. Verifying Node.js installation

5. POSTMAN

Role of Postman configuration in serverless application development is crucial in optimizing the development lifecycle within the domain of serverless application design. It operates as a reliable platform for testing serverless operations, enabling developers to build and run API calls, verify replies, and guarantee the smooth integration of serverless components. The automation features of Postman allow for the building of complex testing workflows, which are crucial for verifying the functioning and performance of serverless apps. An efficient way to develop, test, and document your APIs, Postman is the perfect tool for you. Its user-friendly interface makes the process easy and straightforward, allowing you to focus on building a robust API. Postman streamlines the intricate procedures of API creation by providing user-friendly capabilities, hence enabling developers a comprehensive platform to easily design and oversee APIs.

In addition, Postman enables cooperative development under the serverless paradigm. The inclusion of elements that facilitate the sharing and documentation of APIs promotes effective communication among team members, guaranteeing a unified approach to serverless architecture. Postman enhances the accuracy and dependability of serverless applications by providing features like as environment setting, continuous integration, and extensive monitoring tools. Postman is a crucial tool that helps developers in the ever-changing world of serverless architecture by enabling them to efficiently design, test, and collaborate.

To download and install Postman on your PC (Potti, 2022), First, navigate to the Postman Downloads page by clicking on this URL https://www.postman.com/downloads/ . This will take you to the official Postman website where you can find the necessary files to download.

Next, on the Postman Downloads page, look for the Windows 64-bit download button. It should be located in the bottom section of the page. Click on it to start the download process. A prompt will appear asking you to save the file to your computer.

Double-click on the file "Postman-win64-XXX-Setup.exe" to begin the setup process. Follow the installation wizard, accepting the default settings. This will install Postman on your computer. You can open the Postman application once installation is complete.

Step 4: After opening Postman, you will see a screen with three options: "Create a Free Account", "Sign In", and "Skip". If you are a new user, click "Create a Free Account". For existing users, click "Sign In". Finally, if you want to skip this step and go straight to the app, click on "Skip". Note that you can always create an account later if you choose to skip this step. (refer figure 28).

You are able to view the Scratch Pad screen on your Postman desktop application, which allows you to quickly jot down notes, API requests, or any other relevant information you may need for your project.

You have completed the successful download and installation of Postman on your PC. This is important step towards streamlining your workflow and improving productivity.

Figure 27. Select Windows 64 bit version

Figure 28. The executable for setting up Postman is currently being downloaded

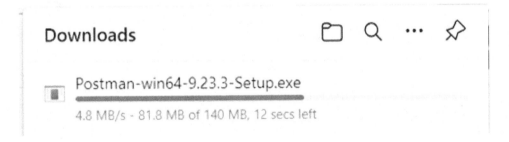

Figure 29. Postman setup executable downloaded successfully

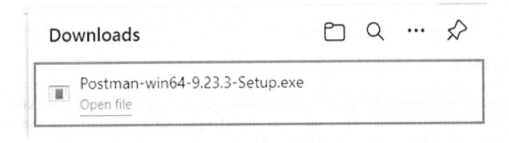

Figure 30. Create postman account

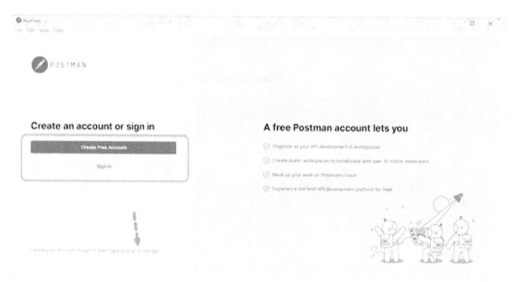

Figure 31. Postman scratch pad

6. SUMMARY

This chapter investigates the development environment, tools, and software development kits (SDKs) relevant to serverless computing. The chapter has covered popular tools, including Visual Studio Code (VSCode), the AWS Toolkit, Node.js, and Postman.

Visual Studio Code (VSCode) emerged as a popular integrated development environment (IDE) used by developers for serverless application development. Its versatility and powerful features allow for more efficient writing, debugging, and deployment. The AWS Toolkit is a significant resource for developers

•

working inside the Amazon Web Services (AWS) environment. It integrates seamlessly with VSCode, allowing for faster creation, testing, and deployment of serverless apps on AWS Lambda.

Node.js, a JavaScript runtime environment, is still a key technology in serverless computing. Its asynchronous and event-driven design suits the serverless paradigm, allowing developers to create scalable and responsive serverless applications easily. Postman has emerged as a key tool for testing and troubleshooting serverless APIs. Its simple interface and extensive features enable developers to automate API testing, monitor performance, and ensure the dependability of serverless applications.

Overall, the chapter emphasizes the importance of these development tools and SDKs in enabling effective and productive serverless application development. By efficiently exploiting these technologies, developers may reap the benefits of serverless computing, such as scalability, cost-efficiency, and faster development cycles.

REFERENCES

Calles, M. A. (2020). *Serverless Security: Understand, Assess, and Implement Secure and Reliable Applications in AWS, Microsoft Azure, and Google Cloud*. Springer International Publishing. doi:10.1007/978-1-4842-6100-2

Chowhan, K. (2018). *Hands-on Serverless Computing: Build, run, and orchestrate serverless applications using AWS Lambda, Microsoft Azure Functions, and Google Cloud functions*. Packt Publishing.

Del Sole, A. (2021). *Visual Studio Code Distilled*. Apress. doi:10.1007/978-1-4842-6901-5

Leipzig, J. (2019). Computational Pipelines and Workflows in Bioinformatics. In S. Ranganathan, M. Gribskov, K. Nakai, & C. Schönbach (Eds.), *Encyclopedia of Bioinformatics and Computational Biology* (pp. 1151–1162). Academic Press. doi:10.1016/B978-0-12-809633-8.20187-8

Potti, A. (2022, October 7). *Postman*. C# Corner: https://www.c-sharpcorner.com/article/how-to-download-and-install-postman-on-your-pc/

Vashishth, T. K., Sharma, V., Sharma, K. K., Kumar, B., Chaudhary, S., & Panwar, R. (2024). *Serverless Computing Real-World Applications and Benefits in Cloud Environments*., doi:10.4018/979-8-3693-0900-1.ch014

VScode Mac. (2022, October 25). *ATA Learning*. Adam the Automator. https://adamtheautomator.com/visual-studio-code-on-mac/

Chapter 16
A Study on the Landscape of Serverless Computing:
Technologies and Tools for Seamless Implementation

T. Kalaiselvi

Department of Computer Science and Engineering, Erode Sengunthar Engineering College, Erode, India

A. V. Santhosh Babu

Department of Information Technology, Vivekanandha College of Engineering for Women, Namakkal, India

G. Saravanan

Department of Artificial Intelligence and Data Science, Erode Sengunthar Engineering College, Erode, India

M. Sakthivel

Department of Computer Science and Engineering, Erode Sengunthar Engineering College, Erode, India

T. Haritha

Department of Information Technology, Vivekanandha College of Engineering for Women, Namakkal, India

Sampath Boopathi

 https://orcid.org/0000-0002-2065-6539

Department of Mechanical Engineering, Muthayammal Engineering College, India

ABSTRACT

This chapter explores serverless computing, a transformative paradigm that revolutionizes application development, deployment, and management. It provides an overview of the core principles and advantages driving its adoption in contemporary technological ecosystems, including function as a service (FaaS) offering, orchestration tools, and serverless frameworks. These technologies enable developers to focus on code execution, abstracting infrastructure management complexities, and serve as a guide for elucidating the efficacy and scalability of serverless architectures. This narrative delves into the evolution of serverless technologies, from early frameworks to sophisticated tools, emphasizing their significance in scalability, operational efficiency, and resource optimization, providing a guide for technologists, developers, and researchers.

DOI: 10.4018/979-8-3693-1682-5.ch016

1. INTRODUCTION

Serverless computing is a significant shift in modern technology, allowing developers to focus on writing code and executing functions without managing servers. This approach enhances agility, scalability, and cost-effectiveness in application development. The foundation of serverless computing is Function as a Service (FaaS), which enables developers to create discrete, independent functions triggered by specific events or requests. These functions execute in stateless, ephemeral containers, dynamically scaling based on demand without manual intervention. This allows developers to respond more rapidly to changes, only paying for the resources consumed during function execution, rather than maintaining continuously running servers (Cassel et al., 2022).

Serverless computing offers several advantages, including the abstraction of infrastructure complexities, which traditional architectures require. This allows developers to focus on application logic, improving productivity and allowing more time for innovative features. Serverless architectures also promote a pay-per-execution billing model, charging users based on actual resource usage, typically measured in milliseconds of function execution and the number of executed functions. This results in cost efficiency, especially for applications with variable workloads, as resources are allocated and billed only when functions are triggered, minimizing idle time and reducing overall infrastructure costs (Shafiei et al., 2022).

Serverless computing faces challenges such as "cold starts" and managing state in a stateless environment, which can impact real-time or latency-sensitive applications. Developers must address design and architectural challenges to effectively orchestrate complex workflows across multiple functions. Serverless computing is a significant advancement in cloud-native application development, offering flexibility, scalability, and cost-efficiency. It abstracts infrastructure complexities and uses a pay-per-execution model, allowing developers to innovate faster and respond to changing demands. This model redefines traditional infrastructure provisioning and management, fostering a more event-driven and reactive programming style. Developers design applications in small, discrete functions triggered by events like HTTP requests, database changes, or file uploads, promoting modular, scalable, and loosely coupled application design, promoting flexibility and agility (Wen et al., 2023).

The shift to serverless architecture offers a new level of scalability, allowing applications to handle sudden spikes in demand. This elastic scalability aligns with modern workloads, providing a responsive and efficient solution. Serverless computing also fosters a microservices-oriented approach, allowing developers to decompose monolithic applications into smaller, specialized functions or microservices. This allows teams to work on discrete components, promoting faster development cycles, easier maintenance, and the ability to update specific functionalities without impacting the entire application (Li et al., 2022). Serverless architectures offer a cloud-agnostic solution, allowing organizations to deploy them in multi-cloud or hybrid environments, reducing vendor lock-in and allowing them to leverage services from different providers. However, these architectures are not suitable for all use cases, especially long-running processes or high-utilization applications. Additionally, security, monitoring, and debugging concerns in distributed and event-driven environments require specialized attention and robust tooling for comprehensive application management.

Serverless computing is a new era in application development, offering scalability, flexibility, and cost-efficiency. Its event-driven nature and cloud-agnostic capabilities make it a compelling choice for modern applications (Kjorveziroski et al., 2021). The evolution of serverless computing began with utility computing, where resources are allocated and consumed based on demand. The term "serverless" gained prominence with the introduction of Function as a Service (FaaS) offerings, such as AWS Lambda in

2014. This shift from managing infrastructure to executing individual functions triggered by events has transformed the way organizations innovate and optimize resource utilization (Rajan, 2020a). Serverless computing has gained significant adoption in recent years, with organizations across industries utilizing it to build scalable, agile, and cost-effective applications. This technology accelerates development cycles, improves resource utilization, and reduces operational overhead. The open-source community has played a crucial role in the evolution and adoption of serverless technologies, with numerous frameworks and tools emerging to democratize access and enable developers to create, deploy, and manage applications more efficiently. This collaborative ecosystem fosters innovation and contributes to the maturation of serverless technologies, catering to diverse use cases and requirements (Grogan et al., 2020).

The serverless landscape is undergoing a convergence of technologies, with service providers expanding beyond FaaS to include serverless databases, messaging systems, and machine learning capabilities. This broadens the scope of serverless computing, catering to diverse application needs across various industries. Serverless computing is based on several core principles, including abstraction, scalability, and cost-effectiveness. Absorption liberates developers from managing infrastructure by abstracting servers and runtime environments, allowing them to focus on writing and deploying functions without the overhead of provisioning or maintaining servers. Scalability allows applications to handle varying loads without manual intervention, optimizing performance and resource utilization (Scheuner & Leitner, 2020). Cost-effectiveness is another advantage, as the pay-per-execution billing model aligns costs directly with usage, eliminating the need for upfront infrastructure investment. This makes serverless computing an attractive option for applications with unpredictable or sporadic workloads.

Serverless computing is a rapidly evolving approach to application development and deployment, driven by its event-driven nature, which allows for quick iterations and deployments. This agile development cycle allows developers to efficiently experiment, test, and iterate on functionalities, accelerating time-to-market for new features. Serverless architectures also enhance fault tolerance and resilience, with distributed architectures ensuring that one function doesn't impact the entire application. Redundancy and auto-scaling capabilities contribute to increased reliability, minimizing downtime, and enhancing application availability. These principles remain fundamental in shaping the future of modern application architectures.

1.1 Function as a Service (FaaS) Offerings

1.1.1 FaaS and its Role in Serverless Computing

Function as a Service (FaaS) is a important component of serverless computing, allowing developers to focus on writing and executing discrete code units without worrying about the underlying infrastructure. Major cloud providers like AWS Lambda, Azure Functions, and Google Cloud Functions offer a scalable, event-driven environment for executing code. Developers upload their functions to these platforms, specifying the events that trigger their execution, resulting in a highly responsive and reactive application architecture (Yussupov et al., 2021). FaaS (Fast Application Services) is a main component in serverless computing, enabling a microservices-oriented approach that breaks down applications into manageable components. It promotes modularity, reusability, and ease of maintenance. FaaS architectures also embrace statelessness, enhancing scalability and resilience. They also introduce a pay-per-execution billing model, charging developers based on the number of function invocations and execution duration. This granular pricing model optimizes cost efficiency and resource utilization, encouraging rapid development cycles without additional costs during idle periods (Yussupov et al., 2019).

FaaS platforms enable developers to create sophisticated applications by integrating with various services and APIs. These integrations include database services, authentication, notifications, and machine learning. FaaS plays a crucial role in the serverless paradigm by providing a scalable environment, allowing developers to focus on writing code. It abstracts infrastructure complexities, encourages modularity, facilitates cost-effective execution, and facilitates seamless integrations. As FaaS offerings evolve, they continue to shape the future of modern application development and deployment (Boopathi, 2024; Sharma et al., 2024; Srinivas et al., 2023).

This chapter delves into the foundations of serverless computing, focusing on concepts like Function as a Service (FaaS), infrastructure management abstraction, and event-driven models. It aims to provide readers with a solid foundation for understanding serverless architectures. The chapter explores the advantages of serverless computing, including scalability, operational efficiency, resource optimization, and rapid development cycles. It highlights the transformative potential of transitioning to serverless architectures for organizations and developers, highlighting the benefits of embracing this technology. The chapter aims to equip readers with a solid foundation for understanding serverless architectures (Agrawal et al., 2023; Boopathi, 2024; Nanda et al., 2024).

This chapter explores the evolution of serverless technologies, from their humble beginnings to the emergence of sophisticated tools and platforms. It provides a historical narrative and highlights key enabling technologies that have shaped the field. The chapter assesses the efficacy and scalability of serverless architectures using real-world scenarios, performance benchmarks, and best practices. It aims to empower readers with the knowledge to make informed decisions regarding the adoption and implementation of serverless architectures, enabling them to make informed decisions in the future (Maguluri et al., 2023).

This chapter aims to provide a practical guide for technologists, developers, and researchers interested in serverless architectures. It offers advice, recommendations, and considerations for designing, developing, and deploying serverless applications effectively, equipping readers with the tools to navigate serverless computing complexities confidently.

2. BACKGROUND

Serverless computing is a revolutionary paradigm in cloud computing, transforming application development, deployment, and management. It abstracts the infrastructure management layer from developers, allowing them to focus on writing code for specific functions or tasks. The core of serverless computing lies in Function as a Service offerings, which allow developers to deploy individual functions or code in response to events or triggers without the need to provision or manage servers (Malathi et al., 2024; Ugandar et al., 2023). The chapter discusses the role of orchestration tools and serverless frameworks in developing and deploying serverless applications, automating scaling, provisioning, and resource management. It highlights the evolution of serverless technologies from their early beginnings to the sophisticated tools and frameworks available today, emphasizing the importance of serverless architectures in achieving scalability, operational efficiency, and resource optimization.

This chapter provides a thorough understanding of serverless computing, its principles, advantages, and implications in various technological contexts, offering valuable insights for practitioners utilizing serverless computing benefits in applications and systems design.

2.1 Objectives

i.   The chapter aims to elucidate the fundamental principles of serverless computing, including Function as a Service (FaaS), abstraction of infrastructure management complexities, and the event-driven model, to provide readers with a solid understanding of the underlying concepts.

ii. It seeks to explore the advantages driving the adoption of serverless architectures, such as scalability, operational efficiency, resource optimization, and rapid development cycles, in order to illustrate the benefits that can be gained by transitioning to serverless computing.

iii. Through a historical narrative, the chapter aims to trace the evolution of serverless technologies from early frameworks to sophisticated tools and platforms, providing insights into the progression of the field and the development of key enabling technologies.

iv. It seeks to assess the efficacy and scalability of serverless architectures in real-world scenarios, by examining case studies, performance benchmarks, and best practices, to provide readers with practical insights into the capabilities and limitations of serverless computing.

v.   Lastly, the chapter aims to serve as a guide for technologists, developers, and researchers interested in adopting serverless architectures, by offering practical advice, recommendations, and considerations for designing, developing, and deploying serverless applications effectively and efficiently.

3. COMPARISON OF MAJOR FAAS PROVIDERS

3.1 AWS Lambda (Taibi et al., 2020)

- **Ecosystem**: Part of Amazon Web Services (AWS), providing a vast ecosystem of cloud services and integrations.
- **Languages Supported**: Supports multiple programming languages including Node.js, Python, Java, C#, and more.
- **Integration**: Seamless integration with other AWS services like S3, DynamoDB, API Gateway, etc.
- **Event Sources**: Offers various triggers, including HTTP requests, database changes (DynamoDB streams), S3 events, and custom events.
- **Scalability**: Highly scalable, automatically managing resources based on demand.
- **Cold Start**: Experiences cold start delays, but warm-up options are available to mitigate this issue.
- **Monitoring & Debugging**: Provides AWS CloudWatch for monitoring and logging, as well as AWS X-Ray for tracing and debugging.
- **Pricing**: Pay-per-invocation and duration of execution, with a free tier available.

3.2 Azure Functions (Jindal et al., 2021)

- **Ecosystem**: Part of Microsoft Azure, providing a suite of cloud services and tight integration with Microsoft tools and technologies.
- **Languages Supported**: Supports languages like C#, F#, Node.js, Python, Java, and PowerShell.
- **Integration**: Integrates well with other Azure services like Azure Storage, Cosmos DB, Event Grid, etc.
- **Event Sources**: Offers triggers for HTTP requests, timers, Azure Storage events, Cosmos DB, and more.
- **Scalability**: Automatically scales based on demand, offering both consumption-based and dedicated hosting plans.
- **Cold Start**: Generally faster cold start times compared to some other FaaS providers.
- **Monitoring & Debugging**: Utilizes Azure Application Insights for monitoring, logging, and diagnostics.
- **Pricing**: Pay-per-execution and resource consumption, with a free tier and multiple pricing plans available.

3.3 Google Cloud Functions (Boopathi, 2024; Sharma et al., 2024; Srinivas et al., 2023)

- **Ecosystem**: Part of Google Cloud Platform (GCP), integrating with various GCP services and tools.
- **Languages Supported**: Supports languages like Node.js, Python, Go, and more.
- **Integration**: Seamlessly integrates with GCP services like Cloud Storage, Firestore, Pub/Sub, etc.
- **Event Sources**: Supports triggers from HTTP requests, Cloud Storage, Pub/Sub, Firebase, and more.
- **Scalability**: Automatically scales based on demand, offering horizontal scaling for concurrent function execution.
- **Cold Start**: Cold start times are present but generally comparable to other providers.
- **Monitoring & Debugging**: Uses Stackdriver for logging, monitoring, and diagnostics.
- **Pricing**: Pay-per-invocation and resources consumed, with a free tier and tiered pricing based on usage.

The selection of a FaaS provider depends on factors such as project requirements, existing infrastructure, preferred programming languages, integration needs, and cost considerations, which can be determined by evaluating these factors (Jindal et al., 2021).

4. USE CASES AND BEST PRACTICES

By considering these use cases and adopting best practices, organizations and developers can effectively harness the capabilities of FaaS offerings, ensuring efficient and scalable application development and deployment in a serverless environment (Agrawal et al., 2023; Hema et al., 2023; Venkateswaran et al., 2023).

4.1 Use Cases

- **Web Applications and APIs**: FaaS can handle HTTP requests efficiently, making it ideal for building web applications and APIs. Each function can handle specific endpoints, enabling a modular and scalable architecture.
- **Event-Driven Processing**: Use FaaS for event-driven processing, such as processing messages from queues (like AWS SQS or Azure Queue Storage), reacting to file uploads in storage services, or handling IoT device data streams.
- **Scheduled Tasks**: Automate tasks through scheduled function invocations, like performing backups, data cleanups, or generating periodic reports at specific times or intervals.
- **Real-time Data Processing**: FaaS can be employed for real-time data processing scenarios, reacting to streaming data changes, and performing computations or transformations on the fly.
- **IoT Applications**: Handle IoT events and sensor data in a scalable manner by using FaaS to process and react to the incoming data from IoT devices.
- **Image or Video Processing**: Use FaaS to perform image resizing, video transcoding, or other media processing tasks triggered by uploads or changes in a storage service.

4.2 Best Practices

- **Granular Functions**: Design functions to be small, focused, and perform specific tasks. This modular approach ensures better reusability, easier maintenance, and efficient scaling.
- **Stateless Design**: Aim for stateless functions to ensure scalability. Minimize reliance on function state between invocations, leveraging external storage or databases for maintaining state when necessary.
- **Optimized Dependencies**: Keep function packages lean by including only necessary dependencies, reducing the function's cold start time and overall execution duration.
- **Error Handling & Logging**: Implement robust error handling mechanisms within functions and ensure comprehensive logging. Utilize logging frameworks provided by the FaaS platform for effective debugging and monitoring.
- **Security Best Practices**: Apply proper security measures such as encryption, access controls, and least privilege principles. Use platform-specific security features and adhere to best practices for securing function code and data.
- **Performance Optimization**: Optimize code for performance to reduce execution times and minimize costs. Use asynchronous operations and caching where appropriate to enhance performance.
- **Cost Monitoring & Optimization**: Continuously monitor function usage and associated costs. Utilize auto-scaling features effectively and consider optimizing execution times to minimize expenses.
- **Testing & Versioning**: Implement thorough testing methodologies and version control for functions. Use staging environments to test and validate changes before deployment to production.

5. ORCHESTRATION TOOLS FOR SERVERLESS ARCHITECTURES

Orchestration tools are essential for managing complex workflows and interactions in serverless architectures, with several notable tools designed specifically for managing serverless environments (Singla & Sathyaraj, 2019a). These orchestration tools facilitate the coordination and management of serverless architectures, allowing developers to build complex workflows, handle asynchronous tasks, and manage interactions between various services and functions in a streamlined and efficient manner. The choice of orchestration tool often depends on specific use cases, ecosystem compatibility, and the desired level of orchestration complexity.

- AWS Step Functions is a visual workflow orchestration tool that allows developers to create state machines to coordinate the execution of multiple AWS services and Lambda functions. It provides a visual interface for defining workflows using various state types, enabling branching, retries, error handling, and coordination of distributed applications. It seamlessly integrates with other AWS services, simplifying complex workflows and enhancing maintainability.
- Azure Logic Apps is a visual tool that allows users to design and automate workflows by connecting Azure services, SaaS applications, and on-premises systems. It offers connectors and triggers for orchestrating workflows, supports conditional logic, loops, and parallel processing, and integrates with multiple Azure services for seamless communication. It simplifies workflow creation and provides extensive monitoring and diagnostics capabilities.
- Google Cloud Workflows is a tool that enables users to define, deploy, and manage serverless workflows linking services, API calls, and other tasks across Google Cloud Platform services. It features a visual editor for creating and managing workflows, direct integration with GCP services, error handling, and retries. It simplifies workflow development, improves visibility, and enables efficient cross-service interaction management.
- The Apache Open Whisk Composer is a programming model that enables developers to create and manage complex, reusable sequences of multiple FaaS functions. It offers a declarative approach, allowing chaining, parallel execution, and conditional branching. Designed specifically for Apache Open Whisk, it promotes modularity and reusability in serverless applications.
- The Serverless Framework Orchestration Plugins extend its capabilities, allowing for the coordination of multiple serverless functions or workflows across various providers. These plugins offer workflow management, coordination, and state management within the framework ecosystem, making them compatible with multiple cloud providers and offering benefits in handling complex workflows.

5.1 Importance of Orchestration in Serverless Environments

Orchestration plays a pivotal role in serverless environments, serving as a linchpin for managing and coordinating the execution of multiple functions, services, and workflows (Arjona et al., 2021). Orchestration in serverless environments enhances component coordination, scalability, reliability, and manageability of distributed systems, allowing developers to concentrate on robust applications while abstracting the complexities of service and function interactions. The importance of Orchestration in Serverless Environments is illustrated in Figure 1.

Figure 1. Importance of orchestration in serverless environments

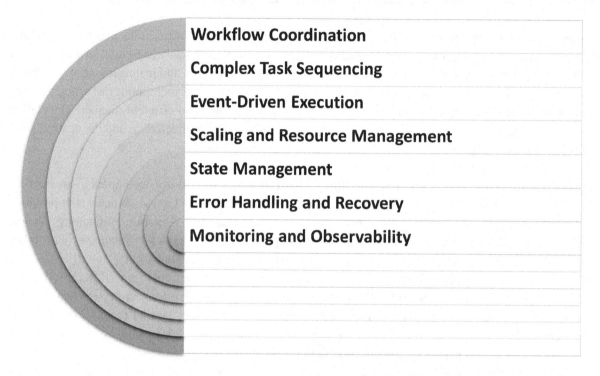

Workflow Coordination: In serverless architectures, applications are often composed of multiple functions and services that need to interact seamlessly. Orchestration tools allow developers to define and manage the sequence of these interactions, ensuring that tasks are executed in the desired order and that dependencies between different components are handled efficiently.

Complex Task Sequencing: Orchestration is essential for handling complex workflows that involve conditional branching, parallel processing, error handling, retries, and timeouts. It enables the arrangement of multiple functions or tasks in a logical sequence, ensuring that each step is executed correctly and that failures are appropriately managed.

Event-Driven Execution: Serverless architectures are inherently event-driven, triggered by various events such as HTTP requests, database changes, file uploads, or timers. Orchestration tools facilitate the handling of these events and the subsequent invocation of the relevant functions or services based on the event triggers.

Scaling and Resource Management: Orchestration helps in managing the dynamic scaling of serverless functions. As the demand for resources fluctuates, orchestration tools automatically provision and scale resources to accommodate varying workloads. This capability ensures optimal resource utilization and efficient scaling without manual intervention.

State Management: In stateless serverless functions, maintaining application state becomes a crucial consideration. Orchestration tools provide mechanisms to manage and pass state between different functions or workflows, enabling the creation of stateful workflows while still leveraging the stateless nature of individual functions.

Error Handling and Recovery: Effective orchestration involves robust error handling mechanisms. Orchestration tools enable the implementation of error recovery strategies, including retries, fallbacks, and handling exceptional scenarios to ensure the reliability and resilience of the entire application.

Monitoring and Observability: Orchestration tools often include monitoring and observability features that provide insights into the execution of workflows. They offer logging, metrics, and tracing capabilities, allowing developers to monitor performance, track the flow of execution, and diagnose issues within the orchestrated processes.

Complexity Management: As serverless architectures evolve and become more complex, orchestration tools simplify the management of this complexity. They provide a centralized mechanism for designing, visualizing, and maintaining intricate workflows, reducing the operational burden on developers.

5.2 Orchestration Tools

The various Orchestration Tools are explained below (Singla & Sathyaraj, 2019b). Each orchestration tool has its unique architecture and functions, aimed at simplifying the creation, management, and coordination of workflows within serverless environments. The choice of tool often depends on specific use cases, preferred workflows, integrations, and the targeted cloud ecosystem as shown in Figure 1.

5.3 AWS Step Functions

Architecture: Uses state machines to define workflows with various states (Task, Choice, Parallel, etc.) connected by transitions. Workflow states represent different actions or tasks to be executed (Jindal et al., 2021; López et al., 2020; Singla & Sathyaraj, 2019a).

5.4 Functions

- **State Management**: Enables defining states, handling retries, branching based on conditions, and managing error handling within workflows.
- **Visual Workflow Designer**: Offers a visual interface for designing and monitoring state machines, facilitating the creation of complex workflows.
- **Integration**: Seamlessly integrates with various AWS services and Lambda functions.

5.5 Azure Logic Apps

Architecture: Visual workflow designer where users create workflows by connecting triggers, actions, and conditions using a graphical interface.

5.6 Functions

- **Connectors and Triggers**: Provides a wide range of connectors to external services and Azure services, enabling workflow orchestration across diverse applications and systems.
- **Conditional Logic and Loops**: Allows the creation of complex workflows with conditional logic, loops, and parallel processing.

- **Integration**: Integration with Azure services and SaaS applications, facilitating seamless communication between services.

5.7 Google Cloud Workflows

Architecture: Uses YAML-based workflow definitions, comprising steps and controls for executing tasks, invoking APIs, and managing conditional logic.

5.8 Functions

- **Visual Editor and YAML Definition**: Offers a visual editor for creating workflows, as well as a YAML-based definition for precise control and versioning.
- **Integration with GCP Services**: Integrates with various Google Cloud Platform services for workflow orchestration and automation.
- **Error Handling and Retries**: Provides features for error handling, retries, and conditional branching within workflows.

5.9 Apache Open Whisk Composer

Architecture: Programming model for composing serverless functions into more complex sequences or workflows using a declarative approach.

5.10 Functions

- **Declarative Composition**: Enables chaining functions together, specifying parallel executions, conditional execution, and managing outputs between functions.
- **Modularity and Reusability**: Promotes modularity by creating reusable compositions of functions, enhancing the overall reusability of serverless logic.
- **Integration with Apache Open Whisk**: Designed specifically to orchestrate functions within the Apache Open Whisk serverless platform.

5.11 Serverless Framework with Orchestration Plugins

Architecture: Extends the Serverless Framework with plugins that provide orchestration and workflow management capabilities.

5.12 Functions

- **Workflow Management**: Offers plugins that facilitate workflow management, coordination, and state management within the Serverless Framework ecosystem.
- **Extensibility and Customization**: Allows developers to extend the framework's capabilities based on specific workflow requirements.
- **Multi-Cloud Support**: Can be used to orchestrate serverless functions across multiple cloud providers supported by the Serverless Framework.

6. SERVERLESS FRAMEWORKS

6.1 Role and Significance of Frameworks in Serverless Development

The various roles of frameworks in serverless development are explained below(Zhang et al., 2020). Serverless frameworks are essential for developers to adopt serverless computing by abstracting complexities, streamlining workflows, optimizing performance, and providing a standardized approach to building and deploying applications. They play a crucial role in the adoption and success of serverless architectures.

Abstraction of Complexity: Serverless frameworks abstract the underlying complexity of serverless architectures, allowing developers to focus on writing code rather than dealing with infrastructure provisioning, scaling, and configuration. They provide higher-level abstractions that enable developers to define and deploy functions without getting mired in the intricacies of cloud-specific configurations.

Facilitation of Development: By providing templates, boilerplate code, and predefined configurations, serverless frameworks expedite the development process. They offer ready-to-use templates for common use cases, reducing the time required for setup and allowing developers to start coding functional logic more swiftly.

Multi-Cloud Support: Many serverless frameworks offer compatibility with multiple cloud providers, allowing developers the flexibility to deploy applications across various cloud environments. This multi-cloud support mitigates vendor lock-in concerns and enables leveraging the strengths of different cloud platforms based on specific project needs.

Streamlined Deployment: Frameworks simplify the deployment process by automating the packaging and deployment of serverless functions. They often integrate with CI/CD pipelines, enabling seamless integration and deployment of code changes, reducing manual intervention, and ensuring a more efficient deployment workflow.

Optimized Performance: Some frameworks offer optimization features that help in reducing cold start times, improving function performance, and managing resource allocation more efficiently. They allow developers to fine-tune configurations for better performance, helping to mitigate latency issues and enhance overall application responsiveness.

Enhanced Testing and Debugging: Serverless frameworks often provide tools for testing and debugging serverless applications locally or in staging environments. This feature aids in identifying and resolving issues during the development phase, ensuring smoother deployments and improved application stability.

Community and Ecosystem Support: Many frameworks have active communities that contribute plugins, extensions, and additional functionalities, enriching the ecosystem around the framework. This support ecosystem can provide additional tools, libraries, and best practices, enhancing the development experience and offering solutions for various use cases.

Cost Optimization: Frameworks often incorporate features that help optimize costs, such as resource allocation, function scaling, and efficient usage of cloud resources. They enable developers to make informed decisions regarding resource utilization, leading to better cost-efficiency for serverless applications.

6.2 Classification of Popular Frameworks

Popular serverless frameworks are categorized based on language support, cloud provider compatibility, and additional functionalities they offer (Palade et al., 2019; Zhang et al., 2020). These classifications showcase the diversity of serverless frameworks available in the ecosystem, catering to specific languages, cloud provider preferences, and additional functionalities required for different application scenarios. Choosing the right framework often depends on factors such as programming language familiarity, cloud platform preference, required features, and deployment complexity. The Figure 2 showcases the classifications of Popular serverless frameworks.

Figure 2. Classification of popular serverless frameworks

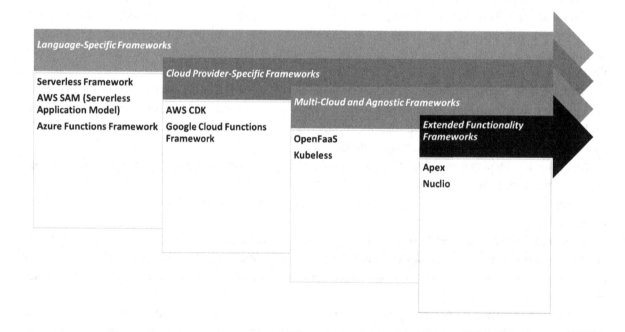

6.2.1 Language-Specific Frameworks

These frameworks are primarily designed for specific programming languages(Boopathi, 2023):

- **Serverless Framework**: Supports multiple cloud providers (AWS, Azure, GCP) and various programming languages like Node.js, Python, Java, and more. It provides a CLI and comprehensive plugins for deployment, resource management, and local testing.
- **AWS SAM (Serverless Application Model)**: Focused on AWS Lambda and related services. Offers a simplified way to define serverless applications using AWS CloudFormation templates, optimized for AWS-specific functionalities.

- **Azure Functions Framework**: Targeted for Microsoft Azure Functions. Offers a local development experience and supports languages like C#, JavaScript, TypeScript, and Java, tailored for Azure-based serverless applications.

6.2.2 Cloud Provider-Specific Frameworks

Frameworks designed to work primarily with a specific cloud provider:

- **AWS CDK (Cloud Development Kit)**: A development framework allowing infrastructure provisioning using programming languages (TypeScript, Python, Java, C#) for AWS. It enables defining cloud resources as code and integrates with AWS services including Lambda.
- **Google Cloud Functions Framework**: Built for Google Cloud Platform (GCP) and supports languages like Node.js, Python, Go, etc. It facilitates local development, testing, and deployment of functions within GCP.

6.2.3 Multi-Cloud and Agnostic Frameworks

Frameworks offering compatibility and support across multiple cloud providers:

- **Open-FaaS**: An open-source serverless framework that works with Kubernetes and supports multiple cloud providers. It allows the creation of functions in any language and provides flexibility in deployment options.
- **Kubeless**: Built on top of Kubernetes, it allows running serverless functions on Kubernetes clusters and supports multiple languages. It's cloud-agnostic, enabling deployment on various cloud platforms or on-premises.

6.2.4 Specialized or Extended Functionality Frameworks

Frameworks providing additional functionalities beyond basic serverless deployment:

- **Apex**: A lightweight framework supporting AWS Lambda. It offers easy deployment and management of Lambda functions and supports Go, Node.js, Python, etc., with additional features like function versions, aliases, and IAM policies.
- **Nuclio**: Focused on real-time and data-centric applications. It optimizes for high-throughput and low-latency functions and targets use cases like stream processing, IoT, and data pipelines.

7. EVOLUTION OF SERVERLESS TECHNOLOGIES

The evolution of serverless technologies has been marked by significant advancements in architecture, functionality, and developer experience (Rajan, 2020b). Serverless technologies enhance application scalability and operational efficiency by offering elastic scalability, reducing overhead, optimizing resources, and enabling faster development cycles, with future advancements expected to further enhance these capabilities. It is illustrated in Figure 3.

7.1 Early Stages

- **Initial Concepts**: The concept of utility computing and cloud services laid the groundwork for serverless computing, emphasizing pay-per-use models and abstracted infrastructure.
- **PaaS and FaaS Beginnings**: Early Platform as a Service (PaaS) offerings, along with the introduction of Function as a Service (FaaS) models, marked the shift towards serverless paradigms. This phase focused on the execution of discrete functions triggered by events.

Emergence of Early Frameworks: Frameworks like AWS Lambda and Azure Functions emerged, providing developers with the foundational tools to deploy functions without managing infrastructure. These frameworks allowed for event-driven architectures but lacked the extensive tooling and maturity seen in modern frameworks.

Figure 3. The evolution of serverless technologies

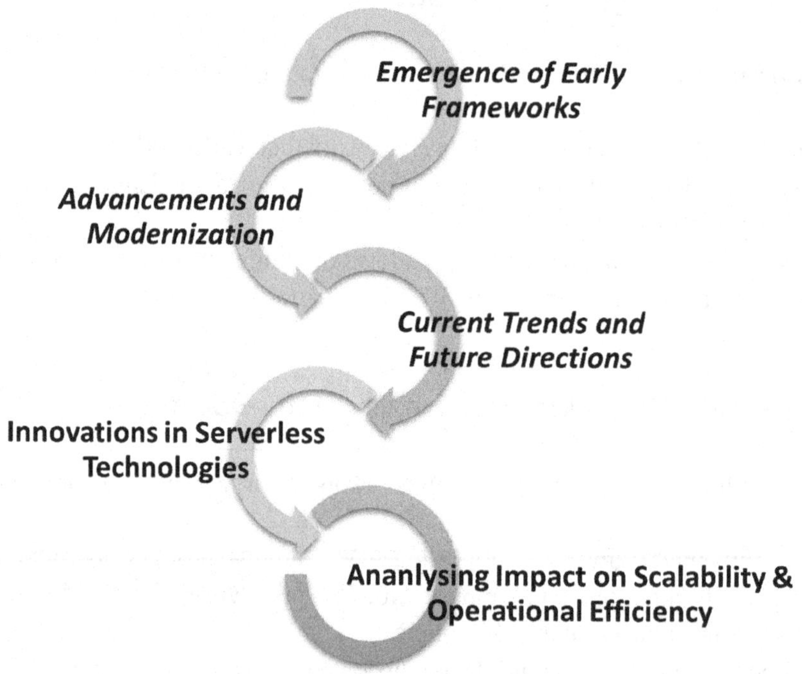

7.2 Advancements and Modernization

- **Expansion of Language Support**: Modern frameworks expanded language support beyond Node.js, incorporating Python, Java, C#, and more, making serverless accessible to a broader developer audience.
- **Richer Toolsets**: Frameworks evolved to offer comprehensive toolsets, CLI capabilities, local development environments, and plugins/extensions for CI/CD, testing, monitoring, and debugging.

- **Abstraction and Multi-Cloud Support**: Frameworks increasingly abstracted infrastructure complexities, enabling multi-cloud deployments and offering higher-level abstractions for infrastructure resources.
- **Orchestration and Workflow Management**: Integration with orchestration tools (AWS Step Functions, Azure Logic Apps) enhanced the management of complex workflows and interactions between functions and services.
- **Optimization and Performance Enhancements**: Ongoing optimization efforts reduced cold start times, improved performance, and provided better resource utilization through fine-tuning and auto-scaling mechanisms.

7.2 Current Trends and Future Directions

Serverless technologies are evolving into mature ecosystems with robust tools, language support, and integrations, enhancing development, scalability, and efficient application management, with potential for innovation and efficiency.

- **Focus on Developer Experience**: Continual improvements in developer experience with emphasis on ease of use, rapid prototyping, and smoother deployment workflows.
- **Hybrid and Edge Computing**: The expansion into hybrid and edge computing, allowing serverless applications to operate closer to end-users for reduced latency and improved performance.
- **Integration with Containers and Kubernetes**: Integration with containerization technologies and Kubernetes-based solutions to combine the benefits of serverless with container orchestration.

7.3 Innovations in Serverless Technologies

- **Event-Driven Architecture**: The shift towards event-driven architectures has been pivotal. Functions execute in response to events like HTTP requests, database changes, or file uploads, fostering modularity and agility.
- **Expanded Language Support**: Early serverless offerings were limited to a few languages. Innovations brought support for multiple languages (Node.js, Python, Java, etc.), making serverless accessible to a broader developer community.
- **Advanced Tooling and Frameworks**: Modern frameworks offer extensive tooling, local development environments, CI/CD integrations, and sophisticated monitoring and debugging tools, enhancing developer productivity.
- **Orchestration and Workflow Management**: The integration of orchestration tools enables the management of complex workflows, facilitating coordination between functions and services.
- **Auto-Scaling and Resource Optimization**: Continuous optimization efforts have improved auto-scaling mechanisms, resource allocation, and performance tuning, resulting in better resource utilization and cost-efficiency.

7.4 Impact on Scalability

- **Elastic Scalability**: Serverless architectures inherently scale based on demand. Functions auto-scale in response to workload fluctuations, ensuring applications handle varying loads without manual intervention.
- **Microservices Architecture**: Serverless encourages a microservices-oriented approach, breaking down monolithic applications into smaller, independent functions or services. This modular design facilitates easier scalability of individual components.
- **Dynamic Resource Allocation**: Serverless platforms dynamically allocate resources per function invocation, optimizing resource allocation and eliminating the need for over-provisioning.

7.5 Impact on Operational Efficiency

- **Reduced Operational Overhead**: Serverless abstracts infrastructure management, allowing developers to focus solely on writing code. This reduction in operational overhead enables teams to be more efficient and productive.
- **Faster Time-to-Market**: With streamlined development workflows and rapid deployment cycles, serverless accelerates the development process, allowing quicker iterations and faster deployment of new features.
- **Cost Optimization**: Pay-per-use pricing models and efficient resource utilization result in cost savings. Organizations pay only for actual resource consumption during function execution, eliminating costs during idle periods.
- **Improved Fault Tolerance**: The distributed nature of serverless architectures enhances fault tolerance. Functions operate independently, reducing the impact of failures on the overall application.

8. SCALABILITY, OPERATIONAL EFFICIENCY, AND RESOURCE OPTIMIZATION

The study explores the impact of serverless architectures on scalability, operational efficiency gains, and strategies for resource optimization in serverless environments(Kumari et al., 2022; Lin & Khazaei, 2020).

8.1 Impact of Serverless Architectures on Scalability

8.1.1 Scalability Advantages

- **Elastic Scaling**: Serverless architectures automatically scale in response to demand, handling varying workloads without manual intervention. Functions scale dynamically based on incoming requests or events.
- **Granular Scaling**: Functions operate independently, allowing for granular scaling where only the required functions scale up/down based on their individual workload.

8.1.2 Benefits to Scalability

- **Efficient Resource Utilization**: Serverless platforms allocate resources precisely as needed per function invocation, avoiding over-provisioning and ensuring optimal resource utilization.
- **High Concurrency Handling**: Serverless can handle a high number of concurrent executions due to its scaling capabilities, making it suitable for scenarios with unpredictable spikes in traffic.

8.2 Operational Efficiency Gains in Serverless Environments

Reduced Operational Overhead: Serverless platforms simplify infrastructure management, allowing developers to concentrate on coding, while automated management handles tasks like provisioning, scaling, and monitoring, streamlining operations and freeing up resources.

Faster Development Cycles: Serverless technology streamlines workflows and automates deployment processes, enabling faster iterations and new features. This enhances developer productivity by reducing infrastructure-related tasks and allowing more focus on core application logic.

8.3 Strategies for Resource Optimization

Fine-Tuning Resource Allocation: Optimize memory and CPU allocation based on workload to improve performance and cost efficiency. Minimize idle time by optimizing function timeouts and utilizing auto-scaling to reduce costs during idle periods.

Optimizing Code and Architectural Design: Optimize code for reduced execution time and resource consumption using efficient algorithms. Design serverless applications for modularity and reusability, improving resource usage and scalability.

Monitoring and Cost Management: Serverless platforms offer monitoring tools for tracking performance metrics, identifying bottlenecks, and optimizing resource allocation. Regular cost analysis involves reviewing usage patterns, adjusting resources, and utilizing cost-effective features.

Implementing these strategies allows organizations to optimize serverless architectures' scalability, operational efficiency, and resource utilization, leading to cost savings and enhanced performance.

9. IMPLEMENTING SERVERLESS COMPUTING IN TECHNOLOGICAL ENVIRONMENTS

The section discusses the practical considerations for adopting serverless computing in technological environments, highlighting challenges and solutions through continuous improvement and iteration (Ivan et al., 2019; Mampage et al., 2022). Organizations can successfully adopt serverless computing benefits by aligning business goals, addressing technical challenges, and fostering continuous improvement through practical considerations and solutions. The various factors have been considered for implementing Serverless Computing in Technological Environments as shown in Figure 4.

Figure 4. Implementing serverless computing in technological environments

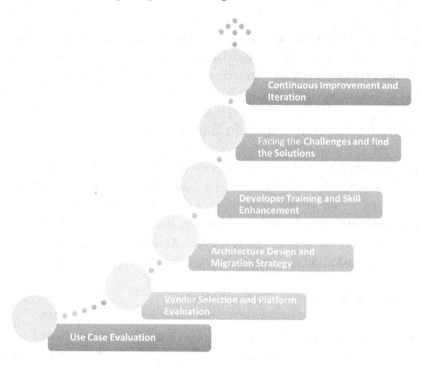

9.1 Practical Considerations for Adoption

- **Use Case Evaluation**: Identify serverless architecture use cases based on workload characteristics, event-driven nature, and scalability requirements, and identify applications or components that benefit from pay-per-use model and auto-scaling capabilities.
- **Vendor Selection and Platform Evaluation**: Choose serverless providers based on language support, services, pricing, ecosystem compatibility, and existing infrastructure, security, compliance, and integration requirements.
- **Architecture Design and Migration Strategy**: Develop a microservices-oriented application design, breaking down functionalities into discrete functions, and devise a migration strategy for transitioning existing applications or components to serverless architecture.
- **Developer Training and Skill Enhancement**: The initiative aims to offer training and resources to developers to effectively utilize serverless paradigms and best practices, enhancing their skills in event-driven programming, serverless frameworks, and cloud-native development.

9.2 Challenges and Solutions

To mitigate vendor lock-in risks, adopt a multi-cloud strategy or use cloud-agnostic frameworks. Address cold start and performance issues by optimizing function initialization and asynchronous processing. Implement robust monitoring and logging using platform-specific tools or third-party solutions for efficient troubleshooting. Implement best practices for securing serverless functions, including access control, encryption, and regular security audits. Utilize auto-scaling, optimize function configurations, and analyze usage patterns for efficient resource allocation and cost management.

Continuous Improvement and Iteration: It emphasizes the importance of continuous iteration on code and architecture to improve performance, reduce latency, and enhance resource utilization. It also encourages feedback from developers and stakeholders to identify areas for improvement and encourages experimentation with new serverless features to drive innovation.

10. CONCLUSION AND FUTURE TRENDS

The chapter explores serverless computing, a paradigm that has transformed application development, deployment, and management. It explores its core principles, advantages, and evolution, providing insights into its impact on scalability, operational efficiency, and resource optimization. Serverless architectures offer scalability, efficiency, and reduced operational overhead by abstracting infrastructure management. They streamline development cycles, boost developer productivity, and enable faster application time-to-market. However, challenges like cold starts, security concerns, and monitoring complexities require careful planning. Adoption strategies include use case evaluation, vendor selection, architectural design, and skill enhancement.

Future trends in serverless computing include hybrid and edge computing, deep container integration, enhanced developer experience, cost optimization, and specialized use cases like IoT, real-time processing, and data analytics. Hybrid and edge environments will allow serverless applications to operate closer to end-users, reducing latency and improving performance. Continuous improvements in developer tooling, local development environments, and debugging capabilities will enhance the developer experience. Serverless technologies will find broader application in these areas. The future of serverless computing is promising for innovation, adoption, and addressing challenges. As the ecosystem matures, focus will be on enhancing developer experience, optimizing performance, and catering to diverse application needs.

11. ABBREVIATIONS

FaaS: Function as a Service
CI/CD: Continuous Integration/Continuous Deployment
AWS: Amazon Web Services
GCP: Google Cloud Platform
PaaS: Platform as a Service
SAM: Serverless Application Model
IoT: Internet of Things
CDK: Cloud Development Kit
IAM: Identity and Access Management
API: Application Programming Interface
Pricing Models: Different pricing models used in serverless computing

REFERENCES

Agrawal, A. V., Shashibhushan, G., Pradeep, S., Padhi, S., Sugumar, D., & Boopathi, S. (2023). Synergizing Artificial Intelligence, 5G, and Cloud Computing for Efficient Energy Conversion Using Agricultural Waste. In Sustainable Science and Intelligent Technologies for Societal Development (pp. 475–497). IGI Global.

Arjona, A., López, P. G., Sampé, J., Slominski, A., & Villard, L. (2021). Triggerflow: Trigger-based orchestration of serverless workflows. *Future Generation Computer Systems*, *124*, 215–229. doi:10.1016/j.future.2021.06.004

Boopathi, S. (2023). Deep Learning Techniques Applied for Automatic Sentence Generation. In Promoting Diversity, Equity, and Inclusion in Language Learning Environments (pp. 255–273). IGI Global. doi:10.4018/978-1-6684-3632-5.ch016

Boopathi, S. (2024). Balancing Innovation and Security in the Cloud: Navigating the Risks and Rewards of the Digital Age. In Improving Security, Privacy, and Trust in Cloud Computing (pp. 164–193). IGI Global.

Cassel, G. A. S., Rodrigues, V. F., da Rosa Righi, R., Bez, M. R., Nepomuceno, A. C., & da Costa, C. A. (2022). Serverless computing for Internet of Things: A systematic literature review. *Future Generation Computer Systems*, *128*, 299–316. doi:10.1016/j.future.2021.10.020

Grogan, J., Mulready, C., McDermott, J., Urbanavicius, M., Yilmaz, M., Abgaz, Y., McCarren, A., MacMahon, S. T., Garousi, V., Elger, P., & … (2020). A multivocal literature review of function-as-a-service (faas) infrastructures and implications for software developers. *Systems, Software and Services Process Improvement: 27th European Conference, 27*, 58–75.

Hema, N., Krishnamoorthy, N., Chavan, S. M., Kumar, N., Sabarimuthu, M., & Boopathi, S. (2023). A Study on an Internet of Things (IoT)-Enabled Smart Solar Grid System. In *Handbook of Research on Deep Learning Techniques for Cloud-Based Industrial IoT* (pp. 290–308). IGI Global. doi:10.4018/978-1-6684-8098-4.ch017

Ivan, C., Vasile, R., & Dadarlat, V. (2019). Serverless computing: An investigation of deployment environments for web apis. *Computers*, *8*(2), 50. doi:10.3390/computers8020050

Jindal, A., Chadha, M., Benedict, S., & Gerndt, M. (2021). Estimating the capacities of function-as-a-service functions. *Proceedings of the 14th IEEE/ACM International Conference on Utility and Cloud Computing Companion*, (pp. 1–8). IEEE.

Kjorveziroski, V., Filiposka, S., & Trajkovik, V. (2021). Iot serverless computing at the edge: A systematic mapping review. *Computers*, *10*(10), 130. doi:10.3390/computers10100130

Kumari, A., Patra, M. K., Sahoo, B., & Behera, R. K. (2022). Resource optimization in performance modeling for serverless application. *International Journal of Information Technology : an Official Journal of Bharati Vidyapeeth's Institute of Computer Applications and Management*, *14*(6), 2867–2875. doi:10.1007/s41870-022-01073-x

Li, Y., Lin, Y., Wang, Y., Ye, K., & Xu, C. (2022). Serverless computing: State-of-the-art, challenges and opportunities. *IEEE Transactions on Services Computing*, *16*(2), 1522–1539. doi:10.1109/TSC.2022.3166553

Lin, C., & Khazaei, H. (2020). Modeling and optimization of performance and cost of serverless applications. *IEEE Transactions on Parallel and Distributed Systems*, *32*(3), 615–632. doi:10.1109/TPDS.2020.3028841

López, P. G., Arjona, A., Sampé, J., Slominski, A., & Villard, L. (2020). Triggerflow: Trigger-based orchestration of serverless workflows. *Proceedings of the 14th ACM International Conference on Distributed and Event-Based Systems*, (pp. 3–14). ACM. 10.1145/3401025.3401731

Maguluri, L. P., Arularasan, A., & Boopathi, S. (2023). Assessing Security Concerns for AI-Based Drones in Smart Cities. In Effective AI, Blockchain, and E-Governance Applications for Knowledge Discovery and Management (pp. 27–47). IGI Global. doi:10.4018/978-1-6684-9151-5.ch002

Malathi, J., Kusha, K., Isaac, S., Ramesh, A., Rajendiran, M., & Boopathi, S. (2024). IoT-Enabled Remote Patient Monitoring for Chronic Disease Management and Cost Savings: Transforming Healthcare. In Advances in Explainable AI Applications for Smart Cities (pp. 371–388). IGI Global.

Mampage, A., Karunasekera, S., & Buyya, R. (2022). A holistic view on resource management in serverless computing environments: Taxonomy and future directions. *ACM Computing Surveys*, *54*(11s), 1–36. doi:10.1145/3510412

Nanda, A. K., Sharma, A., Augustine, P. J., Cyril, B. R., Kiran, V., & Sampath, B. (2024). Securing Cloud Infrastructure in IaaS and PaaS Environments. In Improving Security, Privacy, and Trust in Cloud Computing (pp. 1–33). IGI Global. doi:10.4018/979-8-3693-1431-9.ch001

Palade, A., Kazmi, A., & Clarke, S. (2019). An evaluation of open source serverless computing frameworks support at the edge. *2019 IEEE World Congress on Services (SERVICES)*, *2642*, 206–211. 10.1109/SERVICES.2019.00057

Rajan, A. P. (2020). A review on serverless architectures-function as a service (FaaS) in cloud computing. [Telecommunication Computing Electronics and Control]. *Telkomnika*, *18*(1), 530–537. doi:10.12928/telkomnika.v18i1.12169

Scheuner, J., & Leitner, P. (2020). Function-as-a-service performance evaluation: A multivocal literature review. *Journal of Systems and Software*, *170*, 110708. doi:10.1016/j.jss.2020.110708

Shafiei, H., Khonsari, A., & Mousavi, P. (2022). Serverless computing: A survey of opportunities, challenges, and applications. *ACM Computing Surveys*, *54*(11s), 1–32. doi:10.1145/3510611

Sharma, M., Sharma, M., Sharma, N., & Boopathi, S. (2024). Building Sustainable Smart Cities Through Cloud and Intelligent Parking System. In *Handbook of Research on AI and ML for Intelligent Machines and Systems* (pp. 195–222). IGI Global.

Singla, K. & Sathyaraj, P. (2019). *Comparison of Software Orchestration Performance Tools and Serverless Web Application.*

Srinivas, B., Maguluri, L. P., Naidu, K. V., Reddy, L. C. S., Deivakani, M., & Boopathi, S. (2023). Architecture and Framework for Interfacing Cloud-Enabled Robots. In *Handbook of Research on Data Science and Cybersecurity Innovations in Industry 4.0 Technologies* (pp. 542–560). IGI Global. doi:10.4018/978-1-6684-8145-5.ch027

Taibi, D., El Ioini, N., Pahl, C., & Niederkofler, J. R. S. (2020). *Patterns for serverless functions (function-as-a-service): A multivocal literature review.*

Ugandar, R., Rahamathunnisa, U., Sajithra, S., Christiana, M. B. V., Palai, B. K., & Boopathi, S. (2023). Hospital Waste Management Using Internet of Things and Deep Learning: Enhanced Efficiency and Sustainability. In Applications of Synthetic Biology in Health, Energy, and Environment (pp. 317–343). IGI Global.

Venkateswaran, N., Vidhya, K., Ayyannan, M., Chavan, S. M., Sekar, K., & Boopathi, S. (2023). A Study on Smart Energy Management Framework Using Cloud Computing. In 5G, Artificial Intelligence, and Next Generation Internet of Things: Digital Innovation for Green and Sustainable Economies (pp. 189–212). IGI Global. doi:10.4018/978-1-6684-8634-4.ch009

Wen, J., Chen, Z., Jin, X., & Liu, X. (2023). Rise of the planet of serverless computing: A systematic review. *ACM Transactions on Software Engineering and Methodology*, *32*(5), 1–61. doi:10.1145/3579643

Yussupov, V., Breitenbücher, U., Leymann, F., & Wurster, M. (2019). A systematic mapping study on engineering function-as-a-service platforms and tools. *Proceedings of the 12th IEEE/ACM International Conference on Utility and Cloud Computing*, (pp. 229–240). IEEE. 10.1145/3344341.3368803

Yussupov, V., Soldani, J., Breitenbücher, U., Brogi, A., & Leymann, F. (2021). FaaSten your decisions: A classification framework and technology review of function-as-a-Service platforms. *Journal of Systems and Software*, *175*, 110906. doi:10.1016/j.jss.2021.110906

Zhang, W., Fang, V., Panda, A., & Shenker, S. (2020). Kappa: A programming framework for serverless computing. *Proceedings of the 11th ACM Symposium on Cloud Computing*, (pp. 328–343). ACM. 10.1145/3419111.3421277

Compilation of References

Abraham, A., & Yang, J. (2023, May). A Comparative Analysis of Performance and Usability on Serverless and Server-Based Google Cloud Services. In *International Conference on Advances in Computing Research* (pp. 408-422). Cham: Springer Nature Switzerland. 10.1007/978-3-031-33743-7_33

Adzic, G., & Chatley, R. (2017). Serverless computing: Economic and architectural impact. In *Proceedings of the 2017 11th Joint Meeting on Foundations of Software Engineering (ESEC/FSE 2017)* (pp. 884–889). Association for Computing Machinery. 10.1145/3106237.3117767

Agrawal, A. V., Shashibhushan, G., Pradeep, S., Padhi, S., Sugumar, D., & Boopathi, S. (2023). Synergizing Artificial Intelligence, 5G, and Cloud Computing for Efficient Energy Conversion Using Agricultural Waste. In Sustainable Science and Intelligent Technologies for Societal Development (pp. 475–497). IGI Global.

Ahamad, S., Janani, S., Talukdar, V., Sharma, T., Sahu, A., Pramanik, S., & Gupta, A. (2024). *Apollo Hospital's Proposed Use of Big Data Healthcare Analytics, Big Data Analytics Techniques for Market Intelligence.* IGI Global.

Aksakalli, I. K., Çelik, T., Can, A. B., & Tekinerdoğan, B. (2021). Deployment and communication patterns in microservice architectures: A systematic literature review. *Journal of Systems and Software*, *180*, 111014. https://www.sciencedirect.com/science/article/abs/pii/S0164121221001114. doi:10.1016/j.jss.2021.111014

Al-Ali, Z., Goodarzy, S., Hunter, E., Ha, S., Han, R., Keller, E., & Rozner, E. (2018). Making serverless computing more serverless. In *2018 IEEE 11th International Conference on Cloud Computing (CLOUD)* (pp. 456–459). IEEE. 10.1109/CLOUD.2018.00064

Al-Ameen, M., & Spillner, J. (2019). A systematic and open exploration of FaaS research. In *Proceedings of the European Symposium on Serverless Computing and Applications (CEUR Workshop Proceedings*, (pp. 30–35). CEUR-WS.

Alam, F., Toosi, A. N., Cheema, M. A., Cicconetti, C., Serrano, P., Iosup, A., Tari, Z., & Sarvi, M. (2023). Serverless Vehicular Edge Computing for the Internet of Vehicles. *IEEE Internet Computing*, *27*(04), 40–51. doi:10.1109/MIC.2023.3271641

Aliev, I., Gazul, S., & Bobova, A. (2023, March). Virtualization technologies and platforms: Comparative overview and updated performance tests. In AIP Conference Proceedings. AIP Publishing.

Alouffi, B., Hasnain, M., Alharbi, A., Alosaimi, W., Alyami, H., & Ayaz, M. (2021). A Systematic Literature Review on Cloud Computing Security: Threats and Mitigation Strategies. *IEEE Access*. IEEE.

Alqaryouti, O., & Siyam, N. (2018). Serverless computing and scheduling tasks on cloud: A review. [ASRJETS]. *American Scientific Research Journal for Engineering, Technology, and Sciences*, *40*(1), 235–247.

Alshammari, G., & Alshammari, T. (2021). Containerization technologies: Taxonomies, applications and challenges. *Journal of Cloud Computing (Heidelberg, Germany)*, *10*(1), 1–23. doi:10.1186/s13677-021-00234-3

Alshuqayran, N., Ali, N., & Evans, R. (2016, November). A systematic mapping study in microservice architecture. In *2016 IEEE 9th International Conference on Service-Oriented Computing and Applications (SOCA)* (pp. 44-51). IEEE. https://ieeexplore.ieee.org/abstract/document/7796008/

Aluvalu, R., Muddana, L., Uma Maheswari, V., Channam, K. K., Mudrakola, S., Sirajuddin, M. D., & Syavasya, C. V. R. (2022). Fog Computing: Applications, Chal-lenges, and Opportunities. *Journal of Au-tonomous Intelligence, 5*(2), 24–43. doi:10.32629/jai.v5i2.545

Amazon. (2018). *AWS lambda announces service level agreement.* Amazon Web Services.

Amazon. (n.d.). *AWS Lambda.* Amazon. https://aws.amazon.com/lambda/.

Ambrosino, D., & Xie, H. (2023). Optimization approaches for defining storage strategies in maritime container termi-nals. *Soft Computing, 27*(7), 4125–4137. doi:10.1007/s00500-022-06769-7

Andrushia, A. D., Neebha, T. M., Patricia, A. T., Sagayam, K. M., & Pramanik, S. (2023). Capsule Network based Disease Classification for VitisVinifera Leaves. *Neural Computing & Applications.* doi:10.1007/s00521-023-09058-y

Ao, L., Izhikevich, L., Voelker, G. M., & Porter, G. (2018). Sprocket: A serverless video processing framework. In *Proceedings of the ACM Symposium on Cloud Computing (SoCC '18)* (pp. 263–274). Association for Computing Ma-chinery. 10.1145/3267809.3267815

Apache Software Foundation. (n.d.). *Apache OpenWhisk.* Apache Software Foundation. https://openwhisk.apache. org.

Arjona, A., López, P. G., Sampé, J., Slominski, A., & Villard, L. (2021). Triggerflow: Trigger-based orchestration of serverless workflows. *Future Generation Computer Systems, 124,* 215–229. doi:10.1016/j.future.2021.06.004

Ashisha, G. R., Anitha Mary, X., George, T., & Martin Sagayam, K. (2023). Unai Fernandez-GamizHatıraGünerhan, Uddin, M. N. and Pramanik, S. (2023). Analysis of Diabetes disease using Machine Learning Techniques: A Review. *Journal of Information Technology Management.*

Aske, A., & Zhao, X. (2018). Supporting Multi-Provider Serverless Computing on the Edge. In *Proceedings of the 47th Inter-national Conference on Parallel Processing Companion.* Association for Computing Machinery. 10.1145/3229710.3229742

Assunção, W. K., Krüger, J., & Mendonça, W. D. (2020, October). Variability management meets microservices: six chal-lenges of re-engineering microservice-based webshops. In *Proceedings of the 24th ACM Conference on Systems and Soft-ware Product Line* (pp. 1–6). ACM. https://dl.acm.org/doi/abs/10.1145/3382025.3414942 doi:10.1145/3382025.3414942

Baldini, I., Castro, P., Chang, K., Cheng, P., Fink, S., Ishakian, V., & Suter, P. (2017). Serverless Computing: Current Trends and Open Problems. In Research Advances in Cloud Computing (pp. 1–20). Springer.

Baldini, I., Cheng, P., Fink, S. J., Mitchell, N., Muthusamy, V., Rabbah, R., Suter, P., & Tardieu, O. (2017). The server-less trilemma: Function composition for serverless computing. In *Proceedings of the 2017 ACM SIGPLAN International Symposium on New Ideas, New Paradigms, and Reflections on Programming and Software, Onward! 2017* (pp. 89–103). ACM. 10.1145/3133850.3133855

Bansal, R., Obaid, A. J., Gupta, A., Singh, R., & Pramanik, S. (2021). Impact of Big Data on Digital Transformation in 5G Era. *2nd International Conference on Physics and Applied Sciences (ICPAS 2021).* IOP Science. , 2021.10.1088/1742-6596/1963/1/012170

Barr, J. (2018). *Firecracker - lightweight virtualization for serverless computing.* AWS. https://aws.amazon.com/blogs/aws/firecracker-lightweight-virtualizationfor-serverless-computing,

Barrak, A., Petrillo, F., & Jaafar, F. (2022). Serverless on Machine Learning: A Systematic Mapping Study. *IEEE Access : Practical Innovations, Open Solutions*, *10*, 99337–99352. doi:10.1109/ACCESS.2022.3206366

Baškarada, S., Nguyen, V., & Koronios, A. (2018). Architecting microservices: Practical opportunities and challenges. *Journal of Computer Information Systems*. https://www.tandfonline.com/doi/shareview/10.1080/08874417.2018.1520056

Baumann, A., Barham, P., Dagand, P. E., Harris, T., Isaacs, R., Peter, S., Roscoe, T., Schüpbach, A., & Singhania, A. (2015). The multikernel: A new OS architecture for scalable multicore systems. *Operating Systems Review*, *43*(2), 29–44.

Baumgartner, J., Lillo, C., & Rumley, S. (2023, May). Performance Losses with Virtualization: Comparing Bare Metal to VMs and Containers. In *International Conference on High Performance Computing* (pp. 107-120). Cham: Springer Nature Switzerland. 10.1007/978-3-031-40843-4_9

Bebortta, S., Das, S. K., Kandpal, M., Barik, R. K., & Dubey, H. (2020). Geospatial Serverless Computing: Architectures, tools and future directions. *ISPRS International Journal of Geo-Information*, *9*(5), 311. doi:10.3390/ijgi9050311

Bernstein, D. (2014). Containers and cloud: From lxc to docker to kubernetes. *IEEE cloud computing, 1*(3), 81-84.

Bernstein, D. (2014). Containers and Cloud: From LXC to Docker to Kubernetes. *IEEE Cloud Computing*, *1*(3), 81–84. doi:10.1109/MCC.2014.51

Bhardwaj, P. (2023). *Detecting Container vulnerabilities leveraging the CICD pipeline* [Doctoral dissertation, Dublin, National College of Ireland].

Bhattacharya, A., Ghosal, A., Obaid, A. J., Krit, S., Shukla, V. K., Mandal, K., & Pramanik, S. (2021). Unsupervised Summarization Approach with Computational Statistics of Microblog Data. In D. Samanta, R. R. Althar, S. Pramanik, & S. Dutta (Eds.), *Methodologies and Applications of Computational Statistics for Machine Learning* (pp. 23–37). IGI Global. doi:10.4018/978-1-7998-7701-1.ch002

Bhupathi, J. & Kathirvel, A. (2022). MMF Clustering: A On-demand One-hop Cluster Management in MANET Services Executing Perspective. *International Journal of Novel Research and Development, 8*(4), 127-132.

Billawa, P., Bambhore Tukaram, A., Díaz Ferreyra, N. E., Steghöfer, J. P., Scandariato, R., & Simhandl, G. (2022, August). SoK: Security of Microservice Applications: A Practitioners' Perspective on Challenges and Best Practices. In *Proceedings of the 17th International Conference on Availability* (pp. 1–10). Reliability and Security. https://dl.acm.org/doi/abs/10.1145/3538969.3538986 doi:10.1145/3538969.3538986

Bommala, H., Aluvalu, R., & Mudrakola, S. (2023). Machine learning job failure analysis and prediction model for the cloud environment. *High-Confidence Computing*, *3*(4), 100165. doi:10.1016/j.hcc.2023.100165

Boneder, S. (2023). *Evaluation and comparison of the security offerings of the big three cloud service providers Amazon Web Services, Microsoft Azure, and Google Cloud Platform* [Doctoral dissertation, Technische Hochschule Ingolstadt].

Boopathi, S. (2023). Deep Learning Techniques Applied for Automatic Sentence Generation. In Promoting Diversity, Equity, and Inclusion in Language Learning Environments (pp. 255–273). IGI Global. doi:10.4018/978-1-6684-3632-5.ch016

Boopathi, S. (2024). Balancing Innovation and Security in the Cloud: Navigating the Risks and Rewards of the Digital Age. In Improving Security, Privacy, and Trust in Cloud Computing (pp. 164–193). IGI Global.

Boza, E. F., Abad, C. L., Villavicencio, M., Quimba, S., & Plaza, J. A. (2017). Reserved, on demand or serverless: Model-based simulations for cloud budget planning. In *2017 IEEE Second Ecuador Technical Chapters Meeting (ETCM)*. IEEE. 10.1109/ETCM.2017.8247460

Brenner, S., & Kapitza, R. (2019). Trust more, serverless. In *Proceedings of the 12th ACM International Conference on Systems and Storage (SYSTOR '19)* (pp. 33–43). Association for Computing Machinery. 10.1145/3319647.3325825

Brown, J. (2020). Serverless computing: A beginner's guide. *Tech Radar.* https://www.techradar.com/news/serverless-computing-a-beginners-guide

Brown, E. (2019). *Web development with node and express: leveraging the JavaScript stack.* O'Reilly Media.

Brown, M., & Singh, R. (2023). Implementing robust disaster recovery strategies in multi-cloud environments. *. Cloud Management Insights, 12*(1), 77–89.

Burns, B., Grant, B., Oppenheimer, D., Brewer, E. A., & Wilkes, J. (2016). Borg, Omega, and Kubernetes. *. ACM Queue; Tomorrow's Computing Today, 14*(1), 70–93. doi:10.1145/2898442.2898444

Bushong, V., Abdelfattah, A. S., Maruf, A. A., Das, D., Lehman, A., Jaroszewski, E., Coffey, M., Cerny, T., Frajtak, K., Tisnovsky, P., & Bures, M. (2021). On microservice analysis and architecture evolution: A systematic mapping study. *Applied Sciences (Basel, Switzerland), 11*(17), 7856. https://www.mdpi.com/2076-3417/11/17/7856. doi:10.3390/app11177856

Calles, M. A. (2020). *Serverless Security: Understand, Assess, and Implement Secure and Reliable Applications in AWS, Microsoft Azure, and Google Cloud.* Springer International Publishing. doi:10.1007/978-1-4842-6100-2

Casalicchio, E., & Iannucci, S. (2020). The state-of-the-art in container technologies: Application, orchestration, and security. *Concurrency and Computation, 32*(17), e5668. doi:10.1002/cpe.5668

Casalicchio, E., & Perciballi, V. (2017). Container orchestration: A survey. *Proceedings of the 8th International Conference on Cloud Computing and Services Science.* ACM.

Cassel, G. A. S., Rodrigues, V. F., da Rosa Righi, R., Bez, M. R., Nepomuceno, A. C., & André da Costa, C. (2022). Serverless computing for Internet of Things: A systematic literature review. *Future Generation Computer Systems, 128,* 299–316. doi:10.1016/j.future.2021.10.020

Castro, P., Ishakian, V., Muthusamy, V., & Slominski, A. (2019). *The server is dead, long live the server: Rise of Serverless Computing, Overview of Current State and Future Trends in Research and Industry.* arXiv (Cornell University). https://arxiv.org/pdf/1906.02888

Cerny, T., Donahoo, M. J., & Trnka, M. (2018). Contextual understanding of microservice architecture: Current and future directions. *Applied Computing Review, 17*(4), 29–45. https://dl.acm.org/doi/abs/10.1145/3183628.3183631. doi:10.1145/3183628.3183631

Chahal, D., Ojha, R., Ramesh, M., & Singhal, R. (2020). Migrating Large Deep Learning Models to Serverless Architecture, *2020 IEEE International Symposium on Software Reliability Engineering Workshops (ISSREW)*, Coimbra, Portugal. 10.1109/ISSREW51248.2020.00047

Chau, N. T., & Jung, S. (2018). Dynamic analysis with Android container: Challenges and opportunities. *Digital Investigation, 27,* 38–46. doi:10.1016/j.diin.2018.09.007

Chen, R., Chen, R., & Zhou, Z. (2023, October 26). *Cold starts in serverless computing: A systematic review.* arXiv preprint arXiv:2310.08437. https://ieeexplore.ieee.org/document/9191377

Chen, L. Y., & Ying, W. (2017). A survey of OpenStack technologies. *Journal of Computer and System Sciences, 83*(8), 1514–1530.

Chen, S., Delimitrou, C., & Martínez, J. F. (2019). PARTIES: QoS-aware resource partitioning for multiple interactive services. In *Proceedings of the Twenty-Fourth International Conference on Architectural Support for Programming Languages and Operating Systems, ASPLOS '19*. ACM. 10.1145/3297858.3304005

Chhetri, N. (2016). *A comparative analysis of node. js*. Server-Side Javascript.

Chowhan, K. (2018). *Hands-on Serverless Computing: Build, run, and orchestrate serverless applications using AWS Lambda, Microsoft Azure Functions, and Google Cloud functions*. Packt Publishing.

Cinque, M. (2023). Real-Time FaaS: Serverless computing for Industry 4.0. *Service Oriented Computing and Applications*, *17*(2), 73–75. doi:10.1007/s11761-023-00360-0

CNCF Serverless Working Group. (2018). *Serverless whitepaper v1.0*. Cloud Native Computing Foundation.

Combe, T., Martin, A., & Di Pietro, R. (2016). To Docker or Not to Docker: A Security Perspective. *IEEE Cloud Computing*, *3*(5), 54–62. doi:10.1109/MCC.2016.100

CortezE.BondeA.MuzioA.RussinovichM.FontouraM.BianchiniR. (2017). Resource central: Understanding and predicting workloads for improved resource management in large cloud platforms. In Proceedings of the 26th Symposium on Operating Systems Principles, SOSP '17, (pp. 153–167). ACM. doi:10.1145/3132747.3132772

Dantas, J., Khazaei, H., & Litoiu, M. (2022). Application Deployment Strategies for Reducing the Cold Start Delay of AWS Lambda. *IEEE 15th International Conference on Cloud Computing (CLOUD)*, 1-10. 10.1109/CLOUD55607.2022.00016

Del Sole, A. (2021). *Visual Studio Code Distilled*. Apress. doi:10.1007/978-1-4842-6901-5

Dhamodaran, S., Ahamad, S., Ramesh, J. V. N., Sathappan, S., Namdev, A., Kanse, R. R., & Pramanik, S. (2023). *Fire Detection System Utilizing an Aggregate Technique in UAV and Cloud Computing, Thrust Technologies' Effect on Image Processing*. IGI Global.

Di Francesco, P., Lago, P., & Malavolta, I. (2018, April). Migrating towards microservice architectures: an industrial survey. In *2018 IEEE international conference on software architecture (ICSA)* (pp. 29-2909). IEEE. https://ieeexplore.ieee.org/abstract/document/8417114

Dillon, T., Wu, C., & Chang, E. (2010), Cloud Computing: Issues and Challenges. *2010 24th IEEE International Conference on Advanced Information Networking and Applications*, (pp. 27-33). IEEE.

Du, D., Liu, Q., Jiang, X., Xia, Y., Zang, B., & Chen, H. 2022. Serverless computing on heterogeneous computers. In *Proceedings of the 27th ACM International Conference on Architectural Support for Programming Languages and Operating Systems (ASPLOS '22)*. Association for Computing Machinery. 10.1145/3503222.3507732

Eismann, S., Scheuner, J., Van Eyk, E., Schwinger, M., Grohmann, J., Herbst, N., Abad, C. L., & Iosup, A. (2020a). *A Review of Serverless Use Cases and their Characteristics*. arXiv (Cornell University). https://arxiv.org/pdf/2008.11110

Eismann, S., Scheuner, J., Van Eyk, E., Schwinger, M., Grohmann, J., Herbst, N., Abad, C. L., & Iosup, A. (2020b). *A Review of Serverless Use Cases and their Characteristics*. arXiv (Cornell University). https://arxiv.org/pdf/2008.11110

Eismann, S., Scheuner, J., van Eyk, E., Schwinger, M., Grohmann, J., Herbst, N., Abad, C. L., & Iosup, A. (2021). Serverless Applications: Why, When, and How? *IEEE Software*, *38*(1), 32–39. doi:10.1109/MS.2020.3023302

Felter, W., Ferreira, A., Rajamony, R., & Rubio, J. (2015). An updated performance comparison of virtual machines and Linux containers. *IEEE International Symposium on Performance Analysis of Systems and Software*. IEEE. 10.1109/ISPASS.2015.7095802

Feng, L., Kudva, P., Da Silva, D., & Hu, J. (2018). Exploring serverless computing for neural network training. In *2018 IEEE 11th International Conference on Cloud Computing (CLOUD)* (pp. 334–341). IEEE. 10.1109/CLOUD.2018.00049

Ferdman, M., Adileh, A., Kocberber, O., Volos, S., Alisafaee, M., Jevdjic, D., Kaynak, C., Popescu, A. D., Ailamaki, A., & Falsafi, B. (2012). Clearing the clouds: A study of emerging scale-out workloads on modern hardware. In *Proceedings of the Seventeenth International Conference on Architectural Support for Programming Languages and Operating Systems, ASPLOS XVII* (pp. 37–48). ACM. 10.1145/2150976.2150982

Figiela, K., Gajek, A., Zima, A., Obrok, B., & Malawski, M. (2018, December 10). Performance evaluation of heterogeneous cloud functions. *Concurrency and Computation*, *30*(23), e4792. doi:10.1002/cpe.4792

Fingler, H., Akshintala, A., & Rossbach, C. J. (2019). USETL: Unikernels for serverless extract transform and load why should you settle for less? In *Proceedings of the 10th ACM SIGOPS Asia-Pacific Workshop on Systems, APSys '19* (pp. 23–30). ACM. 10.1145/3343737.3343750

Firecracker Micro VM. (n.d.). *Secure and fast microVMs for serverless computing.* https://firecrackermicrovm.github.io/.

Fontes, J. V., de Almeida, P. R., Hernández, I. D., Maia, H. W., Mendoza, E., Silva, R., Santander, E. J. O., Marques, R. T. S. F., Soares, N. L. N., & Sanches, R. A. (2023). Marine Accidents in the Brazilian Amazon: Potential Risks to the Aquatic Environment. *Sustainability (Basel)*, *15*(14), 11030. doi:10.3390/su151411030

Fouladi, S., Wahby, R. S., Shacklett, B., Balasubramaniam, K., Zeng, W., Bhalerao, R., Sivaraman, A., Porter, G., & Winstein, K. (2017). *Encoding, fast and slow: Low-latency video processing using thousands of tiny threads.* NSDI.

Gackenheimer, C., & Gackenheimer, C. (2013). Understanding Node. js. *Node. js Recipes*, 1-26.

Gadepalli, P. K. (2019). Challenges and opportunities for efficient serverless computing at the edge. *2019 38th Symposium on Reliable Distributed Systems (SRDS)*. IEEE. 10.1109/SRDS47363.2019.00036

Gannon, D., Barga, R., & Sundaresan, N. (2017). Cloud-Native Applications. *IEEE Cloud Computing*, *4*(5), 20–30. doi:10.1109/MCC.2017.4250939

Gan, Y., & Delimitrou, C. (2018). The architectural implications of cloud microservices. *IEEE Computer Architecture Letters*, *17*(2), 155–158. doi:10.1109/LCA.2018.2839189

Gan, Y., Zhang, Y., Cheng, D., Shetty, A., Rathi, P., Katarki, N., Bruno, A., Hu, J., Ritchken, B., Jackson, B., Hu, K., Pancholi, M., Clancy, B., Colen, C., Wen, F., Leung, C., Wang, S., Zaruvinsky, L., Espinosa, M., & Delimitrou, C. (2019). An open-source benchmark suite for microservices and their hardware-software implications for cloud and edge systems. In *Proceedings of the Twenty-Fourth International Conference on Architectural Support for Programming Languages and Operating Systems, ASPLOS '19*. ACM. 10.1145/3297858.3304013

Geng, X., Ma, Q., Pei, Y., Xu, Z., Zeng, W., & Zou, J. (2018). Research on early warning system of power network overloading under serverless architecture. In *2018 2nd IEEE Conference on Energy Internet and Energy System Integration (EI2)* (pp. 1–6). IEEE. 10.1109/EI2.2018.8582355

Ghofrani, J., & Lübke, D. (2018). Challenges of Microservices Architecture: A Survey on the State of the Practice. *ZEUS*, 1-8. https://www.researchgate.net/profile/Christoph-Hochreiner/publication/324517504_Proceedings_of_the_10th_ZEUS_Workshop/links/5ad1c5e9458515c60f5054d3/Proceedings-of-the-10th-ZEUS-Workshop.pdf#page=8

Gibson, J., Rondeau, R., Eveleigh, D., & Tan, Q. (2012). *Benefits and challenges of three cloud computing service models. 2012 Fourth International Conference on Computational Aspects of Social Networks (CASoN)*, Sao Carlos, Brazil. 10.1109/CASoN.2012.6412402

Github. (n.d.-a). *Intel® RDT Software Package.* Github. https://github.com/intel/intel-cmt-cat.

Github. (n.d.-b). *Tesseract Open Source OCR Engine*. https://github.com/tesseract-ocr/tesseract.

Glikson, A., Nastic, S., & Dustdar, S. (2017). Deviceless edge computing: Extending serverless computing to the edge of the network. In *Proceedings of the 10th ACM International Systems and Storage Conference (SYSTOR '17)*. ACM. 10.1145/3078468.3078497

Gobinath, V., Ayyaswamy, K., & Kathirvel, N. (2024). Information Communication Technology and Intelligent Manufacturing Industries Perspective: An Insight. *Asian Science Bulletin*, 2(1), 36–45. doi:10.3923/asb.2024.36.45

Gomez, J. (2022, November 10). *Serverless Computing Vs. Cloud Computing: What's The Difference?* Koombea. https://www.koombea.com/blog/serverless-computing-vs-cloud-computing/

González-Abad, J., López García, Á., & Kozlov, V. Y. (2023). A container-based workflow for distributed training of deep learning algorithms in HPC clusters. *Cluster Computing*, 26(5), 2815–2834. doi:10.1007/s10586-022-03798-7

Götz, B., Schel, D., Bauer, D., Henkel, C., Einberger, P., & Bauernhansl, T. (2018). Challenges of production microservices. *Procedia CIRP*, 67, 167–172. https://www.sciencedirect.com/science/article/pii/S2212827117311381. doi:10.1016/j.procir.2017.12.194

Green, S., & Black, D. (2023). Optimizing cost in cloud-native applications through serverless technologies. *Cloud Economics Review*, 7(4), 98–115.

Grobmann, M., Ioannidis, C., & Le, D. T. (2019). Applicability of serverless computing in fog computing environments for IoT scenarios. In *Proceedings of the 12th IEEE/ACM International Conference on Utility and Cloud Computing Companion (UCC '19 Companion)* (pp. 29–34). Association for Computing Machinery.

Grogan, J., Mulready, C., McDermott, J., Urbanavicius, M., Yılmaz, M., Abgaz, Y. M., McCarren, A., MacMahon, S. T., Garousi, V., Eklund, P., & Clarke, P. M. (2020a). A multivocal literature review of Function-as-a-Service (FAAS) infrastructures and implications for software developers. In Communications in computer and information science (pp. 58–75). Springer. doi:10.1007/978-3-030-56441-4_5

Grogan, J., Mulready, C., McDermott, J., Urbanavicius, M., Yilmaz, M., Abgaz, Y., McCarren, A., MacMahon, S. T., Garousi, V., Elger, P., & ... (2020). A multivocal literature review of function-as-a-service (faas) infrastructures and implications for software developers. *Systems, Software and Services Process Improvement: 27th European Conference*, 27, 58–75.

Gupta, S., & Chaudhary, N. (2023). Security Challenges in Serverless Computing Environments. *Computer Security Journal*, 39(2), 234–250.

Hanuman, R. N., Lathigara, A., Aluvalu, R., & Viswanadhula, U. M. (2023, February). Virtual Machine Load Balancing Using Improved ABC for Task Scheduling in Cloud Computing. In *International Conference on Intelligent Computing and Networking* (pp. 251-264). Singapore: Springer Nature Singapore. 10.1007/978-981-99-3177-4_18

Hassan, B., & Saman, A. (2021). Survey on serverless computing. *Journal of Cloud Computing (Heidelberg, Germany)*, 10(1), 1–29. doi:10.1186/s13677-021-00253-7

Heinrich, R., Van Hoorn, A., Knoche, H., Li, F., Lwakatare, L. E., Pahl, C., & Wettinger, J. (2017, April). Performance engineering for microservices: research challenges and directions. In *Proceedings of the 8th ACM/SPEC on international conference on performance engineering companion* (pp. 223-226). ACM. https://dl.acm.org/doi/abs/10.1145/3053600.3053653

Hellerstein, J. M., Faleiro, J., Gonzalez, J. E., Schleier-Smith, J., Sreekanti, V., Tumanov, A., & Wu, C. (2018). Serverless Computing: One Step Forward, Two Steps Back. http://arxiv.org/abs/1812.03651. Accessed 4 Oct 2021.

Hema, N., Krishnamoorthy, N., Chavan, S. M., Kumar, N., Sabarimuthu, M., & Boopathi, S. (2023). A Study on an Internet of Things (IoT)-Enabled Smart Solar Grid System. In *Handbook of Research on Deep Learning Techniques for Cloud-Based Industrial IoT* (pp. 290–308). IGI Global. doi:10.4018/978-1-6684-8098-4.ch017

Herdrich, A., Verplanke, E., Autee, P., Illikkal, R., Gianos, C., Singhal, R., & Iyer, R. (2016). Cache QoS: From concept to reality in the Intel® Xeon® processor E5-2600 v3 product family. In *High Performance Computer Architecture (HPCA), IEEE International Symposium* (pp. 657–668). IEEE. 10.1109/HPCA.2016.7446102

Hindman, B., Konwinski, A., Zaharia, M., Ghodsi, A., Joseph, A. D., Katz, R., Shenker, S., & Stoica, I. (2011). Mesos: A Platform for Fine-Grained Resource Sharing in the Data Center. *NSDI, 11*, 22–22.

Hyder, M. F., Ahmed, W., & Ahmed, M. (2023). Toward deceiving the intrusion attacks in containerized cloud environment using virtual private cloud-based moving target defense. *Concurrency and Computation, 35*(5), e7549. doi:10.1002/cpe.7549

IBM. (n.d.). *IBM Cloud Functions*. IBM. https://www.ibm.com/cloud/functions.

Ihrig, C. J. (2014). *Pro node. js for developers*. Apress.

Ivan, C., Vasile, R., & Dadarlat, V. (2019). Serverless computing: An investigation of deployment environments for web apis. *Computers, 8*(2), 50. doi:10.3390/computers8020050

Jain, V., Rastogi, M., Ramesh, J. V. N., Chauhan, A., Agarwal, P., Pramanik, S., & Gupta, A. (2023). FinTech and Artificial Intelligence in Relationship Banking and Computer Technology. In K. Saini, A. Mummoorthy, R. Chandrika, N. S. Gowri Ganesh, & I. G. I. Global (Eds.), *AI, IoT, and Blockchain Breakthroughs in E-Governance*. doi:10.4018/978-1-6684-7697-0.ch011

Jain, V., Singh, B., Choudhary, N., & Yadav, P. K. (2023). A Hybrid Model for Real-Time Docker Container Threat Detection and Vulnerability Analysis. *International Journal of Intelligent Systems and Applications in Engineering, 11*(6s), 782–793.

Jaleel, A., Nuzman, J., Moga, A., Steely, S. C., & Emer, J. (2015). High performing cache hierarchies for server workloads: Relaxing inclusion to capture the latency benefits of exclusive caches. In *High Performance Computer Architecture (HPCA), IEEE 21st International Symposium on* (pp. 343–353). IEEE. 10.1109/HPCA.2015.7056045

Jambunathan, B., & Yoganathan, K. (2018). Architecture decision on using microservices or serverless functions with containers. In *2018 International Conference on Current Trends Towards Converging Technologies (ICCTCT)* (pp. 1–7). IEEE. 10.1109/ICCTCT.2018.8551035

Jamshidi, P., Pahl, C., Mendonça, N. C., Lewis, J. W., & Tilkov, S. (2018). Microservices: The journey so far and challenges ahead. *IEEE Software, 35*(3), 24–35. doi:10.1109/MS.2018.2141039

Jayasingh, R. (2022). Speckle noise removal by SORAMA segmentation in Digital Image Processing to facilitate precise robotic surgery. *International Journal of Reliable and Quality E-Healthcare, 11*(1), 1–19. doi:10.4018/IJRQEH.295083

Jindal, A., Chadha, M., Benedict, S., & Gerndt, M. (2021). Estimating the capacities of function-as-a-service functions. *Proceedings of the 14th IEEE/ACM International Conference on Utility and Cloud Computing Companion*, (pp. 1–8). IEEE.

Johnson, L., & Roberts, T. (2023). Advancements in AI and machine learning in serverless computing environments. *International Journal of Advanced Computer Science, 11*(2), 234–249.

Johnson, M. K., & Thompson, H. J. (2023). *Containerization Patterns for Cloud-Native Applications*. Springer Nature.

Jonas, E., Schleier-Smith, J., Sreekanti, V., Tsai, C.-C., & Khandelwal, A. (2019). *Cloud Programming Simplified: A Berkeley View on Serverless Computing*. arXiv. http://arxiv.org/abs/1902.03383

Jones, M. (2021). *What is serverless computing?* RedHat. https://www.redhat.com/en/topics/cloud-native-apps/what-is-serverless-computing

K.aushik, D., Garg, M., Annu, Gupta, A. and Pramanik, S. (2022). Application of Machine Learning and Deep Learning in Cyber security: An Innovative Approach. In M. Ghonge, S. Pramanik, R. Mangrulkar and D. N. Le, (eds.). *Cybersecurity and Digital Forensics: Challenges and Future Trends*. Wiley. doi:10.1002/9781119795667.ch12

Kalske, M., Mäkitalo, N., & Mikkonen, T. (2018). Challenges when moving from monolith to microservice architecture. In *Current Trends in Web Engineering: ICWE 2017 International Workshops, Liquid Multi-Device Software and EnWoT, practi-O-web, NLPIT, SoWeMine*, (pp. 32-47). Springer International Publishing. https://link.springer.com/chapter/10.1007/978-3-319-74433-9_3

Kathirvel, A, Blesso, D., Preetham, S., Hinn, J. T O, Kennedy, R. C, & Immanuel, A. (2023). *Systematic Number Plate detection using improved YOLOv5 detector*. Institute of Electrical and Electronics Engineers Inc. . doi:10.1109/ViTE-CoN58111.2023.10157727

Kathirvel, A. & Pavani, A. (2023). *Machine Learning and Deep Learning Algorithms for Network Data Analytics Function in 5G Cellular Networks*. Institute of Electrical and Electronics Engineers Inc. . doi:10.1109/ICICT57646.2023.10134247

Kathirvel, A. & Shobitha, M. (2023). *Digital Assets Fair Estimation Using Artificial Intelligence*. Institute of Electrical and Electronics Engineers Inc. . doi:10.1109/ViTECoN58111.2023.10157310

Kaur, A., & Singh, S. (2021). Virtualization in Cloud Computing: Moving from Hypervisor to Containerization. *Arabian Journal for Science and Engineering*, 46(8), 8215–8230. doi:10.1007/s13369-021-05553-3

Kelly, D., Glavin, F., & Barrett, E. (2020). Serverless computing: Behind the scenes of major platforms. *2020 IEEE 13th International Conference on Cloud Computing (CLOUD)*. IEEE. 10.1109/CLOUD49709.2020.00050

Kelly, D., Glavin, F. G., & Barrett, E. (2021). Denial of wallet–Defning a looming threat to serverless computing. *Journal of Information Security and Applications*, (60), 2214–2126.

Kelsey, H., & Beyer, B. (2016). *Kubernetes Up and Running: Dive into the Future of Infrastructure*. O'Reilly Media.

Keung, J., & Kwok, F. (2012). *Cloud Deployment Model Selection Assessment for SMEs: Renting or Buying a Cloud*. *IEEE Fifth International Conference on Utility and Cloud Computing*, Chicago, IL, USA. 10.1109/UCC.2012.29

Khan, A. N., & Islam, S. N. (2022, July). Towards a portable serverless framework. In *2022 ACM SIGPLAN International Symposium on Microarchitectures (MICRO)* (pp. 765-778). ACM. https://www.serverless.com/

Khan, A. N., & Islam, S. N. (2023, November 6). *Serverless orchestration: A survey*. arXiv preprint arXiv:2311.13587. https://arxiv.org/pdf/2105.07806

Khan, W. A., Ahmed, S., & Bashir, M. K. (2022, June 29). Serverless Computing: Current Trends and Open Problems. In *Handbook of Research on Serverless Computing and Microservices* (pp. 1-22). IGI Global. https://www.researchgate.net/publication/353174927_Survey_on_serverless_computing

Khanh, P. T., Ngọc, T. H., & Pramanik, S. (2023). Future of Smart Agriculture Techniques and Applications. In A. Khang & I. G. I. Global (Eds.), *Advanced Technologies and AI-Equipped IoT Applications in High Tech Agriculture*. doi:10.4018/978-1-6684-9231-4.ch021

Khanh, P. T., Ngoc, T. T. H., & Pramanik, S. (2024). *AI-Decision Support System: Engineering, Geology, Climate, and Socioeconomic Aspects' Implications on Machine Learning, Using Traditional Design Methods to Enhance AI-Driven Decision Making.* IGI Global. doi:10.4018/979-8-3693-0639-0.ch008

Kim, B., Heo, S., Lee, J., Jeong, S., Lee, Y., & Kim, H. (2021). Compiler-Assisted Semantic-Aware Encryption for Efficient and Secure Serverless Computing. *IEEE Internet of Things Journal, 8*(7), 5645–5656. doi:10.1109/JIOT.2020.3031550

Kim, W. (2009). Cloud Computing: Status and Prognosis. *Journal of Object Technology, 8*(1), 65–72. doi:10.5381/jot.2009.8.1.c4

Kjorveziroski, V., Filiposka, S., & Trajkovik, V. (2021). Iot serverless computing at the edge: A systematic mapping review. *Computers, 10*(10), 130. doi:10.3390/computers10100130

Koller, R., & Williams, D. (2017). Will serverless end the dominance of Linux in the cloud? In *Proceedings of the 16th Workshop on Hot Topics in Operating Systems, HotOS '17* (pp. 169–173). ACM. 10.1145/3102980.3103008

Kounev, S., Herbst, N., Abad, C., Iosup, A., Foster, I., Shenoy, P., Rana, O., & Chien, A. (2023). Serverless Computing: What It Is, and What It Is Not? *Communications of the ACM.*

Krishnamurthi, R., Kumar, A., Gill, S. S., & Buyya, R. (2023). Serverless Computing: New trends and research directions. In Lecture notes on data engineering and communications technologies (pp. 1–13). Springer. doi:10.1007/978-3-031-26633-1_1

Krishnamurthi, R., Kumar, A., Gill, S., & Buyya, R. (2023). *Serverless Computing: Principles and Paradigms.* Springer. doi:10.1007/978-3-031-26633-1

Kritikos, K., & Skrzypek, P. (2018). A review of serverless frameworks. *2018 IEEE/ACM International Conference on Utility and Cloud Computing Companion (UCC Companion).* IEEE. 10.1109/UCC-Companion.2018.00051

Krylovskiy, A., Jahn, M., & Patti, E. (2015, August). Designing a smart city internet of things platform with microservice architecture. In *2015 3rd international conference on future internet of things and cloud* (pp. 25-30). IEEE. https://ieeexplore.ieee.org/abstract/document/7300793

Kuhlenkamp, J., & Werner, S. (2018). Benchmarking FaaS platforms: Call for community participation. In *2018 IEEE/ACM International Conference on Utility and Cloud Computing Companion (UCC Companion)* (pp. 189–194). 10.1109/UCC-Companion.2018.00055

Kulkarni, S. G., Liu, G., Ramakrishnan, K. K., & Wood, T. (2019). Living on the edge: Serverless computing and the cost of failure resiliency. In *2019 IEEE International Symposium on Local and Metropolitan Area Networks (LANMAN)* (pp. 1–6). 10.1109/LANMAN.2019.8846970

Kumari, A., Patra, M. K., Sahoo, B., & Behera, R. K. (2022). Resource optimization in performance modeling for serverless application. *International Journal of Information Technology : an Official Journal of Bharati Vidyapeeth's Institute of Computer Applications and Management, 14*(6), 2867–2875. doi:10.1007/s41870-022-01073-x

Kumar, N., & Thompson, J. (2023). Evaluating the performance of serverless orchestration frameworks. *. Performance Evaluation Review, 31*(2), 45–62.

Lam, M. S., & Schmidt, B. K. (2000). *Supporting ubiquitous computing with stateless consoles and computation caches.* ACM. https://dl.acm.org/citation.cfm?id=932462

Landup, D., & Sanatan, M. (2020). *How to code in Node. JS.* DigitalOcean.

Lee, H., Satyam, K., & Fox, G. (2018). *Evaluation of Production Serverless Computing Environments*. 2018 IEEE 11th International Conference on Cloud Computing (CLOUD), San Francisco, CA, USA, 442-450.

Lee, H., Satyam, K., & Fox, G. (2018). Evaluation of Production Serverless Computing Environments. *IEEE*, 442–450. doi:10.1109/CLOUD.2018.00062

Lee, H., Satyam, K., & Fox, G. (2018). *Evaluation of Production Serverless Computing Environmentts*. 2018 IEEE 11th International Conference on Cloud Computing (CLOUD), San Francisco, CA, USA.

Lee, A., & Kim, B. (2022). Serverless Architecture: A Comprehensive Analysis. *Journal of Cloud Computing Research*, *8*(3), 112–129.

Lee, H., Kwon, S., & Lee, J. H. (2023). Experimental Analysis of Security Attacks for Docker Container Communications. *Electronics (Basel)*, *12*(4), 940. doi:10.3390/electronics12040940

Leipzig, J. (2019). Computational Pipelines and Workflows in Bioinformatics. In S. Ranganathan, M. Gribskov, K. Nakai, & C. Schönbach (Eds.), *Encyclopedia of Bioinformatics and Computational Biology* (pp. 1151–1162). Academic Press. doi:10.1016/B978-0-12-809633-8.20187-8

Leitner, P., Wittern, E., Spillner, J., & Hummer, W. (2019). A mixed-method empirical study of function-as-a-service software development in industrial practice. *Journal of Systems and Software*, *149*, 340–359. doi:10.1016/j.jss.2018.12.013

Lin, C., & Khazaei, H. (2021a). Modeling and optimization of performance and cost of serverless applications. *IEEE Transactions on Parallel and Distributed Systems*, *32*(3), 615–632. doi:10.1109/TPDS.2020.3028841

Liu, G., Gao, X., Wang, H., & Sun, K. (2022) *Exploring the Unchartered Space of Container Registry Typosquatting*. In: USENIX Security Symposium (USENIX Security), USENIX Association, Boston.

Liu, G., Huang, B., Liang, Z., Qin, M., Zhou, H., & Li, Z. (2020, December). Microservices: architecture, container, and challenges. In *2020 IEEE 20th international conference on software quality, reliability and security companion (QRS-C)* (pp. 629-635). IEEE. https://ieeexplore.ieee.org/abstract/document/9282637

Liu, Q., & Yu, Z. (2018). The elasticity and plasticity in semi-containerized co-locating cloud workload: A view from Alibaba trace. In *Proceedings of the ACM Symposium on Cloud Computing, SoCC '18* (pp. 347–360). ACM. 10.1145/3267809.3267830

Li, Y., Hu, H., Liu, W., & Yang, X. (2023). An Optimal Active Defensive Security Framework for the Container-Based Cloud with Deep Reinforcement Learning. *Electronics (Basel)*, *12*(7), 1598. doi:10.3390/electronics12071598

Li, Y., Lin, Y., Wang, Y., Ye, K., & Xu, C. (2022). Serverless computing: State-of-the-art, challenges and opportunities. *IEEE Transactions on Services Computing*, *16*(2), 1522–1539. doi:10.1109/TSC.2022.3166553

Li, Z., Guo, L., Cheng, J., Chen, Q., He, B., & Guo, M. (2022). The serverless computing survey: A technical primer for design architecture. *ACM Computing Surveys*, *54*(10s), 1–34. doi:10.1145/3508360

Lloyd, W., Ramesh, S., Chinthalapati, S., Ly, L. H., & Pallickara, S. (2018). *Serverless Computing: An Investigation of Factors Influencing Microservice Performance*. IEEE. doi:10.1109/IC2E.2018.00039

López, P. G., Arjona, A., Sampé, J., Slominski, A., & Villard, L. (2020). Triggerflow: Trigger-based orchestration of serverless workflows. *Proceedings of the 14th ACM International Conference on Distributed and Event-Based Systems*, (pp. 3–14). ACM. 10.1145/3401025.3401731

Luk, C.-K., Cohn, R., Muth, R., Patil, H., Klauser, A., Lowney, G., Wallace, S., Reddi, V. J., & Hazelwood, K. (2005). Pin: Building customized program analysis tools with dynamic instrumentation. In *Proceedings of the 2005 ACM SIGPLAN Conference on Programming Language Design and Implementation, PLDI '05* (pp. 190–200). ACM. 10.1145/1065010.1065034

Lynn, T., Rosati, P., Lejeune, A., & Emeakaroha, V. (2017). A Preliminary Review of Enterprise Serverless Cloud Computing (Function-as-a-Service) Platforms. *2017 IEEE International Conference on Cloud Computing Technology and Science (CloudCom)*, 162-169. 10.1109/CloudCom.2017.15

Maguluri, L. P., Arularasan, A., & Boopathi, S. (2023). Assessing Security Concerns for AI-Based Drones in Smart Cities. In Effective AI, Blockchain, and E-Governance Applications for Knowledge Discovery and Management (pp. 27–47). IGI Global. doi:10.4018/978-1-6684-9151-5.ch002

Malathi, J., Kusha, K., Isaac, S., Ramesh, A., Rajendiran, M., & Boopathi, S. (2024). IoT-Enabled Remote Patient Monitoring for Chronic Disease Management and Cost Savings: Transforming Healthcare. In Advances in Explainable AI Applications for Smart Cities (pp. 371–388). IGI Global.

Mampage, A., Karunasekera, S., & Buyya, R. (2022). A Holistic View on Resource Management in Serverless Computing Environments: Taxonomy and Future Directions. *ACM Computing Surveys*, 54(11s), 1–36. doi:10.1145/3510412

Manco, F., Lupu, C., Schmidt, F., Mendes, J., Kuenzer, S., Sati, S., Yasukata, K., Raiciu, C., & Huici, F. (2017). My VM is lighter (and safer) than your container. In *Proceedings of the 26th Symposium on Operating Systems Principles, SOSP '17* (pp. 218–233). ACM. 10.1145/3132747.3132763

Marin, Eduard and Perino, Diego and Di Pietro, Roberto (2022) Serverless computing: a security perspective. pp 1–12. Journal of Cloud Computing, SpringerOpen.

Marin, E., Perino, D., & Di Pietro, R. (2022). Serverless computing: A security perspective. *Journal of Cloud Computing (Heidelberg, Germany)*, 11(1), 69. doi:10.1186/s13677-022-00347-w

Martinez, L. F. (2022). The Role of Edge Computing in IoT: Opportunities and Challenges. *Internet of Things Reports*, 5(4), 78-85. https://iotreports.org/edge_computing_challenges

Martinez, A., & Garcia, L. (2023). Exploring the boundaries of edge computing in IoT networks. *Journal of Internet of Things and Edge Computing*, 4(2), 134–150.

McFarling, S. (1993). *Combining branch predictors*. Tech. Rep. TN-36, Digital Western Research Laboratory.

McGrath, G., & Brenner, P. R. (2017). Serverless computing: Design, implementation, and performance. In *2017 IEEE 37th International Conference on Distributed Computing Systems Workshops (ICDCSW)* (pp. 405–410). IEEE. 10.1109/ICDCSW.2017.36

Merkel, D. (2014). Docker: Lightweight linux containers for consistent development and deployment. *Linux Journal*.

Merkel, D. (2014). Docker: Lightweight Linux Containers for Consistent Development and Deployment. *Linux Journal*.

Mirhosseini, A., & Wenisch, T. F. (2019, July). The queuing-first approach for tail management of interactive services. *IEEE Micro*, 39(4), 55–64. doi:10.1109/MM.2019.2897671

Mohan, A., Sane, H., Doshi, K., Edupuganti, S., Nayak, N., & Sukhomlinov, V. (2019). Agile cold starts for scalable serverless. In *11th USENIX Workshop on Hot Topics in Cloud Computing (HotCloud 19)*. USENIX Association.

Mudrakola, S., Uma Maheswari, V., Chennam, K. K., & Kantipudi, M. P. (2023). Fundamentals of Quantum Computing and Significance of Innovation. *Evolution and Applications of Quantum Computing*, 15-30.

Nadareishvili, I., Mitra, R., McLarty, M., & Amundsen, M. (2016). *Microservice Architecture: Aligning Principles, Practices, and Culture*. O'Reilly Media.

Nanda, A. K., Sharma, A., Augustine, P. J., Cyril, B. R., Kiran, V., & Sampath, B. (2024). Securing Cloud Infrastructure in IaaS and PaaS Environments. In Improving Security, Privacy, and Trust in Cloud Computing (pp. 1–33). IGI Global. doi:10.4018/979-8-3693-1431-9.ch001

Nastić, S., Rausch, T., Šćekić, O., Dustdar, S., Gušev, M., Koteska, B., Kostoska, M., Jakimovski, B., Ristov, S., & Prodan, R. (2017). A serverless Real-Time data analytics platform for edge computing. *IEEE Internet Computing*, *21*(4), 64–71. doi:10.1109/MIC.2017.2911430

Newman, S. (2015). *Building Microservices: Designing Fine-Grained Systems*. O'Reilly Media.

Ngọc, T. H., Khanh, P. T., & Pramanik, S. (2023). Smart Agriculture using a Soil Monitoring System. In A. Khang & I. G. I. Global (Eds.), *Advanced Technologies and AI-Equipped IoT Applications in High Tech Agriculture*. doi:10.4018/978-1-6684-9231-4.ch011

O'Neil, P., & Rajan, A. (2023). *Serverless Orchestration and Workflow Management*.

Odun-Ayo, I., Ananya, M., Agono, F., & Goddy-Worlu, R. (2018). *Cloud Computing Architecture: A Critical Analysis*. 2018 18th International Conference on Computational Science and Applications (ICCSA), Melbourne, VIC, Australia.

Pahl, C. (2015). Containerization and the PaaS Cloud. *IEEE Cloud Computing*, *2*(3), 24–31. doi:10.1109/MCC.2015.51

Pahl, C., Brogi, A., Soldani, J., & Jamshidi, P. (2017). Cloud container technologies: A state-of-the-art review. *IEEE Transactions on Cloud Computing*, *7*(3), 677–692. doi:10.1109/TCC.2017.2702586

Palade, A., Kazmi, A., & Clarke, S. (2019). An evaluation of open source serverless computing frameworks support at the edge. *2019 IEEE World Congress on Services (SERVICES)*, *2642*, 206–211. 10.1109/SERVICES.2019.00057

Pandas. (n.d.). *Pandas python data analysis library*. https://pandas.pydata.org.

Pandey, B. K., Pandey, D., Nassa, V. K., George, A. S., Pramanik, S., & Dadheech, P. (2023). Applications for the Text Extraction Method of Complex Degraded Images. In *The Impact of Thrust Technologies on Image Processing*. Nova Publishers. doi:10.52305/ATJL4552

Peinl, R., Holzschuher, F., & Pfitzer, F. (2016). Docker cluster management for the cloud - survey results and own solution. *Journal of Grid Computing*, *14*(2), 265–282. doi:10.1007/s10723-016-9366-y

Pérez, A., Risco, S., Naranjo, D. M., Caballer, M., & Moltó, G. (2019). On-premises serverless computing for event-driven data processing applications. In *2019 IEEE 12th International Conference on Cloud Computing (CLOUD)* (pp. 414–421). 10.1109/CLOUD.2019.00073

Perez, A. (2023). Accelerating and Scaling Data Products with Serverless. In *Serverless Computing: Principles and Paradigms* (pp. 149–173). Springer International Publishing. doi:10.1007/978-3-031-26633-1_6

Pérez, A. G., Moltó, G., Caballer, M., & Calatrava, A. (2018). Serverless computing for container-based architectures. *Future Generation Computer Systems*, *83*, 50–59. doi:10.1016/j.future.2018.01.022

Pietzuch, P. (2016). Securing data processing in untrusted cloud environments. *IEEE Data Eng. Bull.*, *39*(1), 29–40.

Plappert, C., & Fuchs, A. (2023, December). Secure and Lightweight ECU Attestations for Resilient Over-the-Air Updates in Connected Vehicles. In *Proceedings of the 39th Annual Computer Security Applications Conference* (pp. 283-297). ACM. 10.1145/3627106.3627202

Polvi, A. (2015). CoreOS: Linux for the Container World. *Linux Journal.*

Ponce, F., Márquez, G., & Astudillo, H. (2019). Migrating from monolithic architecture to microservices: A Rapid Review. *2019 38th International Conference of the Chilean Computer Science Society (SCCC).* IEEE. 10.1109/SCCC49216.2019.8966423

Potti, A. (2022, October 7). *Postman.* C# Corner: https://www.c-sharpcorner.com/article/how-to-download-and-install-postman-on-your-pc/

Pramanik, S. (2022). Carpooling Solutions using Machine Learning Tools. In *Handbook of Research on Evolving Designs and Innovation in ICT and Intelligent Systems for Real-World Applications, K. K. Sarma, N. Saikia and M. Sharma.* IGI Global. doi:10.4018/978-1-7998-9795-8.ch002

Pramanik, S. (2023). Intelligent Farming Utilizing a Soil Tracking Device. In A. K. Sharma, N. Chanderwal, R. Khan, & I. G. I. Global (Eds.), *Convergence of Cloud Computing, AI and Agricultural Science.* doi:10.4018/979-8-3693-0200-2.ch009

Praveenkumar, S., Veeraiah, V., Pramanik, S., Basha, S. M., Lira Neto, A. V., De Albuquerque, V. H. C., & Gupta, A. (2023). *Prediction of Patients' Incurable Diseases Utilizing Deep Learning Approaches, ICICC 2023.* Springer. doi:10.1007/978-981-99-3315-0_4

Premarathna, D., & Pathirana, A. (2021, September). Theoretical framework to address the challenges in Microservice Architecture. In *2021 International Research Conference on Smart Computing and Systems Engineering (SCSE) (Vol. 4,* pp. 195-202). IEEE. https://ieeexplore.ieee.org/abstract/document/9568346/

Quang, T., & Peng, Y. (2020). *Device-driven On-demand Deployment of Serverless Computing Functions.* 2020 IEEE International Conference on Pervasive Computing and Communications Workshops (PerCom Workshops), Austin, TX, USA.

Raghavendran, V., Naga Satish, G., Suresh Varma, P., & Moses, G. (2016). A Study on Cloud Computing Services. *IJERT.* https://www.ijert.org/research/a-study-on-cloud-computing-services-IJERTCONV4IS34014.pdf

Rahman, M. (2023). *Serverless Cloud Computing: A Comparative Analysis of Performance.* Cost, and Developer Experiences in Container-Level Services.

Rajan, A. P. (2020). A review on serverless architectures-function as a service (FaaS) in cloud computing. [Telecommunication Computing Electronics and Control]. *Telkomnika, 18*(1), 530–537. doi:10.12928/telkomnika.v18i1.12169

Rajan, R. (2018). Serverless architecture-a revolution in cloud computing. *2018 Tenth International Conference on Advanced Computing (ICoAC).* IEEE. 10.1109/ICoAC44903.2018.8939081

Ramírez, A. L., & Romero, D. (2018). Serverless computing for IoT data processing applications. *Internet of Things : Engineering Cyber Physical Human Systems, 3-4,* 18–29.

Ratasich, D., Khalid, F., Geissler, F., Grosu, R., Shafique, M., & Bartocci, E. (2019). A roadmap toward the resilient Internet of Things for cyber-physical systems. *. IEEE Access : Practical Innovations, Open Solutions, 7,* 13260–13283. doi:10.1109/ACCESS.2019.2891969

Rayhan, A., & Rayhan, S. (2023). *Quantum Computing and AI: A Quantum Leap in Intelligence.*

Reddy, R., Latigara, A., & Aluvalu, R. (2023, November). Dynamic load balancing strategies for cloud computing. In AIP Conference Proceedings (Vol. 2963, No. 1). AIP Publishing. doi:10.1063/5.0182748

Reese, W. (2008). Nginx: The high-performance web server and reverse proxy. *Linux Journal, 2008*(173), 2.

Rehemägi, T. (2018, May 14). *Top FaaS Providers (Function As A Service) Guide*. Dashbird. https://dashbird.io/blog/check-out-all-the-faas-providers-developers-have-at-their-disposal-when-going-serverless/

Ruan, B., Huang, H., Wu, S., & Jin, H. (2016). A performance study of containers in cloud environment. In *Asia-Pacific Services Computing Conference* (pp. 343–356). Springer. 10.1007/978-3-319-49178-3_27

Sadaqat, M., Colomo-Palacios, R., & Knudsen, L. E. S. (2018). Serverless Computing: A Multivocal Literature Review. *NOKOBIT - Norsk Konferanse for Organisasjoners Bruk Av Informasjonsteknologi, 26*(1), 1–13.

Samea, F. (2020). A model-driven framework for data-driven applications in serverless cloud computing. *Plos one, 15*(8).

Sanchez, R., & Patel, D. (2024). Evaluating Performance Overheads in Multi-Cloud Strategies. *Proceedings of the 2024 International Conference on Cloud Engineering* (pp. 456-467). IEEE.

Saraswat, M., & Tripathi, R. C. (2020). *Cloud Computing: Analysis of Top 5 CSPs in SaaS, PaaS and IaaS Platforms*. 2020 9th International Conference System Modeling and Advancement in Research Trends (SMART), Moradabad, India.

Saraswathi, A. T., Kalaashri, Y. R., & Padmavathi, S. (2015). Dynamic resource allocation scheme in cloud computing. *Procedia Computer Science, 47*, 30–36. doi:10.1016/j.procs.2015.03.180

Satheesh, M., D'mello, B. J., & Krol, J. (2015). *Web development with MongoDB and NodeJs*. Packt Publishing Ltd.

Savu, L. (2011).Cloud Computing: Deployment Models, Delivery Models, Risks and Research Challenges. *2011 International Conference on Computer and Management (CAMAN)*, Wuhan, China. 10.1109/CAMAN.2011.5778816

Scheuner, J., & Leitner, P. (2020). Function-as-a-service performance evaluation: A multivocal literature review. *Journal of Systems and Software, 170*, 110708. doi:10.1016/j.jss.2020.110708

Schleier-Smith, J., Sreekanti, V., Khandelwal, A., Carreira, J., Yadwadkar, N. J., Popa, R. A., Gonzalez, J. E., Stoica, I., & Patterson, D. A. (2021). What serverless computing is and should become. *Communications of the ACM, 64*(5), 76–84. doi:10.1145/3406011

Schuler, L., Jamil, S., & Kühl, N. (2021). *AI-based Resource Allocation: Reinforcement Learning for Adaptive Autoscaling in Serverless Environments*. 2021 IEEE/ACM 21st International Symposium on Cluster, Cloud and Internet Computing (CCGrid), Melbourne, Australia.

Sewak, M., & Singh, S. (2018). *Winning in the Era of Serverless Computing and Function as a Service*. 2018 3rd International Conference for Convergence in Technology (I2CT), Pune, India.

Sewak, M., & Singh, S. (2018). Winning in the era of serverless computing and function as a service. In 2018 3rd International Conference for Convergence in Technology (I2CT) (pp. 1–5). 10.1109/I2CT.2018.8529465

Shafiei, H., Khonsari, A., & Mousavi, P. (2022). Serverless Computing: A survey of opportunities, challenges, and applications. *ACM Computing Surveys, 54*(11s), 1–32. doi:10.1145/3510611

Shahab, A., Zhu, M., Margaritov, A., & Grot, B. (2018). Farewell my shared LLC! a case for private die-stacked DRAM caches for servers. In *2018 51st Annual IEEE/ACM International Symposium on Microarchitecture (MICRO)* (pp. 559–572). IEEE. 10.1109/MICRO.2018.00052

Shahrad, M., Klein, C., Zheng, L., Chiang, M., Elmroth, E., & Wentzlaff, D. (2017). Incentivizing self-capping to increase cloud utilization. In *Proceedings of the 2017 Symposium on Cloud Computing, SoCC'17*. ACM. 10.1145/3127479.3128611

Sharma, M., Sharma, M., Sharma, N., & Boopathi, S. (2024). Building Sustainable Smart Cities Through Cloud and Intelligent Parking System. In *Handbook of Research on AI and ML for Intelligent Machines and Systems* (pp. 195–222). IGI Global.

Shen, Z., Sun, Z., Sela, G.-E., Bagdasaryan, E., Delimitrou, C., Van Renesse, R., & Weatherspoon, H. (2019). X-Containers: Breaking down barriers to improve performance and isolation of cloud-native containers. In *Proceedings of the TwentyFourth International Conference on Architectural Support for Programming Languages and Operating Systems, ASPLOS '19* (pp. 121–135). ACM. 10.1145/3297858.3304016

Singh, N., Hamid, Y., Juneja, S., Srivastava, G., Dhiman, G., Gadekallu, T. R., & Shah, M. A. (2023). Load balancing and service discovery using Docker Swarm for microservice-based big data applications. *Journal of Cloud Computing (Heidelberg, Germany)*, *12*(1), 1–9. doi:10.1186/s13677-022-00363-w

Singh, S., & Chana, I. (2016). QoS-aware autonomic resource management in cloud computing: A systematic review. *. *ACM Computing Surveys*, *48*(3), 1–46. doi:10.1145/2843889

Singla, K. & Sathyaraj, P. (2019). *Comparison of Software Orchestration Performance Tools and Serverless Web Application.*

Smid, A., Wang, R., & Cerny, T. (2019, September). Case study on data communication in microservice architecture. In *Proceedings of the Conference on Research in Adaptive and Convergent Systems* (pp. 261-267). ACM. https://dl.acm.org/doi/abs/10.1145/3338840.3355659

Smith, A. (2022). *Serverless computing: Advantages and disadvantages.* IBM. https://www.ibm.com/cloud/learn/serverless

Smith, J., & Doe, A. (2023). The impact of Kubernetes on cloud-native computing scalability. *. *Journal of Cloud Computing Research*, *5*(1), 45–60.

Somma, G., Ayimba, C., Casari, P., Romano, S. P., & Mancuso, V. (2020). *When Less is More: Core-Restricted Container Provisioning for Serverless Computing.* IEEE INFOCOM 2020 - IEEE Conference on Computer Communications Workshops (INFOCOM WKSHPS), Toronto, ON, Canada.

Somma, G., Ayimba, C., Casari, P., Romano, S. P., & Mancuso, V. (2020). When less is more: Core-restricted container provisioning for serverless computing. In *IEEE INFOCOM 2020 - IEEE Conference on Computer Communications Workshops (INFOCOM WKSHPS)* (pp. 1153–1159). IEEE.

Söylemez, M., Tekinerdogan, B., & Kolukısa Tarhan, A. (2022). Challenges and solution directions of microservice architectures: A systematic literature review. *Applied Sciences (Basel, Switzerland)*, *12*(11), 5507. https://www.mdpi.com/2076-3417/12/11/5507. doi:10.3390/app12115507

Srinivas, B., Maguluri, L. P., Naidu, K. V., Reddy, L. C. S., Deivakani, M., & Boopathi, S. (2023). Architecture and Framework for Interfacing Cloud-Enabled Robots. In *Handbook of Research on Data Science and Cybersecurity Innovations in Industry 4.0 Technologies* (pp. 542–560). IGI Global. doi:10.4018/978-1-6684-8145-5.ch027

Sriraman, A., & Wenisch, T. F. (2018). uTune: Auto-tuned threading for OLDI microservices. In *13th USENIX Symposium on Operating Systems Design and Implementation (OSDI 18)*. USENIX Association.

Stinner, V. (2022). *The Python Performance Benchmark Suite, Version 0.7.0.* PY Performance. https: //pyperformance.readthedocs.io

Subramanian, V. (2017). *Pro MERN Stack* (Vol. 13). Apress. doi:10.1007/978-1-4842-2653-7

Sudha, D., & Kathirvel, A. (2022a). The effect of ETUS in various generic attacks in mobile ad hoc networks to improve the performance of Aodv protocol. *International Journal of Humanities, Law, and Social Sciences*, *9*(1), 467-476.

Sudha, D., & Kathirvel, A. (2022b). An Intrusion Detection System to Detect and Mitigating Attacks Using Hidden Markov Model (HMM) Energy Monitoring Technique. *Stochastic Modeling an Applications*, *26*(3), 467-476.

Sudha, D., & Kathirvel, A. (2023). The performance enhancement of Aodv protocol using GETUS. *International Journal of Early Childhood Special Education, 15*(2), 115-125. Doi:10.48047/INTJECSE/V15I2.11

Sultan, S., Ahmad, I., & Dimitriou, T. (2019). Container security: Issues, challenges, and the road ahead. *IEEE Access : Practical Innovations, Open Solutions, 7*, 52976–52996. doi:10.1109/ACCESS.2019.2911732

Szalay, M., Matray, P., & Toka, L. (2023). Real-Time FaaS: Towards a Latency Bounded Serverless Cloud. *IEEE Transactions on Cloud Computing, 11*(02), 1636–1650. doi:10.1109/TCC.2022.3151469

Tabrizchi, H., & Kuchaki Rafsanjani, M. (2020). A survey on security challenges in cloud computing: Issues, threats, and solutions. *The Journal of Supercomputing, 76*(12), 9493–9532. doi:10.1007/s11227-020-03213-1

Taibi, D., El Ioini, N., Pahl, C., & Niederkofler, J. R. S. (2020). *Patterns for serverless functions (function-as-a-service): A multivocal literature review.*

Taibi, D., El Ioini, N., Pahl, C., & Niederkofler, J. (2020). Patterns for Serverless Functions (Function-as-a-Service): A Multivocal Literature Review. In *Proceedings of the 10th International Conference on Cloud Computing and Services Science* (pp. 181–192). ScitePress. 10.5220/0009578501810192

Taibi, D., Spillner, J., & Wawruch, K. (2021). Serverless Computing-Where are we now, and where are we heading? *IEEE Software, 38*(1), 25–31. doi:10.1109/MS.2020.3028708

Talukdar, V., Kurniullah, A. Z., Keshwani, P., Khan, H., Pramanik, S., Gupta, A., & Pandey, D. (2023). *Load Balancing Techniques in Cloud Computing, Emerging Trends in Cloud Computing Analytics, Scalability, and Service Models.* IGI Global.

Taneska, M. & Dimkoski, A. (2023). *Microsoft Azure Cloud Computing-Server vs Serverless.* UKIM.

Taviti Naidu, G., & Ganesh, K. V. B. (2023). Technological Innovation Driven by Big Data. Advanced Bioinspiration Methods for Healthcare Standards, Policies, and Reform. IGI Global. doi:10.4018/978-1-6684-5656-9

Thalheim, J., Bhatotia, P., Fonseca, P., & Kasikci, B. (2018). CNTR: Lightweight OS containers. In *2018 USENIX Annual Technical Conference (ATC 18)* (pp. 199–212). ACM.

Trach, B., Oleksenko, O., Gregor, F., Bhatotia, P., & Fetzer, C. (2019). Clemmys: Towards secure remote execution in FaaS. In *Proceedings of the 12th ACM International Conference on Systems and Storage, SYSTOR '19* (pp. 44–54). ACM. 10.1145/3319647.3325835

Turnbull, J. (2016). *The Docker Book: Containerization is the new virtualization.* James Turnbull.

Ugandar, R., Rahamathunnisa, U., Sajithra, S., Christiana, M. B. V., Palai, B. K., & Boopathi, S. (2023). Hospital Waste Management Using Internet of Things and Deep Learning: Enhanced Efficiency and Sustainability. In Applications of Synthetic Biology in Health, Energy, and Environment (pp. 317–343). IGI Global.

van Eyk, E., Toader, L., Talluri, S., Versluis, L., Uță, A., & Iosup, A. (2018, September/October). Serverless is More: From PaaS to Present Cloud Computing. *IEEE Internet Computing, 22*(5), 8–17. doi:10.1109/MIC.2018.053681358

Varghese, B., & Buyya, R. (2018). Next generation cloud computing: New trends and research directions. *Future Generation Computer Systems, 79*, 849–861. doi:10.1016/j.future.2017.09.020

Vashishth, T. K., Sharma, V., Sharma, K. K., Kumar, B., Chaudhary, S., & Panwar, R. (2024). *Serverless Computing Real-World Applications and Benefits in Cloud Environments.*, doi:10.4018/979-8-3693-0900-1.ch014

Vázquez-Poletti, J. L., & Llorente, I. M. (2021). Serverless Computing: From Planet Mars to the Cloud. *Computing in Science & Engineering, 20*(6), 73–79. doi:10.1109/MCSE.2018.2875315

Veeraiah, V., Talukdar, V., Manikandan, K., Talukdar, S. B., Solavande, V. D., Pramanik, S., & Gupta, A. (2023). Machine Learning Frameworks in Carpooling. Handbook of Research on AI and Machine Learning Applications in Customer Support and Analytics. IGI Global.

Veeraiah, V., Shiju, D. J., Ramesh, J. V. N., Ganesh, K. R., Pramanik, S., Pandey, D., & Gupta, A. (2023). *Healthcare Cloud Services in Image Processing, Thrust Technologies' Effect on Image Processing*. IGI Global.

Veeraiah, V., Thejaswini, K. O., Dilip, R., Jain, S. K., Sahu, A., Pramanik, S., & Gupta, A. (2024). *The Suggested Use of Big Data in Medical Analytics by Fortis Healthcare Hospital, Adoption and Use of Technology Tools and Services by Economically Disadvantaged Communities: Implications for Growth and Sustainability*. IGI Global.

Velepucha, V., & Flores, P. (2023). *A survey on microservices architecture: Principles, patterns and migration challenges*. IEEE Access. https://ieeexplore.ieee.org/abstract/document/10220070

Venkateswaran, N., Vidhya, K., Ayyannan, M., Chavan, S. M., Sekar, K., & Boopathi, S. (2023). A Study on Smart Energy Management Framework Using Cloud Computing. In 5G, Artificial Intelligence, and Next Generation Internet of Things: Digital Innovation for Green and Sustainable Economies (pp. 189–212). IGI Global. doi:10.4018/978-1-6684-8634-4.ch009

Verma, A. (2015). Large-scale cluster management at Google with Borg. *European Conference on Computer Systems* (EuroSys).

Vidya Chellam, V., Veeraiah, V., Khanna, A., Sheikh, T. H., Pramanik, S., & Dhabliya, D. (2023). A Machine Vision-based Approach for Tuberculosis Identification in Chest X-Rays Images of Patients. *ICICC 2023*, Springer. doi:10.1007/978-981-99-3315-0_3

Viggiato, M., Terra, R., Rocha, H., Valente, M. T., & Figueiredo, E. (2018). *Microservices in practice: A survey study*. arXiv preprint arXiv:1808.04836. https://arxiv.org/abs/1808.04836

Villamizar, M., Garcés, O., Castro, H., Verano, M., Salamanca, L., Casallas, R., & Gil, S. (2015, September). Evaluating the monolithic and the microservice architecture pattern to deploy web applications in the cloud. In *2015 10th Computing Colombian Conference (10CCC)* (pp. 583-590). IEEE. https://ieeexplore.ieee.org/abstract/document/7333476

Villamizar, M. (2015). Evaluating the Performance and Scalability of the Docker Container Environment. *CLEI Electronic Journal, 18*(3).

Villamizar, M., Garcés, O., Ochoa, L., Castro, H., Salamanca, L., Verano, M., & Lang, M. (2017). Cost comparison of running web applications in the cloud using monolithic, microservice, and AWS Lambda architectures. *Service Oriented Computing and Applications, 11*(2), 233–247. doi:10.1007/s11761-017-0208-y

VS, D. P., Sethuraman, S. C., & Khan, M. K. (2023). Container Security: Precaution Levels, Mitigation Strategies, and Research Perspectives. *Computers & Security*, 103490.

VScode Mac. (2022, October 25). *ATA Learning*. Adam the Automator. https://adamtheautomator.com/visual-studio-code-on-mac/

Wakisaka, S., Chiang, Y.-H., Lin, H., & Ji, Y. (2021). *Timely Information Updates for the Internet of Things with Serverless Computing*. IEEE International Conference on Communications, Montreal, QC, Canada.

Wang, L., Li, M., Zhang, Y., Ristenpart, T., & Swift, M. (2018). Peeking behind the Curtains of Serverless Platforms. In: *USENIX Conference on Usenix Annual Technical Conference (USENIX ATC)*. USENIX Association, Boston.

Wang, L., Li, M., Zhang, Y., Ristenpart, T., & Swift, M. (2018). Peeking behind the curtains of serverless platforms. In *2018 USENIX Annual Technical Conference (ATC 18)*. USENIX Association.

Wang, L., Li, S., & Fu, J. (2023). Self-healing anti-corrosion coatings based on micron-nano containers with different structural morphologies. *Progress in Organic Coatings*, *175*, 107381. doi:10.1016/j.porgcoat.2022.107381

Wang, Y., Kadiyala, H., & Rubin, J. (2021). Promises and challenges of microservices: An exploratory study. *Empirical Software Engineering*, *26*(4), 63. https://link.springer.com/article/10.1007/s10664-020-09910-y. doi:10.1007/s10664-020-09910-y PMID:34149303

Waseem, M., & Liang, P. (2017, December). Microservices architecture in DevOps. In *2017 24th Asia-Pacific Software Engineering Conference Workshops (APSECW)* (pp. 13-14). IEEE. https://ieeexplore.ieee.org/abstract/document/8312518

Wen, J., Chen, Z., Jin, X., & Liu, X. (2017). Serverless Computing: Design, Implementation, and Performance. In *2017 IEEE 37th International Conference on Distributed Computing Systems Workshops (ICDCSW)* (pp. 253-258). IEEE. 10.1109/ICDCSW.2017.27

Wen, J., Chen, Z., Jin, X., & Liu, X. (2023). Rise of the planet of serverless computing: A systematic review. *ACM Transactions on Software Engineering and Methodology*, *32*(5), 1–61. doi:10.1145/3579643

Werner, S., Kuhlenkamp, J., Klems, M., Müller, J., & Tai, S. (2018). *Serverless Big Data Processing using Matrix Multiplication as Example.* 2018 IEEE International Conference on Big Data (Big Data), Seattle, WA, USA.

Werner, S., Kuhlenkamp, J., Klems, M., Müller, J., & Tai, S. (2018). Serverless big data processing using matrix multiplication as example. In *2018 IEEE International Conference on Big Data (Big Data)* (pp. 358–365). IEEE. 10.1109/BigData.2018.8622362

Westerveld, D. (2021). *API Testing and Development with Postman: A practical guide to creating, testing, and managing APIs for automated software testing.* NodeJS. https://nodejs.org/en https://www.npmjs.com/

Williams, C., Patel, H., & Lee, Y. (2023). Security challenges in multi-cloud architectures: A comprehensive review. *Security and Communication Networks*, *16*(3), 112–128.

Williamson, M., & Darbouy, S. (2023). Investigating and Mitigating the Impact of Technical Lag and Different Architectures on Container Image Security.

Wolski, R., Krintz, C., Bakir, F., George, G., & Lin, W.-T. (2019). Cspot: Portable, multi-scale functions-as-a-service for IoT. In *Proceedings of the 4th ACM/IEEE Symposium on Edge Computing (SEC '19)* (pp. 236–249). Association for Computing Machinery. 10.1145/3318216.3363314

Yang, X., Zhang, J., Jiao, W., & Yan, H. (2023). Optimal capacity rationing policy for a container leasing system with multiple kinds of customers and substitutable containers. *Management Science*, *69*(3), 1468–1485. doi:10.1287/mnsc.2022.4425

Yang, Y., Shen, W., Ruan, B., Liu, W., & Ren, K. (2021, December). Security challenges in the container cloud. In *2021 Third IEEE International Conference on Trust, Privacy and Security in Intelligent Systems and Applications (TPS-ISA)* (pp. 137-145). IEEE.

Yarygina, T., & Bagge, A. H. (2018, March). Overcoming security challenges in microservice architectures. In *2018 IEEE Symposium on Service-Oriented System Engineering (SOSE)* (pp. 11-20). IEEE. https://ieeexplore.ieee.org/abstract/document/8359144

Yelam, A., Subbareddy, S., Ganesan, K., Savage, S., & Mirian, A. (2021). CoResident Evil: Covert Communication. In *The Cloud With Lambdas. In: The Web Conference (WWW)* (pp. 1005–1016). Association for Computing Machinery.

Yongyong, W. (2023, April). A Docker-based Operation and Maintenance Method for New-Generation Command and Control Systems. *Journal of Physics: Conference Series*, *2460*(1), 012173. doi:10.1088/1742-6596/2460/1/012173

Young, E. (2019). The true cost of containing: A gVisor case study. In *11th USENIX Workshop on Hot Topics in Cloud Computing (HotCloud 19)*. USENIX Association.

Yu, H., Zhang, H., Shen, J., Geng, Y., Wang, J., Miao, C., & Xu, M. (2023). Serpens: A High Performance FaaS Platform for Network Functions. *IEEE Transactions on Parallel and Distributed Systems*, *34*(08), 2448–2463. doi:10.1109/TPDS.2023.3263272

Yussupov, V., Breitenbücher, U., Leymann, F., & Wurster, M. (2019). A systematic mapping study on engineering function-as-a-service platforms and tools. In *Proceedings of the 12th IEEE/ACM International Conference on Utility and Cloud Computing (UCC'19)* (pp. 229–240). Association for Computing Machinery. 10.1145/3344341.3368803

Yussupov, V., Soldani, J., Breitenbücher, U., Brogi, A., & Leymann, F. (2021). FaaSten your decisions: A classification framework and technology review of function-as-a-Service platforms. *Journal of Systems and Software*, *175*, 110906. doi:10.1016/j.jss.2021.110906

Zhang, H., Li, S., Jia, Z., Zhong, C., & Zhang, C. (2019, March). Microservice architecture in reality: An industrial inquiry. In *2019 IEEE international conference on software architecture (ICSA)* (pp. 51-60). IEEE. https://ieeexplore.ieee.org/abstract/document/8703917

Zhang, W., Fang, V., Panda, A., & Shenker, S. (2020). Kappa: A programming framework for serverless computing. *Proceedings of the 11th ACM Symposium on Cloud Computing*, (pp. 328–343). ACM. 10.1145/3419111.3421277

Zhang, Y., & Kim, W. (2023). Bridging the gap: Integrating container orchestration with microservices. *Software Engineering Trends and Techniques*, *9*(1), 200–215.

Zhou, M., Li, W., & Jiang, W. (2023, November 6). *Cost optimization in serverless computing.* arXiv preprint arXiv:2311.13242. https://arxiv.org/abs/2311.13242

Макеєв, О., & Кравець, Н. (2023). Study Of Methods Of Creating Service-Oriented Software Systems In Azure. *Computer systems and information technologies*, (2), 38-47.

About the Contributors

Rajanikanth Aluvalu (Senior Member, IEEE) received the Ph.D. degree in cloud computing as specialization. He is currently working as Professor and Head, Department of IT, Chaitanya Bharathi Institute of Technology, Hyderabad, India. Formerly, he held positions, including Professor and Head, Department of CSE, Vardhaman College of Engineering, Hyderabad, Volunteered IEEE as Vice-Chair of the Entrepreneurship and Startup Committee, Treasurer and Secretary of the IEEE Computer Society, Hyderabad Section. He is having more than 20 years of teaching experience. He organized various international conferences and delivered keynote addresses. He published more than 100 research papers in various peer-reviewed journals and conferences. He is a Life Member of ISTE and a member of ACM and MIR Labs. He was a recipient of the Best Advisor Award from the IEEE Hyderabad Section as well as the IUCEE Faculty Fellow Award (2018). He an Editorial board member of IJDMMM journal published by Inderscience. He guest edited various books with springer, CRC Press, IGI Global and De Gruyter Publishers. He is reviewer for several SCI, Scopus indexed journals.

Uma Maheswari V (Senior Member, IEEE) received the Ph.D. degree in image analytics and data science from Visveswaraya Technological University, Belgaum. She is currently working as an Associate Professor with the Department of CSE, Chaitanya Bharathi Institute of Technology, Hyderabad. She has published more than 50 research papers in SCI, ESCI, WoS, DBLP, and SCOPUS indexed journals and conferences. She has also published four Indian patents on facial expression analysis in the fields of medical, e-commerce, education, and security. She has done an enormous study and given contributions in facial expression analysis and applications. She constructed feature vector for a given image based on the directions and introduced dynamic threshold values while comparing the images, which helps to analyse any image. She has researched the similarity of images in a given database to retrieve the relevant images. She also worked with convolutional neural networks by giving the pre-processed input image to improve the accuracy. It has been proved that the maximum edge intensity values are enough to retrieve the required feature from the image instead of working on total image data. She has organized various technical programs and served as a technical committee member and a reviewer for various conferences. She has delivered sessions in various capacities. She received the Best Faculty Award under the innovation category from the CSI Mumbai Chapter for the year 2019.

* * *

Kathirvel Ayyaswamy, acquired, B.E.(CSE), M.E. (CSE) from Crescent Engineering College affiliated to University of Madras and Ph. D (CSE.) from Anna University. He is currently working as Professor, Dept of Computer Science and Engineering, Karunya Institute of Technology and Sciences,

Coimbatore. He is a studious researcher by himself, completed 18 sponsored research projects worth of Rs 103 lakhs and published more than 110 articles in journals and conferences. 4 research scholars have completed Ph. D and 3 under progress under his guidance. He is working as scientific and editorial board member of many journals. He has reviewed dozens of papers in many journals. He has author of 13 books. His research interests are protocol development for wireless ad hoc networks, security in ad hoc network, data communication and networks, mobile computing, wireless networks, WSN and DTN. He is a Life member of the ISTE (India), IACSIT (Singapore), Life Member IAENG (Hong Kong), Member ICST (Europe), IAES, etc. He has given a number of guest lecturers/expert talks and seminars, workshops and symposiums.

Swathi Sowmya Bavirthi is currently working as an Assistant Professor in Chaitanya Bharathi Institute of Technology(Autonomous), Gandipet, Hyderabad, Telangana, India. She completed Ph,D. in JNTU Hyderabad, Telangana, India. Her research interests include Data mining, Spatial Mining, Machine Learning, Cloud Computing and Artificial Intelligence and has good number of publications in reputed Journals.

Sampath Boopathi is an accomplished individual with a strong academic background and extensive research experience. He completed his undergraduate studies in Mechanical Engineering and pursued his postgraduate studies in the field of Computer-Aided Design. Dr. Boopathi obtained his Ph.D. from Anna University, focusing his research on Manufacturing and optimization. Throughout his career, Dr. Boopathi has made significant contributions to the field of engineering. He has authored and published over 180 research articles in internationally peer-reviewed journals, highlighting his expertise and dedication to advancing knowledge in his area of specialization. His research output demonstrates his commitment to conducting rigorous and impactful research. In addition to his research publications, Dr. Boopathi has also been granted one patent and has three published patents to his name. This indicates his innovative thinking and ability to develop practical solutions to real-world engineering challenges. With 17 years of academic and research experience, Dr. Boopathi has enriched the engineering community through his teaching and mentorship roles. He has served in various engineering colleges in Tamilnadu, India, where he has imparted knowledge, guided students, and contributed to the overall academic development of the institutions. Dr. Sampath Boopathi's diverse background, ranging from mechanical engineering to computer-aided design, along with his specialization in manufacturing and optimization, positions him as a valuable asset in the field of engineering. His research contributions, patents, and extensive teaching experience exemplify his expertise and dedication to advancing engineering knowledge and fostering innovation.

Vishal Goar is presently working as Assistant Professor in Department of Computer Application at Government Engineering College, Bikaner. Presently he is also Coordinator of Research & Development Department of Government Engineering College, Bikaner. Dr. Goar has contributed many research papers in national and international Conferences and Journals. He has delivered many lectures in International Conferences, Seminars and Workshops. Dr. Goar has published many books from different international and national publishing houses. He has organized many conferences and FDP.

Ankur Gupta has received the B.Tech and M.Tech in Computer Science and Engineering from Ganga Institute of Technology and Management, Kablana affiliated with Maharshi Dayanand University, Rohtak in 2015 and 2017. He is an Assistant Professor in the Department of Computer Science and Engineering at Vaish College of Engineering, Rohtak, and has been working there since January 2019. He has many publications in various reputed national/ international conferences, journals, and online book chapter contributions (Indexed by SCIE, Scopus, ESCI, ACM, DBLP, etc). He is doing research in the field of cloud computing, data security & machine learning. His research work in M.Tech was based on biometric security in cloud computing.

K. Swathi is currently working as an Assistant Professor in Chaitanya Bharathi Institute of Technology(Autonomous), Gandipet, Hyderabad, Telangana, India. She is pursing Ph,D. in JNTU-VZ, AP, India. Her research interests include Network Security, Serverless Computing, Machine Learning, Image Proceesing and Deep Learning and has good number of publications in reputed Journals.

K. Radhika is currently working as a Professor in the Department of Artificial Intelligence and Data Science at Chaitanya Bharathi Institute of Technology, Hyderabad, Telangana, India. She completed B.Tech.(EEE) from VR.Sidhartha Engineering College, Vijayawada, Andhra Pradesh, India. She completed her Post Graduation in Computer Science and Engineering (CSE) from JNTU, Hyderabad. She received her Doctorate from Osmania University for her Research work titled "Efficient Mobile-Centric Vertical Handoff Decision Models for Heterogeneous Wireless Networks". She has a total of about 28 years of experience in both Industry and Academia. She was also the former Head of the Department of Information Technology, CBIT. She was instrumental in establishing a lab for Big Data Analytics with the sponsorship of AICTE and another lab for Internet of Things apart from modernizing the existing laboratories and creating other infrastructural facilities in the Department. Prof. Radhika's research interests include Mobile Computing, Cloud Computing, Machine Learning, Data Science, Decision Support Systems including Game Theory, Multiple Criteria Decision Making-MCDM, Analytic Hierarchy Process-AHP, PCA for Dimensionality Reduction and Blockchain Technology. She has published around 30 research papers in National / International Journals and Conferences. She is currently guiding eight Ph.D. scholars. She is a Member of various Professional bodies and was also a Panel Member and Session Chair for various National and International conferences.

Ramu Kuchipudi is a Life Member of ISTE and Member of IEEE and working as Associate Professor, Department of IT, Chaitanya Bharathi Institute of Technology, Hyderabad, India. He has more than 19 years of teaching experience. He obtained a Ph.D with Wireless Sensor Networks as specialization. He has published more than 28 research articles in various peer-reviewed journals and conferences. He has 6 Patents and Organized Technical Events and Resource person in FDPs. He has authored a textbook on Security in Wireless sensor networks and also published two book chapters. He has guided several B.Tech and M.Tech Projects during his teaching career. He is an active technical reviewer of various International and National journals and conferences of repute including IEEE and Springer.

Ramesh Babu Palamakula joined the Department of Information Technology as an Associate Professor of CBIT in 2022. He received his PhD in Computer Science and Engineering in 2017 from the JNTUA University, Anantapur. Before joining the CBIT, he worked as Professor and Head of the IT department at Siddharth Institute of Engineering & Technology, Puttur affiliated to JNTUA University, Anantapur, A.P. from 2017 to 2021. He has 15 years of experience in the teaching field and 6 years of research work experience. He has published more than 20 research articles in reputed journals and conferences. He has work experience as Controller of Examinations, Director R&D, NBA and NAAC Coordinator at Institute level at SIETK, Puttur, Andhra Pradesh. He is having life membership in professional bodies like ISTE, IAENG.

Kaushikkumar Patel is a distinguished leader in harnessing data-driven strategies within the financial sector, boasting an extensive career that intersects finance and technology. He is pivotal at TransUnion, where he innovates through Big Data, enhancing decision-making processes and financial strategies. His profound knowledge extends to Data Analytics, Financial Technology (FinTech), and Digital Transformation, contributing significantly to advancing tech integration in finance. Based in the United States, Mr. Patel is renowned for his strategic oversight in developing solutions that navigate the complex challenges of data privacy and risk assessment, ensuring compliance and governance in dynamic financial landscapes. His insights have fortified business intelligence, utilizing machine learning and cloud computing solutions to drive organizational success. An influential thought leader, Mr. Patel has shared his expertise and vision through various high-impact publications, shedding light on the transformative power of data in finance. His commitment to excellence was internationally recognized when he was honored with the ET Leadership Excellence Award for his groundbreaking work in Data-Driven Financial Strategies. Mr. Patel's dedication transcends his immediate professional sphere, having a lasting impact on societal well-being. He actively engages in CSR initiatives, leveraging technology to enhance lives and contribute to sustainable development. His unique blend of technical prowess and strategic acumen establishes him as a visionary in his field, continually pushing the boundaries of what's possible at the intersection of finance and technology.

Balakrishna Peesala is a research enthusiastic student pursuing Bachelors of Engineering in Information Technology.

Sabyasachi Pramanik is a professional IEEE member. He obtained a PhD in Computer Science and Engineering from Sri Satya Sai University of Technology and Medical Sciences, Bhopal, India. Presently, he is an Associate Professor, Department of Computer Science and Engineering, Haldia Institute of Technology, India. He has many publications in various reputed international conferences, journals, and book chapters (Indexed by SCIE, Scopus, ESCI, etc). He is doing research in the fields of Artificial Intelligence, Data Privacy, Cybersecurity, Network Security, and Machine Learning. He also serves on the editorial boards of several international journals. He is a reviewer of journal articles from IEEE, Springer, Elsevier, Inderscience, IET and IGI Global. He has reviewed many conference papers, has been a keynote speaker, session chair, and technical program committee member at many international conferences. He has authored a book on Wireless Sensor Network. He has edited 8 books from IGI Global, CRC Press, Springer and Wiley Publications.

Mudrakola Swapna Working as Asst professor at Matrusri Engineering College, Hyd, T.S. Education Qualification pursuing PhD from Osmania University, research area Artificial Intelligence in the medical application. Completed M.Tech in Information Technology and B.Tech in CSE. Total Teaching Experience is 14 years, and my Industry experience is two years as a software engineer. Moto of my life to empowering myself with my sincere hard work. Research Link: Orchid id: Linkedin: Topic: Artificial Intelligence in Bio-Medical Application Email id: swapna0801@gmail.com Mobile no: 9398168896 IEEE membership: 97079376

T. Satyanarayana Murthy acquired his Ph.D., from National Institute of Technology, Tiruchirappalli on the thesis entitled "Effective Algorithms for Privacy Preserving Data Mining" in 2019. He obtained his M. Tech. in Computer Science and Technology with specialization in Artificial Intelligence and Robotics from Andhra University, Visakhapatnam in 2010 and also cleared UGC-NET Lectureship in 2012. He had 16+ Years of Teaching and Research experience in JNTU affiliated colleges and Deemed Universities. He has published around 30+ articles in SCOPUS/ SCI/SCIE/ WOS Indexed Journals and one patent grant. He has participated in various in-house academic projects and training activities on Digital Teaching Techniques, Java Programming, Web Technologies, Data mining and Machine Learning and his current research interest towards Machine Learning, Data Mining, Big Data, NLP and Data Privacy Issues etc.

Satya Kiranmai Tadepalli is currently working as an Assistant professor in Chaitanya Bharathi Institute of Technology(A), Hyderabad, Telangana, India. She is currently pursuing Ph.D. from Gitam University. She has 13 years of teaching experience. Her research interest includes Machine Learning, Artificial Intelligence. She has publications in both National and International Journals and Conferences.

Santhosh Voruganti is currently working as an Assistant Professor in Chaitanya Bharathi Institute of Technology(Autonomous), Gandipet, Hyderabad, Telangana, India. He is pursing Ph,D. in JNTU Kakinada, AP, India. His research interests include Network Security, Serverless Computing, Machine Learning and has good number of publications in reputed Journals.

Nagendra Singh Yadav is a Software Testing professional with experience managing remote teams and leading project teams. His background in software testing, technical writing, Research, Author, blogger, and Project management informs his mindful but competitive approach. Nagendra is fueled by his passion for understanding the project requirements and asking from the stakeholders. He considers himself a 'forever student,' eager to build on his academic foundations as a researcher, technical writer, and blogger, and stays in tune with the latest software testing & project management strategies through continued work experience. He is the Global Assistant General Secretary, International Council of Computer Science (ICCS) at Eudoxia Research Centre and holds degrees in M.C.A, B.C.A & a diploma in Blogging and Content Marketing. He has worked with Infosys Limited for 3 years in the field of software validation solutions as a Test Engineer (2016- 2019).

Index

 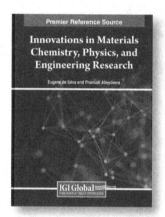 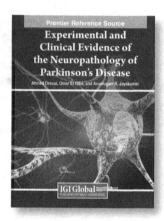 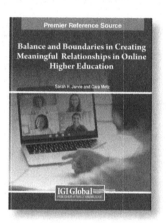

Submit an Open Access Book Proposal

Have Your Work Fully & Freely Available Worldwide After Publication

Seeking the Following Book Classification Types:

Authored & Edited Monographs • Casebooks • Encyclopedias • Handbooks of Research

Gold, Platinum, & Retrospective OA Opportunities to Choose From

Easily Track Your Work in Our Advanced Manuscript Submission System With **Rapid Turnaround Times**

Double-Blind Peer Review by Notable Editorial Boards (*Committee on Publication Ethics (COPE) Certified*

Publications Adhere to All **Current OA Mandates & Compliances**

Affordable APCs *(Often 50% Lower Than the Industry Average)* Including Robust Editorial Service Provisions

Direct Connections with **Prominent Research Funders** & OA Regulatory Groups

Institution Level OA Agreements Available (Recommend or Contact Your Librarian for Details)

Join a **Diverse Community** of 150,000+ Researchers **Worldwide** Publishing With IGI Global

Content Spread Widely to Leading Repositories (AGOSR, ResearchGate, CORE, & More)

? Retrospective Open Access Publishing

You Can Unlock Your Recently Published Work, Including Full Book & Individual Chapter Content to Enjoy All the Benefits of Open Access Publishing

Learn More

Printed in the United States
by Baker & Taylor Publisher Services